Excel Sales Forecasting FOR DUMMIES®

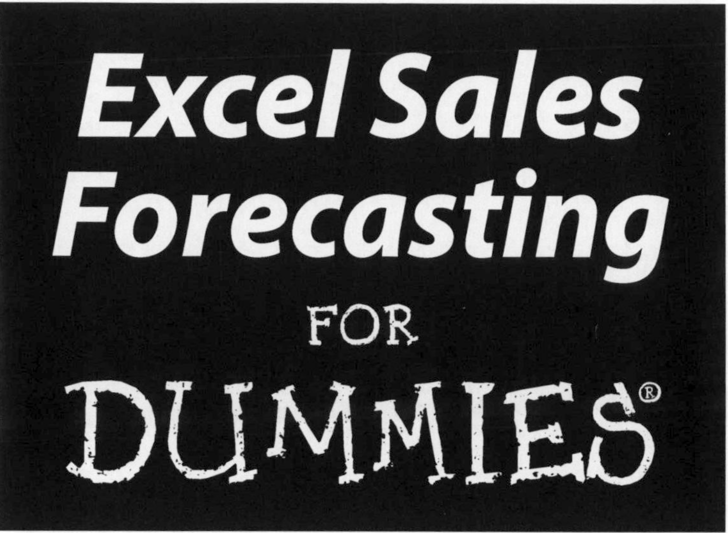

by Conrad Carlberg

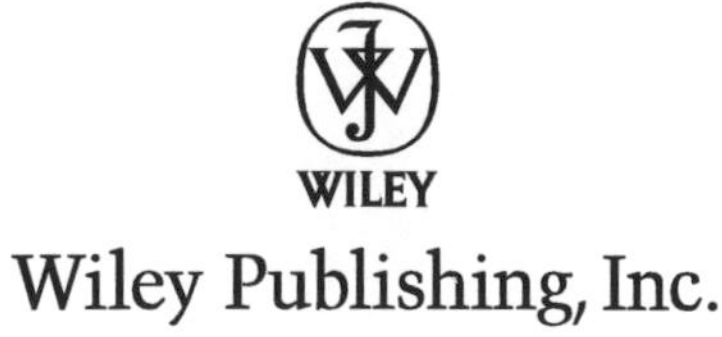

Wiley Publishing, Inc.

Excel Sales Forecasting For Dummies®

Published by
Wiley Publishing, Inc.
111 River Street
Hoboken, NJ 07030-5774

Published by Wiley Publishing, Inc., Indianapolis, Indiana

Published simultaneously in Canada

For general information on our other products and services, please contact our Customer Care Department within the U.S. at 800-762-2974, outside the U.S. at 317-572-3993, or fax 317-572-4002.

For technical support, please visit www.wiley.com/techsupport.

Wiley also publishes its books in a variety of electronic formats. Some content that appears in print may not be available in electronic books.

Library of Congress Control Number: 2005920365

ISBN: 0-7645-7593-7

10 9 8 7 6 5 4 3 2 1

1O/QZ/QT/QV/IN

About the Author

Conrad Carlberg is the author of more than ten books about Microsoft Excel. As a multi-time recipient of Microsoft's MVP designation for Excel, he is a nationally recognized expert on that application.

Carlberg's Ph.D. in statistics involves work in forecasting, as does his work in telecommunications and the health-care industry. He used the techniques in this book to reduce a crushing $24 million inventory owned by a Baby Bell to under $10 million in 18 months. The carrying costs for $24 million in equipment are significant. The point: This forecasting stuff works.

As preparation for starting his consultancy, Carlberg spent two years as a sales engineer for a *Fortune* 500 company. He lives near San Diego, where he tries his best to keep from crashing into other sailboats.

Dedication

For Joe Frazier, Mike Kobluk, and Chad Mitchell: Show me a pretty little number.

Author's Acknowledgments

I want to thank Kathy Ivens, who suggested my name to Wiley for this book and who has been the best coauthor one could hope for on our prior books; Tom Heine, the acquisitions editor who had the idea for this one; Elizabeth Kuball, the development editor, copy editor, project manager, and coach who has brought the book about; and, of course, the technical editor for this book — ladies and gentlemen, give it up for the Excel Trickster, Bob Umlas.

Publisher's Acknowledgments

We're proud of this book; please send us your comments through our online registration form located at www.dummies.com/register/.

Some of the people who helped bring this book to market include the following:

Acquisitions, Editorial, and Media Development

Project Editor: Elizabeth Kuball

Acquisitions Editor: Tom Heine

Technical Editor: Bob Umlas

Editorial Manager: Robyn Siesky

Media Development Supervisor: Richard Graves

Editorial Assistant: Adrienne Porter

Cartoons: Rich Tennant (www.the5thwave.com)

Composition Services

Project Coordinator: Maridee Ennis

Layout and Graphics: Andrea Dahl, Joyce Haughey, Clint Lahnen, Barry Offringa, Lynsey Osborn, Melanee Prendergast, Heather Ryan

Proofreaders: Leeann Harney, Jessica Kramer Carl William Pierce, TECHBOOKS Production Services

Indexer: TECHBOOKS Production Services

Publishing and Editorial for Technology Publishing

Richard Swadley, Vice President and Executive Group Publisher

Barry Pruett, Vice President and Publisher, Visual/Web Graphics

Andy Cummings, Vice President and Publisher, Technology Dummies

Mary Bednarek, Executive Acquisitions Director, Technology Dummies

Mary C. Corder, Editorial Director, Technology Dummies

Publishing for Consumer Dummies

Diane Graves Steele, Vice President and Publisher

Joyce Pepple, Acquisitions Director

Composition Services

Gerry Fahey, Vice President of Production Services

Debbie Stailey, Director of Composition Services

Contents at a Glance

Table of Contents

Introduction

You wouldn't have pulled this book off the shelf if you didn't need to forecast sales. And I'm sure that you're not Nostradamus. Your office isn't filled with the smell of incense and your job isn't to predict the date that the world will come to an end.

But someone — perhaps you — wants you to forecast sales, and you find out how to do that here, using the best workbook program around, Microsoft Excel.

About This Book

This book concentrates on using numbers to forecast sales. If you're a salesperson, or a sales manager, or someone yet higher up the org chart, you've run into forecasts that are based not on numbers but on guesses, sales quotas, wishful thinking, and Scotch.

I get away from that kind of thing here. I use numbers instead. Fortunately, you don't need to be a math major to use Excel for your forecasting. Excel has a passel of tools that will do it on your behalf. Some of them are even easy to use, as you'll see.

That said, it's not all about numbers. You still need to understand your products, your company, and your market before you can make a sensible sales forecast, and I have to trust you on that. I hope I can. I think I can. Otherwise, start with Part I, which talks about the context for a forecast.

You can hop around the chapters in this book, as you can in all books that have the guy with the triangle head on the cover. There are three basic approaches to forecasting with numbers — moving averages, smoothing, and regression — and you really don't have to know much about one to understand another. It helps to know all three, but you don't really need to.

Foolish Assumptions

The phrase *foolish assumptions* is of course redundant. But here are the assumptions I'm making:

- **I'm assuming that you know the basics of how to use Excel.** Entering numbers into a worksheet, like numbers that show how much you sold in August 2005; entering formulas in worksheet cells; saving workbooks; using menus; that sort of thing.

  If you haven't ever used Excel before, don't start here. Do buy this book, but also buy *Excel 2003 For Dummies* by Greg Harvey (published by Wiley), and dip into that one first.
- **I'm assuming that you have access to information on your company's sales history, and the more the better.** The only way to forecast what's about to happen is to know what's happened earlier. Doesn't really matter where that information is — it can be in a database, or in an Excel workbook, or even in a simple text file. As long as you can get your hands on it, you can make a forecast. And I talk about how you can get Excel's "hands" on it.
- **I'm assuming you don't have a phobia about numbers.** You don't have to be some kind of egghead to make good forecasts. But you can't be afraid of numbers, and I really doubt that you are. Except maybe your quarterly sales quota.
- **Oh yeah, I'm also assuming you have Excel on your computer.** I'm *not* assuming you have the latest version. Little in this book requires you to have anything more recent than Excel 95.

How to Use This Book

Do you have a couple of variables at hand? They might be something such as the number of cable subscribers in your region, and your revenues from selling cable services. If so, try looking at the chapters on forecasting by regression. If you know how many subscribers you have, then you're probably well on your way to forecasting revenues using the regression approach.

Do you have just one variable? If your company sells, say, sporting goods, you may not know how many customers you have, but you very likely know how much revenue you've recognized over the past few years. Then you may want to adopt a moving-average approach, maybe by tracking monthly sales dollars. Chapter 13 is probably the right place to start.

And, even with just one variable, you can do something called *exponential smoothing*. Don't worry, it's a lot easier than it sounds, and Excel has a tool that handles it for you if you want. It's a way of using bad forecasts that happened earlier in order to improve your next forecast. Visit Chapter 15 for more.

How you use this book depends on the sort of data you have, and you know that much better than I do.

How This Book Is Organized

All Gaul was divided into three parts. This book is divided into five.

Part I: Understanding Sales Forecasting and How Excel Can Help

I used to have a client who didn't believe in forecasting. He couldn't see why looking at the past could help you understand the future. The chapters in this part of the book explain what I couldn't get my client to understand. (I wish I'd written this book earlier — the client I mentioned has been, well, reassigned.) You also see in this part why Excel is a fine application to use for making your forecasts.

Part II: Organizing the Data

You need to know how to put your existing sales data together in order to get a good forecast (and how to defend that forecast when your management puts you on the griddle). In Excel, the basis for doing that is a *list.* That's kind of a rudimentary term, I know, but lists are really important in Excel. In this part, you also see how to choose and arrange your data.

Part III: Making a Basic Forecast

You can't forecast without knowing what's already happened. And you can't forecast sensibly without getting your data together. Lists, discussed in Part II, are the fundamentals, but pivot tables are the way to manage the data to prepare for a basic forecast. This part shows you how to get your existing sales data together from lists so you can make sensible forecasts.

Here you also get an introduction to the Analysis ToolPak, which you get as a free gift (another redundancy) when you buy Microsoft Excel. You see how you can use the Analysis ToolPak to make your forecast for you. And in this part, I try to convince you to put your data into charts so you can see what's going on.

Part IV: Making Advanced Forecasts

Advanced forecasts are a little more complicated when it comes to the math and the functions you use, but they can shed more light on what's going on in your sales flow. This section walks you through how to do your forecasts using worksheet functions rather than the Analysis ToolPak. As a result, you have more control over what's happening. And more control is better control, if you're willing to take the time to use it.

Part V: The Part of Tens

Part V was fun for me to write. I've been using Excel since the early 1990s and I've written a lot about it, both in online newsgroups and in books, and Part V gives me a chance both to extol its virtues and rant about its faults. Very satisfying emotionally. The Part of Tens talks about my favorite stuff and my pet peeves. Because pivot tables are so important to doing forecasts, it also talks about troubleshooting pivot table problems. And I get to bring my favorite Excel tools to your attention.

Icons Used in This Book

In the margins of this book, you find icons — little pictures that are designed to draw your attention to particular kinds of information. Here's what the icons mean:

Anything marked with this icon will make things easier for you, save you time, get you home in time for dinner. You get some of what I've distilled from all my years browsing those blasted newsgroups.

Not a lot of warnings in this book, but there are a few. These tell you what to expect if you do something that Microsoft hasn't sufficiently protected you against. And there are some of those.

A string around your finger. There are some things to keep in mind when you're doing your forecasts, and it's usually easier to remember them than to have to look them up over and over. I do want you to read this book over and over, as I do with murder mysteries, but you'll get your work done faster if you remember this stuff.

Speaking of stuff, anything marked with this icon is stuff you can probably ignore — but if you're having trouble getting to sleep you may want to read these. I don't get into heavy-duty mathematical issues here, but you see some special things about how Excel prepares your forecasts. Sleep tight.

Where to Go from Here

Are you looking for information about the basics of forecasting? Why it works? Why it's not just an exercise in numeric analysis? Start at Chapter 1.

Do you want to know how to put your data together in a workbook? Head to Chapter 5 to find out more about baselines, and then check out the chapters on using lists in Excel.

If you're already up on forecasting basics and lists, head for Chapter 8, where you'll see how to use pivot tables to set up the baseline for your forecast.

And if you know all that stuff already, just go to Chapter 10 and start looking at how to manage your forecasts yourself, without relying on the various tools that take care of things for you. You'll be glad you did.

Part I

Understanding Sales Forecasting and How Excel Can Help

"Great! It comes with Excel. Now we can forecast and find out where all the money around here is going."

In this part . . .

In Part I, I talk about why forecasting sales can help your business in ways that seem to have little to do with sales. Part I also tells you why forecasting isn't simply a matter of using formulas to crunch numbers. But, face it, some numbers have to be crunched, and here you find an introduction to baselines — which are the basis for the number-crunching. I try to convince you that forecasting really does work, and I back up that claim by showing you how.

Chapter 1

A Forecasting Overview

In This Chapter

- Knowing the different methods of forecasting
- Arranging your data in an order Excel can use
- Getting acquainted with the Analysis ToolPak
- Going it alone

A sales forecast is like a weather forecast: It's an educated guess at what the future will bring. You can forecast all sorts of things — poppy-seed sales, stock market futures, the weather — in all sorts of ways: You can make your own best guess; you can compile and composite other people's guesses; or you can forecast on the basis of wishful thinking.

Unfortunately, all three of these options are less than desirable. If you want to do better more often than you do worse, you need to take advantage of some better options. Lucky for you, there are different ways to forecast, ways that have proven their accuracy over and over. They're a little more time consuming than guessing, but in the long run I've spent more time explaining bad guesses than doing the forecasts right in the first place.

Microsoft Excel was originally developed as a spreadsheet application, suited to figuring payment amounts, interest rates, account balances, and so on. But as Microsoft added more and more functions — for example, AVERAGE and TREND and inventory-management stuff — Excel became more of a multipurpose analyst than a single-purpose calculator.

Excel has the tools you need to make forecasts, whether you want to prepare something quick and dirty (and who doesn't from time to time?) or something sophisticated enough for a boardroom presentation.

The tools are there. You just need to know which tool to choose and know how to use it. You need to know how to arrange data for the tool. And you need to know how to interpret what the tool tells you — whether that tool's a basic one or something more advanced.

Understanding Excel Forecasts

If you want to forecast the future — next quarter's sales, for example — you need to get a handle on what's happened in the past. So you always start with what's called a *baseline* (that is, past history — how many poppy seeds a company sold last year, where the market futures wound up last month, what the temperature was today).

Unless you're going to just roll the dice and make a guess, you need a baseline for a forecast. Today follows yesterday. What happens tomorrow generally follows the pattern of what happened today, last week, last month, last quarter, last year. If you look at what's already happened, you're taking a solid step toward forecasting what's going to happen next. (Part I of this book talks about forecast baselines and why they work.)

An Excel forecast isn't any different from forecasts you make with a specialized program. But Excel *is* a very useful application for making sales forecasts, for a variety of reasons:

- **You often have sales history recorded in an Excel worksheet.** When you already keep your sales history in Excel, basing your forecast on the existing sales history is easy — you've already got your hands on it.
- **Excel's charting features make it much easier to visualize what's going on in your sales history and how that history defines your forecasts.**
- **Excel has tools (found in what's called the Analysis ToolPak) that make generating forecasts easier.** You still have to know what you're doing and what the tools are doing — you don't want to just jam the numbers through some analysis tool and take the result at face value, without understanding what the tool's up to. But that's what this book is here for.
- **You can take more control over how the forecast is created by skipping the Analysis ToolPak's forecasting tools and entering the formulas yourself.** As you get more experience with forecasting, you'll probably find yourself doing that more and more.

You can choose from several different forecasting methods, and it's here that judgment begins. The three most frequently used methods, in no special order, are moving averages, exponential smoothing, and regression.

Method #1: Moving averages

Moving averages may be your best choice if you have no source of information other than sales history — but you *do* need to know your sales history. Later in this chapter, I show you more of the logic behind using moving averages. The underlying idea is that market forces push your sales up or down. By averaging your sales results from month to month, quarter to quarter, or year to year, you can get a better idea of the longer-term trend that's influencing your sales results.

For example, you find the average sales results of the last three months of last year — October, November, and December. Then you find the average of the next three-month period — November, December, and January (and then December, January, and February; and so on). Now you're getting an idea of the general direction that your sales are taking.

Method #2: Exponential smoothing

Exponential smoothing is closely related to moving averages. Just as with moving averages, exponential smoothing uses past history to forecast the future. You use what happened last week, last month, and last year to forecast what will happen next week, next month, or next year.

The difference is that when you use smoothing, you take into account how bad your previous forecast was — that is, you admit that the forecast was a little screwed up. (Get used to that — it happens.) The nice thing about exponential smoothing is that you take the error in your last forecast and use that error, so you hope, to improve your next forecast.

If your last forecast was too low, exponential smoothing kicks your next forecast up. If your last forecast was too high, exponential smoothing kicks the next one down.

The basic idea is that exponential smoothing corrects your next forecast in a way that would have made your *prior* forecast a better one. That's a good idea, and it usually works well.

Method #3: Regression

When you use regression to make a forecast, you're relying on one variable to predict another. For example, when the Federal Reserve raises short-term interest rates, you might rely on that variable to forecast what's going to happen to bond prices or the cost of mortgages. In contrast to moving averages or exponential smoothing, regression relies on a *different* variable to tell you what's likely to happen next — something other than your own sales history.

Getting the Data Ready

Which method of forecasting you use does make a difference, but regardless of your choice, in Excel you have to set up your baseline data in a particular way. Excel prefers it if your data is in the form of a *list.* In Part II, I fill you in on how to arrange your data so that it best feeds your forecasts, but following is a quick overview.

Using lists

There's nothing mysterious about an Excel list. A list is something very much like a database. Your Excel worksheet has columns and rows, and if you put a list there, you just need to manage three requirements:

- **Keep different variables in different columns.** For example, you can put sales dates in one column, sales amounts in another column, sales reps' names in another, product lines in yet another.
- **Keep different records in different rows.** When it comes to recording sales information, keep different sales records in different rows. Put information about a sale that was made on January 15 in one row, and information about a sale made on January 16 in a different row.
- **Put the names of the variables in the list's first row.** For example, you might put "Sales Date" in column A, "Revenue" in column B, "Sales Rep" in column C, and "Product" in column D.

Figure 1-1 shows a typical Excel list.

Why bother with lists? Because many Excel tools, including the ones you use to make forecasts, rely on lists. Charts — which help you visualize what's going on with your sales — rely on lists. Pivot tables — which are the most powerful way you have for summarizing your sales results in Excel — rely heavily on lists. The Analysis ToolPak — a very useful way of making forecasts — relies on lists, too.

You find a lot more about creating and using lists in Chapter 6. In the meantime, just keep in mind that a list has different variables in different columns, and different records in different rows.

Ordering your data

"Ordering your data" may sound a little like "coloring inside the lines." The deal is that you have to tell Excel how much you sold in 1999, and then how much in 2000, and in 2001, and so on. If you're going to do that, you have to put the data in chronological order.

Sales Date	Revenue	Sales Rep	Product
10/6/2005	$ 9,150.38	Wilson	Software
10/17/2005	$ 2,799.29	Anderson	Hardware
10/16/2005	$ 7,524.88	James	Software
10/7/2005	$ 8,127.68	Anderson	Services
10/13/2005	$ 8,625.87	Wilson	Maintenance
10/18/2005	$ 8,762.56	Turgidson	Maintenance
10/21/2005	$ 2,227.09	Anderson	Software
10/8/2005	$ 9,136.42	Jones	Software
10/18/2005	$ 4,122.04	Coulter	Software
10/10/2005	$ 5,141.18	Anderson	Maintenance
10/22/2005	$ 3,057.58	Jones	Hardware
10/13/2005	$ 8,595.78	Tafoya	Software
10/10/2005	$ 1,088.58	Tafoya	Hardware
10/21/2005	$ 7,781.21	Turgidson	Warranty
10/15/2005	$ 5,571.73	Coulter	Hardware
10/7/2005	$ 6,147.57	Turgidson	Hardware
10/20/2005	$ 4,477.92	Wilson	Hardware
10/5/2005	$ 7,683.13	James	Maintenance
10/14/2005	$ 7,920.99	Turgidson	Services
10/19/2005	$ 3,627.68	James	Services
10/11/2005	$ 7,307.49	Coulter	Warranty
10/11/2005	$ 4,690.90	Turgidson	Software
10/22/2005	$ 1,551.36	Coulter	Services
10/16/2005	$ 1,113.69	Wilson	Warranty
10/14/2005	$ 7,447.74	Anderson	Warranty
10/17/2005	$ 3,353.07	Tafoya	Services
10/12/2005	$ 9,359.40	James	Hardware
10/12/2005	$ 6,401.29	Jones	Services
10/8/2005	$ 1,707.77	Coulter	Maintenance
10/20/2005	$ 3,292.47	Tafoya	Maintenance
10/15/2005	$ 8,284.11	Jones	Maintenance
10/9/2005	$ 4,202.45	Wilson	Services
10/9/2005	$ 1,711.83	James	Warranty
10/19/2005	$ 6,192.25	Jones	Warranty

Figure 1-1: You don't have to keep the records in date order — you can handle that later.

The best — and I mean the *best* — way to put your data in chronological order in Excel is by way of pivot tables. A pivot table takes individual records that are in a list (or in an external database) and combines the records in ways that you control. You may have a list showing a year's worth of sales, including the name of the sales rep, the product sold, the date of sale, and the sales revenue. If so, you can very quickly create a pivot table that totals sales revenue by sales rep and by product across quarters. Using pivot tables, you can summarize tens of thousands of records, quite literally within seconds. If you haven't used pivot tables before, this book not only introduces the subject but also makes you dream about them in the middle of the night.

There are a couple of wonderful things about pivot tables:

- **They can accumulate for you all your sales data — or, for that matter, your data on the solar wind, but this book is about sales forecasting.** If you gather information on a sale-by-sale basis, and you then want to know how much your reps sold on a given day, in a given week, and so on, a pivot table is the best way to do so.
- **You can use a pivot table as the basis for your next forecast, which saves you a bunch of time.**
- **They have a unique way of helping you group your historical data — by day, by week, by month, by quarter, by year, you name it.** Chapter 8 gives you much more information on pivot tables, including troubleshooting some common problems.

Making Basic Forecasts

Part III gets into the business of making actual forecasts, ones that are based on historical data (that is, what's gone on before). You see how to use the Analysis ToolPak to make forecasts that you can back up with actuals — given that you've looked at Part II and set up your actuals correctly. (Your *actuals* are the actual sales results that show up in the company's accounting records — say, when the company recognizes the revenue.)

The Analysis ToolPak (often abbreviated ATP) is a gizmo that has shipped with Excel ever since 1995. The ATP is a convenient way to make forecasts, as well as to do general data analysis. The three principal tools Excel's ATP gives you to make forecasts are:

- Moving Averages
- Exponential Smoothing
- Regression

All the news that's fit to print — and then some

You may not be familiar with newsgroups, and if you're not, I think you should be. ***Newsgroups*** are what used to be called bulletin boards before the Internet and the Web came along. They're places where you can post questions (for example, about Excel) and a little later on read answers that other users have posted. (Unfortunately, because newsgroups are largely public, you also see a lot of garbage.) One good way to get familiar with newsgroups is to use Google:

1. **Go to** `www.google.com`.
2. **Click on Groups, and then click Advanced Groups Search.**

   The Advanced Groups Search link is in really small print to the right of the Search Groups button.
3. **Enter** Microsoft.Public.Excel.* **in the Return Only Messages from the Group box.**

   The asterisk returns all public newsgroups beginning with Microsoft.Public.Excel.
4. **Enter a word or phrase you want to look for in one of the Find Messages boxes.**

   For example, you can type **add-in** to search specifically for newsgroups about Excel add-ins.
5. **Click the Google Search button.**

   You'll see all the questions — and all the answers — concerning the word or phrase you entered that have shown up in those newsgroups.

Newsgroups are a great way to find out about Excel — or, for that matter, any other application.

Those are the three principal forecasting methods, and they form the basis for the more-advanced techniques and models. So it's no coincidence that these tools have the same names as the forecasting methods mentioned earlier in this chapter.

The Analysis ToolPak is an *add-in.* An add-in does tasks, like forecasting, on your behalf. An add-in is much like the other tools that are a part of Excel — the difference is that you can choose whether to install an add-in. For example, you can't choose whether the Goal Seek tool (Tools ➪ Goal Seek) is available to you. If you decide to install Excel on your computer, Goal Seek is just part of the package. Add-ins are different. You can decide whether to install them. When you're installing Excel — and in most cases this means when you're installing Microsoft Office — you get to decide which add-ins you want to use.

The following sections offer a brief introduction to the three ATP tools.

Given a good baseline, the ATP can turn a forecast back to you. And then you're responsible for evaluating the forecast, for deciding whether it's a credible one, for thinking the forecast over in terms of what you know about your business model. After all, Excel just calculates — you're expected to do the thinking.

Putting moving averages to work for you

You may already be familiar with moving averages. They have two main characteristics, as the name makes clear:

- **They move.** More specifically, they move over time. The first moving average may involve Monday, Tuesday, and Wednesday; in that case, the second moving average would involve Tuesday, Wednesday, and Thursday; the third Wednesday, Thursday, and Friday, and so on.
- **They're averages.** The first moving average may be the average of Monday's, Tuesday's, and Wednesday's sales. Then the second moving average would be the average of Tuesday's, Wednesday's, and Thursday's sales, and so on.

The basic idea, as with all forecasting methods, is that something regular and predictable is going on — often called the *signal.* Sales of ski boots regularly rise during the fall and winter, and predictably fall during the spring and summer. Beer sales regularly rise on NFL Sundays and predictably fall on other days of the week.

But something else is going on, something irregular and unpredictable — often called *noise.* If a local sporting goods store has a sale on, discounting ski boots from May through July, you and your friends may buy new boots during the spring and summer, even though the regular sales pattern (the signal) says that people buy boots during the fall and winter. As a forecaster, you can't predict this special sale. It's random and tends to depend on things like overstock. It's noise.

Let's say you run a liquor store, and a Thursday night college football game that looked like it would be the Boring Game of the Week when you were scheduling your purchases in September has suddenly in November turned into one with championship implications. You may be caught short if you scheduled your purchases to arrive at your store the following Saturday, when the signal in the baseline leads you to expect your sales to peak. That's *noise* — the difference between what you predict and what actually happens. By definition, noise is unpredictable, and for a forecaster it's a pain.

If the noise is random, it averages out. Some months, your stores will be discounting ski boots for less than the cost of an arthroscopy. Some months, a new and really cool model will come on line, and they'll be taking every possible advantage. The peaks and valleys even out. Some weeks there will be an extra game or two and you'll sell (and therefore need) more bottles of beer. Some weeks there'll be a dry spell from Monday through Friday, you won't need so much beer, and you won't want to bear the carrying costs of beer you're not going to sell for a while.

The idea is that the noise averages out, and that what moving averages show you is the signal. To misquote Johnny Mercer, if you accentuate the signal and eliminate the noise, you latch on to a pretty good forecast.

So with moving averages, you take account of the signal — the fact that you sell more ski boots during certain months and fewer during other months, or that you sell more beer on weekends than on weekdays. At the same time you want to let the random noises — also termed *errors* — cancel one another out. You do that by averaging what's already happened in two, three, four, or more previous consecutive months. The signal in those months is emphasized by the averaging, and that averaging also tends to minimize the noise.

Suppose you decide to base your moving averages on two-month records. That is, you'll average January and February, and then February and March, and then March and April, and so on. So you're getting a handle on the signal by averaging two consecutive months and reducing the noise at the same time. Then, if you want to forecast what will happen in May, you hope to be able to use the signal — that is, the average of what's happened in March and April.

Figure 1-2 shows an example of the monthly sales results and of the two-month moving average.

Chapter 14 goes into more detail about using moving averages for forecasting.

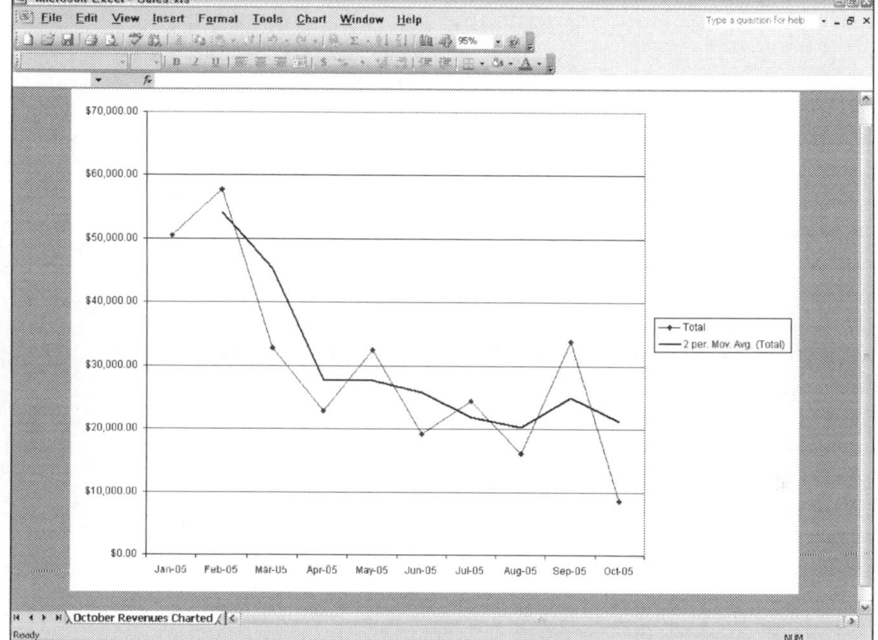

Figure 1-2: The moving average shows the general direction of the sales (the signal), and deemphasizes the random variations (the noise).

Making sense of exponential smoothing

I know, the term *exponential smoothing* sounds intimidating and pretentious. I guess it's both — although I'm not responsible for it, I swear. (If you really want, you can find out why it's called that in Chapter 15.) In any event, don't worry about what it's called — it's just a kind of self-correcting moving average.

Suppose that in June, you forecast $100,000 in sales for July. When the July sales results are in, you find that your July forecast of $100,000 was $25,000 too low — you actually made $125,000 in sales. Now you need to forecast your sales for August. The idea behind this approach to forecasting is to adjust your August forecast in a way that would have made the *July* forecast more accurate. That is, because your July forecast was too low, you increase your August forecast above what it would have been otherwise.

More generally:

- If your most recent forecast turned out to be an underestimate, you adjust your next forecast upward.
- If your most recent forecast turned out to be an overestimate, you adjust your next forecast downward.

You don't make these adjustments just by guessing. There are formulas that help out, and the ATP's Exponential Smoothing tool can enter the formulas for you. Or you can roll your own formulas if you want. Turn to Chapter 15 to see how to do that.

Figure 1-3 shows what you would forecast if your prior forecast (for July) was too low — then you boost your forecast for August.

And if your prior, July forecast was too high (you optimist!), you cool your jets a little bit in your August forecast, as shown in Figure 1-4.

Using regression to get what you want

The term *regression* doesn't sound as bad as *exponential smoothing,* but it is — I admit — more complicated, at least in terms of the math.

And that's why the ATP is convenient. It takes responsibility for the math, just as it does with moving averages and exponential smoothing. ***Remember:*** You still have to give a good baseline to the ATP to get accurate results.

Here's a quick look at forecasting with regression. (You can find a more detailed look in Chapter 11.)

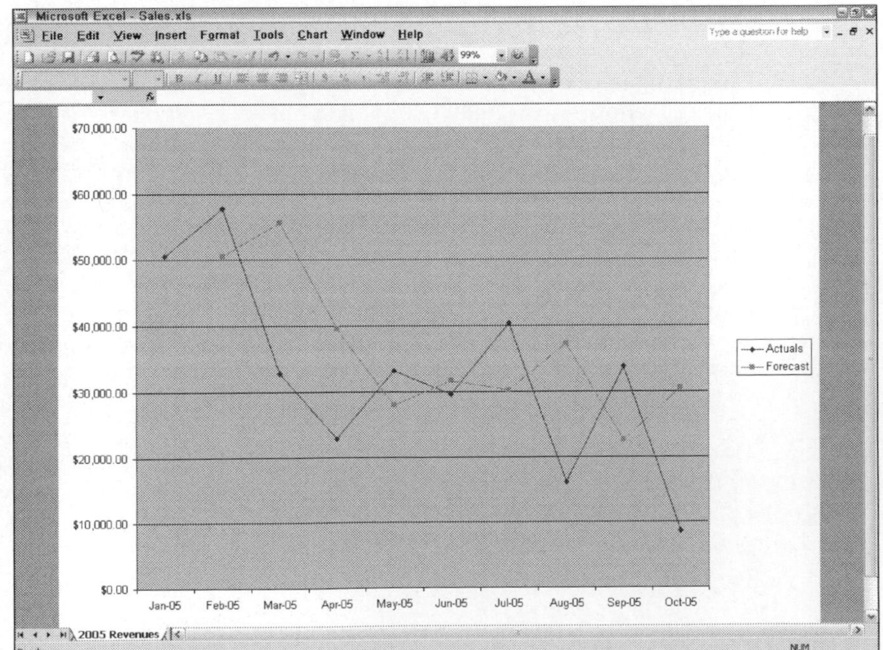

Figure 1-3: Here's what happens if your forecast for July was an underestimate. Notice that the August forecast is kicked up.

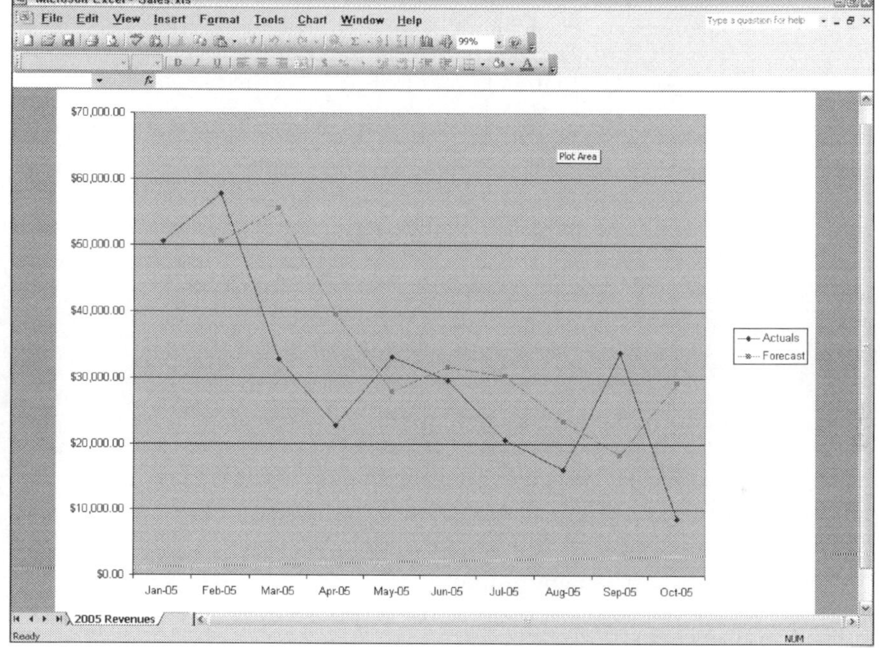

Figure 1-4: Your prior forecast was too high, so exponential smoothing makes you back off your next forecast.

The idea behind regression is that one variable has a relationship with another variable. When you're a kid, for example, your height tends to have a relationship to your age. So if you want to forecast how tall you'll be next year — at least, until you quit growing — you can check how old you'll be next year.

Of course, people differ. When they're 15 years old, some people are 5 feet tall, some are 6 feet tall. On average, though, you can forecast with some confidence how tall someone will be at age 15. (And you can almost certainly forecast that a newborn kidlet is going to be under 2 feet tall, even wearing lifts.)

The same holds true with sales forecasting. Suppose your company sells consumer products. It's a good bet that the more advertising you do, the more you'll sell. At least it's worth checking out whether there's a relationship between the size of your advertising budget and the size of your sales revenue. If you find that there's a dependable relationship — and if you know how much your company is willing to spend on advertising — you're in a good position to forecast your sales.

Or suppose your company markets a specialty product, such as fire doors. (A *fire door* is one that's supposed to be resistant to fire for some period of time, and there are a lot of them in office buildings.) Unlike consumer products, something such as a fire door doesn't have to be a particular off-the-shelf color or have a fresher-than-fresh aroma. If you're buying fire doors, you want to get the ones that meet the specs and are the cheapest.

So if you're selling fire doors, as long as your product meets the specs, you'd want to have a look at the relationship between the price of fire doors and how many are sold. Then you check with your marketing department to find out how much they want you to charge per door, and you can make your forecast accordingly.

The point is that more often than not you can find a dependable relationship between one variable (advertising dollars or unit price) and another (usually, sales revenue or units sold).

You use Excel's tools to quantify that relationship. In the case of regression forecasts, you give Excel a couple of baselines. To continue the examples we've used so far in this section:

- Historical advertising expenses and historical sales revenues
- How much you charged per fire door and how many doors you sold

If you give Excel good baselines, it will come back to you with a formula.

- Excel will give you a number to multiply times how much you expect to spend on advertising, and the result will be your expected sales revenue.
- Or, Excel will give you a number to multiply times the unit cost per door, and the result will be the number of doors you can expect to sell.

It's just a touch more complicated than that. Excel also gives you a number, called a *constant,* that you need to add to the result of the multiplication. But as Chapter 11 shows, you can get Excel to do that for you.

Charting Your Data

I've been doing this stuff for a long time, and I can't tell you how critical it is to chart your baseline and your forecast. Being able to visualize what's going on is important for several reasons.

Using Excel's charts, you can see how your actuals are doing (see Figure 1-5). And by charting your actuals, you can see how well your sales forecasts do against the actual sales results. Figure 1-6 shows a forecast that's based on moving averages, against the monthly actuals.

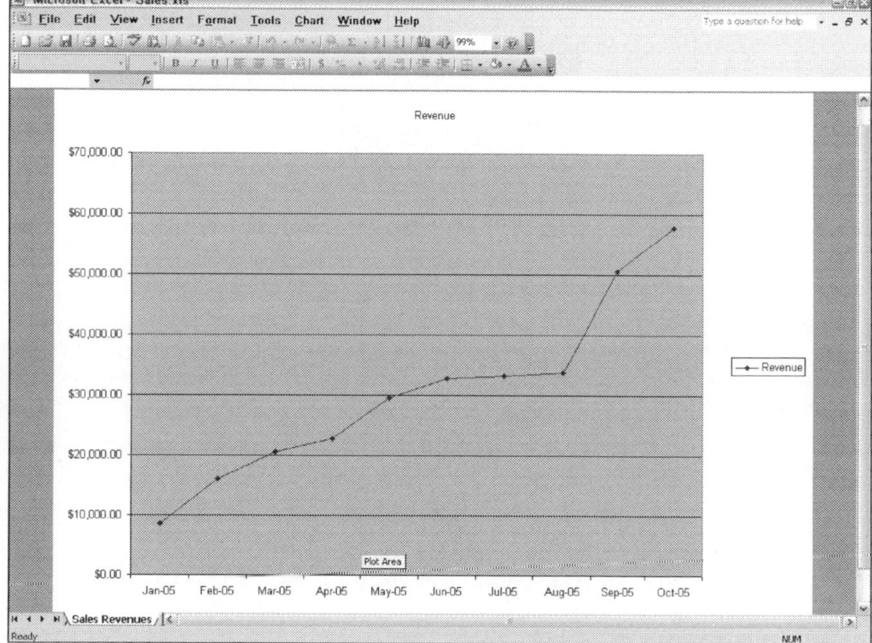

Figure 1-5: An Excel chart makes it much easier to see how your sales are doing.

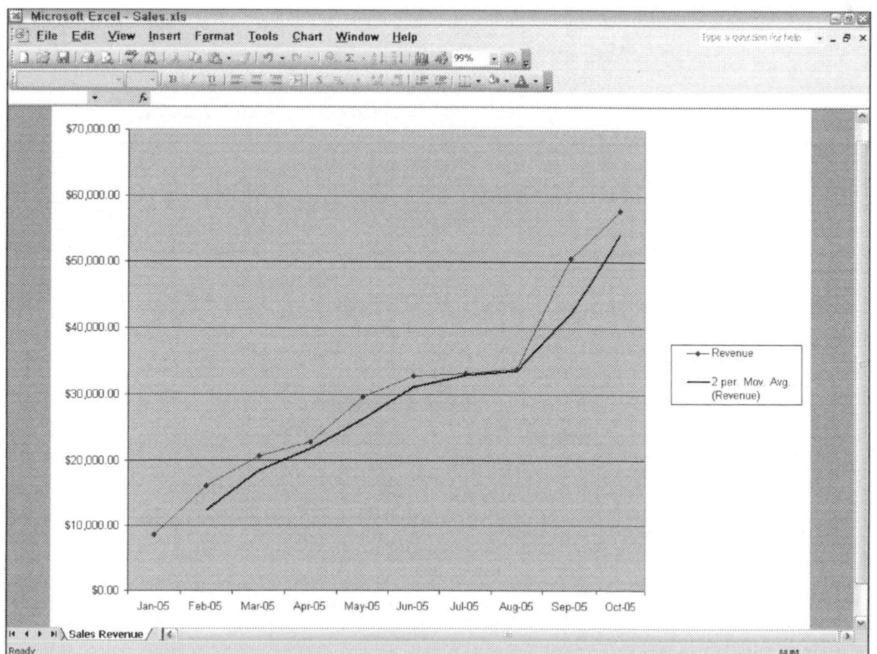

Figure 1-6: Notice how the moving average lags behind the actual results.

A word or two about Excel versions

Pivot tables were first introduced in Excel 95. This book has a good bit to say about basing charts on pivot tables, much of which has been made redundant by Excel 2000 and its pivot charts — beginning with Excel 2000, you can create not only pivot tables but also pivot charts.

Many companies continue to use Excel 97, though, and for good reason. The principal argument for upgrading to Excel 2000, 2002, or 2003 is that ***other*** software might rely on Excel to handle calculations, and that other software requires a version of Excel that's more recent than 1997. A company that doesn't have to do the upgrade, though, usually doesn't — the cost-benefit equation doesn't say "Upgrade now!"

So, if like many others your company still uses Excel 97, you'll want to know how to create charts based on pivot tables. If your company uses Excel 2000 or later, Chapter 9 shows you how to create pivot charts, as well as how to create standard charts that are based on pivot tables.

By charting your baseline and your forecasts, you can:

- **See how your actual results are doing.** A chart is almost always more revealing than a table of numbers.
- **See how well your forecasts predict actual results.** Your eye is a good gauge of the quality of your forecasts.
- **See how well a different variable — advertising dollars or the Consumer Price Index — predicts the sales of your product.**

Yes, an R squared or some other summary statistic can give you a concise estimate of how well your forecasts are working. But there's nothing, *nothing*, like a chart to tell you if you're forecasting results or if you're forecasting junk. Chapter 9 shows you how to set up charts with Excel.

Forecasting with Advanced Tools

There's a lot to be said for using the Analysis ToolPak to create your forecasts. The ATP is quick, it does the heavy lifting for you, and it's pretty comprehensive, taking care of the math and some of the charting.

But there's nothing like doing it yourself. When you wave goodbye to the ATP, you establish and maintain control over what's going on with the forecast. If you have formulas in your worksheet cells — formulas that support your forecasts — you can change those formulas as your forecasting needs change. And you can change — or add to — the baseline and immediately see what the effect doing so has on your forecast.

When the ATP does not give you formulas but static values instead, you can't experiment with the forecasts or see the effect of modifying the baseline. And the ATP's Regression tool gives you just the static values. The Exponential Smoothing tool is a little better, but it mixes formulas with static values. And the Moving Averages tool forces you to start over if you want to change the number of records in the baseline that make up a moving average.

Suppose that you have the number 3 in cell A1 and the number 5 in cell A2. In cell A3 you can enter the sum of those two numbers, 8. But if you now change the number 3 in cell A1 to, say, 103, you still have 8 in A3. It's a constant — a number, not a formula. It doesn't react to what's in cell A1 or A2: You're still going to see the number 8 in cell A3.

On the other hand, suppose you have this in cell A3:

```
=A1 + A2
```

That's a formula, not a constant, and it tells Excel to add whatever's in A1 to whatever's in A2. So if you change what's in A1, or what's in A2, Excel recalculates the result and shows it — in this example — in A3.

The point to keep in mind is that the ATP's regression tool gives you numbers, not formulas. It calculates your forecast, and the underlying figures, and writes numbers onto your worksheet. That means, regardless of how you change the numbers in your baseline, you're still going to be looking at the same forecast as offered by the ATP.

But — and it's a big one — if you make the forecast yourself instead of relying on the ATP, you can enter the formulas that the ATP denies you. Why is this important? By entering the formulas yourself, you have more control over what's going on with the forecast.

Relying on the ATP, which is a good toolbox, and one that you can generally trust, is perfectly okay. However, if you enter formulas, ones that react to changes in your baseline, you can make a change in the baseline and see what happens to the forecast. You can change this month's result from $100,000 to $75,000 and see whether your forecast for next month changes substantially. You can't do that with the ATP's Regression tool, because it doesn't give you formulas. To a smaller degree, the same is true of the Exponential Smoothing tool.

But the more important reason, the reason for you to consider entering the formulas yourself, is that you're relying on your own knowledge of how and why forecasting works. In Part IV, I show you how to use functions like LINEST and TREND to do your regression-based forecasts. You also see how to use array formulas to get the most out of those Excel functions.

You don't need to enter all the formulas yourself to make good forecasts. The ATP is a good tool. But if you do enter the formulas yourself, not only can you be more confident that you know what's going on with your forecast, but you can also exercise more control over what your forecast says is going to happen. In a business as tricky and trappy as forecasting, the more control you have, the better.

Chapter 2

Forecasting: The Basic Issues

In This Chapter

- Knowing why you need to forecast
- Understanding the language of forecasting
- Seeing what Excel can do for you

Unless you really enjoy playing with numbers (and, in that case, you probably have your first slide rule mounted on your wall), you need a good reason to bother with forecasting sales. In this chapter, I tell you some of the business reasons to forecast, beyond the fact that your Vice President of Sales makes you do it.

Like all specialties, forecasting uses terms that are unfamiliar to those who haven't yet been inducted into the secret society. This chapter introduces you to some of the important sales forecasting terminology.

If you're going to make a credible forecast, you need access to a bunch of historical data that isn't necessarily easy to access. You'll often find it right there in an Excel workbook, but sometimes it isn't there; instead, it's in your company's accounting database, and someone will have to exhume it. In this chapter, you'll see some of the reasons to put yourself (or your assistant) through that particular form of agony.

Excel offers several methods of forecasting. Each method works best — and some work *only* — if you set up a baseline using what Excel terms a *list configuration.* Depending on the method you choose, that list may occupy only one column, or two (or more) columns. This chapter gives you an overview of those methods, along with a brief explanation of why you might use just one column of data for your baseline, or two or more columns, depending on your choice of forecasting method.

Excel is an ideal general-purpose analysis program to use for forecasting, in part because it has functions and tools that are intended to help you make your forecasts, and in part because you often store the necessary data in Excel anyway — so, it's right there, ready for you to use. In this chapter, you find out what's so great about Excel and how to put it to use for you.

Why Forecast?

People tend to think of the process of sales forecasting as a knee-jerk response to a frantic call for reassurance from some nervous, jumpy, excitable VP who's worried about having to dust off the résumé. And often, you have some reason to believe that's *exactly* what's going on.

But there are plenty of more productive reasons to go to the trouble of gathering up baseline data, getting it into the right shape to support a credible forecast, do the analysis, and then interpret it than just responding to a VP who's afraid his job is on the line. Here are a few of those reasons.

To plan sales strategies

If you can use sales forecasts to get a handle on either future revenues, or unit sales, or both, you can help groups like Marketing, Product Management, and Production make decisions about activities such as promotion, pricing, and purchasing — each of which influences your company's sales results.

Suppose you take a look at quarterly sales results over a period of several years, and you see that during that time the sales of a particular product have been gently declining. (If the decline had been steep, you wouldn't have to look at a baseline — everyone from the sales force to the CEO would have been rattling your cage.) Your forecast indicates that the decline is likely to continue. Is the market for the product disappearing? That depends. You need to ask and answer some other questions first.

- **Is the product a commodity?** Some business analysts sneer at commodities — they're not very glamorous, after all — but commodities can be very profitable products if you dominate the market. If you don't dominate the market, maybe you shouldn't be in the market. So, have your competitors been cutting into your market share, or is the total size of the market shrinking? If the problem is the competition, maybe you want to do something to take back your share, even if that requires putting more resources into the product line — such as retooling its manufacture, putting more dollars into promotions, or cutting the price. But if the total market itself is shrinking, it may just be time to bail out.
- **How old is the product?** Products do have life cycles. When products are bright and shiny, the sales revenues can grow sharply over a fairly short time frame. When products reach maturity, the sales flatten out. And then, as newer, better, fancier products arrive, the sales start to drop. Think DVD versus VHS. Get Marketing and Product Management to assess whether the product is getting long in the tooth. If it is, it may be

time to get out. Or, it may be smart to spruce up the product and differentiate it from the competition's versions, in order to squeeze some more profitable revenue out of it before you give up on it. Forecasting can support that kind of decision, although it can't make it for you.

- **How will Sales support the product?** If your company decides that it's not yet time to abandon the product, Sales Management needs to make some decisions about how to allocate its resources — that is, its sales reps. One way to do that, of course, is to take the product out of some reps' bags and replace it with another, more robust product. (Keep in mind that some reps *prefer* older products because they can use familiar sales strategies.)
- **Is it possible that the decline in sales is due more to large-scale economic conditions than to problems with the product itself?** If so, you may decide to hang in and wait for the economy, consumer confidence, or the index of leading economic indicators to improve, instead of making a drastic decision to drop a product line.

There's at least one good aspect to a product that's entering the final stage of its life cycle: You very likely have lots of historical data on its sales figures. And in general, the more historical data you have to base a forecast on, the more confidence you can place in that forecast.

To size inventories

During the late 1980s, I worked for a Baby Bell — one of the companies that was spun off by the AT&T breakup. For a couple of years, I was in charge of managing resale equipment inventories at that Baby Bell.

My staff and I reduced the size of the equipment intended for sale to customers from a grotesque $24 million to a more reasonable $9 million in 18 months, without resorting to write-downs. We did it by forecasting sales by product line. This helped us tell which products we could expect to have high *turns ratios* (the speed with which the product line would sell) and we'd buy those in quantities that increased our discounts from our suppliers.

The products that we forecast would have low turns ratios we refused to buy until we were almost out of them. It didn't matter how piteous the pleadings of the sales managers who wanted them on hand for fast delivery just in case a customer decided to buy one and wanted it installed right now. (Getting a huge PBX out of warehouse storage in West Eyesocket, Connecticut, and shipping it to Broken Pelvis, Montana, can take longer than you may think. For one thing, you may have to pressure Connecticut's Regional VP into letting go of it.)

Plus, the annual carrying costs for equipment inventory in the late 1980s averaged around 15 percent of the cost of the equipment, including storage, cost of money, obsolescence, and so on. So by reducing the total inventory cost by $15 million, we saved the company $2.25 million each year. (That savings actually covered the cost of our salaries, by the way.)

Simply reducing the size of inventory isn't the end of the story, though. Sales forecasting helps you plan just-in-time (JIT) inventory management, so you can time your purchases to correspond to when sales need to be fulfilled. The less time inventory spends in the warehouse, the less money you're paying to let it just sit there waiting to be sold.

Talking the Talk: Basic Forecasting Lingo

You need to get a handle on the specialized terminology used in forecasting for a couple very practical reasons. One is that you may be asked to explain your forecasts to your boss or in a meeting of, for example, sales managers. In those situations you want to say things like, "We decided to use regression on the baseline because it turned out to be more accurate." You *don't* want to find yourself saying "Jeff found a formula in a book he has, and we used it on this thingy here. Seems to work okay."

Another good reason is that Excel uses many of these terms, as do other programs, and figuring out what's going on is a lot easier if you know what the terms mean. Okay, deep breath.

Autoregressive integrated moving averages (ARIMA)

I mention autoregressive integrated moving averages (ARIMA) here not because this book is going to use it or even talk much about it. But if you're going to do forecasting, some smart aleck will eventually ask you if you used ARIMA, and you should know how to reply. ARIMA is in part a forecasting method, and also a way of evaluating your baseline so that you can get quantitative evidence that supports using a regression approach, a moving-average approach, or a combination of both. Unless you really take to this forecasting stuff, you'll usually do just fine without it, even though it's an excellent, if complex, diagnostic tool.

By the way, your answer to the smart aleck should be, "No. I've been working with this baseline for so long now that I know I get my best results with exponential smoothing."

Baseline

A *baseline* is a sequence of data arranged in chronological order. In terms of this book's basic topic, the forecasting of sales, some examples of baselines include total monthly revenues from January 2000 through December 2004, number of units sold weekly from January 1, 2005, through December 31, 2005, and total quarterly revenues from Q1 1995 through Q4 2005. Data arranged like this is sometimes called a *time series,* but in this book I use the term *baseline.*

Correlation

A *correlation* coefficient expresses how strongly two variables are related. Its possible values range from –1.0 to +1.0, but in practice you never find correlations so extreme. The closer a correlation coefficient is to +/–1.0, the stronger the relationship between the two variables. A correlation of 0.0 means no relationship. So, you might find a correlation of +0.7 (fairly strong) between the number of sales reps you have and the total revenue they bring in: the greater the number of reps, the more that gets sold. And you might find a correlation of –0.1 (quite weak) between how much a rep sells and his weight.

A special type of correlation is the *autocorrelation,* which calculates the strength of the relationship between one observation in a baseline and an earlier observation (usually, but not always, the relationship between two consecutive observations). The autocorrelation tells you the strength of the relationship between what came before and what came after. This in turn helps you decide what kind of forecasting technique to use. Here's an example of how to calculate an autocorrelation that might make the concept a little clearer:

```
=CORREL(A2:A50,A1:A49)
```

This Excel formula uses the CORREL function to show how strong (or how weak) a relationship there is between whatever values are in A2:A50 and those in A1:A49.

Cycle

A *cycle* is similar to a seasonal pattern (see the "Seasonality" section, later in this chapter), but you don't consider it in the same way as you do seasonality. The upswing might span several years, and the downswing might do the same. Furthermore, one full cycle might take four years to complete, and the next one just two years. A good example is the business cycle: Recessions chase booms, and you never know just how long each is going to last.

Damping factor

The *damping factor* is a fraction between 0.0 and 1.0 that you use in exponential smoothing to determine how much of the error in the prior forecast will be used in calculating the next forecast.

Actually, the use of the term *damping factor* is a little unusual. Most texts on exponential smoothing refer to the *smoothing constant*. The damping factor is 1.0 minus the smoothing constant. It really doesn't matter which term you use; you merely adjust the formula accordingly. This book uses *damping factor* where necessary because it's the term that Excel uses.

Exponential smoothing

Stupid term, even if technically accurate. Using *exponential smoothing,* you compare your prior forecast to the prior *actual* (in this context, an *actual* is the sales result that Accounting tells you —after the fact —that you generated). Then you use the error — that is, the difference between the prior forecast and the prior actual — to adjust the next forecast and, you hope, make it more accurate than if you hadn't taken the prior error into account. In Chapter 15, I show you how really intuitive an idea this is, despite its pretentious name.

Forecast period

The *forecast period* is the length of time that's represented by each observation in your baseline. The term is used because your forecast usually represents the same length of time as each baseline observation. If your baseline consists of monthly sales revenues, your forecast is usually for the upcoming month. If the baseline consists of quarterly sales, your forecast is usually for the next quarter. Using the regression approach, you can make forecasts farther into the future than just one forecast period, but the farther your forecast gets from the most recent actual observation, the thinner the ice.

Moving average

You've probably run into the concept of moving averages somewhere along the line. The idea is that averaging causes noise in the baseline to cancel out, leaving you with a better idea of the *signal* (what's really going on over time, unsullied by the inevitable random errors). It's an *average* because it's the average of some number of consecutive observations, such as the average of the sales in January, February, and March. It's *moving* because the time periods that are averaged move forward in time — so, the first moving average could include January, February, and March; the second moving average could include February, March, and April; and so on.

There's no requirement that each moving average include three values — it could be two, or four, or five, or conceivably even more. (Chapter 13 fills you in on the effects of choosing more or fewer periods to average.)

Predictor variable

You generally find this term in use when you're forecasting with regression. The *predictor variable* is the variable you use to estimate a future value of the variable you want to forecast. For example, you may find a dependable relationship between unit sales price and sales volume. If you know how much your company intends to charge per unit during the next quarter, you can use that relationship to forecast the sales volume for next quarter. In this example, unit sales price is the predictor variable.

Regression

If you use the *regression* approach to forecasting, it's because you've found a dependable relationship between sales revenues and one or more predictor variables (see the preceding section for more information). You use that relationship, plus your knowledge of future values of the predictor variables, to create your forecast.

How would you know those future values of the predictor variables? If you're going to use unit price as a predictor, one good way is to find out from Product Management how much it intends to charge per unit during each of the next, say, four quarters. Another way involves dates: It's entirely possible, and even common, to use dates such as months within years as a predictor variable. Even I can figure out what the next value is in a baseline that ends with November 2005.

Seasonality

During the span of a year, your baseline might rise and fall on a seasonal basis. Perhaps you sell a product whose sales rise during warm weather and fall during cold. If you can see roughly the same pattern occur within each year over a several-year period, you know you're looking at *seasonality*. You can take advantage of that knowledge to improve your forecasts.

Trend

A *trend* is the tendency of the level of a baseline to rise or fall over time. A rising trend is, of course, good news for sales reps and sales management, to say nothing of the rest of the company. A falling baseline, although seldom good news, can inform Marketing and Product Management that some decisions, perhaps painful ones, need to be made and acted on. Regardless of the direction of the trend, the fact that a trend exists can cause problems for your forecasts in some contexts — but there are ways of dealing with those problems. Chapter 17 shows you some of those ways.

Understanding the Baseline

A *baseline* is a series of observations — more to the point, a *revenue stream* — that you use to form a forecast. There are three typical forecasts, depending on what the baseline looks like:

- **If the baseline has held steady,** your best forecast will probably be close to the average of all the sales amounts in the baseline.
- **If the baseline has been rising,** your forecast will likely be higher than the most recent sales amount.
- **If the baseline has been falling,** your forecast will probably be lower than the most recent sales amount.

Note: Those weasely words *likely* and *probably* are there because when there's a seasonal aspect to the sales that doesn't yet appear in your baseline, the next season might kick in at the same point as your forecast and reverse what you'd expect otherwise.

Why is a baseline important? Because it elevates your forecast above the status of a guess. When you use a baseline, you recognize that — absent special knowledge such as the fact that your per-unit price is about to change drastically — your best guide to what happens next is often what happened before.

There's another weasel word: *often*. You'll have plenty of opportunities to use one variable, such as the total of sales estimates from individual sales representatives, to forecast the variable you're really interested in, sales revenues. In that case, you might get a more accurate forecast by using Excel to figure the formula that relates the two variables, and then use that formula to forecast the next value of sales revenues.

Depending on the strength of the relationship between the two variables, that formula can be a better guide than looking solely to the baseline of sales history. It's still a baseline, though: In this case, the baseline consists of two or more variables, not just one.

Charting the baseline

The eye is a great guide to what's going on in your baseline. You can take advantage of that by making a chart that shows the baseline. There are a couple of possibilities:

- **If you're making your forecast solely on the basis of previous sales revenues,** a good choice is a Line chart, like the one shown in Figure 2-1. You can see that thc revenues are flat over time, even though they jump around some. The baseline's pattern in the chart is a clue to the type of forecast to use: in Figure 2-1, that type could be exponential smoothing.
- **If you're using another variable** — such as the total of the sales estimates provided by individual sales reps — you'd probably use an XY (Scatter) chart, like the one shown in Figure 2-2. Notice that the actuals track fairly well against the sum of the individual estimates, which may convince you to use the regression approach to forecasting the next period, especially because you can get your hands on the next estimate from the sales force to forecast from.

If you're going to base your next forecast on information from individual sales reps, don't make your forecast periods too short. If you do, you'll have the reps spending more time making estimates than making sales, which means their commissions decline, and the next thing you know they're working for your competition — and you can flush your forecast down the toilet.

If you're using any version of Excel through Excel 97, you'll need to put your data in the form of a list (such as in columns A and B in Figure 2-1 and Figure 2-2) and then use the Chart button (or choose Insert ⇨ Chart). If you're using any Excel version *after* Excel 97, you can start with the same list and create a pivot chart. The pivot chart gives you some flexibility that standard Excel charts don't offer.

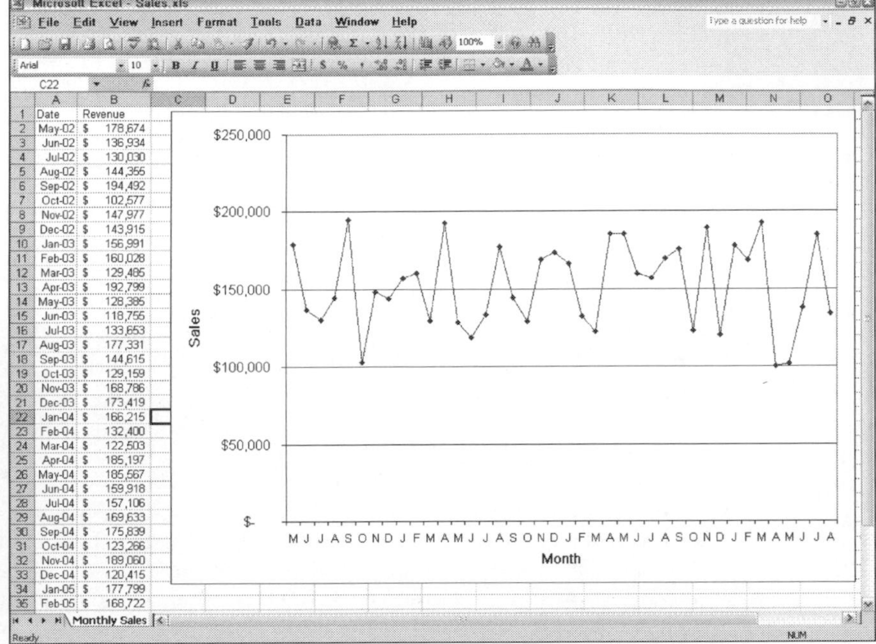

Figure 2-1: The Line chart is ideal for just one variable, such as sales revenues.

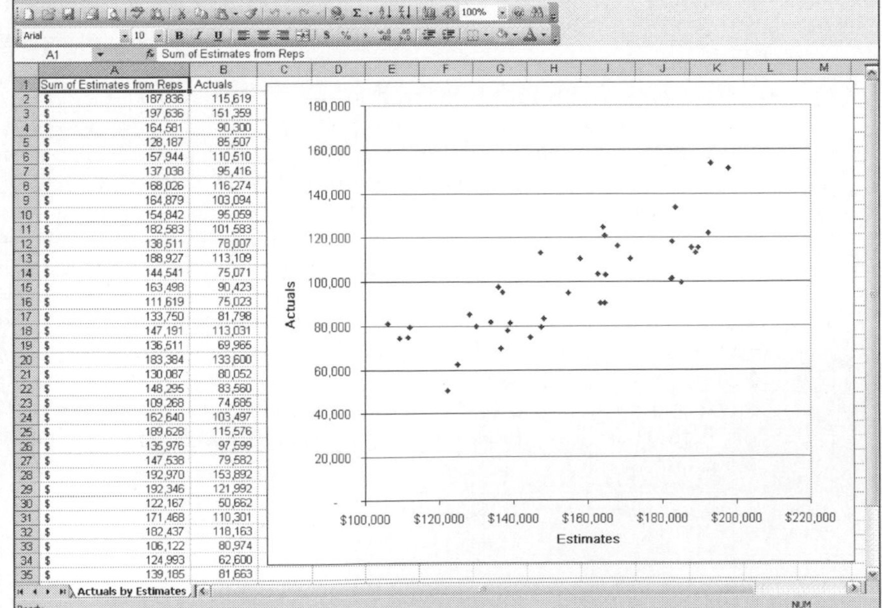

Figure 2-2: In this case, a positive relationship exists between the sum of individual estimates and the actual results.

Looking for trends

Trends are important in forecasting. For one thing, knowing if there's a trend in your baseline is critical to knowing more about what's going on in the product line. For another, the presence of a trend sometimes tells you that you have to do more preparation. If you've decided to use exponential smoothing, for example, you often want to remove the trend first (see Chapter 17 for more information on trends).

If you pored over the baseline shown in column A of Figure 2-3, it wouldn't take you long to conclude that there's an upward trend in the sales revenues. But if you exert the tiny bit of effort needed to chart the baseline, also shown in Figure 2-3, not only do you immediately see the trend, but you get a good intuitive idea of where the sales are headed and how fast they're getting there.

Be careful when you see a trend such as the one shown in Figure 2-3. If these are weekly results, it may just be the first part of a seasonal pattern (or a cycle) that's about to head back down. Notice that the final seven periods look as though the results may be getting ready to do just that. Bummer.

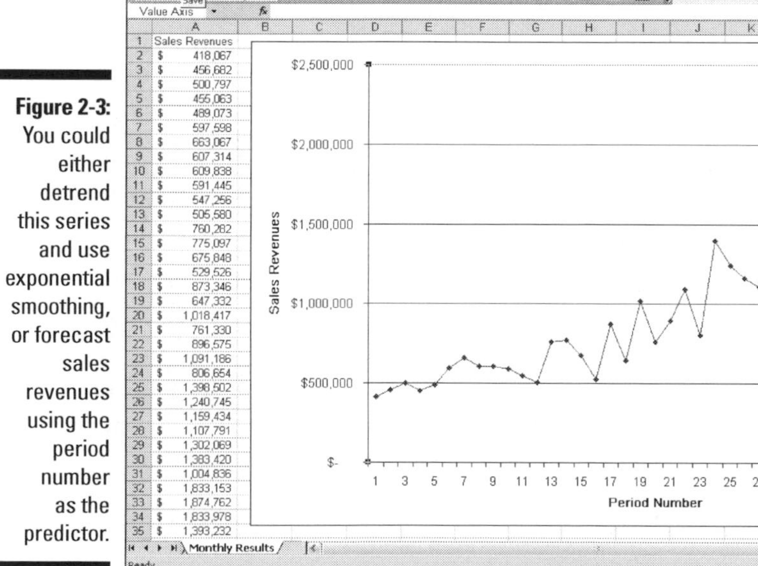

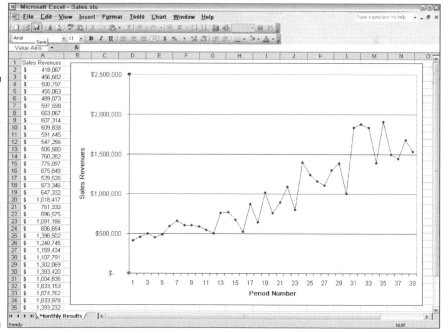

Figure 2-3: You could either detrend this series and use exponential smoothing, or forecast sales revenues using the period number as the predictor.

Setting Up Your Forecast

The most straightforward way of getting a forecast is to lay out your baseline on a worksheet in a list configuration (see Chapter 6) and then call on the Analysis ToolPak to generate a forecast for you. The Analysis ToolPak (ATP) accompanies Microsoft Office; it also accompanies Excel if you get Excel as a stand-alone application. (You can find information about installing the ATP in Chapter 7.)

The ATP is good news and bad news — more good than bad, actually. It hasn't changed substantially since Excel 1995, except that now the code is written using Visual Basic rather than the old weird Excel 4.0 macro language. It can be quirky, as you'll see if you decide to use it. And I think you should decide to use it, because, despite its quirks, it can save you a lot of time and spare you the errors that inevitably occur when you roll your own forecasts (at least, they inevitably occur when I roll my own).

The ATP has 19 different numeric and statistical analysis tools. Using the ATP, if you lay out your data in the right way, you can point one of its tools at your data and get a fairly complete and usually correct analysis — including autocorrelation analyses, moving-average forecasts, exponential-smoothing forecasts, and regression forecasts. It does the hard work for you, and because it's all precoded, you don't need to worry about, say, getting a formula wrong.

Smoothing data

If you decide to use exponential smoothing to create your forecast (I help you make that decision in Chapter 10), all you'll need is your baseline of historic sales revenues. Each observation in the baseline should be from the same sort of forecast period — as often as not, revenue totals on a monthly basis.

You need no variable other than your sales results because, using smoothing, you're going to use one period's result to forecast the next — which is one reason you'll use the ATP's Correlation tool to determine the amount of autocorrelation in the baseline before you do the forecast. Substantial autocorrelation will tend to lead you toward using the Exponential Smoothing tool as your forecasting method — and it will help you determine what damping factor to use in developing your forecast.

Regression: It's all about relationships

If you have available some variable in addition to sales revenues or units sold, and you suspect that it's strongly related to the sales results, you should take a closer look at the relationship.

Suppose you can lay your hands on historical data that shows — by year and month, say — the unit price that you've charged and the number of units you've sold. If you're interested in forecasting the number of units you'll sell next month, the ATP's Regression tool can ease your task, as shown in Figure 2-4.

(In Figure 2-4, I modified the appearance of the chart as the ATP creates it to make it easier to gauge the relationship between price and volume. You can see how to do this in Chapter 11.)

With this baseline, including unit price and units sold, your interest doesn't focus on revenues. After all, it's pretty clear from the chart that the higher the unit price, the fewer the units sold — and that will tend to minimize the variation in quarterly revenue. Instead, this analysis speaks to production. If you know how you'll set your unit price for next quarter, you can use the ATP's Regression tool to forecast the number of units you'll sell next quarter. That forecast might well inform your Production department about how to allocate its resources.

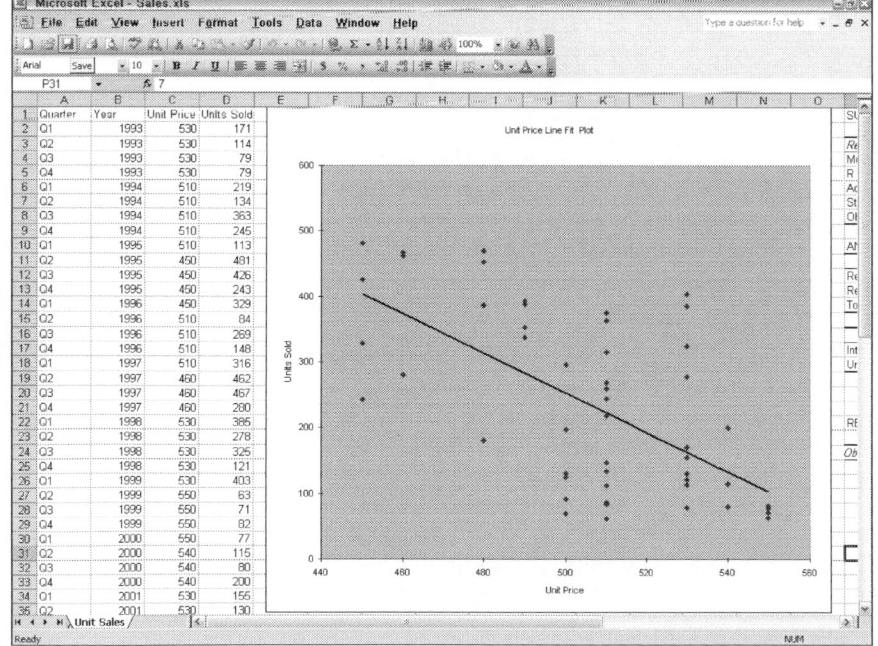

	A	B	C	D
1	Quarter	Year	Unit Price	Units Sold
2	Q1	1993	530	171
3	Q2	1993	530	114
4	Q3	1993	530	79
5	Q4	1993	530	79
6	Q1	1994	510	219
7	Q2	1994	510	134
8	Q3	1994	510	363
9	Q4	1994	510	245
10	Q1	1995	510	113
11	Q2	1995	450	481
12	Q3	1995	450	426
13	Q4	1995	450	243
14	Q1	1996	450	329
15	Q2	1996	510	84
16	Q3	1996	510	269
17	Q4	1996	510	148
18	Q1	1997	510	316
19	Q2	1997	460	462
20	Q3	1997	460	467
21	Q4	1997	460	280
22	Q1	1998	530	385
23	Q2	1998	530	278
24	Q3	1998	530	325
25	Q4	1998	530	121
26	Q1	1999	530	403
27	Q2	1999	550	63
28	Q3	1999	550	71
29	Q4	1999	550	82
30	Q1	2000	550	77
31	Q2	2000	540	115
32	Q3	2000	540	80
33	Q4	2000	540	200
34	Q1	2001	530	155
35	Q2	2001	530	130

Figure 2-4: The chart gives you a visual of what's going on between the two variables: Unit Price and Units Sold.

By the way, Excel terms the solid line shown in Figure 2-4 a *trendline.* When you see a trendline run from the upper left to the lower right, as in Figure 2-4, you know that the correlation between the two variables is negative (and in this case, the correlation between unit price and units sold is –0.65). A *negative correlation* means that the higher the level of one of the variables, the lower the corresponding value of the other variable. If the trendline runs from the lower left to the upper right, you know that the correlation is positive. A *positive correlation* means that lower values on one variable are associated with lower values on the other, and that higher values on one are associated with higher values on the other.

Using Your Revenue and Cost Data

If your ecological niche is in your company's sales management chain, it's likely that you keep a record in Excel of the company's sales results, or you have someone keep it for you. If your products are doing well, you like to fire up Excel, look at those results, and sigh contentedly. If your products aren't performing as they should, you reflexively fire up Excel, look at those results, and wonder how to fix what's gone wrong. Either way, the data is probably in an Excel workbook already, and that makes doing your forecasting easy.

The novelist Rex Stout once had a character complain to his boss, with heavy sarcasm, "When I meekly mention that the science of bookkeeping has two main branches, first addition, and second subtraction. . . ." Your interest may very well focus on the addition branch — that is, sales revenues. But profits are really what it's about, and you may want to take a look at profit forecasts. In that case, you also need to look at the subtraction branch — that is, cost of sales.

Building revenue baselines is pretty straightforward. You decide on your *forecast period* (the length of time that's represented by each observation in your baseline) and if necessary use Excel to figure the total revenue for each period in your baseline. Now you're ready to forecast how much you'll bring in during the upcoming period.

Figuring costs, particularly cost of sales, is trickier. Should you include the cost of goods sold? Of course, you'll include the costs of sales reps' salaries and commissions, of product promotions, of leave-behinds, of trash-and-trinkets, of travel and entertainment. What about indirect costs?

One way to proceed is to subtract those costs, for each period in your baseline, from the revenues for the same period to get a profit estimate for the period. This creates a new, profit baseline that you can use to forecast the next period's profit.

But what about opportunity costs? When you spend money to support the sales of one product line, you're diverting resources from another product line. That's an opportunity cost: You had the opportunity to spend that money in support of Gidgets rather than Widgets, and you might have created more revenue and more profit if you'd used the money to help sell Widgets.

No rule of accounting tells you whether to include opportunity costs in your profit calculations. Here, you're not *doing* accounting, you're *using* it to help lay your plans.

Figure 2-5 illustrates how forecasting can help you plan how to support product lines.

In Figure 2-5, the data on Widgets and Gidgets is pretty straightforward. The figure shows the actual revenue and the actual direct costs of supporting each product line during each month from January 2004 through July 2006, in row 3 through row 33. The worksheet gets the profit figures simply by subtracting the costs from the revenues.

Microsoft Excel - Sales.xls

F35 =TREND(F3:F33,G3:G33,G35)

	A	B	C	D	F	G	H
1	Sales Date		Widgets			Gidgets	
2		Revenue	Cost	Profit	Revenue	Cost	Profit
3	Jan-04	$ 42,597	$ 39,928	$ 2,669	$ 32,074	$ 28,712	$ 3,362
4	Feb-04	$ 42,127	$ 33,368	$ 8,759	$ 32,869	$ 27,071	$ 5,798
5	Mar-04	$ 42,149	$ 36,961	$ 5,188	$ 30,969	$ 28,633	$ 2,336
6	Apr-04	$ 49,931	$ 39,494	$ 10,437	$ 30,437	$ 26,565	$ 3,872
7	May-04	$ 32,456	$ 34,591	$ (2,135)	$ 34,405	$ 27,901	$ 6,504
8	Jun-04	$ 32,418	$ 31,241	$ 1,177	$ 33,146	$ 27,633	$ 5,513
9	Jul-04	$ 41,145	$ 39,917	$ 1,228	$ 34,046	$ 28,943	$ 5,103
10	Aug-04	$ 42,301	$ 36,917	$ 5,384	$ 33,644	$ 25,359	$ 8,285
11	Sep-04	$ 46,239	$ 34,729	$ 11,510	$ 31,548	$ 26,885	$ 4,663
12	Oct-04	$ 44,551	$ 31,316	$ 13,235	$ 30,885	$ 25,249	$ 5,636
13	Nov-04	$ 30,346	$ 34,504	$ (4,158)	$ 33,458	$ 25,091	$ 8,367
14	Dec-04	$ 34,663	$ 38,765	$ (4,102)	$ 34,772	$ 25,515	$ 9,257
15	Jan-05	$ 49,297	$ 35,631	$ 13,666	$ 34,757	$ 27,213	$ 7,544
16	Feb-05	$ 43,048	$ 39,893	$ 3,155	$ 33,979	$ 26,701	$ 7,278
17	Mar-05	$ 30,915	$ 28,513	$ 2,402	$ 33,116	$ 28,501	$ 4,615
18	Apr-05	$ 32,256	$ 32,969	$ (713)	$ 34,340	$ 25,751	$ 8,589
19	May-05	$ 42,774	$ 34,884	$ 7,890	$ 34,175	$ 25,519	$ 8,656
20	Jun-05	$ 42,456	$ 33,729	$ 8,727	$ 32,810	$ 25,292	$ 7,518
21	Jul-05	$ 30,816	$ 31,726	$ (910)	$ 33,538	$ 28,948	$ 4,590
22	Aug-05	$ 35,752	$ 35,281	$ 471	$ 30,789	$ 25,152	$ 5,637
23	Sep-05	$ 42,581	$ 31,034	$ 11,547	$ 33,970	$ 26,771	$ 7,199
24	Oct-05	$ 30,558	$ 26,096	$ 4,462	$ 34,794	$ 26,761	$ 8,033
25	Nov-05	$ 35,397	$ 34,742	$ 655	$ 32,328	$ 25,428	$ 6,900
26	Dec-05	$ 33,096	$ 36,986	$ (3,890)	$ 34,564	$ 26,332	$ 8,232
27	Jan-06	$ 38,513	$ 30,147	$ 8,366	$ 31,150	$ 27,571	$ 3,579
28	Feb-06	$ 37,458	$ 37,797	$ (339)	$ 31,932	$ 25,165	$ 6,767
29	Mar-06	$ 45,450	$ 30,604	$ 14,846	$ 32,344	$ 26,023	$ 6,321
30	Apr-06	$ 47,390	$ 35,605	$ 11,785	$ 31,551	$ 26,861	$ 4,690
31	May-06	$ 30,946	$ 32,511	$ (1,565)	$ 32,095	$ 27,619	$ 4,476
32	Jun-06	$ 49,998	$ 37,388	$ 12,610	$ 31,014	$ 26,570	$ 4,444
33	Jul-06	$ 47,794	$ 39,361	$ 8,433	$ 31,783	$ 25,004	$ 6,779
35	Aug-06 Forecast	$ 42,515	$ 38,386	$ 4,128	$ 32,741	$ 25,540	$ 7,201

Widgets and Gidgets

Figure 2-5: The TREND worksheet function is based on linear regression — here, using the historical relationship between costs and revenues.

Row 35 shows forecasts for August 2006. Here's how it gets them:

1. **It forecasts the costs for August 2006 using exponential smoothing (see Chapter 15 for more information).**

   The cost forecasts are shown in cells C35 and G35.

2. **For each product, it forecasts the revenues for August 2006 by using the *regression* approach (where you use a dependable relationship between sales revenues and one or more predictor variables to make your forecast), in the guise of the TREND worksheet function.**

   Using information about the historic relationship between the costs and revenues for each product, it forecasts in cells B35 and F35 what the revenues would be, given the cost forecasts.

3. **It forecasts the profits for August 2006 by subtracting the forecast cost from the forecast revenue.**

   Adding the forecast profits for both product lines results in a total profit for August 2006 of $11,329.

Now, what if you took the opportunity costs of supporting Widgets into account, and instead poured them into Gidgets? In Figure 2-6, you can see the effect of abandoning Widgets and putting its costs — the resources your company spends supporting Widgets — into supporting Gidgets only.

Microsoft Excel - Sales.xls

J35 =TREND(J3:J33,K3:K33,K35)

	A	B	C	D	F	G	H	J	K	L
1	Sales Date		Widgets			Gidgets		Support Gidgets Only		
2		Revenue	Cost	Profit	Revenue	Cost	Profit	Revenue	Cost	Profit
3	Jan-04	$ 42,597	$ 39,928	$ 2,669	$ 32,074	$ 28,712	$ 3,362	$ 76,677	$ 68,640	$ 8,037
4	Feb-04	$ 42,127	$ 33,368	$ 8,759	$ 32,869	$ 27,071	$ 5,798	$ 73,384	$ 60,439	$ 12,945
5	Mar-04	$ 42,149	$ 36,961	$ 5,188	$ 30,969	$ 28,633	$ 2,336	$ 70,945	$ 65,594	$ 5,351
6	Apr-04	$ 49,931	$ 39,494	$ 10,437	$ 30,437	$ 26,565	$ 3,872	$ 75,687	$ 66,059	$ 9,628
7	May-04	$ 32,456	$ 34,591	$ (2,135)	$ 34,405	$ 27,901	$ 6,504	$ 77,060	$ 62,492	$ 14,568
8	Jun-04	$ 32,418	$ 31,241	$ 1,177	$ 33,146	$ 27,633	$ 5,513	$ 70,620	$ 58,874	$ 11,746
9	Jul-04	$ 41,145	$ 39,917	$ 1,228	$ 34,046	$ 28,943	$ 5,103	$ 81,001	$ 68,860	$ 12,141
10	Aug-04	$ 42,301	$ 36,917	$ 5,384	$ 33,644	$ 25,359	$ 8,285	$ 82,622	$ 62,276	$ 20,346
11	Sep-04	$ 46,239	$ 34,729	$ 11,510	$ 31,548	$ 26,885	$ 4,663	$ 72,300	$ 61,614	$ 10,686
12	Oct-04	$ 44,551	$ 31,316	$ 13,235	$ 30,885	$ 25,249	$ 5,636	$ 69,191	$ 56,565	$ 12,626
13	Nov-04	$ 30,346	$ 34,504	$ (4,158)	$ 33,458	$ 25,091	$ 8,367	$ 79,468	$ 59,595	$ 19,873
14	Dec-04	$ 34,663	$ 38,765	$ (4,102)	$ 34,772	$ 25,515	$ 9,257	$ 87,601	$ 64,280	$ 23,321
15	Jan-05	$ 49,297	$ 35,631	$ 13,666	$ 34,757	$ 27,213	$ 7,544	$ 80,266	$ 62,844	$ 17,422
16	Feb-05	$ 43,048	$ 39,893	$ 3,155	$ 33,979	$ 26,701	$ 7,278	$ 84,746	$ 66,594	$ 18,152
17	Mar-05	$ 30,915	$ 28,513	$ 2,402	$ 33,116	$ 28,501	$ 4,615	$ 66,246	$ 57,014	$ 9,232
18	Apr-05	$ 32,256	$ 32,969	$ (713)	$ 34,340	$ 25,751	$ 8,589	$ 78,305	$ 58,720	$ 19,585
19	May-05	$ 42,774	$ 34,884	$ 7,890	$ 34,175	$ 25,519	$ 8,656	$ 80,892	$ 60,403	$ 20,489
20	Jun-05	$ 42,456	$ 33,729	$ 8,727	$ 32,810	$ 25,292	$ 7,518	$ 76,565	$ 59,021	$ 17,544
21	Jul-05	$ 30,816	$ 31,726	$ (910)	$ 33,538	$ 28,948	$ 4,590	$ 70,294	$ 60,674	$ 9,620
22	Aug-05	$ 35,752	$ 35,281	$ 471	$ 30,789	$ 25,152	$ 5,637	$ 73,977	$ 60,433	$ 13,544
23	Sep-05	$ 42,581	$ 31,034	$ 11,547	$ 33,970	$ 26,771	$ 7,199	$ 73,349	$ 57,805	$ 15,544
24	Oct-05	$ 30,558	$ 26,096	$ 4,462	$ 34,794	$ 26,761	$ 8,033	$ 68,723	$ 52,857	$ 15,866
25	Nov-05	$ 35,397	$ 34,742	$ 655	$ 32,328	$ 25,428	$ 6,900	$ 76,497	$ 60,170	$ 16,327
26	Dec-05	$ 33,096	$ 36,986	$ (3,890)	$ 34,564	$ 26,332	$ 8,232	$ 83,113	$ 63,318	$ 19,795
27	Jan-06	$ 38,513	$ 30,147	$ 8,366	$ 31,150	$ 27,571	$ 3,579	$ 65,210	$ 57,718	$ 7,492
28	Feb-06	$ 37,458	$ 37,797	$ (339)	$ 31,932	$ 25,165	$ 6,767	$ 79,893	$ 62,962	$ 16,931
29	Mar-06	$ 45,450	$ 30,604	$ 14,846	$ 32,344	$ 26,023	$ 6,321	$ 70,382	$ 56,627	$ 13,755
30	Apr-06	$ 47,390	$ 35,605	$ 11,785	$ 31,551	$ 26,861	$ 4,690	$ 73,373	$ 62,466	$ 10,907
31	May-06	$ 30,946	$ 32,511	$ (1,565)	$ 32,095	$ 27,619	$ 4,476	$ 69,875	$ 60,130	$ 9,745
32	Jun-06	$ 49,998	$ 37,388	$ 12,610	$ 31,014	$ 26,570	$ 4,444	$ 74,655	$ 63,958	$ 10,697
33	Jul-06	$ 47,794	$ 39,361	$ 8,433	$ 31,783	$ 25,004	$ 6,779	$ 81,815	$ 64,365	$ 17,450
35	Aug-06 Forecast	$ 42,515	$ 38,386	$ 4,128	$ 32,741	$ 25,540	$ 7,201	$ 77,932	$ 63,927	$ 14,005

Widgets and Gidgets

Figure 2-6: What happens when you abandon Widgets and put its costs into supporting Gidgets.

In Figure 2-6, columns A through H are identical to those in Figure 2-5. Columns J through K show the effect of taking the resources away from Widgets and using them to support Gidgets. The following steps show how to get those projections:

1. **In cell K3, enter** =C3+G3 **and copy and paste the formula into cells K4 through K33, and into cell K35.**

   Column K now has the sum of the actual costs for the two product lines from January 2004 through July 2006, plus the sum of the forecast costs in K35.

2. **In cell J3, enter** =(F3/G3)*K3 **and copy and paste the formula into cells J4 through J33.**

   This formula gets the ratio of revenue to cost for Gidgets in January 2004, and multiplies it by the total costs shown in cell K3. The effect is to apply one measure of gross margin to a higher measure of costs, and estimate what the revenue for Gidgets would be in that case.

3. **In cell J35, enter this formula** =TREND(J3:J33,K3:K33,K35).

   This forecasts the revenues for Gidgets in August 2006, given the relationship between the projections of revenues and costs in J3 through K33, if you decided to support Gidgets only.

4. **To get a forecast of profit for Gidgets only in August 2006, enter** =J35-K35 **in cell L35.**

Notice that the sum of the profit in August 2006 for Widgets and Gidgets is $4,128 + $7,201 = $11,329. But if you committed your Widget resources to Gidgets, your profit for August 2006 would be $14,005 — $2,676 more. In raw dollars, that doesn't seem like much, but it's a 24 percent increase. Generations of European casino owners have grown wealthy on much smaller advantages.

The reason, of course, is that the gross margin on Gidgets is larger than that on Widgets, even though your revenue on Widgets is almost 30 percent greater than on Gidgets. To summarize:

- In column K, you act as though you had committed all your resources to Gidgets only, from January 2004 through July 2006. The effect is to remove all support from Widgets and adds it to the support given to Gidgets.
- In column J, you estimate the revenues you'd earn if you supported Gidgets only, using the historical margin for Gidgets.
- Using the TREND function, you regress the revenue estimates in J3 through J33 onto the costs in K3 through K33, and apply the result to the estimated cost in K35. Subtract K35 from J35 to get a forecast of profit if you recognized your opportunity costs and supported Gidgets only.

Using two different scenarios — Widgets with Gidgets, and Gidgets alone — makes this example a little more difficult to follow. But it's a realistic illustration of how you can use the basic forecasting function TREND to help make an informed decision about resource allocation.

Of course, other considerations would factor into a decision to shift resources from one product line to another — sunk costs, possible retooling to support added manufacturing capacity in a product line, the necessity of ongoing support for customers who have invested in Widgets, and so on. But one of the criteria is almost always financial estimates, and if you can forecast the financials with confidence, you're ahead of the game.

Chapter 3

Understanding Baselines

In This Chapter

- Putting your forecast in context with qualitative data
- Avoiding common errors in sales forecasting
- Understanding the effects of seasons and trends

You build your sales forecast on something called a *baseline* — that is, data that describes your level of sales, usually in prior months, quarters, or years. But creating a numeric forecast without looking at the context isn't a good idea. You need to make sure you have a handle on product management's plans, marketing's promotional budget, sales management's intentions for hiring (or firing), and so on.

Even with a good context and a good baseline, several common errors can send your forecast reeling off course. Recognizing and avoiding these errors is easy if you know what they are, and in this chapter I point them out for you.

Your baseline will often reflect both an ongoing trend (sales have been heading generally up or down) and seasons (sales reliably spike or drop at certain times of the year). In this chapter, I let you know the reasons that context, common errors, trends, and seasonality contribute to good forecasts — and bad ones.

Using Qualitative Data

Qualitative data is information that helps you understand the background for quantitative data. Of course, that begs the question: What's quantitative data? I really want to focus on this issue early, because it's an important one, and one that makes a real difference to the value of your sales forecasts.

Quantitative data is numeric data — the number of units your team sold during the prior quarter, or the revenue that your team brought in during March. With quantitative data, you can use Excel to calculate the number of units sold per month, or the fewest, or the most. You can use Excel to figure a moving average of the revenue your sales team has earned, or its minimum revenue, or the percentage of annual revenue earned during October.

In contrast, *qualitative data* doesn't have an average, a minimum, or a maximum. It's information that helps you *understand* quantitative data. It puts the numbers into a context. It helps to protect you against making really dumb mistakes. I've made my share of dumb mistakes in forecasts, and they've often happened because I haven't paid enough attention to the qualitative data — to my regret.

The right mindset can help you keep all the numbers in perspective. Knowing what questions to ask about your company's direction is key, of course. And you can better decide how to structure your numbers if you understand how your company wants to use your forecast. Here's a closer look at those issues.

Asking the right questions

Suppose that your VP of Sales asks you to forecast how many cars your agency will sell during the next year. If your agency sells mostly Fords, it's reasonable to take a whack at a forecast. If, up until last year, your agency sold mostly Duesenbergs, making a forecast is unreasonable. You can't sell any Duesenbergs because nobody's making them anymore.

That example is admittedly extreme, but it's not entirely stupid. You need to know what your company is going to bring to market during the time period that you want to forecast into. Otherwise, your sales history — your baseline — just isn't relevant. And you can't make an accurate forecast that's based on an irrelevant baseline.

Here are some questions you should ask before you even start thinking about putting a baseline together:

- **How many salespeople will your company make available to you?** Will you have more feet on the street than you did last year? Fewer? About the same? The size of the sales force makes a difference. To make a decent forecast, you need to know what sales resources you're going to have available.
- **Will the commission levels change during the forecast period?** Is your company incentivizing its sales force as it has during, say, the last 12 months? If so, you don't need to worry about this in making forecasts. But if the business model has changed and commission rates are going to drop because the competition has dropped — or rates are going up because the competition has stiffened — your forecast needs to take that into account.

- **Will the product pricing change during this forecast period?** Will your product line's prices jump? If so, you probably need to build some pessimism into your forecast of units sold. Will they drop? Then you can be optimistic. (Keep in mind that pricing usually affects units sold more than it does revenue.)

You can't use forecasting to answer questions like these. And yet their answers — which qualify as qualitative data — are critical to making good forecasts. You can have a lengthy, well-behaved baseline, which is really key to a good forecast. And then you can get completely fooled if your company changes its product line, or reduces its sales force, or changes its commission structure so much that the sales force walks, or lowers its prices so far that the market can't keep its collective hands off the product line. Any of these is going to make your forecast look like you shrugged and rolled a couple of dice. Albert Einstein said that God doesn't play dice; Stephen Hawking says that God does. In either case, you don't want to be thought of as a high roller.

You can't depend entirely on a baseline to make a sales forecast. You need to pay attention to what your company is doing in its marketing, its pricing, its management of people, its response to the competition, in order to make a good sales forecast.

This book shows you how to make good forecasts *under the conditions in place when you got your baseline.* If those conditions are still in place, your forecast can be an accurate one. If not, it can't. So understanding as much as possible about the conditions that will be in place during your forecast period is important.

Keeping your eye on the ball: The purpose of your forecast

Set up your baseline to reflect the period you want to forecast into. That is, if you want to forecast one month's sales, your baseline should show your sales history in months. If the purpose of the forecast is to help guide financial projections such as earnings estimates, you probably want to forecast a quarter's results, and your baseline should be organized into quarters. Chapter 8 shows you an easy way to turn data on individual sales into summaries for the time period you're after.

Figure 3-1 shows an example of a useful baseline.

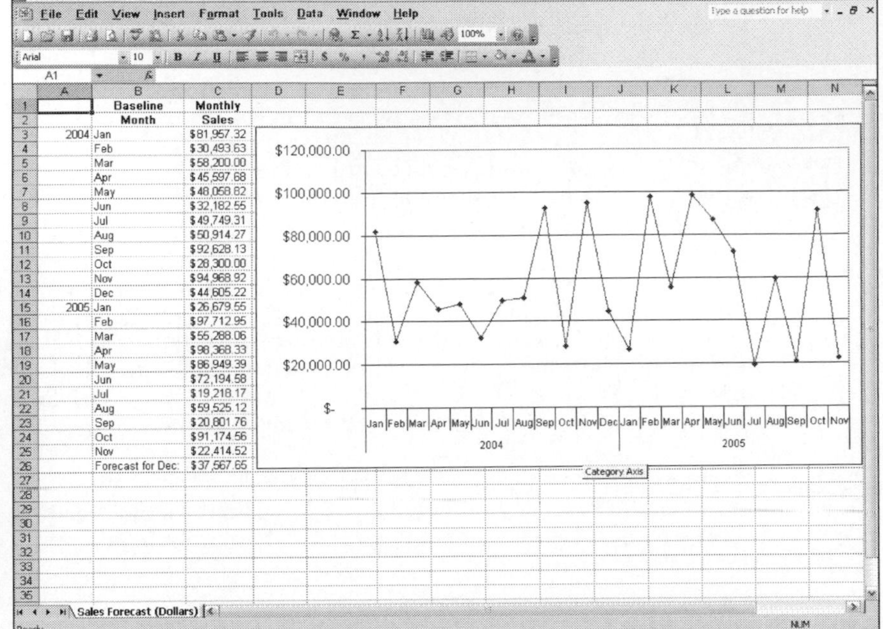

Figure 3-1: The forecast is for the next month, so the baseline provides monthly sales history.

You could easily create the list of month names in column B of Figure 3-1. You would select cell B3 and type **January**, or **Jan**, as shown in the figure. Press Enter, and if necessary reselect cell B3 (or press Ctrl+Enter). Notice the small black square in the lower-right corner of the cell — it's called the *fill handle.* Move your mouse pointer over the fill handle. You'll see the pointer change to crosshairs. Now, although you can still see the crosshairs, press the mouse button, continue holding it down, and drag down as far as you want. Excel fills in the names of the months for you. This also works for days of the week.

There are some rules of thumb about building a baseline that you'll find it useful to keep in mind.

- **Use time periods of the same length in your baseline.** Using one period covering February 1 through February 14, and the next period covering February 15 through March 31 is odd. I've seen it done, though, just because it turned out to be convenient to put the data together that way. But that throws things off, because the apparent February revenues are an underestimate and the apparent March revenues an overestimate. Regardless of the forecast approach you use, that's going to be a problem. (You can safely ignore small differences, such as 28 days in February and 31 days in March.)

- **Make sure the time periods in your baseline are in order, earliest to latest.** Several popular forecasting techniques, including two described in this book, rely on the relationship between one period's measurement and the next period's measurement. If your time periods are out of time order, your forecast will be out of whack.
- **Account for all time periods in the baseline.** If your baseline starts in January 2000, you can't leave out February 2000, even if the data is missing. If the remaining months are in place, skip January 2000 and start with March 2000. Why? Because you want to make sure you're getting the relationship right between one period and the next.

Recovering from Mistakes in Sales Forecasting

Forecasting can be tricky business. You can do everything right and wind up with a forecast that completely misses the mark. It's not pure math. Human factors, the economy, the weather, technology — they all conspire to make your forecast look bad. This section discusses some reasons for mistakes that are beyond your control, and some that you should be able to get your arms around.

Getting over it

In the forecasting dodge, you have to get used to being wrong. The best you can do is get close. More often than not you're going to miss the target. Fortunately, in sales forecasting, close is usually all that's needed. You just can't tell what's going to happen in the marketplace tomorrow, next month, next year. The best you can do is to act on these recommendations. It will help to get your management used to that idea. Then, they won't be too surprised when the forecast is off base.

And it will be. You can use the past as a guide to the future, but it won't always be a *reliable* guide. Because the future doesn't always respond to the past, your forecasts will sometimes be, well, wrong.

The problem is that the market doesn't stand still, for reasons like these:

- Customers make new choices.
- Product lines change.
- Marketing strategies change.
- Pricing strategies change.

Given all that, you just can't expect to nail your forecasts time and again.

But — and this is a big but — you usually have some lead time. Market conditions tend not to change suddenly. Customers don't all shift to ordering exclusively Hewlett-Packard computers on Tuesday, when they've been ordering both Hewlett-Packard and Dell computers up through Monday.

These things happen more gradually, and that's why your baseline is so important. The forecasting tools that this book describes take that into account. They take note of the fact that one product's market share is gently declining, while another's is gently rising.

Using revenue targets as forecasts

Here's how sales forecasts frequently come about: The Sales VP at corporate needs to tell the CFO what the revenues are going to be for Q2 2006. As those of us who have been in sales all know:

> Little bugs have littler bugs
>
> Upon their backs to bite 'em,
>
> And littler bugs have littler still,
>
> And so on, ad infinitum.

So the Sales VP gets after the regional sales directors, who get after the district sales managers, and so on, for Q2 2006 sales forecasts.

Now, suppose I'm a district sales director or a branch sales manager, and I'm supposed to come up with a sales forecast for Q2 2006. If I'm like some of the sales managers I've worked with in the past, here's how I do it:

1. **I check my quota for the second quarter.**

   Turns out that's $1,500,000.

2. **I phone in my forecast, which coincidentally is also $1,500,000.**

   An experienced sales manager would also build in a fudge factor.

Now that's a sorry way of forecasting. It's bad business and it chases its own tail. One major purpose of forecasting is to set sales quotas on a regional, branch, and personal basis. And here companies are rolling up quotas to set forecasts.

So you shouldn't take a quota and pretend it's a forecast. Of course, people do it all the time, but that doesn't make it a good idea.

A good idea is to look at the qualitative aspects of your product line, your sales force, your market, and your competition, to make sure you're on point for your forecast period. Then, if you still feel comfortable with those, take your baseline and extend it using one of the methods you'll read about starting with Chapter 10.

Recognizing Trends and Seasons

Baselines are often *stationary:* They tend to stay centered around an average value, even though they don't stick right to that average. Figure 3-2 has an example of a stationary baseline.

But baselines also often move up or down — the sales figures for a product generally rise or drop with some fluctuation in the direction, but overall you can see what's happening. These are baselines that have *trend.* You can see a baseline with an upward trend in Figure 3-3.

There are also baselines with *seasonality.* These baselines tend to move up and down regularly over time, usually in ways that correspond to seasons. Sales of fruit rise in the spring and summer, and drop back down in the fall and winter (unless you live in the southern hemisphere). Figure 3-4 shows a baseline of seasonal sales.

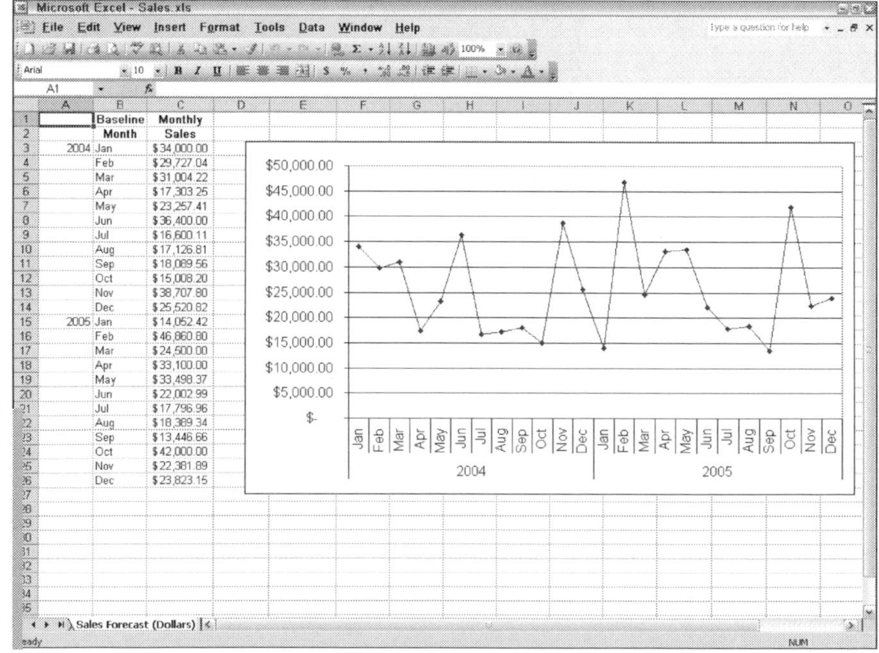

Figure 3-2: There's no clear trend in this baseline. It sticks close to home.

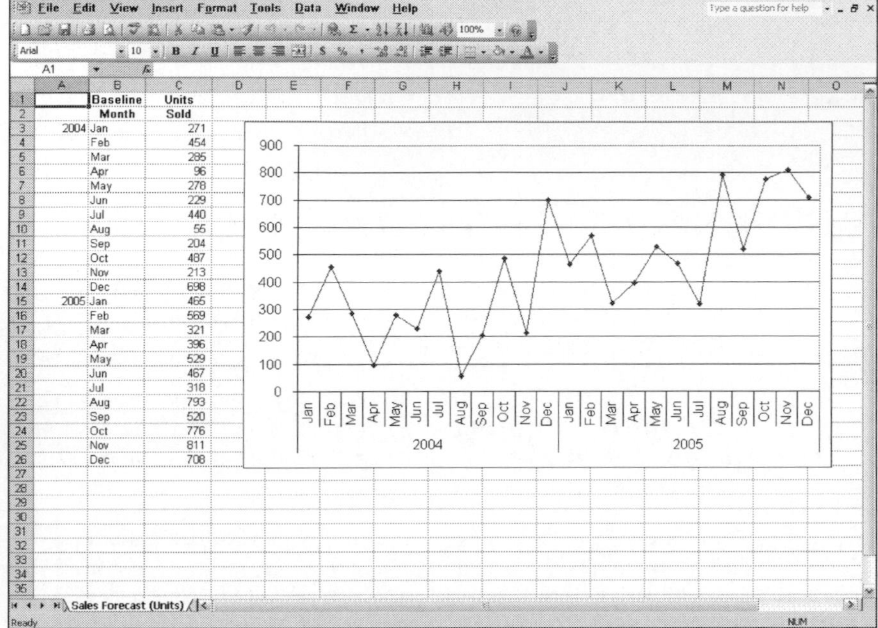

	Baseline Month	Units Sold
2004	Jan	271
	Feb	454
	Mar	285
	Apr	96
	May	278
	Jun	229
	Jul	440
	Aug	55
	Sep	204
	Oct	487
	Nov	213
	Dec	698
2005	Jan	465
	Feb	569
	Mar	321
	Apr	396
	May	529
	Jun	467
	Jul	318
	Aug	793
	Sep	520
	Oct	776
	Nov	811
	Dec	708

Figure 3-3: This baseline has trend. It wanders some, but you can see that the direction is generally up.

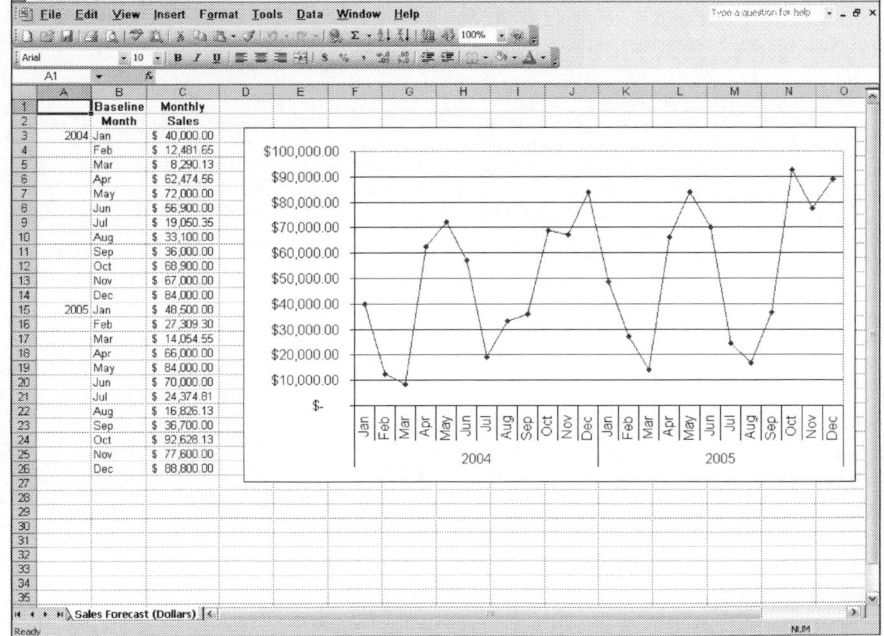

	Baseline Month	Monthly Sales
2004	Jan	$ 40,000.00
	Feb	$ 12,481.65
	Mar	$ 8,290.13
	Apr	$ 62,474.56
	May	$ 72,000.00
	Jun	$ 56,900.00
	Jul	$ 19,050.35
	Aug	$ 33,100.00
	Sep	$ 36,000.00
	Oct	$ 68,900.00
	Nov	$ 67,000.00
	Dec	$ 84,000.00
2005	Jan	$ 48,500.00
	Feb	$ 27,309.30
	Mar	$ 14,054.55
	Apr	$ 66,000.00
	May	$ 84,000.00
	Jun	$ 70,000.00
	Jul	$ 24,374.81
	Aug	$ 16,826.13
	Sep	$ 36,700.00
	Oct	$ 92,628.13
	Nov	$ 77,600.00
	Dec	$ 88,800.00

Figure 3-4: The size of the season's effect on sales varies, but it's there quarter after quarter.

The next two sections help you understand why recognizing trends and seasons is important.

Identifying trends

A baseline with a trend generally heads up (refer to Figure 3-3) or down. Chapter 4 discusses how trends can make forecasting trickier, as well as the steps you can take to make the forecast more accurate. For the time being, though, understanding what trends are about is a good idea.

In sales, trends tend to follow changes in customers' behavior. For good or ill, trends are an economic fact. In looking for trends, bear in mind the following:

- **People stop using certain products or services.** There are lots of ways that society encourages people to purchase some products — an upward trend — and discourages them from purchasing other products — a downward trend. Over time, upward trends often turn into downward trends due to changing market conditions. For example, someone who sells tobacco, whether retail or wholesale, probably wants to see an upward trend — but as consumers have more information about the dangers of smoking, fewer of them will buy the product. (Some will always buy, but not in the numbers seen decades ago.)
- **People want the newer, faster versions.** DSL? Cable? Your very own fiber loop? Doesn't matter. People are impatient and they want to get stuff to and from the Internet faster than they used to. They go from 1,200 bps (yes, my children, people used to send and receive at 1,200 bps, and slower yet) to 9,600 to 56,000 to whatever your phone or cable company offers. The number of people subscribing to higher-speed communications increases, as a trend, over time. The same is true of many other technological improvements.
- **People spend more dollars, but they may not spend more constant dollars.** Here's the deal: In 2005, a sawbuck doesn't buy as many boxes of Good & Plenty as it did in 1955. Blame it on inflation. Or blame it on the bossa nova — the fact is that things cost more than they used to. There are ways to deal with this, such as converting prices to constant dollars, but unless you do so you're going to be looking at a trend, and a meaningless one at that.
- **People spend more for the things they want.** For example, people generally pay whatever gasoline costs, even as the cost continues to rise at a high rate. There are lots of reasons for the increasing cost of gasoline, ranging from South American politics to thirsty SUVs to exploding economies in the Far East. Shrinking or static supply, blended with increased demand, creates upward revenue trends; expanding supply, and static or decreased demand, creates downward trends.

One of the problems with a trend is that there's a mathematical relationship between one figure and the next in the baseline. The two main approaches to forecasting that this book covers — smoothing and regression — deal with those relationships differently. You tend not to worry about the relationship between one figure and the next if you're using the regression method of sales forecasting. If you're using smoothing, you usually want to remove the trend from the baseline. You can find more about removing trends in Chapter 17.

Understanding seasonality

A *seasonal* baseline is one that rises and falls regularly. For example, one that has higher sales revenue during the summer and lower sales revenue during the winter (such as Speedo swimsuits), or higher during the first and third quarters, and lower during the second and fourth quarters (such as a line of textbooks for a course that is offered every other quarter).

A seasonal baseline can be a special case of a *cyclical* baseline. Cyclical baselines rise and fall but not necessarily on a regular basis. A good example is the business cycle as it's related to recessions. Recessions come and go, but nothing requires them to follow the calendar. The U.S. economy contracted, big time, in the late 1860s, the early and mid 1880s, the 1910s, and of course during the Great Depression of the late 1920s and early 1930s. But there is nothing regular about when these contractions occurred. They're *cyclical,* not *seasonal.*

Contrast that with a baseline that rises and falls along with a calendar grouping. Sales that depend on the season of the year are both cyclical *and* seasonal. They follow a cycle, and it's a regular, seasonal cycle. Depending on the product and the time of year, the seasonal cycle might rise and fall every 3 months, or every 6 months, or even every 12 months.

A trap may be lurking. Suppose that you're dealing with a cyclical or seasonal series that looks like the one in Figure 3-5. How serious the trap is depends on how long your baseline is, and on how far out you want to forecast. Suppose you build your baseline on a weekly basis, from January 1 through March 12. It could look like the one in Figure 3-6, which shows a subset of the baseline in Figure 3-5.

If you want to forecast into March 19, you're probably okay — although you don't yet know it on March 12, the series is still on its way up. But if on March 19 you want to forecast beyond into March 26, you're going to have a problem — although you don't know it yet, the series is starting down because of its seasonality.

Generally, the longer your baseline, the better your forecast. If your baseline is as shown in Figure 3-5, where you have six months' worth of data to forecast from, then you can tell the trend is seasonal and allow for that in your forecast. If the baseline extends from January 1 through March 19, though, you're going to get fooled.

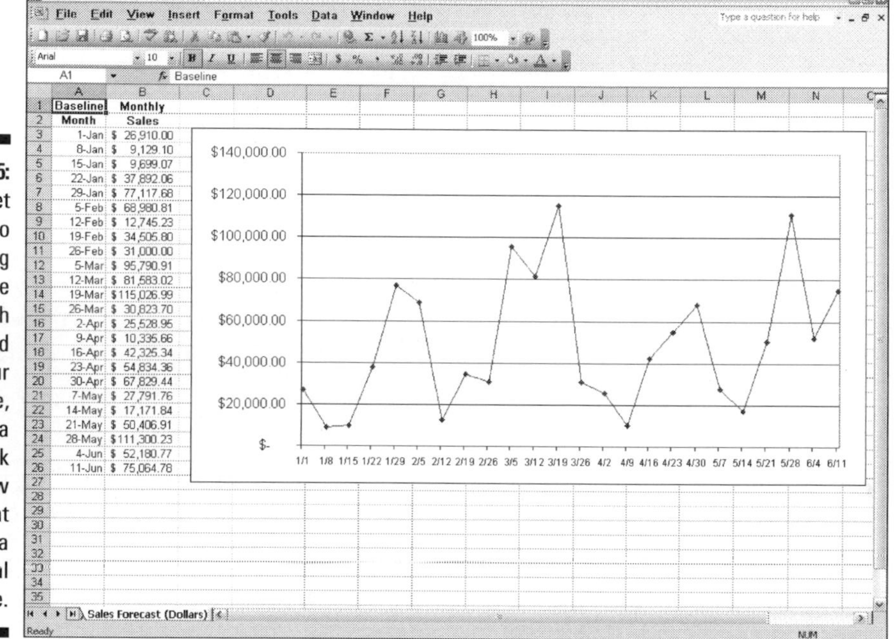

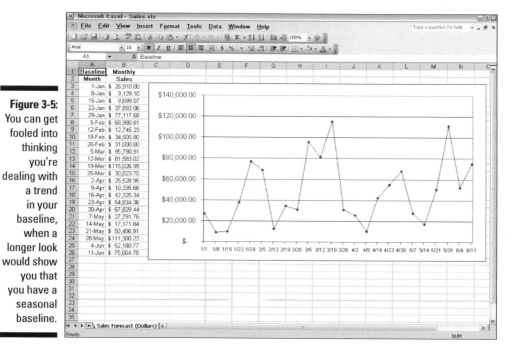

Figure 3-5: You can get fooled into thinking you're dealing with a trend in your baseline, when a longer look would show you that you have a seasonal baseline.

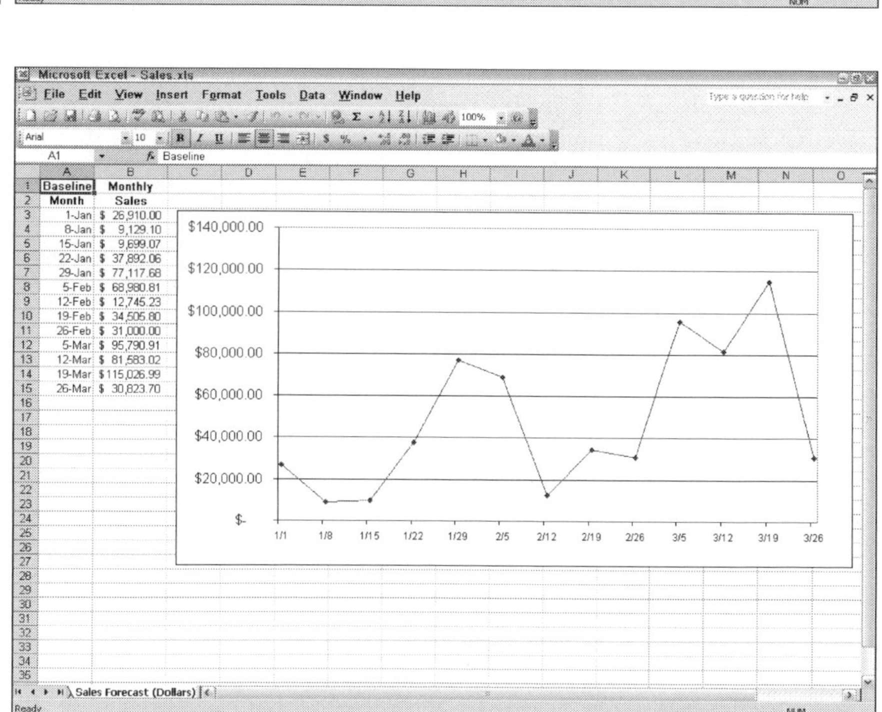

Figure 3-6: Here, your baseline is the upward trend of the seasonal series shown in Figure 3-5.

Chapter 4

Predicting the Future: Why Forecasting Works

In This Chapter

- Finding trends in your data
- Looking at a mess of data and finding relationships that make sense

Many baselines of sales history rise during the early stages of a product's release, and fall as technology and fashions move on. During a product's middle age, the sales flatten out. Your forecasts' accuracy improves if you understand the nature of those trends and whether you should detrend the baseline. Excel offers methods of testing for trends, to help you decide whether you're looking at something real or just random variation.

Relationships in your sales baselines are the key to any forecast, whether the relationship is between one month's results and the next month's, or between historical sales results and some other variable such as advertising costs. In this chapter, I show you how to use Excel to quantify those relationships using Excel's worksheet functions and the Analysis ToolPak.

Understanding Trends

Unfortunately, many decision-makers have no faith in sales forecasting. Their image of a forecaster is a combination of the meteorologist on Channel 7 and someone gazing into a crystal ball, probably wearing a pointy hat.

But quantitative forecasting works because of sound mathematical and logical reasons, and you can find plenty of examples of forecasts working in practice. If someone looks at you suspiciously when you trot out your sales forecast, you'll want to understand the reasons that forecasts aren't some kind of magic. One of those reasons is that many baselines — particularly baselines of sales revenues — involve *trends*.

A trend is easy to define, if not always easy to manage. A trend has two main characteristics:

- **It goes up (good, if you're measuring revenues) or it goes down (not good).** It may fluctuate — for example, you'll see some temporary downturns in a baseline that's mainly trending up — but in the main it's going in one direction. If you see many consecutive increases followed by many consecutive decreases, you're probably dealing with a seasonal or cyclic baseline, and certainly not a trend.
- **The trend lasts much longer than the forecast period.** Suppose you use the results of four calendar quarters to forecast a fifth quarter. You may find that the trend established for the first four is substantially different from the one you'd get when the fifth quarter's actuals are in. But a trend figured on, say, 20 calendar quarters is unlikely to change much in the 21st quarter, unless a sudden and major sea change occurs in the market.

What causes trends? There are as many reasons for trends as you care to think up. Just a few examples:

- **Products go out of style.** Smoked a cigarette, pipe, or cigar lately? If you have, you're out of step. The society you belong to is frowning and wagging its finger at you. You're having difficulty lighting up after a meal in a restaurant. The trend, my friend, is down: People don't want to smell your smoke anymore (mine either, and thank heaven for the nicotine patch).
- **Inflation sets in.** As this book is written, the United States has had very low inflation for several years. During the 1970s and into the 1980s (when high interest rates finally slowed it down) there was serious inflation in the U.S. economy. The inflation caused prices — and therefore revenues — to trend upward.
- **Technology improves productivity.** When your parents or grandparents or even great-grandparents were small children, they might have set aside one day a week to do the wash, outdoors in a big metal drum filled with soapy water that they'd churn with a big stick. Then along came washing machines. Washing machines were initially very expensive compared to a metal drum and a stick, and the demand for washing machines was, therefore, fairly low. But as economies of scale kicked in, and unit prices came down, what was once only for the wealthy became the norm, and the increase in revenues far outweighed the decrease in unit cost, until washing machines became commodities — then revenues flattened out. But there was a significant trend for decades because of increased productivity and demand.
- **Products become more popular.** There are more cars, trucks, and SUVs on the road than there were last year, and last year there were more than the year before, and so on, all the way back to the Model T and even earlier. And each year that a census has been taken, the population of the United States has increased. You get more people, you get more people wanting to drive, you get more cars and trucks and SUVs.

The rest of this chapter gets into some of the effects of trends (and there are in reality many, many more baselines that have trends than baselines that are stationary). Trends are a principal reason that forecasting works. But if you can tell that a baseline is stationary — trending neither up nor down — you can do every bit as well as you can with a trend, if you handle things correctly.

Watching revenues go up — and down

One reason that forecasting skeptics are, well, skeptical is that they tend not to understand how what happens in baselines tells us about the future.

Consider rain clouds. They don't just appear overhead all of a sudden and start pouring water down on you. They form gradually, or the prevailing winds bring them over your area. In either case, if you're watching the sky, you have advance warning that you're going to get wet.

It's the same with baselines. They don't go screaming up and then suddenly, with no warning, go screaming down. Unless the forecast period you're using is shorter than a year (not recommended) you'll seldom if ever see a baseline that looks like the one shown in Figure 4-1.

Of course, the situation shown in Figure 4-1 *could* occur, especially if some convulsion occurred in, say, the company's production facilities, or if the FDA announced that the company's main over-the-counter medication caused consumers' left legs to shrink by 3 inches. But, in either case, you'd know about that ahead of time.

Much more likely is the situation shown in Figure 4-2. Compare the changes in the trend's direction in Figures 4-1 and 4-2. The change in Figure 4-1 is abrupt and dramatic. Unless repeated due to seasonality, sales revenues just don't behave that way in the normal course of events. As in Figure 4-2, revenues slow, flatten, and finally decline. The point is that you have time to notice what's going on, and so does your forecasting technique.

If you're using a single-variable method, such as moving averages or exponential smoothing, your forecast builds recent sales data into your forecast. By the time the sixth data point has entered the baseline, the forecast has built in the fourth and fifth data points, and if the actuals had been shooting up, the forecast would pull in its horns. If the more recent actuals are beginning to fall off, it's not long before the forecast notices and starts to drop in response. Figure 4-3 shows the baseline in Figure 4-2 with a forecast line overlaid.

As I've said, it's unusual for baselines to resemble the one shown in Figure 4-1, but what if you do run into one and you use smoothing on it? Figure 4-4 has the Figure 4-1 data, including a forecast line from exponential smoothing.

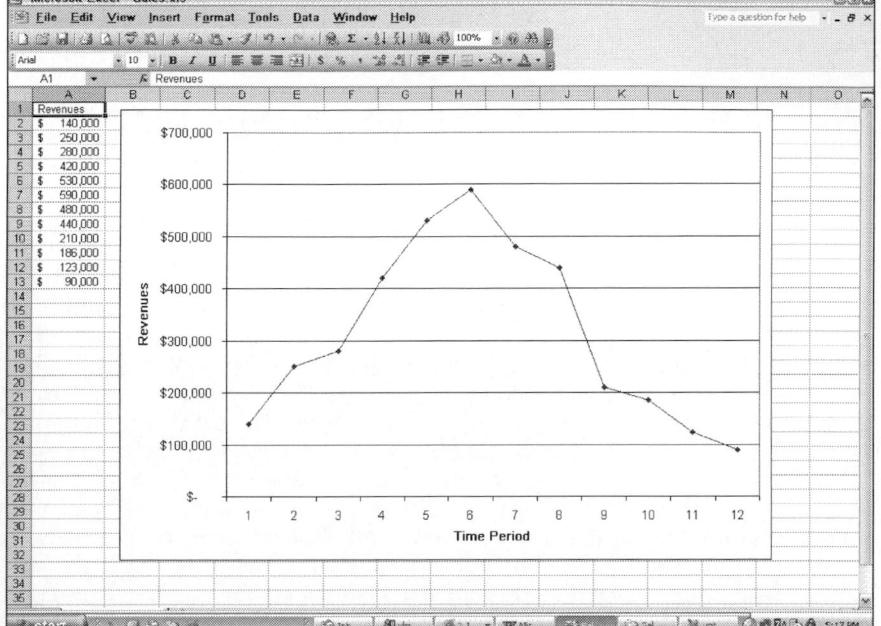

Figure 4-1: A realistic forecaster or user of forecasts doesn't worry about this sort of nonsense.

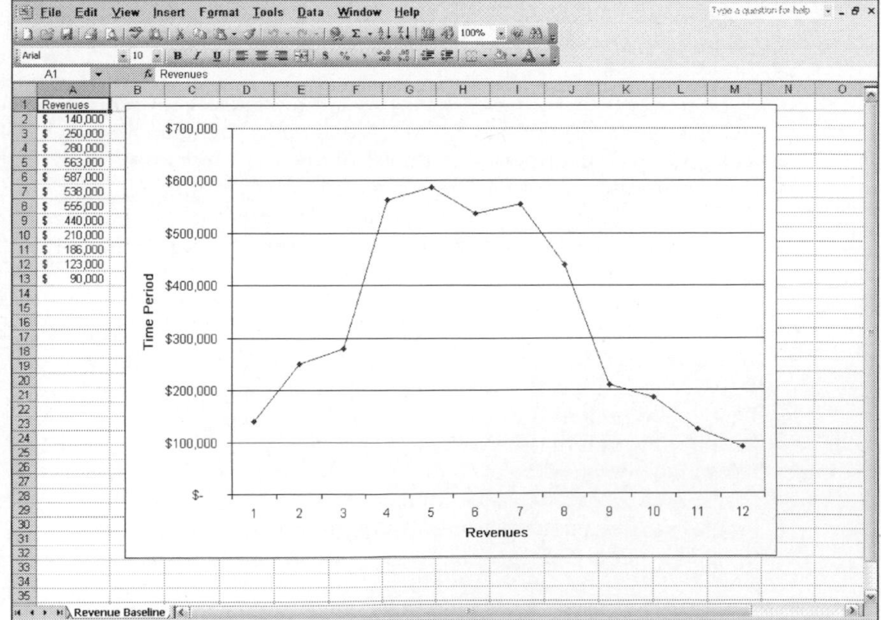

Figure 4-2: When a trend turns, it's usually due to seasonality or to movement through the product's life cycle.

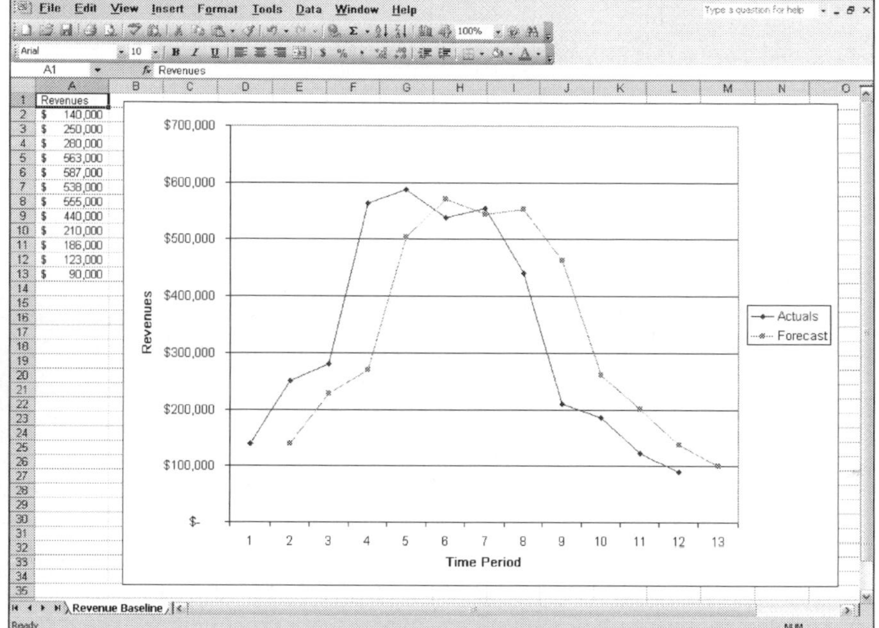

Figure 4-3: Smoothing and moving average forecasts typically lag a bit behind the actuals.

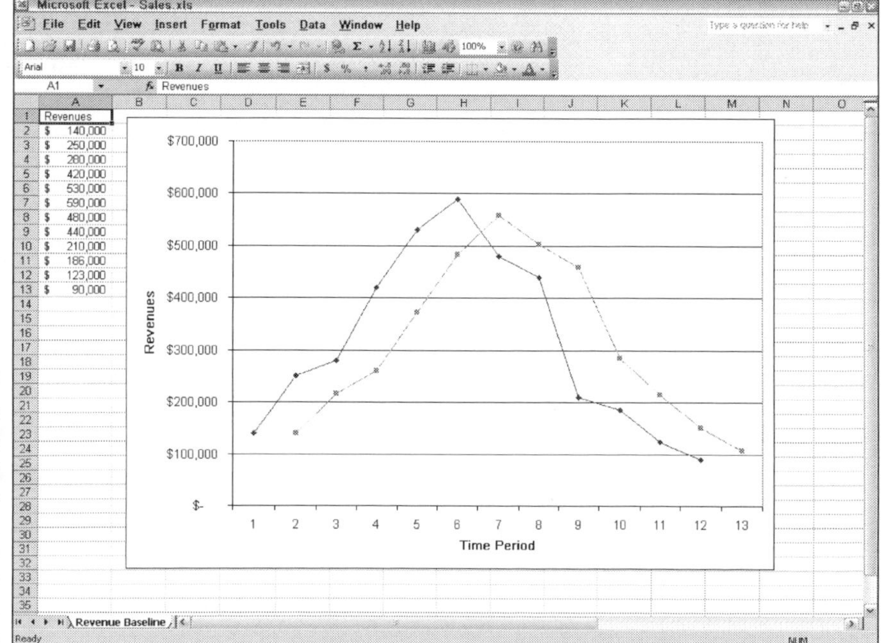

Figure 4-4: The forecast catches up with the change in direction pretty quickly.

So, when the worm turns at period 6 and drops $90,000 between periods 6 and 7, the forecast for period 7 is off by $80,000. And because this sort of forecast always lags behind a bit, it continues to be an overestimate through the end of the baseline.

There's nothing magical about quantitative forecasting. The process doesn't just pull numbers out of the worksheet like rabbits from a hat. It looks at what has gone before and makes its best estimate as to what the history suggests will happen next. Even if an abrupt change occurs in the series, the forecast catches up in a hurry.

Standard regression forecasts don't work so well — in fact, they don't work at all — in catching up with changes in the baseline's direction: They provide straight-line (linear) projections, as shown in Figure 4-5. Autoregression forecasts, in which you regress a baseline on itself, are an exception. They catch up just like moving averages and smoothing.

Testing for trends

How do you know whether a trend is real? If you see a baseline that looks like it's drifting up or down, does that represent a real trend or is it just random variation? To answer those questions, we have to get into probability and statistics. Fortunately, we don't have to get into them too far — wrist-deep, maybe.

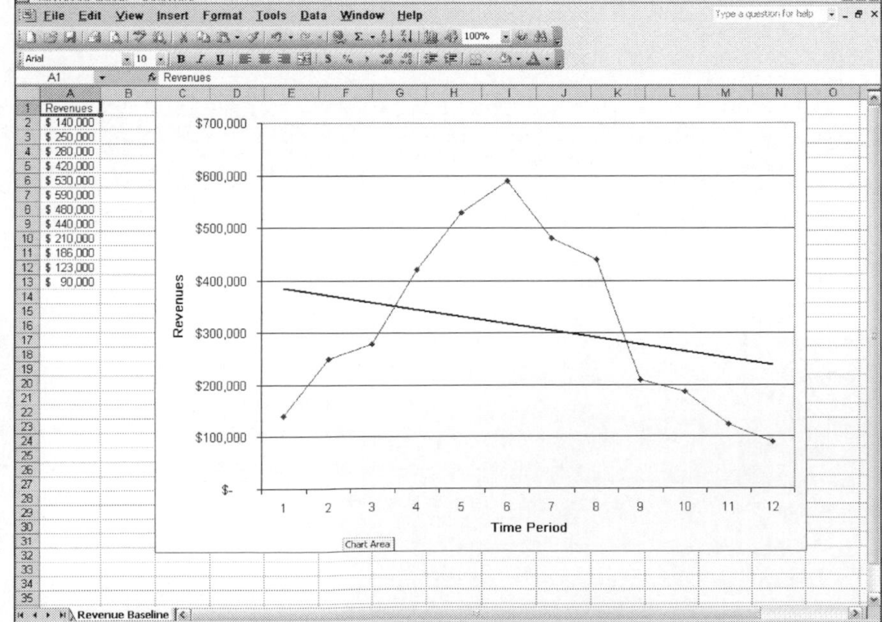

Figure 4-5. A straight-line, regression forecast doesn't help you account for seasons or cycles.

The basic train of thought goes like this:

1. **I use Excel to tell me what the correlation is between sales revenues and a time period.**

   It doesn't matter if I represent that time period as January 2000, February 2000, March 2000 . . . December 2005, or as 1, 2, 3 . . . 72.

2. **If there's no relationship, as measured by the correlation, between revenues and time period, there's no trend and I don't need to worry about it.**

3. **If there *is* a relationship between revenues and time period, I have to choose the best way to handle the trend.**

4. **After Excel calculates the correlation, I have to decide whether it represents a real relationship between time period and revenue amount, or whether it's just a lucky shot.**

   If the probability that's it's just luck is less than 5 percent, I'll decide it's a real trend. (Nothing magic about 5 percent, either — it's conventional. Some people prefer to use 1 percent as their criterion — it's more conservative than 5 percent, and they feel a little safer.) This raises the issue of statistical significance: What level of probability do you require before you decide that something (here, a correlation) is the real McCoy?

There are various methods for testing the statistical significance of a correlation coefficient. Here are three popular methods:

- Test the correlation directly and compare the result to the normal distribution.
- Test the correlation directly and compare the result to the *t-distribution* (the t-distribution, although similar to the normal curve, assumes that you're using a smallish sample rather than an infinitely large population).
- Convert the correlation with the *Fisher transformation* (which converts a correlation coefficient to a value that fits in the normal curve) and compare the result to the normal distribution.

Other popular methods for testing the statistical significance of a correlation coefficient exist. Each returns a slightly different result. In practice, you'll almost always make the same decision (the correlation is or is not significantly different from zero), regardless of the method you choose.

Let's run through the process of testing a correlation's statistical significance. Figure 4-6 shows the basic data: the time period in column A and the sales revenues in column B, along with the standard — and very useful — chart of revenues by time period to show you more of what's going on.

The numbers that identify the time periods are in cells A2 through A40. The sales revenue figures for each time period are in cells B2 through B40.

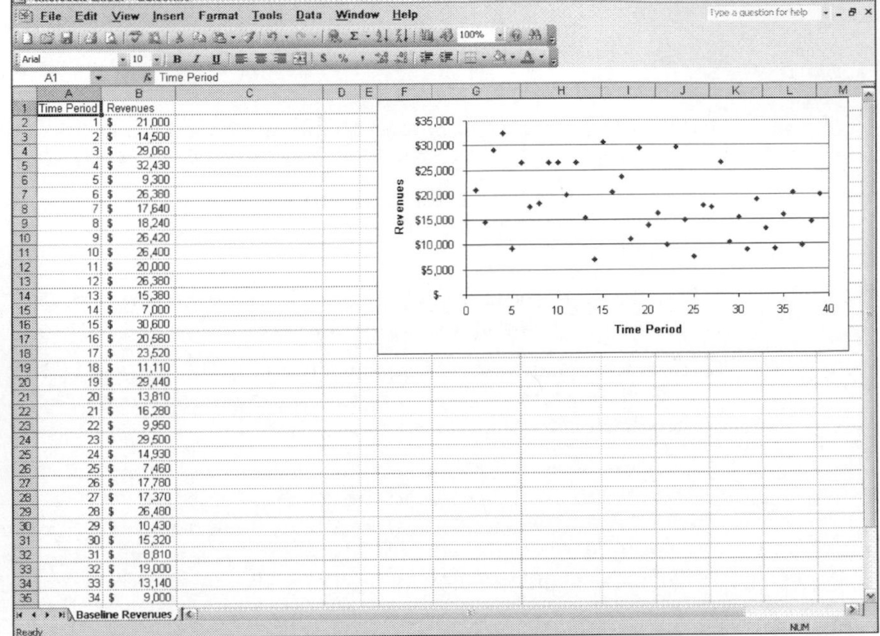

Time Period	Revenues
1	$ 21,000
2	$ 14,500
3	$ 29,060
4	$ 32,430
5	$ 9,300
6	$ 26,380
7	$ 17,640
8	$ 18,240
9	$ 26,420
10	$ 26,400
11	$ 20,000
12	$ 26,380
13	$ 15,380
14	$ 7,000
15	$ 30,600
16	$ 20,560
17	$ 23,520
18	$ 11,110
19	$ 29,440
20	$ 13,810
21	$ 16,280
22	$ 9,950
23	$ 29,500
24	$ 14,930
25	$ 7,460
26	$ 17,780
27	$ 17,370
28	$ 26,480
29	$ 10,430
30	$ 15,320
31	$ 8,810
32	$ 19,000
33	$ 13,140
34	$ 9,000

Figure 4-6: Notice that revenues gently decline over time in the chart, from upper left toward lower right, so the correlation is negative.

With the data on the worksheet, get the formulas in place:

1. **Select a blank cell — say, D2 — and enter** =CORREL(A2:A40,B2:B40)**.**

   In plain English, show the correlation between the period number in cells A2 through A40, and the sales revenues in cells B2 through B40. I don't have words to express how great this is. I don't want to make myself sound like a geezer, but when I took my first statistics course, calculating this correlation could take as long as 20 minutes, because we had to do it on a Burroughs adding machine that had a crank on its side (and another sitting in front of it). Now, with Excel, it takes all of 10 seconds.

   The correlation is –0.38. Is that likely to be real or just random variation? In other words, if you extended the periods maybe another 40 or so back in time, would you get a correlation similar to the one you have here? A negative correlation somewhere between, say, –0.25 and –0.5? Or would you get a correlation somewhere between –0.1 and +0.1 (that is, no real relationship)?

2. **To find out whether the correlation is real or random, enter** =D2/(1/SQRT(COUNT(A2:A40)-1)) **in, say, cell D4.**

   The formula assumes that the CORREL formula from Step 1 is in cell D2.

   This returns something called a *z-value* or *z-statistic.* It tells you where the correlation in D2 lies on a normal curve. A negative z-value lies below the normal distribution's average value.

3. **To find out how many different data sets, if you repeated this test with 100 different data sets, would have z-values as large as the one in cell D4, enter** =NORMSDIST(D4) **in cell D6.**

   This formula returns the value 0.98 percent. That's less than 1 percent. In plain English, this means that if the true correlation were 0, you'd expect to get a calculated correlation as far from 0 as –0.38 in only 1 of those hypothetical 100 data sets. It's more rational to assume that the correlation between revenue and time period is truly nonzero than it is to assume that it's the one out of 100 that's an aberration.

When you've taken the three steps just described, the worksheet looks like the one shown in Figure 4-7. It has three formulas not yet displayed in Figure 4-6, which taken together tell you whether the trend in the sales data is more likely to be a real one or is more likely to be a ghost. You're converting the correlation to a z-value, which is one that you can use in conjunction with the normal curve.

When you're testing correlations for statistical significance, as steps 1 through 3 did, keep in mind that two issues determine the probability you calculate: the size of the correlation and the number of data points that go into it. Here you have a correlation of moderate size *and* a reasonably large number of data points, so getting a statistically significant result isn't surprising.

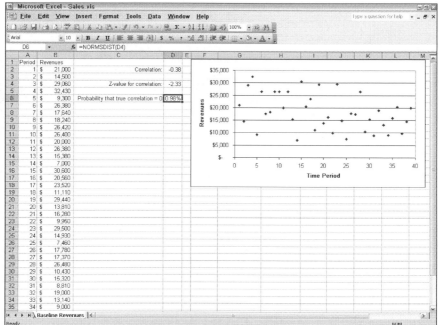

D6 =NORMSDIST(D4)

Period	Revenues		
1	$ 21,000	Correlation:	-0.38
2	$ 14,500		
3	$ 29,060	Z-value for correlation:	-2.33
4	$ 32,430		
5	$ 9,300	Probability that true correlation = 0	0.98%
6	$ 26,380		
7	$ 17,640		
8	$ 18,240		
9	$ 26,420		
10	$ 26,400		
11	$ 20,000		
12	$ 26,380		
13	$ 15,380		
14	$ 7,000		
15	$ 30,600		
16	$ 20,560		
17	$ 23,520		
18	$ 11,110		
19	$ 29,440		
20	$ 13,810		
21	$ 16,280		
22	$ 9,950		
23	$ 29,500		
24	$ 14,930		
25	$ 7,460		
26	$ 17,780		
27	$ 17,370		
28	$ 26,480		
29	$ 10,430		
30	$ 15,320		
31	$ 8,810		
32	$ 19,000		
33	$ 13,140		
34	$ 9,000		

Figure 4-7: Because you've calculated the correlation's z-value in cell D4, you can compare it to the normal standard distribution (NORMSDIST) in cell D6.

If you conclude that the trend the correlation measures is real (and when the probability is less than 1 percent that the correlation is a ghost, you probably should accept that conclusion), you have two more questions to ask yourself:

- **Should I use a forecasting approach that handles trends well?** You'd think that if you detected a trend, you should use a forecasting approach that handles trends well. That's often true, but not necessarily. Suppose that instead of using time period as one of the variables in your correlation analysis, you used something such as sales revenues made by the *competition.*

  If the competition's revenues are slipping as yours are, you'll find a likely significant correlation between your revenues and the competition's. But it's quite possible — even likely — that there's no real, causal relationship between their revenues and yours. It's just that both yours and theirs are correlated with the real causal factor: The overall market is getting smaller. In that case, you would be much better off using a measure of overall market size as your predictor variable. In this scenario, market size has a direct, causal relationship to your revenue, whereas your competition's revenue has only an indirect relationship to your revenue.

- **Should I detrend the data?** A hidden variable, such as a consistent change in the overall size of a market, can lead you to believe that a predictor variable and the variable you want to forecast are directly related, when in fact they're not. Or the predictor and the forecast may change in similar ways because they're both related to *time.*

  The way to handle this sort of situation is to detrend both variables first by means of a transformation. (I show you how to do that in Chapter 17.)

  Or you may prefer to make your forecast using an approach that doesn't handle trends well, such as moving averages or exponential smoothing. One reason for doing this is that you may find the regression approach with your data set isn't as accurate a forecaster as moving averages or smoothing. Again, see if you can transform the data to remove the trend.

Matchmaker, Matchmaker: Finding Relationships in the Data

When you make a *quantitative forecast* (a forecast that uses a numeric baseline rather than something like expert opinions), you're always looking for relationships. Suppose you're considering using regression to forecast. You can get your hands on several possible predictor variables, any one (or any combination) of which might give you your best forecast.

In the sales arena, this means looking for relationships between sales and some other variables like size of sales force, time period, or unit price. (Expert opinions, as long as they come from a real expert, are valuable, too — even if you use them only to provide a context for your quantitative forecast.)

The relationship between sales revenue for one time period and a prior time period is also frequently of interest. This is called an *autocorrelation* and is close conceptually to *autoregression*. Calculating an autocorrelation can help you make many decisions, including the following:

- Which forecasting method to use
- Whether you'd be misled by a moving-average forecast
- How to structure an exponential-smoothing forecast
- Whether to detrend a baseline

Especially if you have a sizable number of possible predictor variables, calculating the relationships one by one can be a real pain. For that, you'll want to use the Analysis ToolPak (ATP).

One of the tools you'll find in the ATP is the Correlation tool. (For more information about installing the ATP into Excel, see Chapter 7.) If you set up your baseline as an Excel list, the Correlation tool takes most of the agony out of calculating the correlations.

Figure 4-8 begins an example that this section works through. It shows:

- Sales revenues (the variable you want to forecast)
- Time period
- Unit price
- Size of sales force
- Advertising dollars
- Total of sales managers' revenue estimates

Your goal is to decide which (if any) of the last five variables to consider as predictor variables in a regression forecast. To begin that work, calculate each of the correlation coefficients. I show you how to do that in the next section.

Choosing the predictors

One of the goals of the regression approach is *parsimony* — a highfalutin way of saying that you don't want to use more predictor variables than are needed, when you *are* using more than one. Suppose that one of your predictor variables is unit price and another is units sold. These two variables tend to be strongly related: the lower the price, the more units you'll sell.

Sales ($000)	Time Period	Unit Price	Sales Force	Advertising ($000)	Revenue Estimates
$ 251,897	1	$ 240	52	$ 3,149	$ 121,806
$ 154,426	2	$ 265	56	$ 19,303	$ 160,487
$ 237,450	3	$ 255	59	$ 23,745	$ 215,323
$ 201,980	4	$ 281	58	$ 50,495	$ 251,289
$ 271,298	5	$ 257	54	$ 13,565	$ 132,589
$ 260,171	6	$ 247	54	$ 65,043	$ 158,200
$ 243,231	7	$ 275	51	$ 24,323	$ 104,498
$ 281,218	8	$ 265	53	$ 31,637	$ 330,361
$ 330,765	9	$ 260	59	$ 66,153	$ 238,259
$ 289,533	10	$ 273	50	$ 21,715	$ 361,302
$ 332,443	11	$ 253	53	$ 12,467	$ 350,477
$ 241,126	12	$ 262	55	$ 12,056	$ 118,257
$ 153,515	13	$ 278	41	$ 23,027	$ 184,314
$ 119,390	14	$ 276	22	$ 4,477	$ 131,311
$ 200,280	15	$ 287	33	$ 40,056	$ 204,771
$ 141,599	16	$ 264	20	$ 5,310	$ 135,308
$ 210,875	17	$ 258	22	$ 18,452	$ 240,851
$ 285,605	18	$ 281	22	$ 42,841	$ 221,149
$ 298,577	19	$ 272	23	$ 11,197	$ 106,862
$ 259,678	20	$ 242	20	$ 9,738	$ 161,538
$ 255,948	21	$ 287	56	$ 22,395	$ 278,345
$ 303,582	22	$ 260	32	$ 37,948	$ 149,876
$ 235,109	23	$ 270	22	$ 35,266	$ 94,001
$ 256,463	24	$ 254	32	$ 57,704	$ 165,103
$ 281,613	25	$ 255	55	$ 10,560	$ 279,605
$ 276,382	26	$ 286	56	$ 27,638	$ 83,172

Figure 4-8: This is too much data to calculate conveniently with worksheet functions.

So, in a regression situation, you'd want to use one or the other, but probably not both. Suppose you use time period and unit price together to forecast revenue. In that case, you normally wouldn't want to add units sold to the forecast equation, because it would add little information to what's provided by unit price.

And adding units sold to the equation would come at a cost: some technical stuff about degrees of freedom and something awful called multicollinearity, and some more-practical stuff about a misleadingly high Multiple R (see Chapter 11 for more information on all of this).

Your initial correlation analysis should look at the strength of the relationship between each predictor variable and sales revenues, because if the relationship is weak, you don't want it in your forecast equation. But you should also look at the strength of the relationship between each pair of predictors, because if that's too strong, you'll wind up with more variables than you need or want in the equation.

There are six variables in the baseline list. That means you need to calculate 30 correlation coefficients. If you use the worksheet function CORREL to calculate them, you waste your time and risk making errors. And because I've done that myself — that is, I've calculated the correlations one by one using CORREL — I can tell you it leads to lower-back pain later on.

If you want to know how many different correlations you'll need for any given number of variables, use this formula, where NC is the number of correlations and NV is the number of variables:

```
NC = NV * (NV - 1) / 2
```

Here's how to get what's called a *correlation matrix* (which is a table of correlation coefficients) with the ATP's correlation tool, using the data shown in Figure 4-8:

1. **With the ATP installed in Excel, choose Tools ➪ Data Analysis.**

   The Data Analysis dialog box appears.

2. **In the Analysis Tools drop-down list, choose Correlation, and click OK.**

   The Correlation dialog box appears.

3. **Click in the Input Range box and drag through your entire input range, including the labels at the top of each column.**
4. **Make sure that the Columns radio button is selected.**
5. **Select the Labels in First Row check box.**
6. **Click the Output Range button.**

   The ATP might make the Input Range box active again when you click the Output Range button. If it does, click in the Output Range box and drag across any cell address that might already appear there before you enter the cell where you want the output to start.

7. **Click OK.**

   The ATP takes over and produces the triangular matrix of correlations shown in Figure 4-9.

For correlations, the ATP gives you nine decimal places. That's too much for present purposes and it makes the matrix harder to read. To change the number of decimal places:

1. **Select the full matrix.**
2. **Choose Format ➪ Cells.**
3. **Select the Number tab.**
4. **In the Category drop-down list, select Number.**
5. **Accept the default of two decimal places (or change it if you want) and click OK.**

   This changes the 1 integers in the main diagonal to show as 1.00. You can select them one by one and reduce the decimal places to zero, but that's a little pointless.

	A	B	C	D	E	F	G
1		*Sales ($000)*	*Time Period*	*Unit Price*	*Sales Force*	*Advertising ($000)*	*Revenue Estimates*
2	Sales ($000)	1.00					
3	Time Period	0.56	1.00				
4	Unit Price	-0.30	-0.03	1.00			
5	Sales Force	0.18	-0.42	-0.13	1.00		
6	Advertising ($000)	0.57	0.40	-0.17	0.08	1.00	
7	Revenue Estimates	0.40	0.24	0.03	0.16	0.28	1.00
8							
9		**Sales ($000)**	**Time Period**	**Unit Price**	**Sales Force**	**Advertising ($000)**	**Revenue Estimates**
10		$ 251,897	1	$ 240	52	$ 3,149	$ 121,806
11		$ 154,426	2	$ 265	56	$ 19,303	$ 160,487
12		$ 237,450	3	$ 255	59	$ 23,745	$ 215,323
13		$ 201,980	4	$ 281	58	$ 50,495	$ 251,289
14		$ 271,298	5	$ 257	54	$ 13,565	$ 132,589
15		$ 260,171	6	$ 247	54	$ 65,043	$ 158,200
16		$ 243,231	7	$ 275	51	$ 24,323	$ 104,498
17		$ 281,218	8	$ 265	53	$ 31,637	$ 330,361
18		$ 330,765	9	$ 260	59	$ 66,153	$ 238,259
19		$ 289,533	10	$ 273	50	$ 21,715	$ 361,302
20		$ 332,443	11	$ 253	53	$ 12,467	$ 350,477
21		$ 241,126	12	$ 262	55	$ 12,056	$ 118,257
22		$ 153,515	13	$ 278	41	$ 23,027	$ 184,314
23		$ 119,390	14	$ 276	22	$ 4,477	$ 131,311
24		$ 200,280	15	$ 287	33	$ 40,056	$ 204,771
25		$ 141,599	16	$ 264	20	$ 5,310	$ 135,308
26		$ 210,875	17	$ 258	22	$ 18,452	$ 240,851
27		$ 285,605	18	$ 281	22	$ 42,841	$ 221,149
28		$ 298,577	19	$ 272	23	$ 11,197	$ 106,862
29		$ 259,678	20	$ 242	20	$ 9,738	$ 161,538
30		$ 255,948	21	$ 287	56	$ 22,395	$ 278,345
31		$ 303,582	22	$ 260	32	$ 37,948	$ 149,876
32		$ 235,109	23	$ 270	22	$ 35,266	$ 94,001
33		$ 256,463	24	$ 254	32	$ 57,704	$ 165,103
34		$ 281,613	25	$ 255	55	$ 10,560	$ 279,605
35		$ 276,382	26	$ 286	56	$ 27,638	$ 83,172

Figure 4-9: The correlations of 1.00 appear because the correlation of a variable with itself is always 1.00.

The principal goal of analyzing the correlations is to start the process of eliminating unnecessary predictor variables.

Analyzing the correlations

What does all this preliminary correlation analysis tell you? The first thing I see is that I want to start by using time period and advertising as predictors, at least for a first run. They have respectable correlations with sales: 0.56 and 0.57 in cells B3 and B6 of Figure 4-9.

And I probably want to eliminate Unit Price and Sales Force as predictor variables — they both have relatively low correlations with sales. Further, Sales Force has a moderate correlation with Time Period, which I've already tentatively decided to keep. So, Sales Force might not add much information beyond that supplied by Time Period.

My next step would be to use the ATP's Regression tool to create a forecast. (See Chapter 11 and Chapter 16 for more information on using the Regression tool.) And I'd start by using Time Period, Advertising, and Revenue Estimates as my predictor variables. (Bear in mind that when you use more than one predictor variable, you still wind up with one forecasting equation. For each predictor variable that you add, Regression just adds another factor to the equation.)

I'm not utterly confident of my judgments about the correlations. So I'd continue by using the Regression tool two or three more times: once adding Unit Price to the predictors, once adding Sales Force. And depending on those results, I might add them both in to the predictors and use the Regression tool on all the possible predictors. If I had a much shorter baseline, I'd be worried about that.

I like to have at least eight times as many time periods in the baseline as predictor variables in the regression equation — but that's just a rule of thumb.

Figure 4-10 shows the results of using the ATP's Regression tool with Time Period, Advertising, and Revenue Estimates as the predictor variables.

A lot of information is wrapped up in this analysis. At the outset, the most important item to look at is the R-squared number in cell G5. It can range from 0 to 1.0, and the closer it is to 1.0, the more accurate you can expect your forecast to be. An R-squared of 0.5 isn't bad. That means that 50 percent of the variability in sales can be predicted using the regression forecast equation.

Microsoft Excel - Sales.xls

File Edit View Insert Format Tools Data Window Help

F1 SUMMARY OUTPUT

	A	B	C	D	E	F	G	H	I	J	
1	Sales ($000)	Time Period	Advertising ($000)	Revenue Estimates		SUMMARY OUTPUT					
2	$ 251,897	1	$ 3,149	$ 121,806							
3	$ 154,426	2	$ 19,303	$ 160,487		*Regression Statistics*					
4	$ 237,450	3	$ 23,745	$ 215,323		Multiple R	0.71				
5	$ 201,980	4	$ 50,495	$ 251,289		R Square	0.50				
6	$ 271,298	5	$ 13,565	$ 132,589		Adjusted R Square	0.46				
7	$ 260,171	6	$ 65,043	$ 158,200		Standard Error	60930.45				
8	$ 243,231	7	$ 24,323	$ 104,498		Observations	40				
9	$ 281,218	8	$ 31,637	$ 330,361							
10	$ 330,765	9	$ 66,153	$ 238,259		ANOVA					
11	$ 289,533	10	$ 21,715	$ 361,302			*df*	*SS*	*MS*	*F*	*Signi*
12	$ 332,443	11	$ 12,467	$ 350,477		Regression	3	132875201027	44291733676	11.93	
13	$ 241,126	12	$ 12,056	$ 118,257		Residual	36	133650707260	3712519646		
14	$ 153,515	13	$ 23,027	$ 184,314		Total	39	266525908288			
15	$ 119,390	14	$ 4,477	$ 131,311							
16	$ 200,280	15	$ 40,056	$ 204,771			*Coefficients*	*Standard Error*	*t Stat*	*P-value*	*Low*
17	$ 141,599	16	$ 5,310	$ 135,308		Intercept	140811.89	27410.23	5.14	0.00	
18	$ 210,875	17	$ 18,452	$ 240,851		Time Period	2577.40	918.94	2.80	0.01	
19	$ 285,605	18	$ 42,841	$ 221,149		Advertising ($000)	1.21	0.43	2.81	0.01	
20	$ 298,577	19	$ 11,197	$ 106,862		Revenue Estimates	0.18	0.11	1.66	0.11	
21	$ 259,678	20	$ 9,738	$ 161,538							
22	$ 255,948	21	$ 22,395	$ 278,345							
23	$ 303,582	22	$ 37,948	$ 149,876							
24	$ 235,109	23	$ 35,266	$ 94,001							
25	$ 256,463	24	$ 57,704	$ 165,103							
26	$ 281,613	25	$ 10,560	$ 279,605							
27	$ 276,382	26	$ 27,638	$ 83,172							
28	$ 252,487	27	$ 18,937	$ 237,505							
29	$ 296,596	28	$ 48,197	$ 385,426							
30	$ 206,751	29	$ 18,091	$ 220,722							
31	$ 191,277	30	$ 4,782	$ 203,258							
32	$ 195,784	31	$ 7,342	$ 224,831							
33	$ 252,467	32	$ 53,649	$ 106,609							
34	$ 343,489	33	$ 55,817	$ 123,247							
35	$ 344,420	34	$ 81,800	$ 331,416							

Regression Forecast

Figure 4-10: Either the Multiple R or the R Square figure tells you that this regression forecast will be reasonably reliable.

Depending on where you look, you'll find that Excel and Excel-related documents use the terms *R Square* and *R-squared.* They're the same thing.

In Figure 4-10, you'll find the coefficients for the forecast equation in cells G17 through G20. Rounding them a little, your equation would be:

```
Sales = 140812 + (2577 * Time Period) + (1.2 *
        Advertising) + (Revenue Estimates * 0.18)
```

Just plug the next period's values of Time Period, Advertising, and Revenue Estimates into the equation to get your Sales forecast for the next period.

The correlation analysis just gives you a place to start with your choice of predictor variables. With 5 possible predictors, there are 31 different combinations including 1, 2, 3, 4, or 5 variables, and you need a place to start. An analysis of the relationships between the variables is a good one.

Part II
Organizing the Data

"The funny thing is he's spent 9 hours organizing his computer desktop."

In this part . . .

Part II gets into how to set up your data as the basis for a forecast. Understanding your product line, your company's sales strategy, and the marketplace that you and your people are selling into is really important. It's equally important to have a sales history that you can use to make your numeric forecast. Part II shows you how to set up that sales history, so Excel can take best advantage of those numbers.

Chapter 5

Choosing Your Data: How to Get a Good Baseline

In This Chapter

- Knowing when you need to pay attention to order — and when you can ignore it
- Recognizing the importance of time periods
- Making your time periods equal

In most cases, you'll get the most out of your historical baseline of sales data if you put it in chronological order. And because you're going to forecast into the future, the order should be ascending chronological order. This chapter shows you the easiest way to arrange that order for your baseline.

Your forecast will be for a particular period of time. To some extent, your baseline's time periods determine the length of time your forecast will cover. For example, if your baseline's time periods are years, forecasting revenues for the next month is tough. On the other hand, if you need to forecast a year, you may have to jiggle your baseline some. In either case, the length of each time period in your baseline is important.

When you forecast, you're trying to separate the *signal* (the regular, dependable component of your baseline) from the *noise* (the irregularities that come from unpredictable events, like sales reps being out sick, random changes in your customers' buying patterns, and so on). To help with this separation, you want to impose some order on the chaos. One of the ways you do this is to use equally spaced time periods of nearly equal length.

Early to Bed: Getting Your Figures in Order

One of the characteristics of a useful baseline is that the data is in a rational *order.* For some purposes, you may have a list of monthly sales revenues that's sorted in order of magnitude. That is, you might show the largest monthly revenue first, and then the next largest, and so on. That would tend to highlight the most (and, at the bottom, the least) successful time periods.

When it comes to forecasting, you need your baseline to be in order, and in a particular kind of order: chronological.

Why order matters: Moving averages

When you forecast using moving averages, you're taking the average of several consecutive results — in this book, I look at sales results, but I could just as easily be tracking the number of traffic accidents over time. So, you may get the moving averages like this:

- **First moving average:** The average of months January, February, and March
- **Second moving average:** The average of months February, March, and April
- **Third moving average:** The average of months March, April, and May

Notice that the moving averages each combine an equal number of months (three apiece) and that each consecutive moving average *begins* with the next consecutive month. Figure 5-1 has an example.

In Figure 5-1, columns C through F show where each moving average comes from, as well as the moving averages themselves. For example, the third moving average is 42,745 (in cell E7), and it's the average of the values in cells B4, B5, and B6.

Suppose you decide that each moving average will be based on three baseline values. The first moving average *must* be based on the first three, chronologically consecutive values. The baseline values *should* be in chronological order, as shown in Figure 5-1. It's possible to make the first moving average consist of January, February, and March even if the baseline is in some random order — but doing so is tedious and error prone. If you sort the baseline in chronological order, you can use a simple cut and paste, or AutoFill, to create the moving averages.

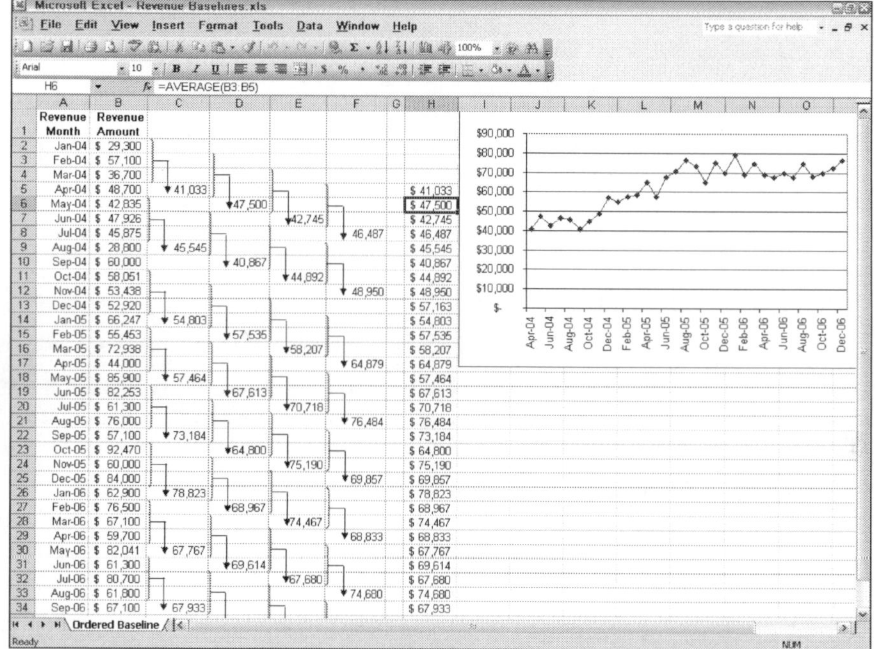

Figure 5-1: The moving averages show how the baseline's level, or *trend*, is gradually increasing.

Figure 5-1 shows how the moving averages *should* look: The baseline in columns A and B is in order. The level of the baseline is gradually increasing over time, and the chart of moving averages reflects that increase.

Here's how easy it is to get the moving averages shown in Figure 5-1:

1. **In cell H5, type** =AVERAGE(B2:B4) **and press Enter.**
2. **Select cell H5 and choose Edit ➪ Copy.**
3. **Select the range of cells H6:H37 and choose Edit ➪ Paste.**

That's all there is to it. (AutoFill is even quicker on the worksheet, but to describe it takes more words on the printed page.)

On the other hand, Figure 5-2 shows what can happen when the data in your baseline is out of order.

In Figure 5-2, there's no rhyme or reason to the order in which the baseline data appear — and this is just the sort of thing that can happen if you've gotten the baseline data from monthly reports that have been stuffed into a file drawer, or even if you pasted them into your worksheet from a database that stores the monthly results in some other order.

The chart does show the averages in chronological order, but when the averages are based on a random sequence of months, that's not much help. Notice in Figure 5-2 that the moving averages in the chart form a line that shows no trend — but we know from Figure 5-1 that the trend is gently up.

If you do get data in some sort of random order, as in columns A and B of Figure 5-2, the problem is easily fixed. Take these steps:

1. **Click any cell in the baseline in column A or column B — for example, cell B17.**
2. **Choose Data ➪ Sort.**

   The Sort dialog box, shown in Figure 5-3, appears.
3. **If your layout is as shown in Figures 5-1 and 5-2, with text labels in the first row, make sure that the Header Row button is selected. If you don't have labels in the first row, click the No Header Row button.**
4. **Choose Revenue Month in the Sort By drop-down list.**
5. **Click OK.**

   Your baseline will now be sorted into chronological order, and your moving averages will make sense.

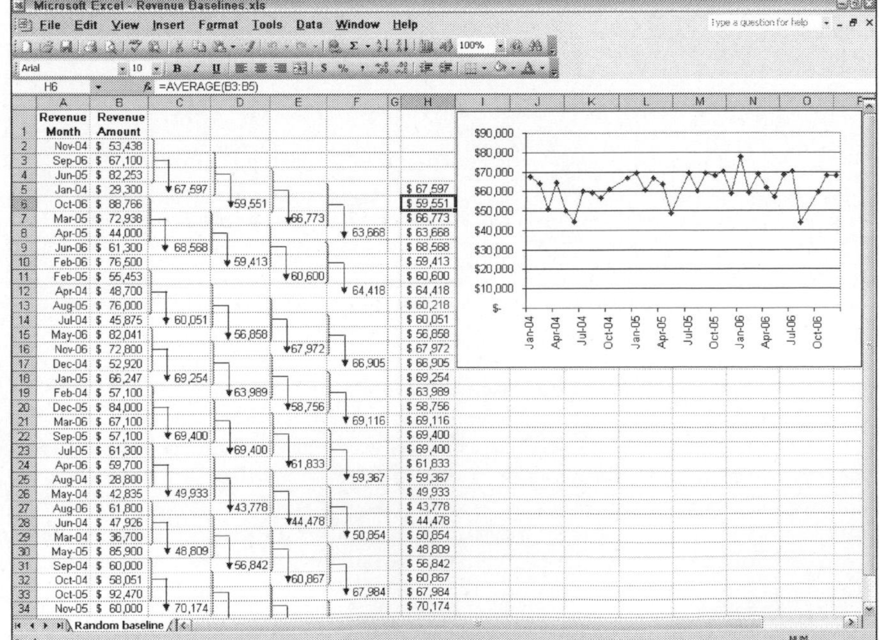

Figure 5-2: Your moving averages can jump all over the place if you haven't tended to your baseline's order.

Figure 5-3: If you don't have labels in the first row, click the No Header Row button.

Why order matters: Exponential smoothing

The idea behind exponential smoothing is a near neighbor to the idea behind moving averages. In both cases, you forecast what's going to happen next on the basis of what happened before. For example, in a three-period moving average, you would get an April forecast by averaging January, February, and March actuals, or a fourth-quarter forecast by averaging the actuals from the first, second, and third quarters.

And with moving averages, you generally give each period that goes into an average the same weight: Q4 forecast = (Q1 + Q2 + Q3) ÷ 3. In exponential smoothing, the farther back you go in the baseline, the less the impact of the actuals. For example, to get a forecast for July using exponential smoothing, the following factors are plausible:

- June exerts 100 percent influence on the July forecast.
- May exerts 70 percent influence.
- April exerts 50 percent influence.
- March exerts 34 percent influence.
- February exerts 24 percent influence.

So the farther back into the baseline you go, the less the influence an actual result exerts on the next forecast. This is an intuitively appealing approach: You've probably had experience with how, say, a fashion in clothing has less and less impact on your choices in apparel as more and more months go by. Leisure suits, for example. Jeans with holes in them.

The formula that you use to do exponential smoothing is deceptively simple. See Figure 5-4 for an example.

	Revenue Month	Revenue Amount	Forecast
2	Jan-04	$ 29,300	#N/A
3	Feb-04	$ 57,100	$ 29,300
4	Mar-04	$ 36,700	$ 37,640
5	Apr-04	$ 48,700	$ 37,358
6	May-04	$ 42,835	$ 40,761
7	Jun-04	$ 47,926	$ 41,383
8	Jul-04	$ 45,875	$ 43,346
9	Aug-04	$ 28,800	$ 44,105
10	Sep-04	$ 60,000	$ 39,513
11	Oct-04	$ 58,051	$ 45,659
12	Nov-04	$ 53,438	$ 49,377
13	Dec-04	$ 52,920	$ 50,595
14	Jan-05	$ 66,247	$ 51,293
15	Feb-05	$ 55,453	$ 55,779
16	Mar-05	$ 72,938	$ 55,681
17	Apr-05	$ 44,000	$ 60,858
18	May-05	$ 85,900	$ 55,801
19	Jun-05	$ 82,253	$ 64,831
20	Jul-05	$ 61,300	$ 70,057
21	Aug-05	$ 76,000	$ 67,430
22	Sep-05	$ 57,100	$ 70,001
23	Oct-05	$ 92,470	$ 66,131
24	Nov-05	$ 60,000	$ 74,033
25	Dec-05	$ 84,000	$ 69,823
26	Jan-06	$ 62,900	$ 74,076
27	Feb-06	$ 76,500	$ 70,723
28	Mar-06	$ 67,100	$ 72,456
29	Apr-06	$ 59,700	$ 70,849
30	May-06	$ 82,041	$ 67,505
31	Jun-06	$ 61,300	$ 71,865
32	Jul-06	$ 80,700	$ 68,696
33	Aug-06	$ 61,800	$ 72,297

Figure 5-4: This becomes tedious in a hurry if your baseline isn't in chronological order.

You can tell from looking at the formula in the Formula Bar that a forecast is a weighted average of the prior actual and the prior forecast. Again, after you've entered the formula once, at the top of the baseline, it's just a matter of copying and pasting it down to the end of the baseline.

But that's because the baseline is in chronological order, with the earliest actual results shown first. If the baseline were in some random order, as in Figure 5-2, you *could* do exponential smoothing, but it would take forever to get the formulas right.

Why order doesn't matter: Regression

With moving averages and exponential smoothing, the argument for putting the baseline in chronological order is based on the fact that you're using the forecast variable itself to make the next forecast. You're averaging, or otherwise combining, prior values of sales revenues so as to forecast the next revenue figure. Therefore, having the baseline in chronological order is helpful.

The same thing can happen with the regression approach, where you get an application such as Excel to look at your baseline and develop an equation that you use for your forecasts. Used this way, it's called *autoregression* because, once again, you're forecasting from past actuals. Autoregression really likes the baseline to be in chronological order.

Another example of regression in forecasting is the use of another variable to forecast sales — something such as the size of your sales force, your changing market share, unit price, even month and year during which your sales reps made those sales. Many variables can affect your sales revenues or number of units sold. And here, finally, it doesn't matter what order your baseline is in. Figure 5-5 shows the principal reason.

You're not making your forecast based on earlier values of your sales baseline. Your forecast is based on another variable entirely. If you're going to get more sales reps, your analysis might forecast higher revenues. This is due to the historic relationship between number of sales reps and amount of revenue. Regression analysis gives you an equation (shown in the chart in Figure 5-5). You pop the upcoming number of sales reps into the equation, and out pops your revenue forecast.

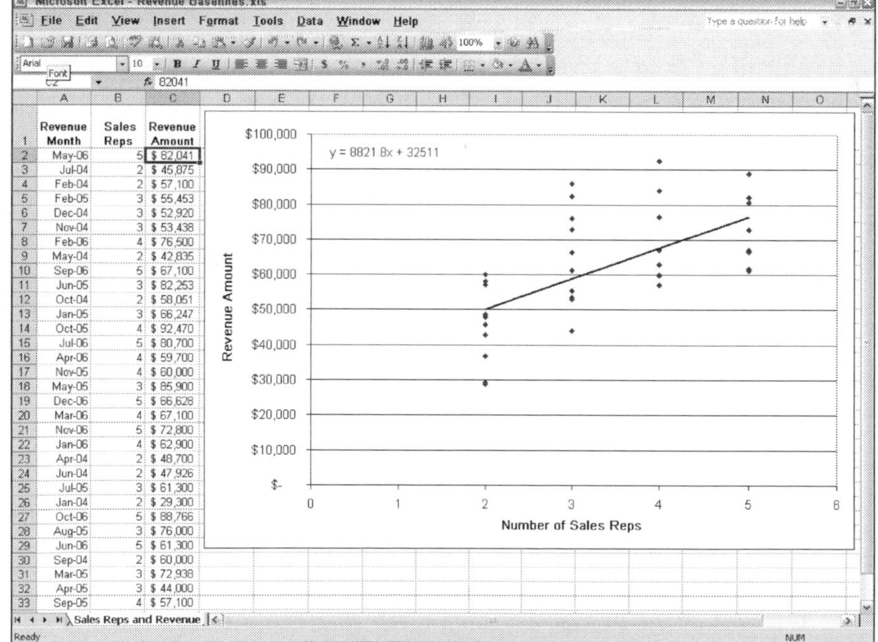

Revenue Month	Sales Reps	Revenue Amount
May-06	5	$ 82,041
Jul-04	2	$ 45,875
Feb-04	2	$ 57,100
Feb-05	3	$ 55,453
Dec-04	3	$ 52,920
Nov-04	3	$ 53,438
Feb-06	4	$ 76,500
May-04	2	$ 42,835
Sep-06	5	$ 67,100
Jun-05	3	$ 82,253
Oct-04	2	$ 58,051
Jan-05	3	$ 66,247
Oct-05	4	$ 92,470
Jul-06	5	$ 80,700
Apr-06	4	$ 59,700
Nov-05	4	$ 60,000
May-05	3	$ 85,900
Dec-06	5	$ 66,628
Mar-06	4	$ 67,100
Nov-06	5	$ 72,800
Jan-06	4	$ 62,900
Apr-04	2	$ 48,700
Jun-04	2	$ 47,926
Jul-05	3	$ 61,300
Jan-04	2	$ 29,300
Oct-06	5	$ 88,766
Aug-05	3	$ 76,000
Jun-06	5	$ 61,300
Sep-04	2	$ 60,000
Mar-05	3	$ 72,938
Apr-05	3	$ 44,000
Sep-05	4	$ 57,100

Figure 5-5: The chart, an XY (Scatter) chart, doesn't require that the baseline be in any particular order.

Because regression analysis doesn't require you to have your baseline in chronological order, you can get away with even a random order. But why would you? I suppose if that's how your data comes in and you only want to use regression, you might pass on sorting it first.

Staying Inside the Lines: Why Time Periods Matter

Two terms in particular are important to this section:

- **Baseline:** I use this term a little loosely (shame on me). It's commonly used to mean historical data, going back some undefined distance from the present day, and consisting of at least one variable — the one that will be forecast. The baseline can have other measures, too, such as the dates that the forecast variable was measured, and other variables of interest like unit price or number of sales reps. But *baseline* can also be used to mean just the forecast variable itself. You can almost always tell from the context which usage someone means.
- **Time period:** This is the period that you've split your baseline into. In sales forecasting, that's usually months and quarters, although some businesses recognize revenue weekly. (Doesn't matter, by the way: All sales figures are grist for this mill.)

In the following sections, I go into more detail on time periods.

Deciding how far to forecast

When you're asked to make a forecast, one of the first things you need to consider is how far into the future you want to peer. Some forecasting techniques put you in a position to forecast farther out than do others. Figure 5-6 shows two techniques that let you forecast just one time period ahead.

Other chapters (such as Chapter 13 and Chapter 15) show you much more about how and why the formulas in Figure 5-6 make for good forecasts. For now, notice what happens when you stretch them too far: Like rubber bands, they break and snap back at you.

Look first at cell D5 in Figure 5-6. It's the average of cells B2, B3, and B4, and it's what the moving-average approach forecasts for September 2004. That is, the way this forecast is set up, the forecast for September is the average of June, July, and August. You can see the forecast of $40,867 in cell D5, and the formula itself for illustration in cell E5.

	A	B	C	D	E
1	Revenue Month	Actual Revenue Amount		Moving Averages	
2	Jun-04	$ 47,926			
3	Jul-04	$ 45,875		#N/A	
4	Aug-04	$ 28,800		#N/A	
5	Sep-04	$ 60,000		$ 40,867	=AVERAGE(B2:B4)
6	Oct-04	$ 58,051		$ 44,892	
7	Nov-04	$ 53,438		$ 48,950	
8	Dec-04	$ 52,920		$ 57,163	
9	Jan-05	$ 66,247		$ 54,803	
10	Feb-05	$ 55,453		$ 57,535	
11	Mar-05	$ 72,938		$ 58,207	
12	Apr-05	$ 44,000		$ 64,879	
13	May-05	$ 85,900		$ 57,464	
14	Jun-05	$ 82,253		$ 67,613	
15	Jul-05	$ 61,300		$ 70,718	
16	Aug-05	$ 76,000		$ 76,484	
17	Sep-05	$ 57,100		$ 73,184	
18	Oct-05	$ 92,470		$ 64,800	
19	Nov-05	$ 60,000		$ 75,190	
20	Dec-05	$ 84,000		$ 69,857	
21	Jan-06	$ 62,900		$ 78,823	
22	Feb-06	$ 76,500		$ 68,967	
23	Mar-06	$ 67,100		$ 74,467	
24	Apr-06	$ 59,700		$ 68,833	
25	May-06	$ 82,041		$ 67,767	
26	Jun-06	$ 61,300		$ 69,614	
27	Jul-06	$ 80,700		$ 67,680	
28	Aug-06		Forecast:	$ 74,680	=AVERAGE(B25:B27)
29	Sep-06		Forecast:	$ 71,000	=AVERAGE(B26:B28)

Figure 5-6: Moving averages are usually limited to one-step-ahead forecasts.

This formula is copied and pasted down through cell D28, where it provides the "real" forecast for August 2006. I'm using "real" in the sense that I haven't yet seen an actual value for that month — my most recent actual value is for July 2006. The formula itself is shown in cell E28.

But if I copy and paste the formula one more row down, to try for a forecast for September 2006, I've stretched it too far. Now it's trying to average the actual results for June through August 2006, and I have no actual for August. Because of the way that Excel's AVERAGE works, it ignores cell B28 and the formula returns the average of B26 and B27.

The District Attorney will decline to prosecute if you're found shifting suddenly from a three-month moving average to a two-month moving average, but you really shouldn't. If you do, you're inviting an apple to mix with the oranges.

And if you take your forecast much farther down, it'll start returning the really nasty error value `#DIV/0!`. (That exclamation point isn't mine, it's Excel's, and it's meant to get your attention. Excel is yelling at you, "You're trying to divide by zero!")

A similar situation occurs with exponential smoothing, and it's shown in Figure 5-7. The formula for smoothing is different from the formula for moving averages, but something similar happens when you get past the one-step-ahead forecast in cell D28.

Notice that the formula in cell D29 (the formula is shown in E29; the value that the formula returns appears in D29) uses the values in cells B28 and D28. But because we don't yet have an actual for August, the "forecast" for September 2006 is faulty: In fact, it's nothing more than the forecast for August multiplied by 0.7. Again, in this sort of exponential smoothing, you're limited to a one-step-ahead forecast.

Figure 5-8 shows a different situation, where the forecast is built using regression rather than moving averages or exponential smoothing.

Using regression (see Chapter 11 for the basics and Chapter 16 for some refinements), you're in a different position than with moving averages and exponential smoothing. As Figure 5-8 shows, you can create your forecasts using date itself as a predictor: Each forecast value there is based on the relationship in the baseline between date and revenue.

Because I know the value of the next two dates, August and September 2006, I can use the relationship between date and revenue in the baseline on the next two dates to get a forecast. The forecast values appear in cells C28 and C29 and show up in the chart as the final two points in the Forecast series.

	A	B	C	D	E
1	Revenue Month	Actual Revenue Amount		Exponenial Smoothing	
2	Jun-04	$ 47,926		#N/A	
3	Jul-04	$ 45,875		$ 47,926	
4	Aug-04	$ 28,800		$ 47,311	
5	Sep-04	$ 60,000		$ 41,757	=0.3*B4+0.7*D4
6	Oct-04	$ 58,051		$ 47,230	
7	Nov-04	$ 53,438		$ 50,476	
8	Dec-04	$ 52,920		$ 51,365	
9	Jan-05	$ 66,247		$ 51,831	
10	Feb-05	$ 55,453		$ 56,156	
11	Mar-05	$ 72,938		$ 55,945	
12	Apr-05	$ 44,000		$ 61,043	
13	May-05	$ 85,900		$ 55,930	
14	Jun-05	$ 82,253		$ 64,921	
15	Jul-05	$ 61,300		$ 70,121	
16	Aug-05	$ 76,000		$ 67,474	
17	Sep-05	$ 57,100		$ 70,032	
18	Oct-05	$ 92,470		$ 66,152	
19	Nov-05	$ 60,000		$ 74,048	
20	Dec-05	$ 84,000		$ 69,833	
21	Jan-06	$ 62,900		$ 74,083	
22	Feb-06	$ 76,500		$ 70,728	
23	Mar-06	$ 67,100		$ 72,460	
24	Apr-06	$ 59,700		$ 70,852	
25	May-06	$ 82,041		$ 67,506	
26	Jun-06	$ 61,300		$ 71,867	
27	Jul-06	$ 80,700		$ 68,697	
28	Aug-06		Forecast:	$ 72,298	=0.3*B27+0.7*D27
29	Sep-06		Forecast:	$ 50,608	=0.3*B28+0.7*D28

Figure 5-7: If you want to forecast farther ahead, consider a regression forecast.

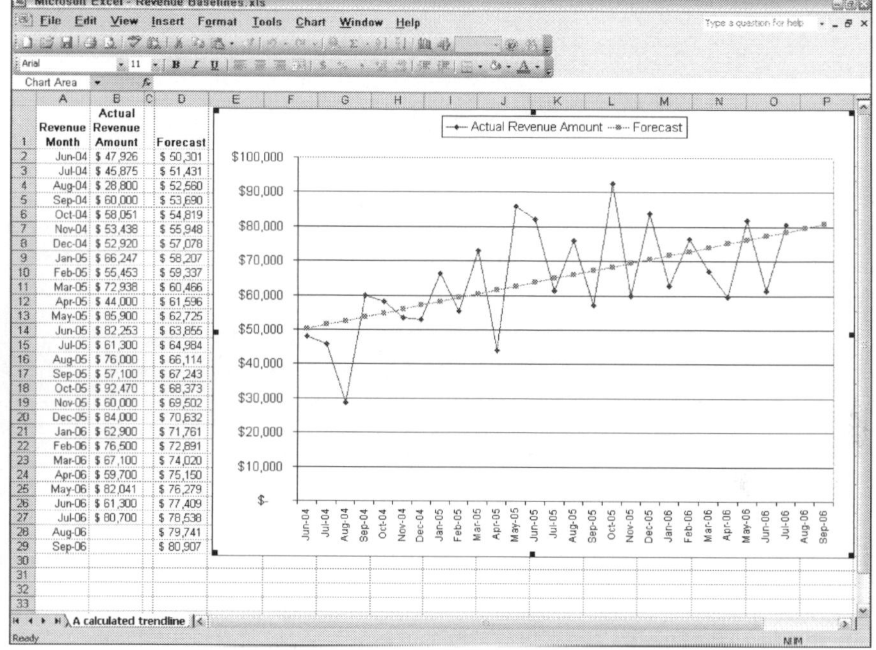

	A	B	C	D
1	Revenue Month	Actual Revenue Amount		Forecast
2	Jun-04	$ 47,926		$ 50,301
3	Jul-04	$ 45,875		$ 51,431
4	Aug-04	$ 28,800		$ 52,560
5	Sep-04	$ 60,000		$ 53,690
6	Oct-04	$ 58,051		$ 54,819
7	Nov-04	$ 53,438		$ 55,948
8	Dec-04	$ 52,920		$ 57,078
9	Jan-05	$ 66,247		$ 58,207
10	Feb-05	$ 55,453		$ 59,337
11	Mar-05	$ 72,938		$ 60,466
12	Apr-05	$ 44,000		$ 61,596
13	May-05	$ 85,900		$ 62,725
14	Jun-05	$ 82,253		$ 63,855
15	Jul-05	$ 61,300		$ 64,984
16	Aug-05	$ 76,000		$ 66,114
17	Sep-05	$ 57,100		$ 67,243
18	Oct-05	$ 92,470		$ 68,373
19	Nov-05	$ 60,000		$ 69,502
20	Dec-05	$ 84,000		$ 70,632
21	Jan-06	$ 62,900		$ 71,761
22	Feb-06	$ 76,500		$ 72,891
23	Mar-06	$ 67,100		$ 74,020
24	Apr-06	$ 59,700		$ 75,150
25	May-06	$ 82,041		$ 76,279
26	Jun-06	$ 61,300		$ 77,409
27	Jul-06	$ 80,700		$ 78,538
28	Aug-06			$ 79,741
29	Sep-06			$ 80,907

Figure 5-8: The trendline in the chart is taken from the worksheet. You can also get one from the Chart menu.

Now, the farther out into the future you forecast using regression, the thinner the ice gets (or, if you prefer the earlier metaphor, the more strain you're putting on the rubber band). The farther you get from the end of your baseline, the more opportunities there are for the actuals to change direction — for example, to turn down or to level off.

If you have a real need to forecast, say, 12 months into the future on a monthly basis, and if you think there's a dependable relationship between date and revenue amount, then regression may be your best choice. But keep in mind that things get flaky out there in the future.

Another method to push your forecast out beyond a one-step-ahead approach is seasonal smoothing. This approach, which depends on a seasonal component in your baseline, can support a forecast that goes that year into the future. It ain't necessarily so, but it's possible. (Chapter 18 has information on the seasonal approach.)

Choosing your time periods

Suppose that you *do* need to forecast out a ways from the present — a year, for instance. Here's where judgment enters the picture, along with the nature of your requirements.

If your baseline consists of several years, with actuals broken out by months, one thing you may consider is to change the baseline's time period from months to years. Then you can forecast the entire next year — although your forecasts would not be month-by-month. You would get the one-step-ahead forecast, and that one step would be the entire year (see Figure 5-9).

Here's what's going on in Figure 5-9:

- Column A contains the month during which revenue was recognized. It extends down past the bottom of the visible worksheet area to December 2006.
- Column B contains the revenue for each month.
- The range D3:E9 contains a pivot table. (Excel's pivot tables are huge assets for forecasting, and you can find out how to use them in Chapter 8.) This pivot table converts the monthly data in columns A and B to annual data — the sum of the revenue for each year.
- The forecast for each year, using moving averages, is in the range G4:H10. Your one-step-ahead forecast for 2007 is in cell H10. In this case, the forecasts are based on two-year moving averages, rather than the three-period averages that appear in Figure 5-6.

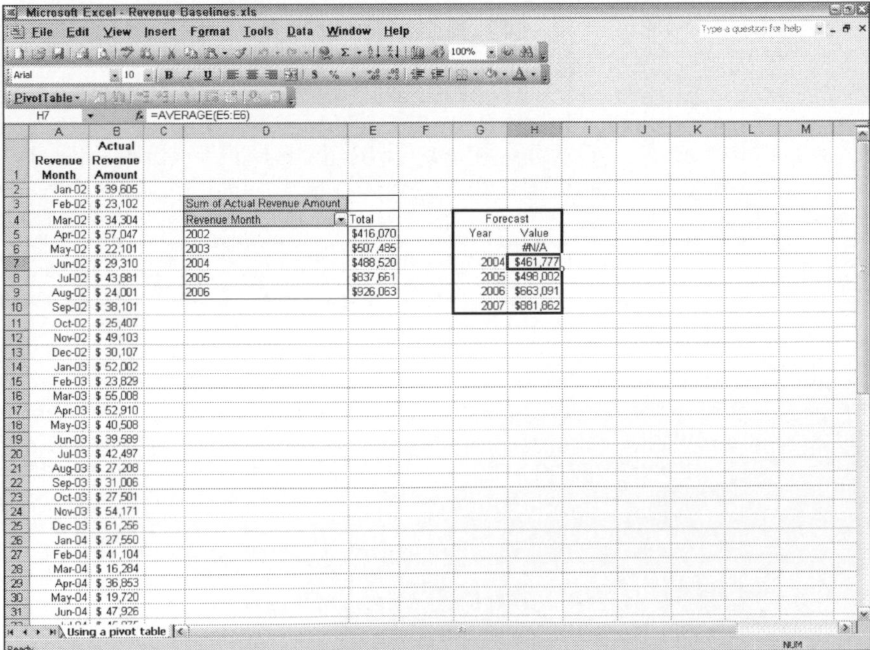

Figure 5-9: Pivot tables are useful for summarizing baseline data into longer time periods.

The approach in Figure 5-9 has a couple drawbacks:

- **Your baseline goes from 60 observations (monthly revenue over 5 years, a good long baseline) to 5 observations (yearly revenue over 5 years, a short baseline indeed).** Reducing the length of your baseline so drastically often causes misleading results. But because the monthly revenues show the same gradual growth as the annual totals, you can have some confidence in the annuals.
- **Whoever requested the forecast — an accountant, a bank, a sales manager, a sales VP — could want to see the forecast for 2007 on a monthly basis.** If so, you're probably going to have to back up to the monthly baseline and use regression (*probably,* because you may be able to find the seasonality in the baseline that would support seasonal smoothing).

Spacing Time Periods Equally

Getting your baseline's time periods to line up properly is important. It's also important that, within reason, each time period in your baseline represents the same length of time. Here's a closer look at each of these two issues.

Using periodic relationships

Over time, a baseline tends to display consistent behavior: Its level is increasing, decreasing, or remaining stationary (or it may be seasonal or cyclic). The relationships between time periods help measure this behavior: the relationship between one month and the next, or between one quarter and the next, or between one quarter and the same quarter in the prior year.

Your baseline might mix up the relationships between its time periods for various reasons, some good and some bad. A couple of examples:

- Whoever assembled the baseline data (not you, certainly) overlooked the sales revenues for June 15 through June 30. This is a real problem, and it's really indefensible. "The dog ate my homework" doesn't cut it here.
- The warehouse burned to the ground and nobody could sell anything until the factory could catch up with the loss of inventory. Again, a real problem, but it doesn't help your forecast even if the police do catch the arsonist.

The reason is this: If almost all of your baseline consists of monthly revenues, and one time period represents just half a month, any forecast that depends on the entire baseline will be thrown off. Figure 5-10 shows an example of what can happen.

Microsoft Excel - Revenue Baselines.xls

A1 Revenue Month

	A	B	C	H	I	J
1	Revenue Month	Actual Revenue Amount		Revenue Month	Actual Revenue Amount	
2	Jun-04	$ 47,926	#N/A	Jun-04	$ 47,926	#N/A
3	Jul-04	$ 45,875	$ 47,926	Jul-04	$ 45,875	$ 47,926
4	Aug-04	$ 28,800	$ 47,311	Aug-04	$ 28,800	$ 47,311
5	Sep-04	$ 60,000	$ 41,757	Sep-04	$ 60,000	$ 41,757
6	Oct-04	$ 58,051	$ 47,230	Oct-04	$ 58,051	$ 47,230
7	Nov-04	$ 53,438	$ 50,476	Nov-04	$ 53,438	$ 50,476
8	Dec-04	$ 52,920	$ 51,365	Dec-04	$ 52,920	$ 51,365
9	Jan-05	$ 66,247	$ 51,831	Jan-05	$ 66,247	$ 51,831
10	Feb-05	$ 55,453	$ 56,156	Feb-05	$ 55,453	$ 56,156
11	Mar-05	$ 72,938	$ 55,945	Mar-05	$ 72,938	$ 55,945
12	Apr-05	$ 44,000	$ 61,043	Apr-05	$ 44,000	$ 61,043
13	May-05	$ 85,900	$ 55,930	May-05	$ 85,900	$ 55,930
14	Jun-05	$ 82,253	$ 64,921	Jun-05	$ 82,253	$ 64,921
15	Jul-05	$ 61,300	$ 70,121	Jul-05	$ 61,300	$ 70,121
16	Aug-05	$ 76,000	$ 67,474	Aug-05	$ 76,000	$ 67,474
17	Sep-05	$ 57,100	$ 70,032	Sep-05	$ 57,100	$ 70,032
18	Oct-05	$ 92,470	$ 66,152	Oct-05	$ 92,470	$ 66,152
19	Nov-05	$ 60,000	$ 74,048	Nov-05	$ 60,000	$ 74,048
20	Dec-05	$ 84,000	$ 69,833	Dec-05	$ 84,000	$ 69,833
21	Jan-06	$ 62,900	$ 74,083	Jan-06	$ 62,900	$ 74,083
22	Feb-06	$ 76,500	$ 70,728	Feb-06	$ 76,500	$ 70,728
23	Mar-06	$ 67,100	$ 72,460	Mar-06	$ 67,100	$ 72,460
24	Apr-06	$ 59,700	$ 70,852	Apr-06	$ 59,700	$ 70,852
25	May-06	**$82,041**	$ 67,506	May-06	**$41,020**	$ 67,506
26	Jun-06	$ 61,300	$ 71,867	Jun-06	$ 61,300	$ 59,560
27	Jul-06	$ 80,700	$ 68,697	Jul-06	$ 80,700	$ 60,082
28	Aug-06 Forecast		$ 72,298	Aug-06 Forecast		$ 66,268

Inconsistent revenues in May-06

Figure 5-10: Bad data from a recent time period can lead to a bad forecast.

In Figure 5-10, cells A1:B27 contain a baseline with accurate revenues throughout. Exponential smoothing gives the forecast for August 2006 in cell C28.

Also in Figure 5-10, cells H1:I27 have the same baseline, except for cell I25. For some reason (careless accounting, that warehouse fire, or something else), the revenue for May 2006 has been underreported. The result is that the forecast for August 2006 is more than $6,000 less than it is when the May 2006 revenues are the result of neither an error nor a one-time incident. Six thousand dollars may not sound like a lot, but in this context it's an 8 percent difference. And it's even worse right after the problem occurs: The difference in the two forecasts is 17 percent in June 2006.

If this happened to me, I'd send someone back to the files — whether hard- or soft-copy — to fill in the missing data for May 2006.

If the missing data can't be located, due perhaps to an accounting error, or if no error was made but some really unusual incident interrupted the sales process during May 2006, I'd probably estimate the actuals for May. A couple of reasonable ways to do that:

- Take the average of April and June and assign that average to May.
- Use January 2004 through April 2006 as a baseline, and forecast May 2006. Then use that May 2006 forecast in your full baseline, January 2004 through July 2006.

Chapter 9 stresses the importance of charting your baseline. This situation is another good reason. Just looking at the baseline, you might not notice that May 2006 is an oddball. But it jumps right out at you if you chart the baseline.

Don't worry about small differences in the length of the baseline's time periods. March has one more day in it than April does, but it's not worth worrying about. Two missing weeks is another matter.

When missing data causes unequal time periods

When you're working with forecasts that are based on moving averages and on exponential smoothing, you're working with forecasts that depend on a baseline with consecutive time periods. You might have a sequence of monthly sales revenues that make for a good, sound forecast into the next month, due to the relationship between the sales in consecutive months. But if some of those months are missing, you could be in trouble. Figure 5-11 shows how a full baseline works.

Notice the straight line in the chart in Figure 5-11. It's called a *trendline.* The trendline indicates how well the gradual growth in revenues tracks against the dates when the revenues were recognized. Just what you like to see. Generally, the greater the incline in the trendline, the stronger the relationship between the time period and the revenue, and this is a pretty decent result.

Contrast the chart in Figure 5-11 with the one in Figure 5-12.

The dates and revenues in Figure 5-12 are the same as in Figure 5-11, except that seven months are missing, some from the start of the baseline and a few from well into the baseline. Now, the relationship between the time period and its revenue has been disrupted by the missing periods, and the trendline in the chart has become nearly horizontal, indicating a much weaker relationship.

You wouldn't be able to put much trust in a forecast constructed from the baseline in Figure 5-12, even though the data that's in it is the same as the data in Figure 5-11. The lesson: Arrange for a baseline that's chock-full of consecutive time periods — or don't bother with a forecast.

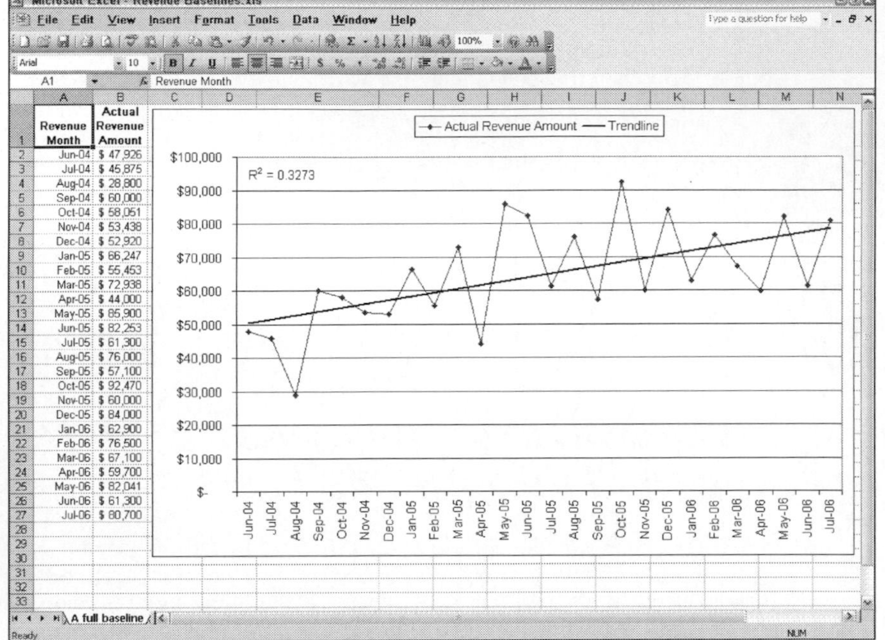

Figure 5-11: Excel can calculate the trendline and the equation for you.

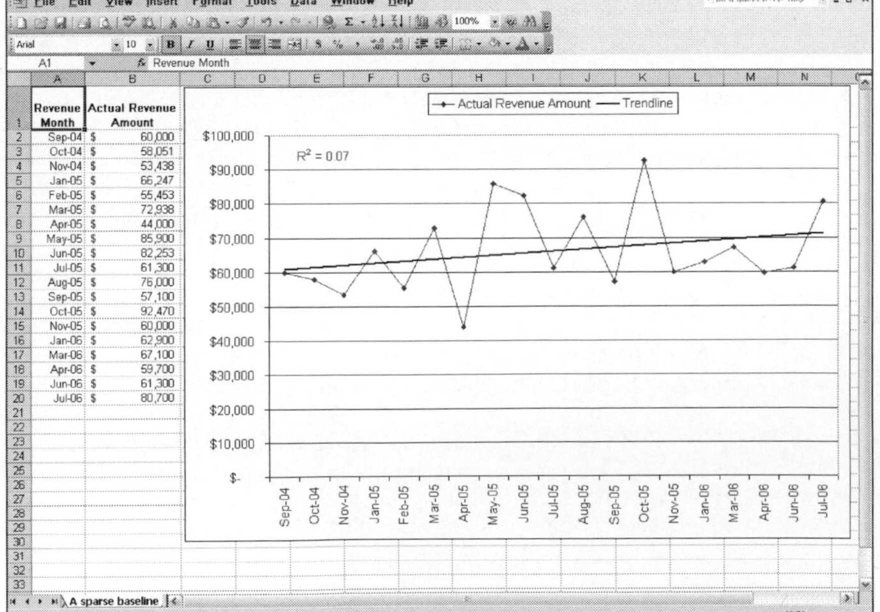

Figure 5-12: The smaller the R-squared value, the less dependable the forecast. An R-squared of 0.07 is small.

Chapter 6

Setting Up Lists in Excel

In This Chapter

- Knowing how lists are structured
- Working with Excel's List command
- Looking at the records you're interested in
- Getting your data into an Excel list

Excel is *not* a database program like Access or SQL Server or Oracle. Sure, you can store data in it, but it's really not intended to store large amounts of data or to manage relationships between different data sets.

Still, Excel has a way, called a *list,* to store your data, whether it's sales data or something else. Lists are important as the basis for your forecasts: Sometimes you use them directly, and sometimes you use them indirectly as the basis for pivot tables. In this chapter, I show you how to set up lists and how to filter them so you can focus on specific sets of records.

You can use a new command in Excel 2003 to set particular options in your lists, such as new record rows and total rows. This chapter shows you how to use the Data menu's List command.

Because you sometimes want to forecast on the basis of a subset of the data in a list (for example, a sales forecast for the Northwest region only, or a sales forecast for dishwasher detergents only), you sometimes want to filter out those subsets. I show you how to do that here.

The process of importing data from another application such as a database can be time consuming and tedious unless you know the most effective way. This chapter shows you how to automate importing the data.

Understanding List Structures

An Excel list has a fairly simple structure. It has these characteristics:

- **Different fields, also known as *variables*, are in different columns.** Notice in Figure 6-1 that three columns contain data, and each column contains a different field. Keeping the same sort of data — such as sales dates, product lines, sales regions, and so on — in one column is a good idea. Don't stick a markup percent in a column full of names of product lines.
- **Different records are in different rows.** Each row in the list represents a different record. In this case, each record is a different sale, and the date, the sales rep, and the revenue is shown for each sales record.
- **The columns have labels.** Each column in the list has a label in the first row. Here, the labels are Date, Sales Rep, and Revenue.

Within the limits of an Excel worksheet's size (256 columns and 65,536 rows), there's no limit to the size of a list. It could have anywhere from 1 to 256 columns, and anywhere from 2 to 65,536 rows. Of course, you'd have to be nuts to put that much data in a worksheet — if you have that much data, use a true database instead.

Speaking of databases, if you're familiar with how tables look in a database, you'll see the resemblance between the Excel list and the database table: fields in columns, records in rows, labels at the tops of the columns. In fact, an Excel list is really just what, years ago, Excel called a database.

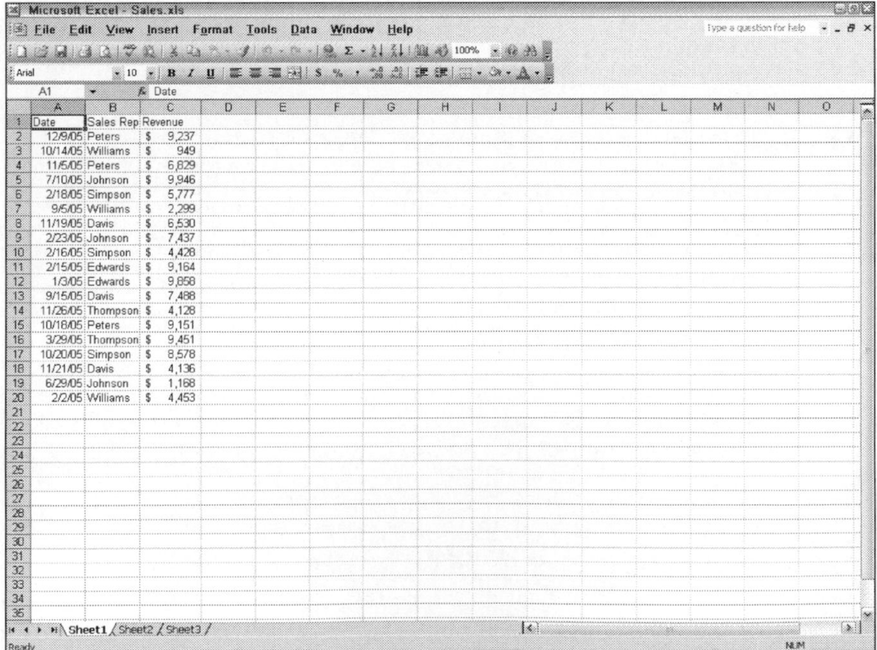

	A	B	C
1	Date	Sales Rep	Revenue
2	12/9/05	Peters	$ 9,237
3	10/14/05	Williams	$ 949
4	11/5/05	Peters	$ 6,829
5	7/10/05	Johnson	$ 9,946
6	2/18/05	Simpson	$ 5,777
7	9/5/05	Williams	$ 2,299
8	11/19/05	Davis	$ 6,530
9	2/23/05	Johnson	$ 7,437
10	2/16/05	Simpson	$ 4,428
11	2/15/05	Edwards	$ 9,164
12	1/3/05	Edwards	$ 9,858
13	9/15/05	Davis	$ 7,488
14	11/26/05	Thompson	$ 4,128
15	10/18/05	Peters	$ 9,151
16	3/29/05	Thompson	$ 9,451
17	10/20/05	Simpson	$ 8,578
18	11/21/05	Davis	$ 4,136
19	6/29/05	Johnson	$ 1,168
20	2/2/05	Williams	$ 4,453

Figure 6-1: The range A1:C20 contains a list.

In Figure 6-1, the records aren't sorted by date, sales rep, or revenue. A list doesn't have to be sorted to be a list.

Why would you want to put a list like the one in Figure 6-1 into an Excel worksheet? Because a list is the basis for many kinds of analysis, including forecasting. For example:

- **If you *do* want to sort the records in the list, Excel makes it easy.** You just click any cell in the list and choose Data ➪ Sort. Excel lets you sort on up to three fields. In Figure 6-1, for example, you could sort first on the sales rep, and within each sales rep's records sort on the date.
- **Lists make filtering your data easy.** You just click any cell in the list and choose, say, Data ➪ Filter ➪ AutoFilter. You'll get a drop-down list at the top of each field where you can select a particular value. Figure 6-2 shows how the list in Figure 6-1 has been filtered to show just the top ten sales in terms of revenue. You could also use the drop-down list in the Sales Rep column to show, say, just Simpson's sales. (To get rid of the autofilter, just choose Data ➪ Filter ➪ AutoFilter again.)
- **Pivot tables make summarizing data in a list easy.** Pivot tables that group the records by date (week, month, quarter, or year) are the basis for the forecasting techniques that this book describes. But if you're building a pivot table, using data in an Excel worksheet, the data has to be structured as a list. Figure 6-3 shows a pivot table based on the list you've been looking at.

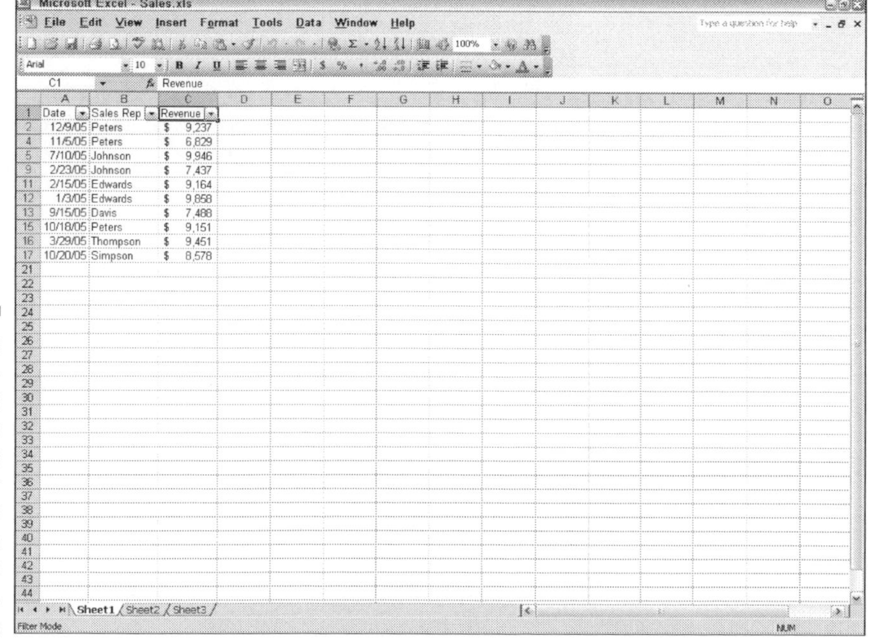

	Date	Sales Rep	Revenue
2	12/9/05	Peters	$ 9,237
4	11/5/05	Peters	$ 6,829
5	7/10/05	Johnson	$ 9,946
9	2/23/05	Johnson	$ 7,437
11	2/15/05	Edwards	$ 9,164
12	1/3/05	Edwards	$ 9,858
13	9/15/05	Davis	$ 7,488
15	10/18/05	Peters	$ 9,151
16	3/29/05	Thompson	$ 9,451
17	10/20/05	Simpson	$ 8,578

Figure 6-2: The drop-down lists offer you the values in their columns as well as a top-ten option.

Date	Sales Rep	Revenue
12/9/05	Peters	$ 9,237
10/14/05	Williams	$ 949
11/5/05	Peters	$ 6,829
7/10/05	Johnson	$ 9,946
2/18/05	Simpson	$ 5,777
9/5/05	Williams	$ 2,299
11/19/05	Davis	$ 6,530
2/23/05	Johnson	$ 7,437
2/16/05	Simpson	$ 4,428
2/15/05	Edwards	$ 9,164
1/3/05	Edwards	$ 9,858
9/15/05	Davis	$ 7,488
11/26/05	Thompson	$ 4,128
10/18/05	Peters	$ 9,151
3/29/05	Thompson	$ 9,451
10/20/05	Simpson	$ 8,578
11/21/05	Davis	$ 4,136
6/29/05	Johnson	$ 1,168
2/2/05	Williams	$ 4,453

Sum of Revenue	
Sales Rep	Total
Davis	$18,154
Edwards	$19,022
Johnson	$18,551
Peters	$25,217
Simpson	$18,783
Thompson	$13,579
Williams	$7,701
Grand Total	$121,007

Figure 6-3: The pivot table automatically sorts itself by the data in the Row field — here, that's the sales rep's name.

You have to follow the list structure carefully if you're preparing to create a pivot table. For example, if you forgot to put a label at the top of one of the columns, Excel would not create the pivot table for you — instead, you'd get an error message telling you that one of your field names wasn't valid.

If for some reason you want to omit a record — that is, have a blank row in the middle of the list — that's okay. But you shouldn't have blank columns, at least not if you're going to create a pivot table using the list. Blank columns result in the same problem you get if you forget to label one of the list's columns — you get an error message.

The List Command

Excel 2003 has a new command in the Data menu — List — and it has some nice features. After you've created a list, click a cell inside the list and choose Data ➪ List ➪ Create List. The Create List dialog box, shown in Figure 6-4, appears.

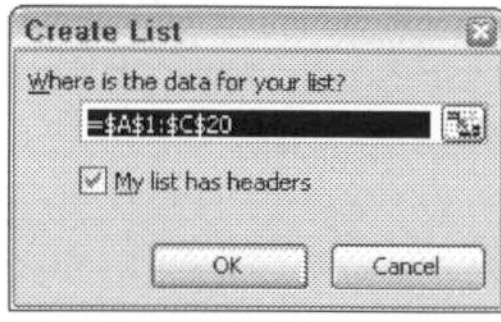

Figure 6-4: If you start by clicking in the list, Excel automatically proposes the full list range.

Notice that the dialog box in Figure 6-4 makes a liar out of me. I've been telling you that you need to put labels at the top of each column in your list. But the Create List dialog box has a My List Has Headers check box, which allows you specify whether your list has *headers* (one way that Excel refers to those column labels). The truth? You *can* have a list that doesn't have column labels. In fact, you can sort a list that's missing one or more column labels, and you can filter a list with missing labels. But use them anyway. Why? Because you can't build a pivot table if a label is missing. And if all the labels are missing, Excel will assume that the first row of data contains the field names for the pivot table, and that leads to ridiculous results.

If you leave the My List Has Headers check box cleared, Excel puts headers in on your behalf. It shifts the list down a row and inserts the labels Column1, Column2, and so on. So be careful: If for some other reason you need the list to stay where it was, be sure that you've provided your own column labels.

After you're sure that Excel has figured out properly where your list is, and you've select the My List Has Headers check box (if appropriate), click OK. You'll see something similar to Figure 6-5.

When you click any cell in the list, Excel does two things:

- **It adds a row at the bottom of the list, with an asterisk at its left edge.** This enables you to add new data to the list, and the list will expand automatically.
- **AutoFilter drop-down lists appear in the cells with the column labels, so you can focus in on just certain records if you want.**

Excel lets you do some special things with lists that you've set up with the Create List command. I go into these special features in the following sections.

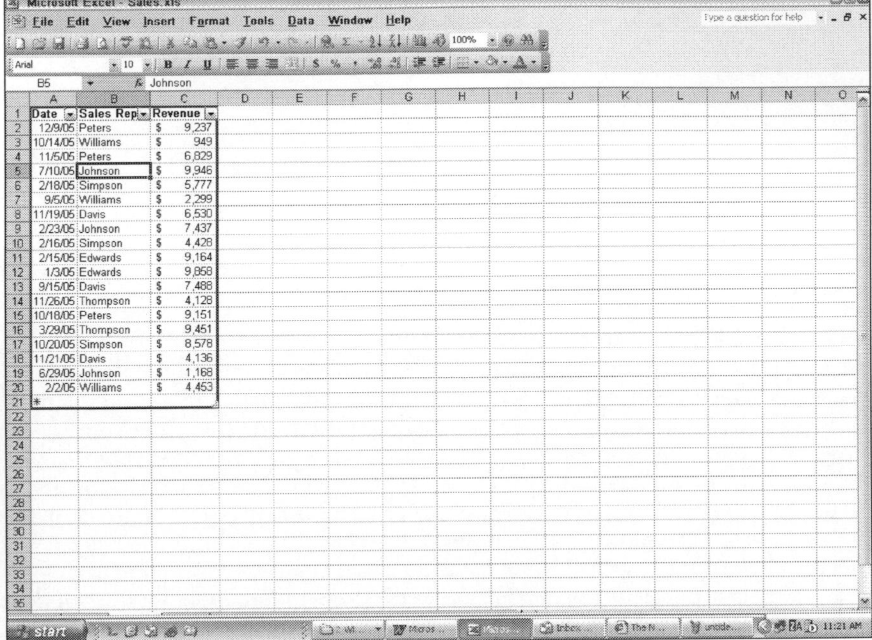

Figure 6-5: The List command puts borders around your list and gives you AutoFilter drop-down lists.

Using the Total Row

Click in the list and choose Data ➪ List ➪ Total Row. You'll get a new row below the list. The new row shows you summaries for your data (see Figure 6-6).

The Total Row automatically gives you a summary of the rightmost column in the list. If the column contains numeric data only, you'll get a sum. If it contains text data, you'll get a count of the values.

But each cell in the Total Row displays a drop-down list if you click in it. And if you click that drop-down list, you'll see a selection of summary statistics that you can choose from, similar to the summaries you can choose in a pivot table:

- **None:** The user wants a total row, but doesn't want it to display a summary.
- **Average:** The sum of the numeric values divided by the number of numeric values.
- **Count:** How many values there are, whether numeric or text.
- **Count Nums:** How many numeric values there are.
- **Max:** The largest numeric value.

- **Min:** The smallest numeric value.
- **Sum:** The total of the numeric values.
- **StdDev:** A quantity that describes how much variability, or spread, there is around the field's average value.
- **Var:** The square of the standard deviation.

You can use Count Nums if a column in the list mixes numeric values with text values. Having a column that mixes numeric and text values usually doesn't make much sense, though — you normally want to store the same kind of information in each column, and if you've mixed text and numeric values, then you probably haven't done that.

So, you can arrange for a total in each cell of the Total Row. In the list we've been looking at, you could get the earliest sales date, a count of the sales reps, and the sum of the revenue (see Figure 6-7).

Suppose you begin to build a pivot table based on a list with a Total Row. You select a single cell inside the list and choose Data ➪ PivotTable and PivotChart Report. When Step 1 of the PivotTable and PivotChart Wizard appears, you choose Microsoft Office Excel List or Database as the data location. In response, Excel selects your entire list but omits both the row for new records and the total row.

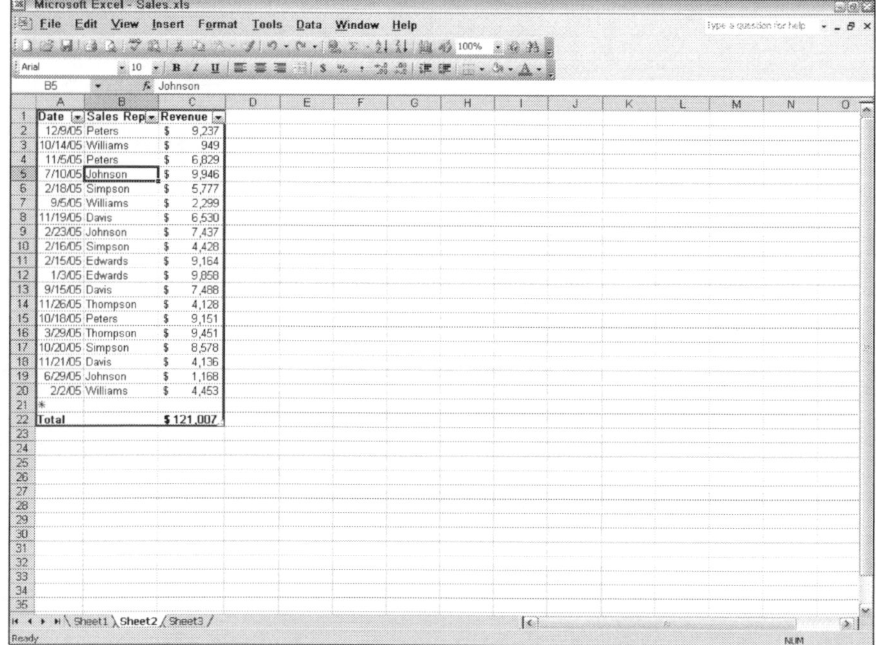

Figure 6-6: The Total Row remains in place after you select some cell outside the list.

Microsoft Excel - Sales.xls

A22 =SUBTOTAL(105,A2:A20)

	Date	Sales Rep	Revenue
2	12/9/05	Peters	$ 9,237
3	10/14/05	Williams	$ 949
4	11/5/05	Peters	$ 6,829
5	7/10/05	Johnson	$ 9,946
6	2/18/05	Simpson	$ 5,777
7	9/5/05	Williams	$ 2,299
8	11/19/05	Davis	$ 6,530
9	2/23/05	Johnson	$ 7,437
10	2/16/05	Simpson	$ 4,428
11	2/15/05	Edwards	$ 9,164
12	1/3/05	Edwards	$ 9,858
13	9/15/05	Davis	$ 7,488
14	11/26/05	Thompson	$ 4,128
15	10/18/05	Peters	$ 9,151
16	3/29/05	Thompson	$ 9,451
17	10/20/05	Simpson	$ 8,578
18	11/21/05	Davis	$ 4,136
19	6/29/05	Johnson	$ 1,168
20	2/2/05	Williams	$ 4,453
21	*		
22	1/3/05	19	$ 121,007

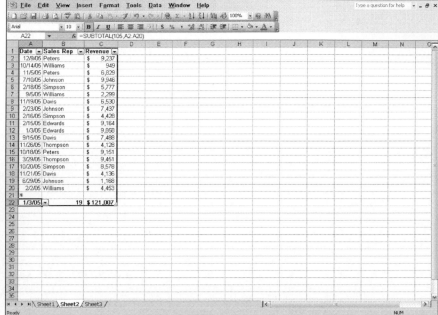

Figure 6-7: You can get the earliest date by choosing the Min summary for the Date column.

This process — starting with a cell inside the list, starting by selecting one cell only, and then starting the PivotTable and PivotChart Wizard — is usually the way to begin building a pivot table from a list. If you start with a cell outside the list, you'll need to type or drag through the list to show the PivotTable Wizard where your data is. You'll also need to be careful not to include the Total Row in the range of cells you provide to the wizard — you don't want to duplicate totals in your pivot table.

Trying out other new List features

Using the Data menu's List command, you can do three other things with lists that you may find handy:

- **Delete the border.** Excel puts a border around the list when you use the List command to create it. If you'd rather not see the border when you're working outside the list, click in the list and then choose Data ⇨ List ⇨ Hide Border of Inactive Lists. The border will appear when a cell in the list is active, and disappear otherwise.

- **Convert a list back into just a normal range.** Click inside a list that you've created with the List command, and choose Data ⇨ List ⇨ Convert to Range. It will still be a list, but the special features of a list that you created by choosing Data ⇨ List ⇨ Create List — the border, the new record row, the AutoFilter drop-down lists — will be gone. If you included a Total Row, its summaries stay in place.
- **Include new data in the list.** If you enter a new column of data to the right of an existing list, you can easily include the new data in the list. You'll see a resize handle in the rightmost column and the bottom row of the list. Move your pointer over it until the pointer turns to a double-headed arrow. Click and hold your mouse down, and drag the edge of the list over the new data to incorporate it in the list. (You can also choose Data ⇨ List ⇨ Resize List, which gives you more control over which cells to include in the list.)

Filtering Lists

You frequently want to filter a list so as to look more closely at specific records. Excel offers you a couple of ways to do this. One is quick and easy, and the other takes just a little more time, but you get more ways to filter.

Using Excel's AutoFilter

You can use the AutoFilter with a so-called "normal" list — that is, a list that you haven't subjected to the Data ⇨ List command. As the previous section mentions, when you choose Data ⇨ List, Excel automatically puts AutoFilter drop-down lists in the cells that contain the column labels.

To use AutoFilter, click somewhere in the list and choose Data ⇨ Filter ⇨ AutoFilter. The AutoFilter drop-down lists appear at the top of each column. When you click a drop-down list, you'll see a list box containing all the unique values in that column, plus a few special options (see Figure 6-8). In the figure, to focus in on just one sales rep, you would click the rep's name.

The sorting capability of the AutoFilter drop-down lists isn't as sophisticated as you get by choosing Data ⇨ Sort, but it's quick. You can sort by only one column at a time, whereas Data ⇨ Sort lets you sort by as many as three columns at once.

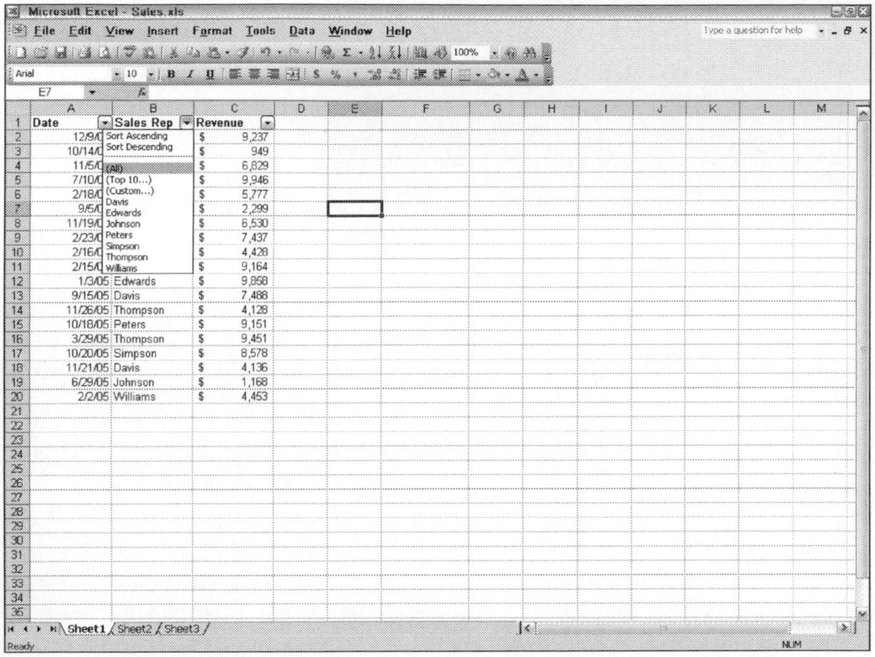

Figure 6-8: Notice that the list box offers you another way to sort your list — either ascending or descending.

If you've already used AutoFilter on your list and you want to see all the records again, select (All) in the list box. You can tell which drop-down lists are being used to filter your data, because the triangle on the drop-down list turns blue when it's in use.

If you're filtering on a numeric field, such as Revenues, you may want to focus on the largest or the smallest value. Select (Top 10 . . .) from the drop-down list. You'll get the Top 10 AutoFilter dialog box, as shown in Figure 6-9.

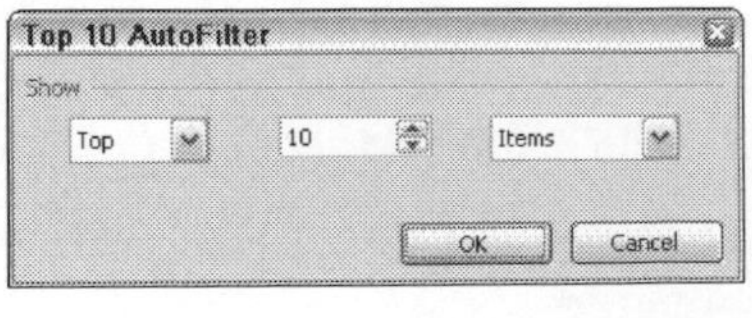

Figure 6-9: The Top 10 AutoFilter dialog box allows you to show either a number of items or a percent of items.

To use the Top 10 AutoFilter, follow these steps:

1. **In the leftmost drop-down list, select either Top (the largest values) or Bottom (the smallest values).**
2. **In the center drop-down list, select however many values you want to see.**
3. **In the rightmost drop-down list, select either Items or Percent.**

For example, in Figure 6-9, if you chose Top, 10, and Items, respectively, you'd see the largest ten Revenue values. If you chose Top, 20, and Percent, respectively, you'd see the top 20 percent of Revenue values.

Selecting (Custom . . .) from the drop-down list (refer to Figure 6-8) lets you select two filtering criteria from the column. In Figure 6-8, clicking the drop-down list at the top of the Sales Rep column and selecting (Custom . . .) displays the Custom AutoFilter dialog box shown in Figure 6-10.

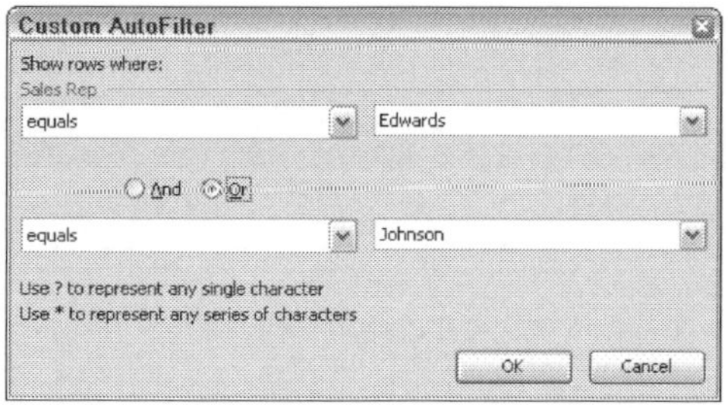

Figure 6-10: The Custom AutoFilter enables you to select two sales reps and filter out the others.

Using the Equals operator in both cases, clicking the Or button, and selecting Edwards and Johnson, you can focus in on their records only. (If you use And rather than Or, you see no records because no one in the list is named both Edwards *and* Johnson.) Other operators are available to you in the Custom AutoFilter dialog box, several of which make sense for use with numeric fields, such as Is Greater Than and Is Less Than.

Using the Advanced Filter

If you want to do a little more in the way of filtering a list, choose Data ➪ Filter ➪ Advanced Filter. The Advanced Filter dialog box, shown in Figure 6-11, appears.

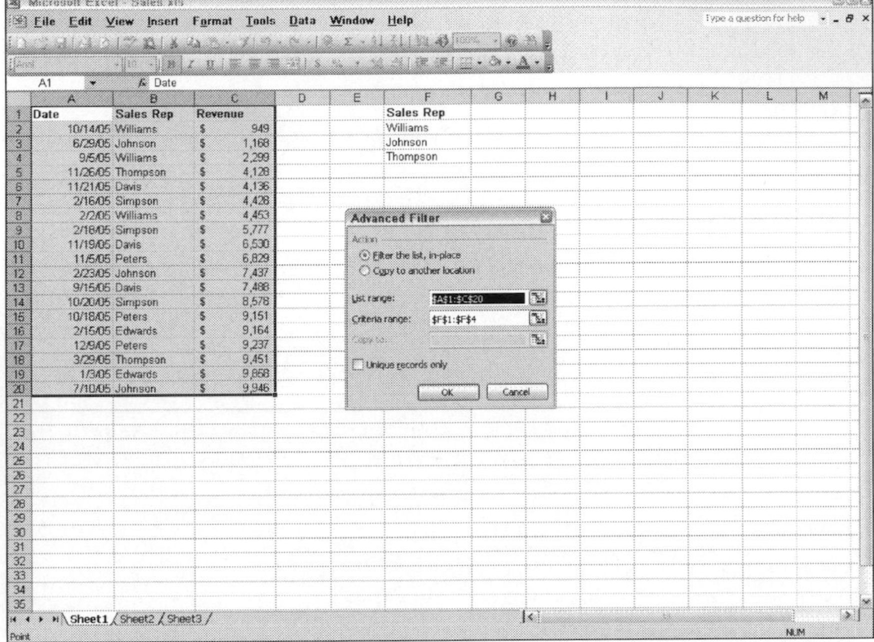

Figure 6-11: The Advanced Filter dialog box allows you to do a little more in the way of filtering.

The Advanced Filter dialog box allows you to filter for more than the two specific values that the AutoFilter offers you with the (Custom . . .) item. Suppose you wanted to see just the sales belonging to Williams, Johnson, and Thompson. You set up a criteria range in a different part of the worksheet — F1:F4 in Figure 6-11. Put the column label for the column you want to filter on in the first row of the criteria range, and underneath it put the values you want to display.

Then click one of the list's cells and choose Data ➪ Filter ➪ Advanced Filter. The Advanced Filter dialog box will automatically fill the List Range box with the address. Click in the Criteria Range box and drag through the cells where you put the criteria range. Click OK, and you'll see the records that meet your criteria.

To get all the records back, choose Data ➪ Filter ➪ Show All.

You can use more than one set of criteria. If in addition to the sales rep criteria you wanted to see only records since June 2005, you could enter **Date** in cell G1 and **>6/30/2005** in each cell in the range G2:G4. Adjust the criteria range address in the Advanced Filter dialog box to F1:G4, and click OK.

If you want to create a new list from the filtered data, select the Copy to Another Location radio button. The Copy To box becomes enabled, so you can click in it and then click in a worksheet cell where you want your new list to start.

Suppose you wanted a list of the sales reps' names, but you didn't want them repeated as they are in your original list. Follow these steps:

1. **Choose Data ⇨ Filter ⇨ Advanced Filter.**
2. **Click in the List Range box and — as the data is laid out in Figure 6-11 — drag through B1:B20 to capture the column label and the sales reps' names.**
3. **Choose to copy the filtered list to another location and indicate that location.**
4. **Select the Unique Records Only check box and click OK.**

   You now have a new list that contains the sales reps' names, one apiece.

Importing Data from a Database to an Excel List

If you're setting up a list so you can use it to help forecast sales, there's a good chance that the data is stored in your company's accounting system. Many companies use a database management system for accounting purposes and Excel for financial analysis. If you're in that situation, or a similar one, there's an easy way to get the data out of the database and into an Excel list. Take these steps:

1. **Choose Data ⇨ Import External Data ⇨ Import Data.**

   The Select Data Source dialog box, shown in Figure 6-12, appears.

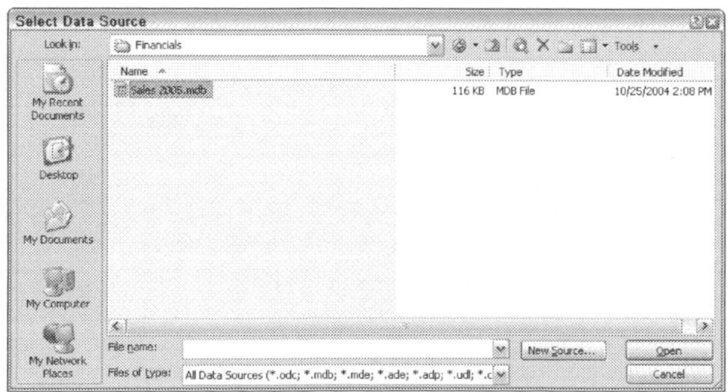

Figure 6-12: Use the Select Data Source dialog box to browse to the location where your database is stored.

2. **When you've located your data source, select it and click OK.**

   If more than one table is in the data source, you'll see the Select Table dialog box, shown in Figure 6-13.

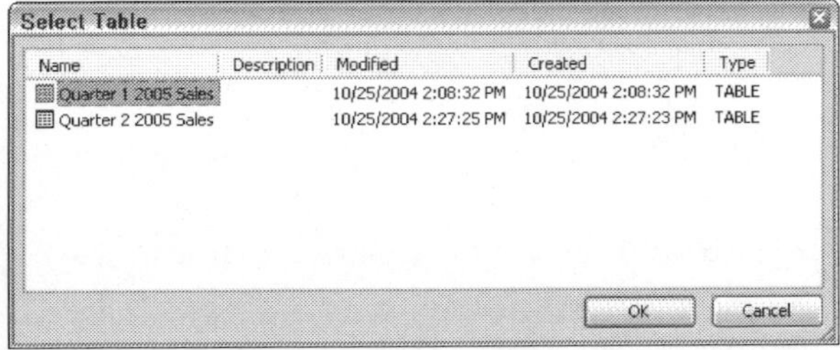

Figure 6-13: In the Select Table dialog box, pick the table (or query or view) that you want to import from.

3. **Select the table you want and click OK.**

   Any data that's in the table will be imported into a list, and the Import Data dialog box, shown in Figure 6-14, appears.

4. **Select where you want to put the data and click OK.**

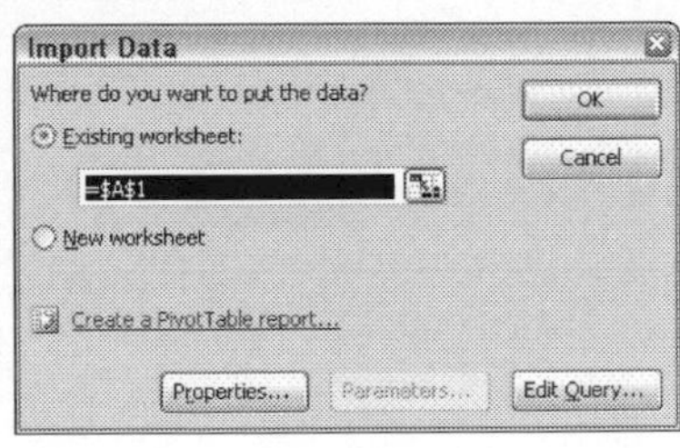

Figure 6-14: Use the Properties button to control various aspects of the list, which will occupy an *external data range.*

You could, of course, open the database directly, open the table, and do a copy and paste — and that probably seems easier. But the nice thing about doing it the longer way is that your list will save not only the data, but also information about the database's location. The next time you want to bring the data into your worksheet, just click a cell in that list, choose Data ➪ Refresh Data, and the most current information will flow from the database into the list.

Chapter 7

Working with Lists in Excel

In This Chapter

- Figuring out how to make charts from your lists
- Putting the Analysis ToolPak to work for you
- Sidestepping the Analysis ToolPak's pitfalls

In Chapter 6, I show you how to set up a list — what a list's structure is like, how to get Excel to help you manage it, and how to focus on specific items in the list. In other words, the dull routine of data management. Not fun, not always interesting, but necessary.

In this chapter, I get into more interesting things — certainly more colorful things. Excel's charts are great ways to visualize what's going on with the data in your list. They put you in a position to see patterns that are buried in the numbers. And you can use charts in some subtle ways to get more deeply into the business of sales forecasting.

I also show you how to use Excel's Analysis ToolPak, how it interacts with lists, and how it helps you build your forecasts (as well as some annoying traps to avoid).

Turning Lists into Charts

Excel has a laundry list of charts for you to choose from — click the Chart button or choose Insert ⇨ Chart to see your options. Looking at them, you may think that making the choice is just a matter of which type looks prettiest — and, truth to tell, the decision *is* partly a matter of what you like to look at. But you need to know about some issues beyond appearance, especially if you're going to use charts to help you forecast sales.

And using charts to help forecast sales is a good idea. In fact, if you and I were in the same room right now, I'd grab you by your shoulders, look you in the eye, and in an insistent tone of voice I'd say, "Using charts is a good idea."

Understanding chart types

Most Excel charts have at least two axes. The axes are represented by the chart's left, vertical border and its bottom, horizontal border. Figure 7-1 shows an example.

The chart in Figure 7-1 is a *Line chart.* Excel has names for the two different types of axes: the category axis and the value axis. In Figure 7-1, the horizontal axis with the months is called a *category axis,* and the vertical axis with the revenues is called a *value axis.*

The idea is that different *categories* (here, months) have different numeric *values* (here, revenues). You show the category values on one axis and the numeric values on the other axis.

But the categories aren't always shown on the horizontal border and the values aren't always shown on the vertical. For example, Figure 7-2 shows a *bar chart.* With a bar chart, the categories are on the vertical axis and the values are on the horizontal axis.

Each of the charts shown in Figure 7-1 and Figure 7-2 has one category axis (date) and one value axis (revenue). But another type of Excel chart has not just one but two value axes: the XY (Scatter) chart. The XY (Scatter) chart (see Figure 7-3) is an important type of chart because it helps you understand what's going on when you forecast by using regression.

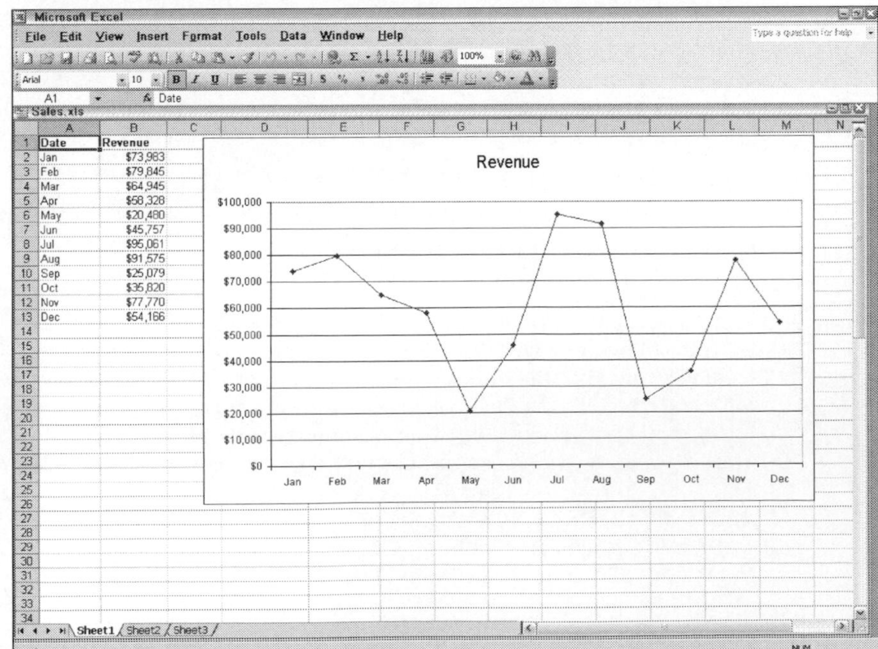

Figure 7-1: You can tell the amount of revenue for each month by checking the values on the two axes.

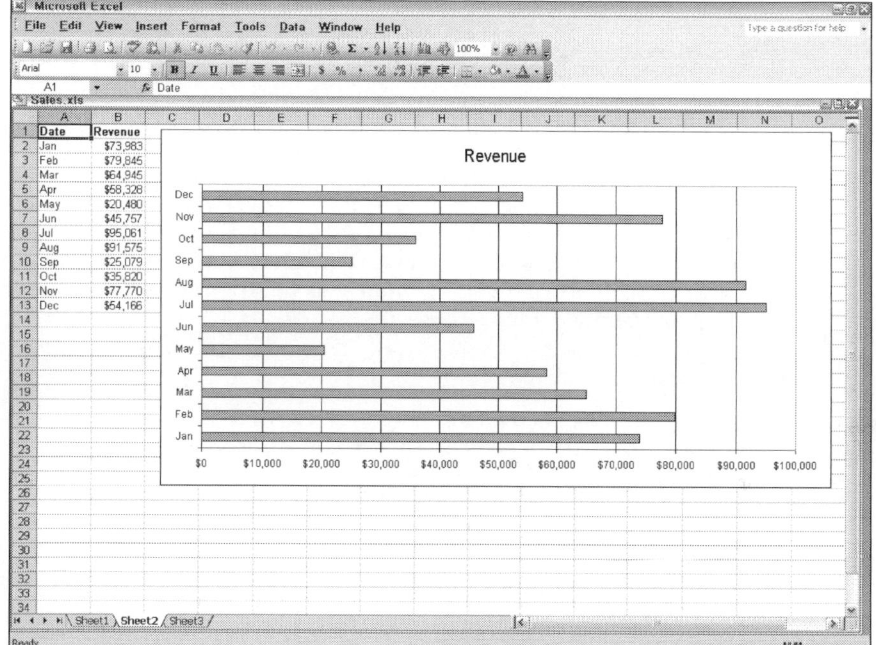

Figure 7-2: The categories show up on the vertical axis in a bar chart.

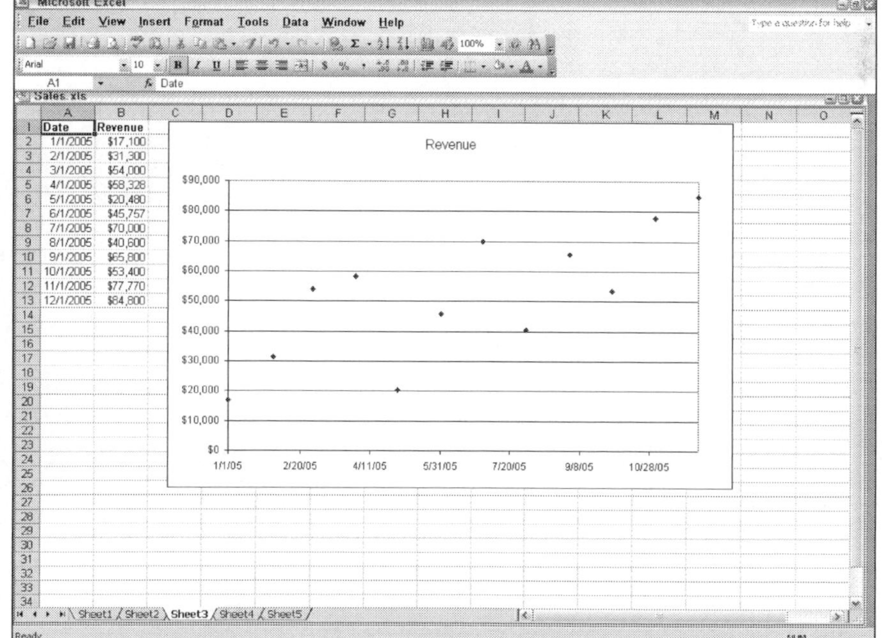

Figure 7-3: The XY (Scatter) chart resembles a Line chart, but both the horizontal and the vertical axes are value axes.

When you're forecasting sales, you often pair up dates — usually months or years — with a measure of sales revenue. Revenues are of course numbers, so they belong on a value axis. Dates are also numbers (Excel measures dates by counting the number of days since January 1, 1900). When both fields are numbers, putting them both on value axes is often correct — so, you end up with an XY (Scatter) chart.

Here's one reason that you often want to have two value axes on a chart: You can then use meaningful *trendlines*. A trendline shows the relationship between the two variables. In Figure 7-3, that would be the relationship between the date on the horizontal axis and the revenues on the vertical axis. To get a trendline, follow these steps:

1. **Select the chart.**

   If the chart is on its own sheet, select that sheet. If the chart is embedded in a worksheet, click on the embedded chart.

2. **Choose Chart ⇨ Add Trendline.**
3. **In this case, accept the default Linear trendline.**
4. **Select the Options tab, and fill at least two check boxes: Display Equation on Chart and Display R-Squared Value on Chart.**
5. **Click OK.**

Figure 7-4 shows the result, based on the original chart from Figure 7-3.

Three new sources of information in Figure 7-4 come from adding the trendline:

- **The R-squared value:** This tells you how closely the date is related to the revenues. The farther that the R-squared value is from zero, the stronger the relationship. Zero means no relationship — and you may want to try a forecast with one of the other approaches that this book discusses: moving averages or exponential smoothing. Plus 1.0 is a perfect relationship, and if you get it, you can name your own ticket. Sorry, but that's not going to happen.
- **The equation:** This tells you how to forecast the next revenue value. Plug the next date value into the equation in place of the equation's *x* value, and the result is your forecast. The better the R-squared value — the farther it is away from zero — the more confidence you can have in that forecast value.
- **The trendline itself:** It shows you what the equation forecasts in revenues for any given date value. And, of course, it shows you whether your revenues are increasing, decreasing, or flat over time. As the figure shows, I'm assuming your revenues are increasing. That trendline's heading up: You've got a good product, good sales reps, or a good ad firm.

The chart trendline is a handy way to find the relationship between sales and another variable such as date, as in Figure 7-4, or some other predictor such as advertising budget. But if you're going to use the equation to make a forecast, you should also use the LINEST function on the worksheet. That will give you the equation in worksheet cells, which makes it easier to create the forecast. Chapter 16 discusses LINEST and regression in more depth.

You can get a trendline on a chart that's not an XY (Scatter) chart, such as a Line chart. It might well look like the trendline on an XY (Scatter) chart. But if you look at the equation, it will probably be very different. The reason is that in a Line chart, Excel calculates the equation not by relating the revenues to the actual date values, but to the category number (1, 2, 3, and so on). That's why I recommend that you use an XY (Scatter) chart if you're going to use it to have a look at the trendline, equation, and R-squared to evaluate the relationship. Later, if you want to put the equation on the worksheet by using LINEST, it will match the one in your chart.

Creating the chart from your list

Excel makes it easy to create a chart from a list. Here's how you can create the chart in Figure 7-4 from the list in cells A1:B13:

1. **Click the Chart Wizard button on the Standard toolbar, or choose Insert ➪ Chart.**

   The Chart Wizard dialog box, shown in Figure 7-5, appears.

2. **In the Chart Type list box, click XY (Scatter) chart.**
3. **Accept the default subtype, which has no lines connecting the dots, and click Next.**
4. **In Step 2 of the Chart Wizard, make sure that the Data Range box is active, and drag through the range of worksheet cells that have your data.**

   In Figure 7-4, that's A1:B13.

5. **Click Finish.**

If you click Finish at this point, you can't set other chart options while you're using the Chart Wizard — options such as its location, whether the plot area has a pattern, whether it has a legend, and so on. Instead, click Next to set those options now. I just want you to know how fast you can create a chart. Going through four steps doesn't take too long. You can set the other options after creating the chart by first selecting the chart, and then choosing Chart ➪ Chart Options.

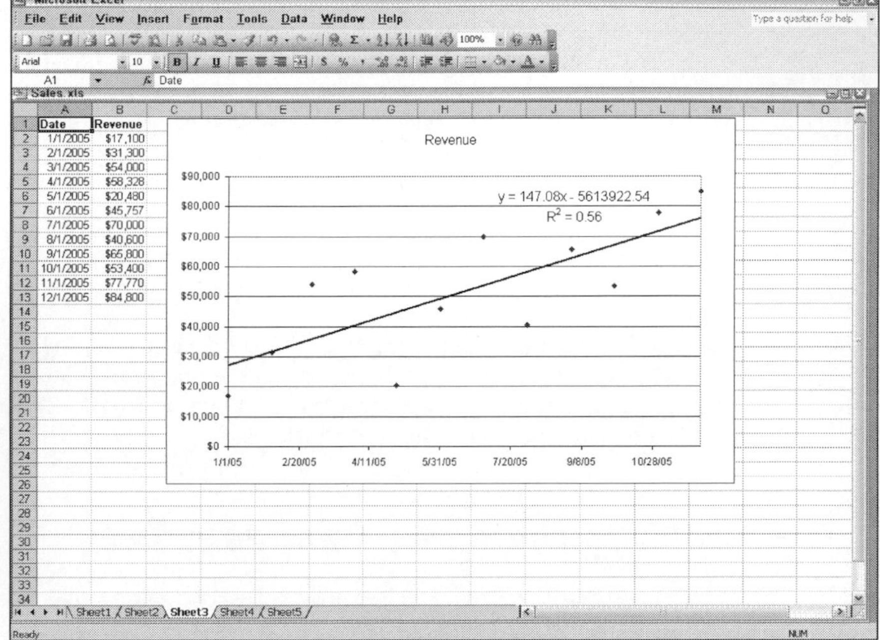

Figure 7-4: By showing the equation on the chart you can preview what the LINEST function would show on the worksheet.

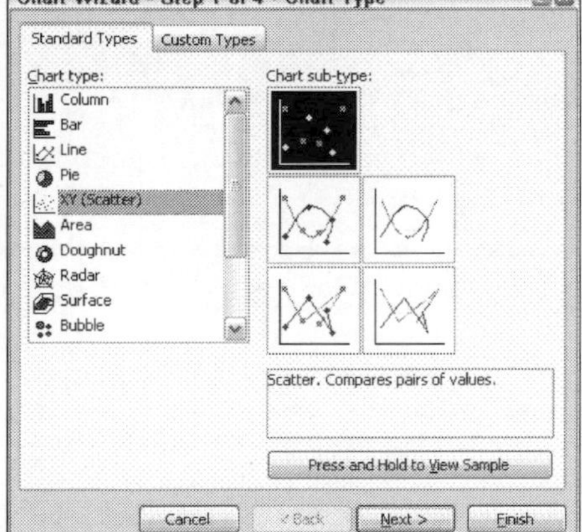

Figure 7-5: Select the type of chart you want in Step 1 of the Chart Wizard.

No matter what type of chart — Line, XY (Scatter), Column, or something else — you select, if one of your list's fields is a date field, you'll get each individual date from that list on the chart. In Figures 7-1 through 7-5, I've been careful to show each date as a separate month. If your data source provides sales dates on a daily basis, charting that list will drive you nuts. You'll be looking at a chart that shows daily sales, and those records are so full of noise that they're almost impossible to interpret. Chapter 8 shows you how to group your records to get summaries by week, month, quarter, or year. After they're grouped, you'll be able to create a chart that's easier to interpret.

Refining charts

I go on and on about charts here, and I write even more in other chapters in this book, because I've always found representing my baseline data visually very important. Looking at how the baseline falls out over time is important to how you analyze it. The chart may very well convince you to use a completely different approach to creating your forecast — such as smoothing or moving averages rather than regression.

After you've created a chart, you can revise it in different ways to make it more informative. Here are some of them.

Using the Chart menu

Start off in one of two ways. If you left the chart embedded in a worksheet, as shown in Figure 7-4, click on the chart to activate it. If you put the chart in its own sheet, all by itself, select that sheet. You'll get a new menu, named Chart. Click that menu and you'll see the following menu items:

- **Chart Type:** Choosing this menu item brings up the first step of the Chart Wizard, as shown in Figure 7-5. Use this to change from, for example, a Line chart to an XY (Scatter) chart, or to change a chart's subtype.
- **Source Data:** This menu item enables you to change the location of the data that feeds the chart. If more data becomes available, you can use this to expand the data range that the chart uses. You can also use the Series tab to rename the data series on the chart, and to fine-tune the locations of the categories and the values that go into the chart.
- **Chart Options:** When you choose Chart Options, you get the Chart Options dialog box, as shown in Figure 7-6.

  Use Chart Options to:

  - Add or change the titles for the chart and for the axes.
  - Change how the axes are based.
  - Control whether the axes have gridlines.
  - Control whether there's a legend with the data series names and, if so, where to put it.
  - Control whether and how to label individual data points.
  - Control whether to show the data that underlies the chart in a table *on* the chart. (If the chart is embedded in the worksheet that contains the data, you probably don't want to use a data table in the chart. The data's already visible on the worksheet itself.)

- **Location:** This menu item lets you switch back and forth between putting the chart in its own sheet, all by itself, or embedding it in a worksheet along with other things that you may want to see at the same time.
- **Add Data:** Use this as a quick alternative to the Source Data menu item if you want to add more information to the chart.
- **Add Trendline:** This menu item is how you start to add a trendline, an equation, and an R-squared value to your chart.
- **3D-View:** You're unlikely to find use for this option in a forecasting context.

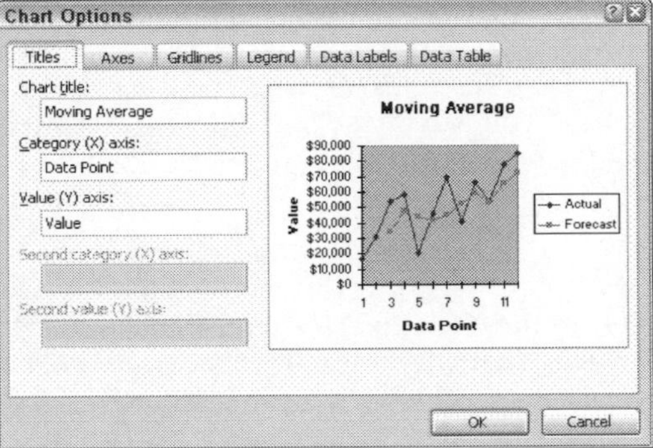

Figure 7-6: The Chart Options dialog box puts you in a position to change much of the way your chart appears.

Formatting the axes

You can control more about your chart's appearance if you click one of the axes — you'll know you've seized the axis if you see square blocks, called *selection handles,* at each end of the axis. Then choose Format⇨Selected Axis. You can change these aspects of the axis by selecting any of five tabs:

- **Patterns:** Whether the axis has tick marks and, if so, how many, as well as the style, color, and weight of any lines
- **Scale:** For example, the minimum and maximum values to show for a value axis
- **Font:** Whether to use Times New Roman or Bauhaus 93 (or some other font)
- **Number:** Stuff like whether to show the axis labels as Currency, Date, Percentage, whatever
- **Alignment:** Whether the axis labels should be horizontal, vertical, or on an angle

Using the Analysis ToolPak with Lists

The Analysis ToolPak (ATP) helps you do statistical analyses of all sorts — and sales forecasting is definitely one sort of statistical analysis.

The ATP is an add-in. An add-in is a hidden workbook containing Visual Basic code: a program written in a version of BASIC that Excel can run. It's password protected, locked up so that you don't get to look at the code itself. That's okay — you probably wouldn't want to see it any more than you'd want to look at legislation or sausage making.

You need to install the ATP on your computer from your Office installation CD. You'll find it among the Add-Ins under Excel if you do a custom installation, or it will be installed automatically if you do a complete installation.

But installing the ATP on your computer doesn't mean it's installed in Excel; so far you've just installed it on your hard drive. As with all add-ins, you need to bring it to Excel's attention. To do so, follow these steps:

1. **In Excel, choose Tools ➪ Add-Ins.**
2. **Select the check box for Analysis ToolPak.**

   If you don't see that check box, you'll have to rerun the Excel installation routine from the CD and make sure you install the ATP.
3. **Click OK.**

   Now you'll find a new menu item, Data Analysis, in Excel's Tools menu. Click that item to get at the ATP's tools.

With the ATP installed both on your computer and in Excel, you'll find 19 analysis tools. Suppose you want to wield the Moving Average tool on your list. Do this:

1. **Choose Tools ➪ Data Analysis.**

   The Data Analysis dialog box, shown in Figure 7-7, appears.
2. **Scroll down the Analysis Tools list box and click Moving Average, and then click OK.**

   The Moving Average dialog box, shown in Figure 7-8, appears.
3. **Click in the Input Range field and, using your mouse pointer, drag through the Revenues part of your list.**
4. **If you include the column label in the Input Range, select the Labels in First Row check box.**
5. **Click in the Interval field and enter the number of months you want to base your moving average on.**

   For example, to base your moving average on a three-month interval, enter 3. If you want to base it on a two-month interval, enter 2.

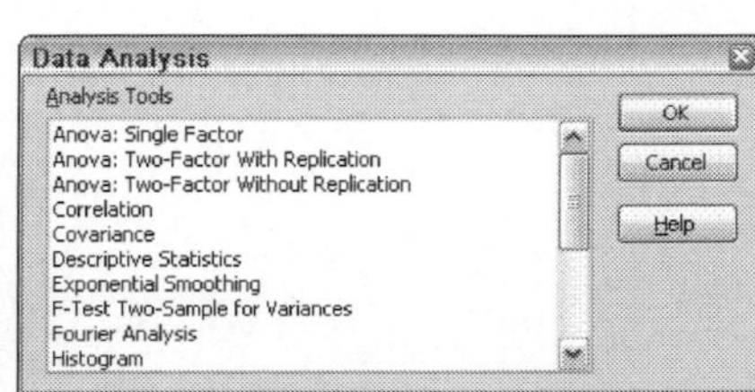

Figure 7-7: Not all the analysis tools are useful for doing forecasting. The three best are Exponential Smoothing, Moving Average, and Regression, but you'll want to use others for other purposes.

6. **Click in the Output Range field, and then click the worksheet cell where you want the results to start showing up.**

7. **If you want to see a chart of the moving average (and I'm grabbing your shoulders and telling you that you do), select the Chart Output check box.**

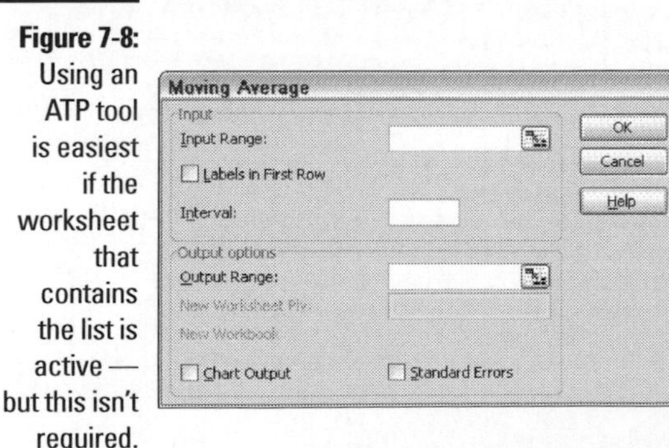

Figure 7-8: Using an ATP tool is easiest if the worksheet that contains the list is active — but this isn't required.

8. **Click OK.**

   You'll see the results shown in Figure 7-9.

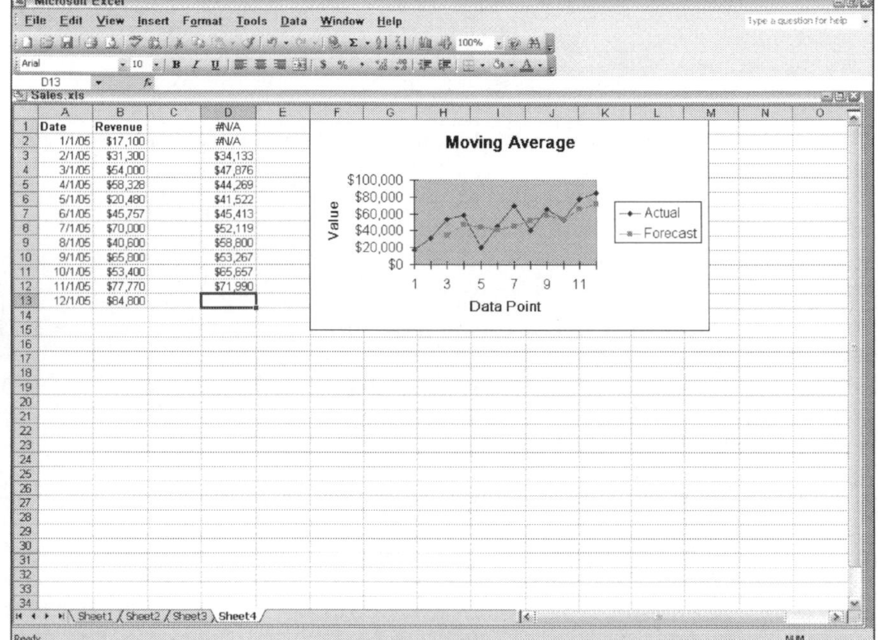

Figure 7-9: This moving average is based on three intervals — that is, each average consists of three months.

You get #N/A values at the start of a moving average forecast because at the start of the sequence there are never enough values to complete the average.

Notice how the moving average smoothes out the individual observations. This tends to suppress the *noise* (the random variation in each of your list's records) and to emphasize the *sound* (the main direction of the baseline).

Also notice how much easier it is to see what's going on when you look at the chart than when you just look at the list. The lesson: Chart your baselines.

There's more, much more, to moving averages, and you can find it in Chapters 13 and 14. But now you know the basics of getting and charting a moving average from a list.

Avoiding the Analysis ToolPak's Traps

For years, some of the ATP's tools (for example, the Regression tool) have confused the input range with the output range. As you find in Chapter 16, if you're going to forecast by means of regression you need at least two variables: a predictor variable (such as date or advertising dollars) and a predicted variable (in this context, something such as sales revenues or unit sales).

The ATP's Regression tool refers to the predictor variable's values as the Input X Range, and the predicted variable's values as the Input Y Range.

Now, suppose you do this:

1. **Choose Tools ➪ Data Analysis, click on Regression and then click OK.**
2. **Click in the Input Y Range field, and then drag through something such as your sales revenues values on the worksheet.**
3. **Click in the Input X Range box, and then drag through something such as the date values on the worksheet.**

   Notice that the default option for the Output Range is New Worksheet Ply.

If you now override the default option and click the Output Range option button (which lets you put the Regression output on the same sheet with your list), the focus snaps back to Input Y Range. If you then click in some worksheet cell, that cell becomes the Input Y Range. Because you normally want to use an empty range for the output, you certainly won't select a cell with input values in it. So you choose an empty cell, and because of the change in focus, that cell becomes the Input Y Range.

In other words, the ATP is trying to get you to choose a range, or cell, without any data in it to supply your Input Y Range — that is, the predicted values.

If you're not aware of what's going on, this can cost you time and unnecessary skull sweat. Unfortunately, there's no good solution — remember, you can't open the code that drives the ATP — other than to be aware that it happens, and to know you have to click the Output Range option button and then its associated field again to reset the focus.

Several tools in the ATP have this problem. Take care when you're identifying an output range for an ATP tool.

The other main problem with the ATP is that its output is often static. The Regression tool, for example, puts calculated values in cells rather than formulas that can recalculate when the inputs change. If you get new or changed input values, you'll have to rerun the tool to get the revised results.

Other tools, such as Moving Average and Exponential Smoothing, report their results as formulas, so they'll recalculate if you change the inputs. If you have new values for these tools to use (for example, your input range changes from A1:A20 to A1:A25), you'll need to reset the input range address; but if you're just revising an earlier value, the formulas will recalculate and the charts will redraw without any extra effort on your part.

Part III
Making a Basic Forecast

"The top line represents our revenue, the middle line is our inventory, and the bottom line shows the rate of my hair loss over the same period."

In this part . . .

Excel has some powerful tools to help you make your forecasts. One of them is the PivotTable, which organizes your sales history for you and makes creating your baseline a snap. Another is the PivotChart — it's hard to overemphasize how important a chart is to understand what's going on with your sales. If you can visualize it, you're a lot closer to understanding it. Part III also introduces you to the Analysis ToolPak (which has tools that help you make basic forecasts from one variable) and to regression analysis (a way to forecast sales using some other variable).

Chapter 8

Summarizing Sales Data with Pivot Tables

In This Chapter

- Getting used to the idea of pivot tables
- Putting a pivot table on your worksheet
- Grouping similar records together
- Keeping a pivot table from biting you

If you're going to create good forecasts, you frequently need to match up some amount of revenue with the period that the revenue came in. Or, if you need to deal with the number of units sold rather than revenue, you need to pair a count of units with the period they were sold. Excel's pivot tables give you an excellent method of doing that, if you set your data up right.

When you have your pivot table, it often makes sense to look at your revenues from different viewpoints — usually, in terms of months or quarters or years. Pivot tables refer to this as *grouping.* In this chapter, I cover building pivot tables and grouping dates.

Understanding Pivot Tables

A pivot table summarizes one variable — typically, one that can be counted or summed — in terms of another variable, typically one that comes in categories. Pivot tables in Excel are the most powerful way of summarizing any kind of data, including sales information. That makes pivot tables a useful way to prepare a baseline for your forecast.

A pivot table is often based on an Excel list. (If you're not yet a list maven, check out Chapter 6.) Excel lists put different variables, or *fields,* in different columns and different records in different rows. So if you have daily sales revenues in an Excel list, one column would have the date field (like March 10, 2002) and another column, probably an adjacent one, would have the revenue field (like $5,841). One row would show the revenue for March 10, another would show the revenue for April 4, and so on. Different fields are in different columns, and different records are in different rows.

With a list setup, you can create a pivot table that helps you summarize the information in the list. Pivot tables always have a *data* field. If you have a list giving revenues by month, you would treat the list's revenue field as the pivot table's data field. With revenue in the data field, you've prepared to total up (or summarize) revenue by date.

Also, pivot tables usually have *row* fields. In this same situation, you'd probably decide to use the list's date field as the pivot table's row field. That means that different dates (in this case, different months) show up in different rows of the pivot table, right next to the revenue for each different date.

With that setup, you can *group* the date field so that each row in the pivot table has a broader span than just one day — say, a month, a quarter, or a year. Figure 8-1 gives an example of totaling revenue by month.

	A	B	C	D	E
1	Sales Date	Sales Revenue			
2	1/1/2005	$ 9,484.09			
3	1/2/2005	$ 6,304.72		Sum of Sales Revenue	
4	1/3/2005	$ 9,788.24		Sales Date	Total
5	1/4/2005	$ 2,144.47		Jan	$178,350.33
6	1/5/2005	$ 9,613.29		Feb	$111,079.27
7	1/6/2005	$ 2,480.10		Mar	$149,502.56
8	1/7/2005	$ 2,894.44		Apr	$165,789.70
9	1/8/2005	$ 4,439.56		May	$193,146.34
10	1/9/2005	$ 9,582.37		Jun	$159,608.43
11	1/10/2005	$ 6,477.79		Jul	$145,924.86
12	1/11/2005	$ 5,235.91		Aug	$164,267.67
13	1/12/2005	$ 9,724.71		Sep	$154,837.45
14	1/13/2005	$ 3,387.69		Oct	$157,552.37
15	1/14/2005	$ 9,761.08		Nov	$136,564.52
16	1/15/2005	$ 5,307.74		Dec	$181,530.71
17	1/16/2005	$ 4,900.91		Grand Total	$1,898,154.41
18	1/17/2005	$ 9,951.41			
19	1/18/2005	$ 1,840.75			
20	1/19/2005	$ 8,805.36			
21	1/20/2005	$ 3,504.63			
22	1/21/2005	$ 4,960.41			
23	1/22/2005	$ 8,281.00			
24	1/23/2005	$ 3,701.29			
25	1/24/2005	$ 1,520.66			
26	1/25/2005	$ 1,296.07			
27	1/26/2005	$ 6,912.01			
28	1/27/2005	$ 6,846.61			
29	1/28/2005	$ 2,583.82			
30	1/29/2005	$ 3,960.57			
31	1/30/2005	$ 7,410.90			
32	1/31/2005	$ 5,247.73			
33	2/1/2005	$ 3,265.14			
34	2/2/2005	$ 4,493.51			

Figure 8-1: The list in columns A and B gives daily sales revenues. The pivot table starting in column D summarizes the revenues by month.

Pivot tables are handy in various ways. If you want to chart your sales by week, month, quarter, or year, you can start by using a pivot table to summarize them. If you just want a tabulation, the pivot table gives it to you. And if you want to use Excel's Analysis ToolPak to create a forecast, the pivot table can give you just the layout you'll need.

In the following sections you see how to use pivot tables to support your forecasts, by turning basic sales data into a baseline for your forecast, and getting summaries of revenue data and counts of units sold.

Making baselines out of sales data

Most companies that are in the business of selling products and services record their sales on a daily basis, whether they're recording revenues or the number of units that were sold. You can usually tell from their corporate accounting system how many dollars they brought in on May 4 and on October 12, or how many widgets they sold on February 8 and on August 25.

The accounting system usually breaks out individual sales. So, if the company made ten sales on June 3, you're going to see a different record for all ten of those sales. Seeing those sales one by one is great if you're an accountant, or if you have some other reason to need information about individual sales, or if you're having trouble sleeping. But if you're forecasting, individual records are a nuisance.

You need a way of summarizing all those individual records into a baseline for forecasting. Consider the following ideas while deciding the best way to summarize your sales data:

- **You don't need individual sales records.** If your company made three sales on January 5 — one for $2,500, another for $8,650 and another for $4,765 — an important fact you want to know is that, on January 5, you brought in $15,915.
- **You don't forecast sales on a daily basis.** If your company is like most, you need a bigger picture. To plan your inventory levels, decide how many salespeople your company needs, and figure out what you can expect in revenue and what your company's tax liability will be — you need a longer time period for your forecast.
- **You do need to match the length of your time period with your reasons for forecasting.** Typical time periods are a month, a quarter, or a year, depending on why you're forecasting. For purchasing materials, you may want to forecast your sales for next month. For estimating earnings, you may want to forecast your sales for the next quarter. For hiring decisions, you may want to forecast your sales for the next year.

The point — and, along with Ellen DeGeneres, I do have one — is that if you're going to forecast sales for next month you need to organize your baseline in months: how much you sold in January, in February, in March, and so on. If you're going to forecast sales for next quarter, then that's how you need to organize your baseline: how much you sold in Q1, in Q2, in Q3, and so on.

You need a much longer baseline than just three periods to make a forecast that won't embarrass you.

Excel's pivot tables are ideal for helping you total up your sales data to establish a baseline for forecasting. You feed your raw sales data into Excel, where you can build pivot tables in two primary ways:

- **From an Excel list:** Suppose your Accounting or IT department can send you sales data in a soft copy format, like a `.csv` (comma-separated values) file. You can paste that data into an Excel workbook as a list, and base a pivot table on it.
- **From (what Excel calls) *external data*:** In other words, the underlying data, the individual sales figures, aren't stored in an Excel worksheet. They're kept in a separate database or a text file or even another Excel workbook.

  Building your pivot tables on external data can be handy because the sales data are usually updated routinely in the external data source (in practice, this is often a database). Then when you want to update your forecast, you don't have to get and paste new data into your workbook. The pivot table can update itself automatically from the external data source.

In the following sections, I show you some of the uses for row fields, column fields, and page fields in pivot tables.

Using row fields

Row fields are important in pivot tables, because you can use them to organize your data as a summarized list. In forecasting situations, this means that you have a different record for each row in the pivot table, and that record represents each time period in your baseline.

For example, suppose you want to forecast sales for the next quarter. You set up your pivot table so that each of the quarterly sales totals for the previous, say, ten years shows up in a different row.

To total according to quarters, months, or some other time span, you need to *group* the date field. Turn to the "Grouping Records" section, later in this chapter, for more information.

With your pivot table set up that way, getting the Analysis ToolPak, or the Chart Wizard, to create a forecast is easy. And the time period will be right. Summed up into quarterly totals, you can get the next quarter's estimate. Summed up into monthly totals, you can get the best estimate for the next month. You can't do that if the data is still organized by individual sale, or by specific day.

The way to start is to put the dates that the sales were made into a pivot table's row field. If the company's accounting system, or sales database, already summarizes sales into the time period you want to use, so much the better. Then you don't need to do any grouping of individual dates into months, quarters, or years. If the company's accounting system, or sales database, doesn't already summarize sales into the time period you want to use, you can do that in a snap (see "Grouping Records," later in this chapter).

Using column fields

In setting up your sales data to do forecasting, you're going to have a lot more use for row fields than for column fields, because Excel handles lists so well.

A column field puts different records into different columns — but an Excel list asks you to put different records into different rows. Suppose you have a list that shows date and revenue for each date. You want your pivot table to summarize your sales data by month. If you put the date field into the Column area, you'll wind up with a different month in each column.

That's inconvenient, especially if you want to use the Analysis ToolPak to create a forecast. (It can also be mildly inconvenient if you want to chart your revenues over time.)

In sales forecasting, column fields really come into their own when you have several product lines that you want to analyze. Pivot tables can have row fields *and* column fields (and, by the way, page fields). The combination of a row field with a column field is ideal for forecasting sales of different product lines.

Your list could have three fields: date of sale, product line, and sales revenue. Then your pivot table could use the fields like this (see Figure 8-2):

- **Date of sale as a row field:** Each row in the pivot table corresponds to a different total of sales on a particular date.
- **Product line as a column field:** Each column in the pivot table corresponds to a different product line.
- **Revenue as a data field:** Each cell in the pivot table sums the revenue for a particular product line on a particular date.

Now the pivot table takes on a true list structure. This makes it easy to get a forecast for each product line, whether you're using the Analysis ToolPak to get the forecast or using a trendline in a chart.

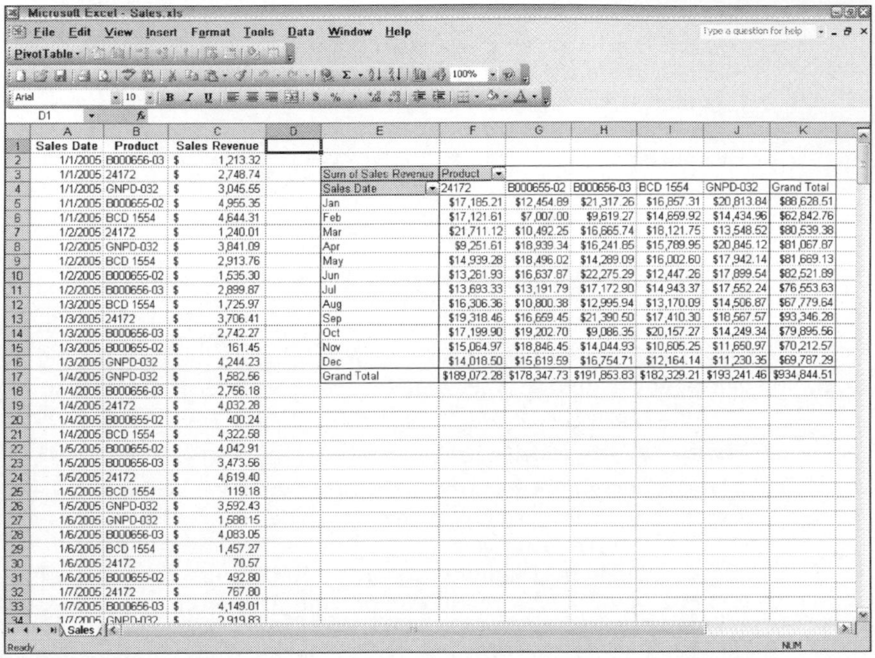
Microsoft Excel - Sales.xls
File Edit View Insert Format Tools Data Window Help
Type a question for help
PivotTable
100%
Arial
10
D1
Sales Date Product Sales Revenue
1/1/2005 B000656-03 $ 1,213.32
1/1/2005 24172 $ 2,748.74
1/1/2005 GNPD-032 $ 3,045.55
1/1/2005 B000655-02 $ 4,955.35
1/1/2005 BCD 1554 $ 4,644.31
1/2/2005 24172 $ 1,240.01
1/2/2005 GNPD-032 $ 3,841.09
1/2/2005 BCD 1554 $ 2,913.76
1/2/2005 B000655-02 $ 1,535.30
1/2/2005 B000656-03 $ 2,899.87
1/3/2005 BCD 1554 $ 1,725.97
1/3/2005 24172 $ 3,706.41
1/3/2005 B000656-03 $ 2,742.27
1/3/2005 B000655-02 $ 161.45
1/3/2005 GNPD-032 $ 4,244.23
1/4/2005 GNPD-032 $ 1,582.56
1/4/2005 B000656-03 $ 2,756.18
1/4/2005 24172 $ 4,032.28
1/4/2005 B000655-02 $ 400.24
1/4/2005 BCD 1554 $ 4,322.58
1/5/2005 B000655-02 $ 4,042.91
1/5/2005 B000656-03 $ 3,473.56
1/5/2005 24172 $ 4,619.40
1/5/2005 BCD 1554 $ 119.18
1/5/2005 GNPD-032 $ 3,592.43
1/6/2005 GNPD-032 $ 1,588.15
1/6/2005 B000656-03 $ 4,083.05
1/6/2005 BCD 1554 $ 1,457.27
1/6/2005 24172 $ 70.57
1/6/2005 B000655-02 $ 492.80
1/7/2005 24172 $ 767.80
1/7/2005 B000656-03 $ 4,149.01
1/7/2005 GNPD-032 $ 2,919.83
Sum of Sales Revenue Product
Sales Date 24172 B000655-02 B000656-03 BCD 1554 GNPD-032 Grand Total
Jan $17,185.21 $12,454.89 $21,317.26 $16,857.31 $20,813.84 $88,628.51
Feb $17,121.61 $7,007.00 $9,619.27 $14,659.92 $14,434.96 $62,842.76
Mar $21,711.12 $10,492.25 $16,665.74 $18,121.75 $13,548.52 $80,539.38
Apr $9,251.61 $18,939.34 $16,241.85 $15,789.95 $20,845.12 $81,067.87
May $14,939.28 $18,496.02 $14,289.09 $16,002.60 $17,942.14 $81,669.13
Jun $13,261.93 $16,637.87 $22,275.29 $12,447.26 $17,899.54 $82,521.89
Jul $13,693.33 $13,191.79 $17,172.90 $14,943.37 $17,552.24 $76,553.63
Aug $16,306.36 $10,800.38 $12,995.94 $13,170.09 $14,506.87 $67,779.64
Sep $19,318.46 $16,659.45 $21,390.50 $17,410.30 $18,567.57 $93,346.28
Oct $17,199.90 $19,202.70 $9,086.35 $20,157.27 $14,249.34 $79,895.56
Nov $15,064.97 $18,846.45 $14,044.93 $10,605.25 $11,650.97 $70,212.57
Dec $14,018.50 $15,619.59 $16,754.71 $12,164.14 $11,230.35 $69,787.29
Grand Total $189,072.28 $178,347.73 $191,853.83 $182,329.21 $193,241.46 $934,844.51
Sales
Ready
NUM

Figure 8-2: This pivot table resembles a true list, and you can use the Analysis ToolPak to create forecasts from it.

Getting subsets with page fields

A page field is fundamentally different from a column, row, or data field. A data field, as I mention in "Understanding Pivot Tables," is the field that you're summing, or averaging, or getting mins and maxs from. Column and row fields give you a way to see something such as the total revenues for Fords versus Chevys, or the units sold for Mixmasters versus Toastmasters.

You use a page field, instead, to get a subset of data. Suppose your sales data looks like that in Figure 8-3.

Click the drop-down list in the page field. In Figure 8-3, that's the one that's labeled Make. You now can choose Ford to see the monthly sales revenue for Fords, or Chevy to see the monthly sales revenue for Chevy, or — and I'm not sure why you'd want to do this, but you could — Yugo to see the monthly sales revenue for Yugo.

The page field is much like an AutoFilter. Use it when you want to zoom in on just one value — Ford, Chevy, whatever — in a field from the pivot table's underlying data source. When you want to combine all the values in the page field, just choose All.

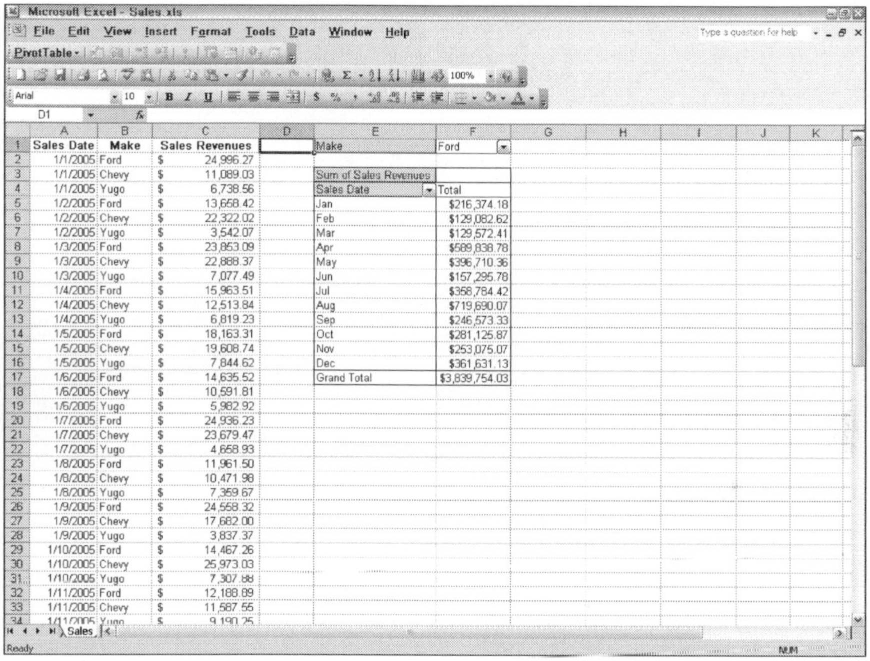

Figure 8-3: The row field breaks revenues down by month. You can use the page field to focus on sales of Fords.

Totaling up the data

In a pivot table, you always have to have a data field. You can manage with no row field or column field or page field — it doesn't make a lot of sense to do so, but technically you can. What you can't do without is a data field. You always have to have a data field that the pivot table can sum, count, or summarize in some other way.

Summing revenues

In sales forecasting, you're in the business of summing revenues and counting units sold. So generally you're going to want to have your data field sum up revenues if it's bucks, or count units if it's the number of items you've sold.

Figure 8-4 shows what your worksheet looks like when you're ready to put a field into the Data area.

Excel stalks you. It's always watching what you're doing. Suppose your data field is revenues. That's a *numeric* field: It's numbers. When you put a numeric field into the Data area, Excel notices that and it automatically gives you a sum. For each value of the row or column field, you'll get a sum of, for example, your sales revenues.

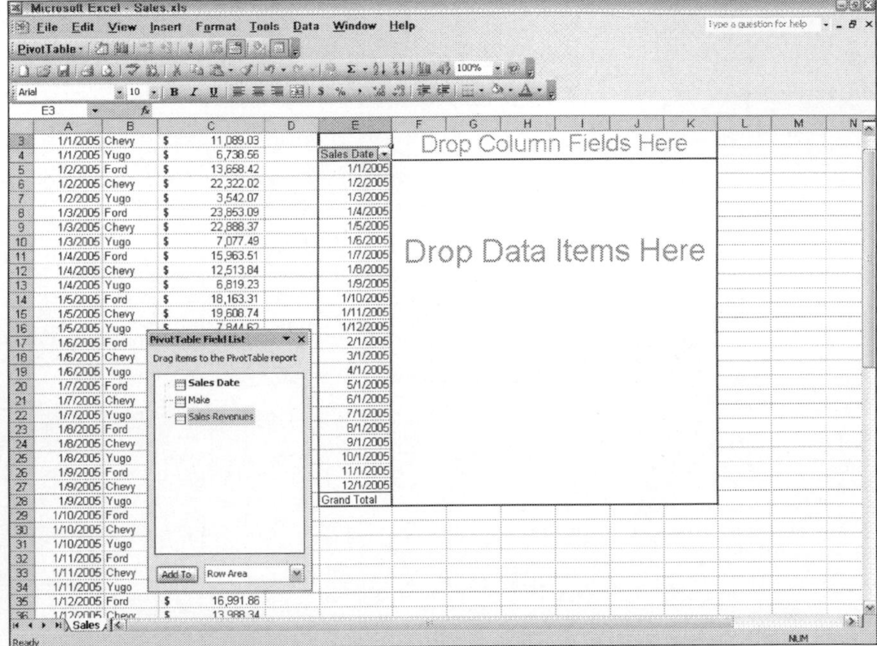

Figure 8-4: You've completed the pivot table as soon as you put a field in the Data area.

You'll almost always have a row, column, or page field in your pivot table. In sales forecasting, you'll usually find yourself using dates as a row field, so January might be in one row, February in the next, and so on.

For each item in the row field, the pivot table's data field will give you the total of all the revenue that goes with that item. Maybe your list shows 50 sales records for February. The pivot table can total the revenue for those 50 records and show the sum of that revenue in one row — which is labeled "February."

Counting units

But what if you want to summarize units sold rather than revenues? Say you sell cars. Then your list might have a field named Make. You'd put that field into the Row area and into the Data area. Because Make is a text field — with values like Ford, Chevy, and Yugo — the pivot table's Data area defaults not to a sum but to a count. After all, it can't add a Ford to a Chevy. But it can count the number of Fords, Chevys, and Yugos that you've sold.

Putting the same field into both the Row area and the Data area may seem a little strange, but that's how it's done. You'll get a different row for each distinct value. And — if you're smart and make sure it's a text field — you'll get a count of records for each row. Figure 8-5 shows an example.

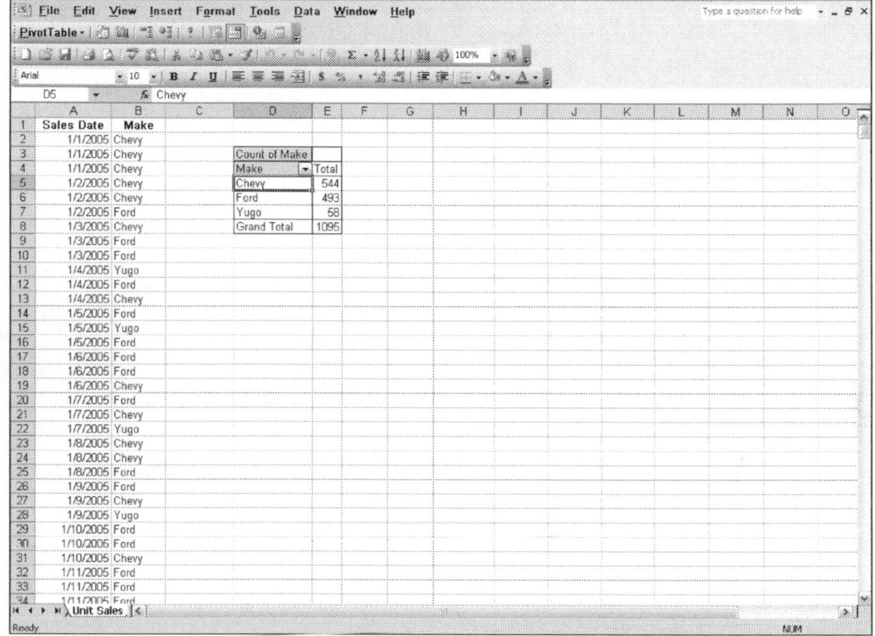

Figure 8-5: Pivot tables use Count as the default when the data field has text values.

Sometimes Excel defaults to the wrong summary. This can happen, for example, when you accidentally wind up with a text value in what you expected to be an entirely numeric field. If Excel finds even one text value in the pivot table's data field, it will default to Count as the summary.

If this happens, you need to do two things:

- Find the text value in the data source and either change it to a number, or delete it.
- Right-click the data field and choose Field Settings from the shortcut menu. Then click on Sum in the Summarize By list box.

Other summaries

When you're forecasting sales, you're generally most interested in total revenues and counts of units sold. But sometimes you want other information, such as the largest single sale made each month, or the smallest number of units sold each quarter.

The pivot table's data field offers you several summaries besides Sum and Count. You can look at a Maximum, a Minimum, and an Average. (There are several other summaries that you're unlikely to have use for in sales forecasting. They have to do mostly with how the individual records in the underlying data set vary around their average value.)

Building the Pivot Table

Okay, it's time to actually create a pivot table and group the date field. You've got your baseline of data, laid out as a list. What now?

Suppose your list looks like Figure 8-6.

The problem is that you don't need to forecast sales by salesperson. And you don't need to forecast sales by day. In this case, the whole idea is to forecast sales by month. Corporate couldn't care less who made the sale, or on which day. They don't want to know how much George Bergstrom sold on February 24. They want you to tell them how much your sales team will sell in January 2006. For that, you don't need daily sales data and you don't need salesperson data.

You do need to know monthly totals. With that information, you can generate a forecast that's rational and credible. You'll get the monthly totals, but first you need to build the pivot table.

1. **Click in a worksheet cell below or to the right of your list.**

   TIP

   When Excel creates the pivot table, it builds it to the right and down from the cell you select. If you start the pivot table to the left of or above your list, Excel will ask you if you really want to overwrite those cells.

Microsoft Excel - Sales.xls

	A	B	C
1	Date	Salesperson	Revenue
2	1/1/2005	Jones	$ 341.55
3	1/1/2005	Smith	$ 109.82
4	1/1/2005	Williams	$ 85.36
5	1/2/2005	Jones	$ 16.11
6	1/2/2005	Smith	$ 58.67
7	1/2/2005	Williams	$ 395.03
8	1/3/2005	Jones	$ 276.51
9	1/3/2005	Smith	$ 214.35
10	1/3/2005	Williams	$ 13.80
11	1/4/2005	Jones	$ 288.78
12	1/4/2005	Smith	$ 157.71
13	1/4/2005	Williams	$ 325.70
14	1/5/2005	Jones	$ 16.62
15	1/5/2005	Smith	$ 374.10
16	1/5/2005	Williams	$ 254.89
17	1/6/2005	Jones	$ 206.17
18	1/6/2005	Smith	$ 227.90
19	1/6/2005	Williams	$ 103.87
20	1/7/2005	Jones	$ 45.21
21	1/7/2005	Smith	$ 108.48
22	1/7/2005	Williams	$ 412.79
23	1/8/2005	Jones	$ 122.24
24	1/8/2005	Smith	$ 262.08
25	1/8/2005	Williams	$ 426.40
26	1/9/2005	Jones	$ 485.89
27	1/9/2005	Smith	$ 442.70
28	1/9/2005	Williams	$ 380.34
29	1/10/2005	Jones	$ 189.07
30	1/10/2005	Smith	$ 358.06
31	1/10/2005	Williams	$ 370.22
32	1/11/2005	Jones	$ 184.47
33	1/11/2005	Smith	$ 421.29
34	1/11/2005	Williams	$ 370.59
35	1/12/2005	Jones	$ 411.55

Daily Sales

Figure 8-6: The list shows sales by date and by salesperson.

2. **Choose Data ➪ PivotTable and PivotChart Report.**

   Your choice will differ if you have a version earlier than Excel 2000. Then you'll want to choose PivotTable Report.

   The window shown in Figure 8-7 appears. This is the first step in the PivotTable and PivotChart Wizard.

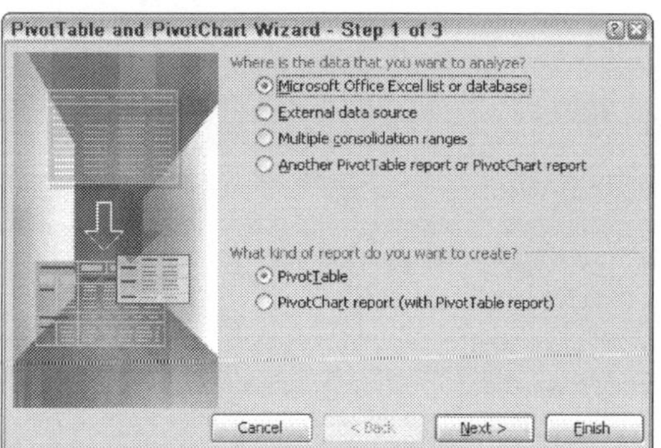

Figure 8-7: This is where you tell Excel how to find the basic data. In this case, your data is already on the worksheet, in the form of an Excel list.

3. **Under Where Is the Data That You Want to Analyze?, choose Microsoft Office Excel List or Database.**

4. **Under What Kind of Report Do You Want to Create?, choose PivotTable, and click Next.**

   The PivotTable and PivotChart Wizard's second step appears. The second step in the PivotTable and PivotChart Wizard depends on where you want it to get the data. When it's in a list, like in this example, it looks like Figure 8-8.

   A Microsoft Excel *database* is just an old term for a *list.*

5. **You can type the range address in the Range field if you want, but it's usually easier to drag through it with the mouse pointer; click Next when you've told Excel where to find the data.**

Figure 8-8: Be sure to include the field names in the Range address.

If you don't include the field names that are in the first row of the list, Excel will have trouble creating the pivot table.

Step 3 of the PivotTable and PivotChart Wizard is shown in Figure 8-9.

6. **Choose to put the pivot table in a new worksheet, or on the existing worksheet.**

   If you started by clicking in the cell where you want the pivot table to start, just click Finish. Otherwise, click in the range box and then in a different cell, and then click Finish.

Figure 8-9: The box below the second option button is the range box.

7. **Drag the field buttons into the areas where you want them.**

   After you click Finish, your worksheet appears, as shown in Figure 8-10. Click the Date button in the PivotTable Field List and drag it into the Row area in the schematic shown on the worksheet.

8. **Drag the Revenue button into the Data area.**

   As soon as you put a field into the Data area, the pivot table completes itself (see Figure 8-11), so it's usually best to leave the Data area for last.

Even if you've formatted a field like revenue as Currency in the underlying list, when it appears in the pivot table it's formatted as regular numbers with decimals. To show it as Currency in the pivot table, follow these steps:

1. **Right-click in a cell in the pivot table field you want to reformat.**

   A shortcut menu appears.

2. **Choose Field Settings.**

   The PivotTable Field dialog box appears.

3. **Click the Number button.**

   The Format Cells dialog box appears.

4. **Click Currency in the Category list box.**
5. **Click OK in the Format Cells dialog box.**
6. **Click OK in the PivotTable Field dialog box.**

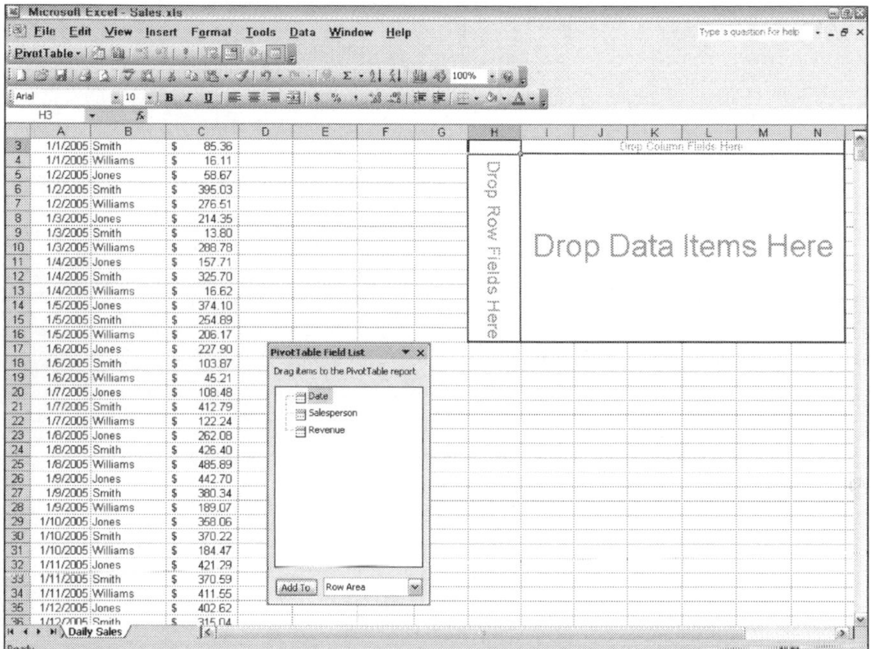

Figure 8-10: A date field often goes into the Row area.

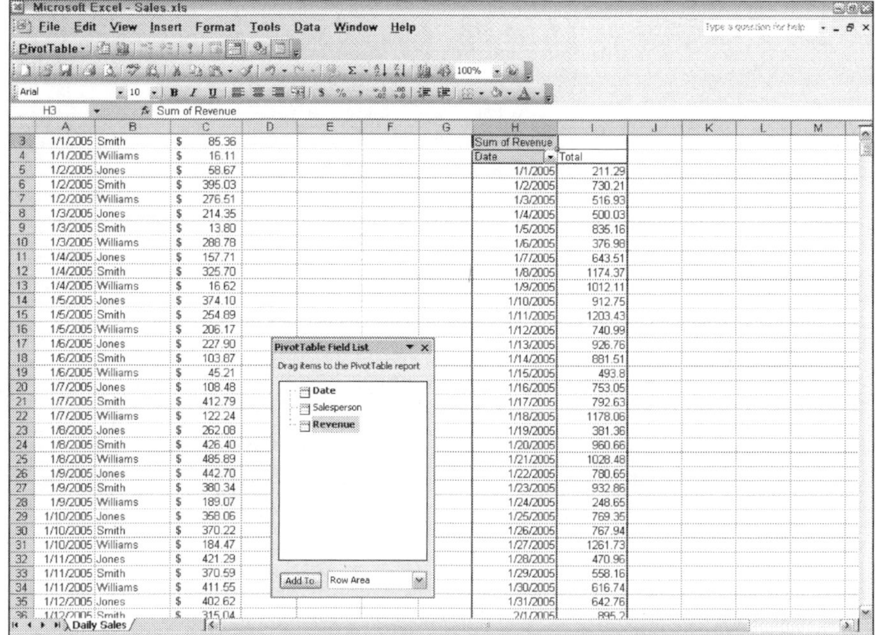

Figure 8-11: You've finished making the pivot table, but it's not very useful yet.

Grouping Records

You can use pivot tables to summarize data. One of the ways that you fine-tune a summary in a pivot table is to *group* a row field or a column field.

When you group a row field or column field, you combine the values in the field. For example, you might have a field that shows the dates when sales were made. Excel's pivot tables make it possible for you to group individual dates like September 4 and September 6 into weeks, like September 1 through September 7. Or you can group into months, or quarters, or years. It all depends upon how you want to forecast — by week, by month, by quarter, by year. Keep your time period in mind.

Knowing when to group records

If you followed the steps in the prior section, you have a pivot table that summarizes revenue, but it still does so day by day. The reason is that the list you've based the pivot table on shows revenue by day. Summarizing revenue by month (or week, or quarter, or year) would be much better. Here's how to do that.

Notice in Figure 8-11 that the underlying list has several identical dates. The pivot table combines those identical dates into just one row, adding up their revenue along the way. One of the things that pivot tables do is to combine identical values in a list into the same item in a row, column, or page field.

But you don't want to forecast by individual dates. That's not the right time period. In this kind of situation, you need to group individual dates that belong to the same, say, month into one row of the pivot table. Then all the revenues for those dates are also totaled.

Of course, you're not restricted to grouping on months. You can use seven-day periods, quarters, years, and others (such as three-day or ten-day periods).

Creating the groups

After you have a pivot table set up, as in Figure 8-11, grouping the individual dates in the row field is simple. Follow these steps:

1. **Click any of the cells in the column of the pivot table that has the dates.**

   In Figure 8-11, that's Column H.

2. **Choose Data ➪ Group and Outline.**

3. **Choose Group.**

   You'll see the Grouping window shown in Figure 8-12.

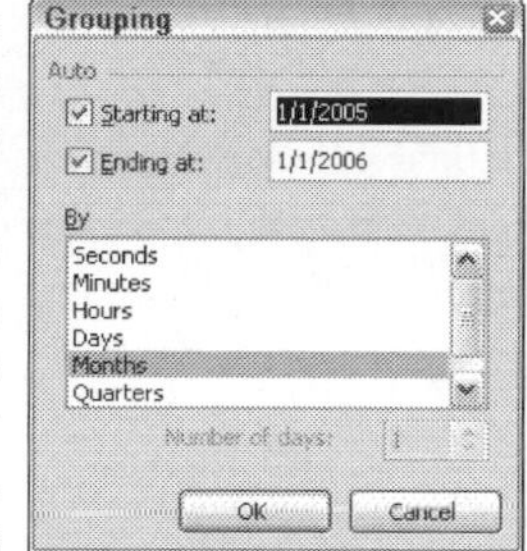

Figure 8-12: You get this window when the field you started with shows dates or times.

4. **Click OK.**

Because you want to summarize your revenues by month, you can accept the default selection, Months. When you click OK, the pivot table changes and looks like the one shown in Figure 8-13.

You always need to know how you're going to get out. If you want to ungroup the records, do this:

1. **Click in a cell with grouped records.**

   In Figure 8-13, that's a cell in the Row area.

2. **Choose Data ➪ Group and Outline.**

3. **Choose Ungroup from the new menu.**

   Now you have the row field back to its original state.

If you want to change a grouping level from, say, Months to Quarters you don't need to ungroup first. Just choose Data ➪ Group and Outline ➪ Group, deselect Months, and select Quarters. Then click OK.

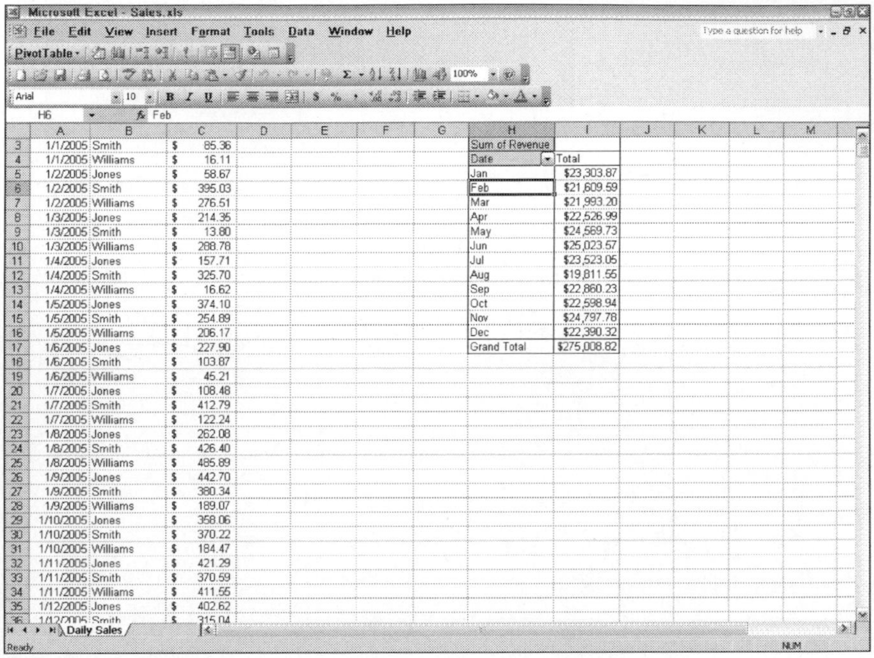

Figure 8-13: Now you can see the total revenue for each month.

Avoiding Grief in Excel Pivot Tables

You need to watch out for a few things if you're grouping on a date field in an Excel pivot table: You may get an error message that doesn't tell you what the problem is; you want to orient your table correctly; you want to make sure that you've chosen enough grouping levels. The next few sections talk about these issues.

Don't use blank dates

Have another look at the list that the pivot table in Figure 8-13 summarizes. All the records in the list have dates. Suppose that one (or more) of the records in the list was missing a date value — that the record just had a blank cell rather than a date.

You could create a pivot table from that list. And one of the rows in the pivot table would show *(blank)* rather than a date. But as soon as you tried to group that field, Excel would whine at you. You'd see a message box that would say `Cannot group that selection`.

When you see that message, it's almost certain that the problem is a missing value (or even a text value) in the field you're trying to group. Here's how to fix it:

1. **Go back to your list and locate the record with the missing value.**

   Maybe you can figure out what the missing value should be.

   If you can't figure out what the missing value should be, you may be better off just removing it from the list.

2. **Fill in the missing data with your best guess.**
3. **Choose Data ➪ Refresh Data.**

   Refreshing the pivot table's data forces it to go back to its source — in this example, the list — and replace the missing value that kept it from grouping.

Any time the underlying data changes, you need to choose Data ➪ Refresh Data to force the pivot table to reflect the change. It doesn't happen automatically.

If you're trying to group by month, it doesn't really matter which day of the month you use — the pivot table will put it into May regardless of whether you call it May 1 or May 31.

If your baseline spans more than one year's worth of dates, consider using Year as well as Month (or Quarter or Days) to group on. If you don't include Year, then March 2004 would be included with March 2005. You might want to treat them together if you were investigating seasonality, but not if you were preparing an actual forecast.

The same thing happens if you are trying to group a standard number field that doesn't have dates in it. Regardless of the type of data you're grouping on, the thing to remember is that Excel won't group a field that has missing values.

Putting dates in the Row area

Excel worksheets are tall and skinny. Think Kobe Bryant in a plaid suit. If you go all the way to the right on a worksheet, you'll see that the final column is named IV — that's not a way of dripping medicine into your veins but the Vth letter into the Ith time through the alphabet. Another way of saying it is it's the 256th (and final) column in the worksheet.

That may seem like plenty of columns — and it is if you're laying your data out right — but if you go all the way down to the bottom of a worksheet, you'll see that it has 65,536 rows. That's 256^2. In other words, an Excel worksheet has 256 times as many rows as it does columns.

Now, if you have a year's worth of sales data, you could easily have 260 or more dates. If you start making your pivot table by putting the date field in the Column area, you're probably going to have a problem. The pivot table will try to accommodate each date, one per column. And if you have more than 256 dates to handle, Excel will run out of columns for the pivot table. It can't put 260 distinct dates into 256 columns.

Again, Excel will whine at you. You'll see a message that says `PivotTable report will not fit on the sheet. Do you want to show as much as possible?` If you click OK, Excel will build the pivot table all the way to column IV, but you won't see all your data. If you have 260 dates, you'll lose a few at the right.

But if you start by putting the date field in the Row area (have a look back at Figure 8-9) then you have plenty of room. You can easily accommodate 260 days, or 365 days, in 65,536 rows. Then, after you've created the pivot table, you can group the date field, reducing it to, say, 12 months.

After you've grouped the date field, you can put it in the Column area if you really want. Pivot the table directly on the worksheet by dragging the date field's button to the top of the table.

Excel has a comfort level with lists — records in rows, fields in columns. So leaving the monthly records in the rows makes sense.

Making multiple groups

What if your list has dates that span more than one year? If your data spans more than one year, and you choose to group just on month, Excel will put March 2004 in with March 2005 and call them both March.

You might decide to group your dates just by month, because it could be interesting to see how your sales revenues vary by month, regardless of the year. If you sell parkas, for example, you might expect to see your sales spike in the fall and winter — and you might have to go on the dole in the spring and summer. (I show you more about forecasting and seasons in Chapter 18.)

But often you'll want to look at the monthly (or quarterly) results for 2005 separately from the monthly results for 2004. That's easy to handle. Just follow these steps:

1. **Click any cell in the date field of the pivot table report and choose Data ➪ Group and Outline ➪ Group.**
2. **As usual, accept the default Months grouping.**

3. **Click Years at the bottom of the list box.**

   You might need to scroll down the list box to find Years.

4. **Click OK.**

   Now you'll be able to see months within years, as in Figure 8-14.

You can deselect any grouping level that's already selected just by clicking it in the Grouping dialog box. For example, Months is the default grouping level for a date field. If you don't want to group Months, just click on it to deselect it, and then group the level you want to use — like Quarters or Years.

You can't group specifically on Weeks. You need to select Days, and then specify 7 with the Number of Days spinner. Excel enables the spinner as soon as you select Days. (A *spinner* is a type of control in a dialog box. You can see one — although it's dimmed — above the Cancel button in Figure 8-12. You use it to increase or decrease the number of days to group by.)

Microsoft Excel - Sales.xls

	Date	Salesperson	Revenue
2	1/2/2004	Jones	$ 161.45
3	1/2/2004	Smith	$ 19.03
4	1/2/2004	Williams	$ 9.94
5	1/3/2004	Jones	$ 59.57
6	1/3/2004	Smith	$ 21.84
7	1/3/2004	Williams	$ 62.15
8	1/4/2004	Jones	$ 228.04
9	1/4/2004	Smith	$ 12.97
10	1/4/2004	Williams	$ 128.80
11	1/5/2004	Jones	$ 6.38
12	1/5/2004	Smith	$ 27.10
13	1/5/2004	Williams	$ 15.54
14	1/6/2004	Jones	$ 293.71
15	1/6/2004	Smith	$ 326.40
16	1/6/2004	Williams	$ 172.24
17	1/7/2004	Jones	$ 248.64
18	1/7/2004	Smith	$ 126.70
19	1/7/2004	Williams	$ 6.63
20	1/8/2004	Jones	$ 76.18
21	1/8/2004	Smith	$ 244.26
22	1/8/2004	Williams	$ 26.88
23	1/9/2004	Jones	$ 219.98
24	1/9/2004	Smith	$ 278.20
25	1/9/2004	Williams	$ 217.69
26	1/10/2004	Jones	$ 358.95
27	1/10/2004	Smith	$ 496.12
28	1/10/2004	Williams	$ 155.91
29	1/11/2004	Jones	$ 266.57
30	1/11/2004	Smith	$ 328.63
31	1/11/2004	Williams	$ 249.85
32	1/12/2004	Jones	$ 417.84
33	1/12/2004	Smith	$ 234.23
34	1/12/2004	Williams	$ 452.66

Sum of Revenue		
Years	Date	Total
2004	Jan	$19,423.57
	Feb	$18,647.03
	Mar	$18,493.64
	Apr	$15,342.14
	May	$18,020.52
	Jun	$19,310.11
	Jul	$18,084.12
	Aug	$14,113.43
	Sep	$16,982.60
	Oct	$17,745.34
	Nov	$17,254.89
	Dec	$18,170.90
2005	Jan	$23,303.87
	Feb	$21,609.59
	Mar	$21,993.20
	Apr	$22,526.99
	May	$24,569.73
	Jun	$25,023.57
	Jul	$23,523.05
	Aug	$19,811.55
	Sep	$22,860.23
	Oct	$22,598.94
	Nov	$24,797.78
	Dec	$22,390.32
Grand Total		$486,597.11

Daily Sales

Figure 8-14: The years appear in an outer row field and the months in an inner row field.

Chapter 9

Charting Your Baseline: It's a Good Idea

In This Chapter

- Figuring out what's going on in your baseline
- Using pivot charts to make your data look good
- Using more than one scale

To make good forecasts — forecasts that your colleagues think of as useful guides to the future — you need to know as much as you can about the baselines that determine those forecasts. You can run all sorts of highfalutin statistical tests on a baseline, but one of your best sources of information is the lowly chart. For example, if your baseline describes an upside-down U, simple regression statistics or correlations aren't going to tell you that. But charting the baseline often results in the well-known interocular impact effect: It hits you right between the eyes.

If you use a version of Excel after Excel 97, you can use a special kind of chart called a pivot chart. Pivot charts are similar to pivot tables in two primary ways:

- You can easily change the role of a variable — for example, moving it from a chart's horizontal axis to its vertical axis.
- You can display a data field as any one of a set of summary options: Count, Sum, Average, and so on.

Sometimes you want to chart more than one data series at once, so you can see how two baseline variables behave over time. If those data series have very different scales, such as monthly sales and monthly sales commissions, the differences in the scales can make it hard to see what's happened during the course of the baseline. Putting two axis scales into your chart can help in this situation.

Digging Into a Baseline

Sometimes you can stare at the numbers in a baseline until they start to swim up at you out of the worksheet and tell you absolutely nothing. But you have to find a way to get a read on what's going on in that baseline. It might be rising, falling, holding steady, or just out for a walk.

At these times — really, at all times — you should think about putting the baseline into a chart. Because of the nature of forecasting, many charts that help you understand the baseline use dates on one chart axis or another. So you may as well start by getting your arms around how Excel keeps track of dates.

Using date and time data in Excel

I feel as though I should apologize for this section but I'm not going to. It's a little dull, and I've looked in vain for ways to spice it up with some jokes that are in questionable taste. The thing is, you have to have a grasp on this stuff if you're going to understand how dates and times work in Excel — and, therefore, how they work in regression forecasts and in charts.

How Excel keeps track of dates

Excel assigns a numeric value to each date since January 1, 1900 (January 1, 1904, on Macintosh computers). You can see this for yourself by following these steps:

1. **Enter** 1 **in a worksheet cell.**
2. **Select that cell.**
3. **Choose Format ⇨ Cells and select the Number tab.**
4. **In the Category list box, choose Date.**
5. **In the Type list box, choose any date format that shows the month, the day, and the year.**
6. **Click OK.**

   Depending on which specific format you selected in Step 5, you'll see something such as 1/1/1900 or January 1, 1900.

Working the other direction, if you enter **1/2/1900** in a worksheet cell and format it as Number (as in Step 3), you'll see the value 2, or 2.00, or however many decimal places you chose when you formatted the value as a number. January 2, 1900, is the second day in the sequence.

So, despite their format on the worksheet, dates in Excel are actually numbers. This fact has implications for using, say, date of sale as a predictor variable in a regression forecast, and for how you view date of sale in an Excel chart.

How Excel keeps track of time

Excel also assigns a number to time of day. It's a fractional value, ranging from 0.000 for midnight, to 0.999 for 11:59 p.m. And Excel adds that fractional value to the integer date value, so you can specify a particular time of day on a particular date. For example, 17804.72917 represents September 28, 1948, at 5:30 p.m.

You probably won't have much use for fractional time values in sales forecasting, but if you do happen to come across a date/time value with a fractional component, you'll know what it's about.

Charting dates and times in Excel

Chapter 7 dips briefly into the topic of using charts in forecasting, just enough to whet your appetite. In this section, I tell you more about the importance of choosing the right chart type when you chart your baseline.

There are at least two axes on most Excel standard chart types (the exceptions are Pie and Doughnut charts). Three-dimensional charts have three axes. The charts that have two axes, as you'd expect, have a vertical axis and a horizontal axis. Figure 9-1 shows the two axes on a Line chart.

A chart axis can display variables of two different types: *value* and *category.* These are Excel's terms, and unfortunately the term *value* is misleading.

A category axis is meant to display labels, like London, Paris, New York, and Boise. There's no intrinsic value in a label. All a label does is name a category, such as London, that's different in some way (perhaps in many ways) from another category, such as Boise.

If there were an intrinsic value to a category, you could put the labels in an order that made sense. But you typically can't do that with categories, except with alphabetical sorting, and now you're dealing not with categories but with letters.

On a Line chart, the horizontal or X axis is designed to display categories, which means that the different categories are equally spaced. If a category has no intrinsic value, neither do the differences between categories, and Excel just puts them on the axis. Figure 9-2 shows an example.

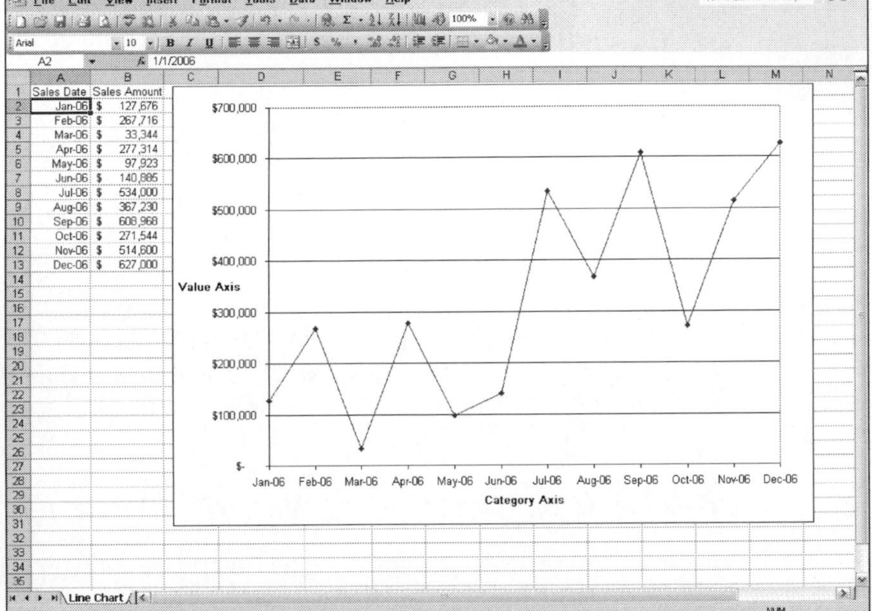

Figure 9-1: The horizontal axis is often termed the *X axis* and the vertical axis the *Y axis.*

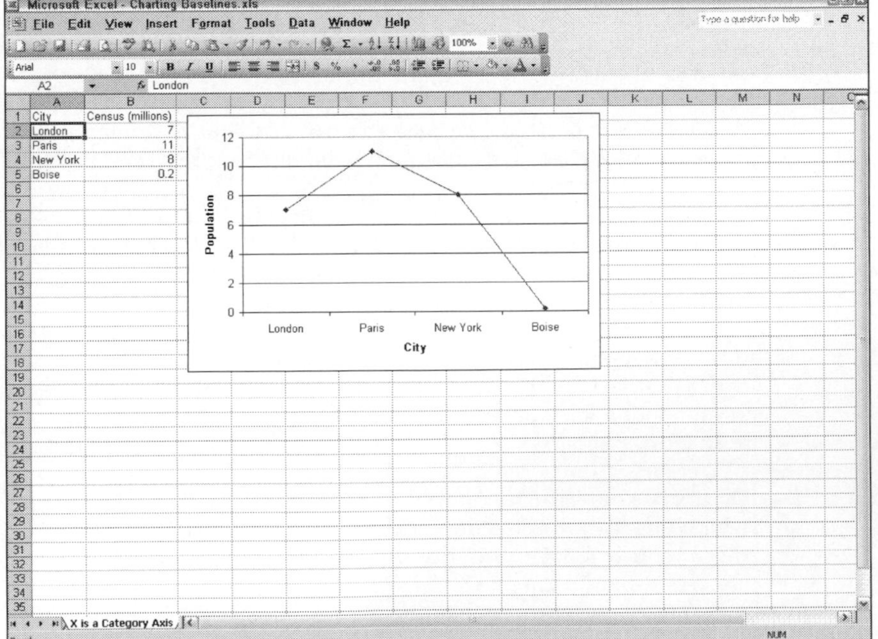

Figure 9-2: The X axis is a category axis in a Line chart.

The other kind of axis, the so-called *value* axis, takes account of intrinsic differences among values. All Line charts, such as the one in Figure 9-2, have a vertical axis that is a value axis. Notice in Figure 9-2 that the vertical distances between the data points reflect their relative values.

I dislike the term *value axis* because it implies that text values (such as London and New York) are not values. They are values; they're just not numeric values. A much better term would have been *numeric axis.* If it sounds like I'm kvetching here, I'm not. Things need to be given names that are descriptive and accurate, or else people get misled. But that's how Excel uses the term, so I'll do the same, under protest.

Excel has 13 standard chart types. I list them here, along with the nature of their axes and some comments:

- **Cylinder, Cone, and Pyramid charts:** One category axis and one value axis. These charts are just 3-D variations on Column and Bar charts. These charts don't truly have three dimensions, but the data markers are formatted to look like 3-D.
- **Pie and Doughnut charts:** A value axis only. Not suited for forecasting due to design and single axis.
- **Radar chart:** One category axis and one value axis. Not suited for forecasting due to nonlinear layout.
- **Area chart:** One category axis and one value axis. The problem is that the Area chart's visual design draws your eye to the area below the data points rather than to the height of the points themselves.
- **Surface chart:** Two category axes and one value axis. A true three-dimensional chart. However, a 3-D chart, if you're forecasting, gives you too much visual information.
- **Column and Bar charts:** One category axis and one value axis. These charts are identical except that a Column chart's X axis is a category axis and a Bar chart's Y axis is a category axis. The data markers — the columns or the bars — draw your eye away from the main issue: the value of the data series at each point on the category axis.
- **Bubble charts:** Two value axes. There is actually a third value axis, represented by the area occupied on the chart by each data marker, so this type is unsuitable for forecasting.
- **Line charts:** One category axis and one value axis. Excellent for forecasting.
- **XY (Scatter) charts:** Two value axes. Excellent for forecasting.

In forecasting, you want the predictor variable to run from left to right along a horizontal axis, and the value of the forecast variable to be tied to the vertical axis. That arrangement is visually the most informative, and it's the one you get with Line charts and XY (Scatter) charts.

One problem with XY (Scatter) charts is that they tend to line up the X-axis labels poorly with the data points for the forecast variable. Figure 9-3 shows what happens.

You don't have as much control over the appearance of a value axis and its labels as you do over a category axis. So, I recommend you use a Line chart if you're charting a variable such as sales revenue or number of units sold over time.

Using Line charts

A closer look at the category axis on a Line chart shows you that things are a little more complicated than they seem. To get a closer look, take these steps:

1. **Click somewhere in a Line chart to activate it.**

   It doesn't matter what part of the chart you select, but make sure that you've activated a Line chart.

2. **Choose Chart ➪ Chart Options.**
3. **Select the Axes tab.**

   The Chart Options dialog box, shown in Figure 9-4, appears.

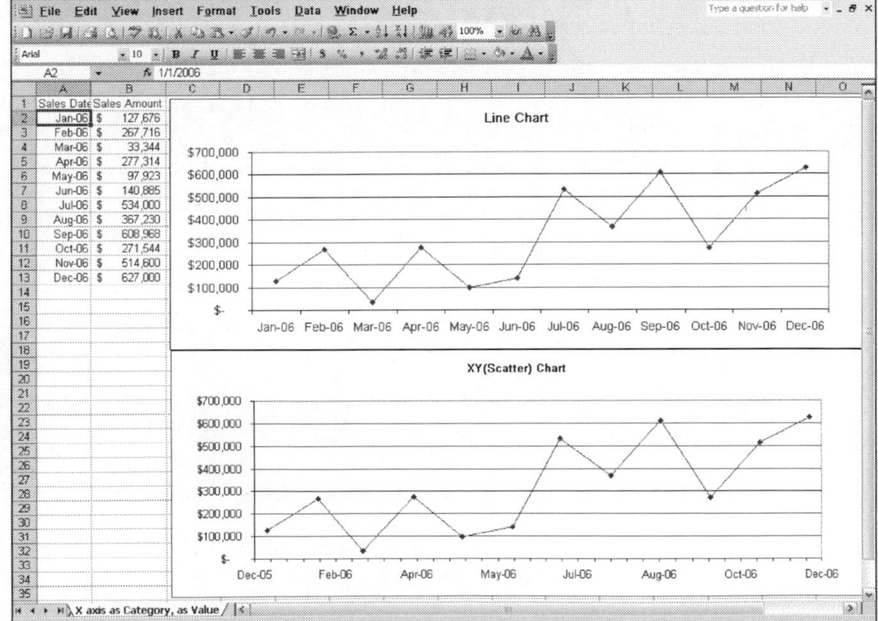

Figure 9-3: The Line chart does a good job of aligning labels with data points; the XY (Scatter) chart does not.

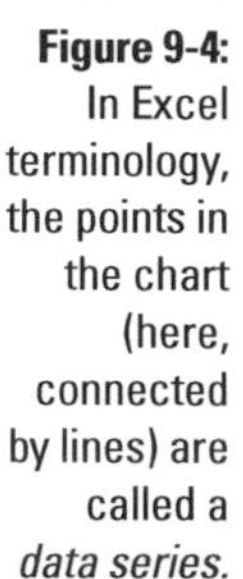

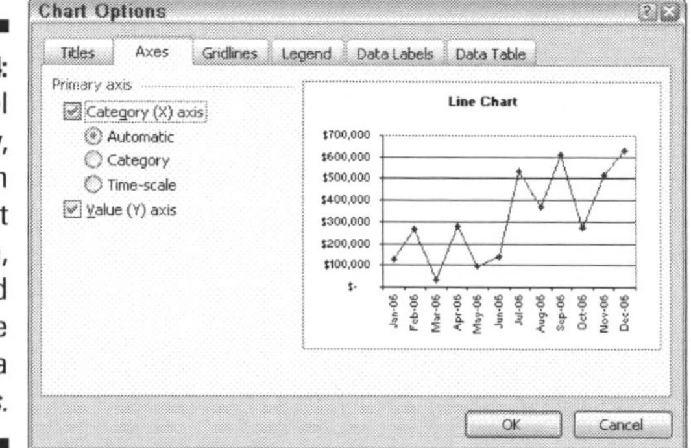

Figure 9-4: In Excel terminology, the points in the chart (here, connected by lines) are called a *data series.*

A category axis can have three subtypes (and this is true of the category axis in any type of chart, given that the chart has a category axis). Suppose you want to use whatever's in A2:A13 as the values for your category axis. On the Axes tab, you can choose from:

- **Category:** Selecting this option forces Excel to treat the values as categories — that is, as though they were text labels. Doesn't matter if the values in A2:A13 are genuinely numeric, either with or without a date format. If you choose this option, Excel treats the values in A2:A13 as text labels, and we're back to London, Paris, and so on.
- **Time-scale:** The only reason you'd select this option is that you have dates in A2:A13, you want to use them on the category axis, and those dates are in a Number rather than a Date format. Figure 9-5 shows the difference between an X axis that's a true category axis, and an X axis that Excel has time-scaled. (This option's name is misleading, by the way: The shortest time span it can handle is one day. So both 1:00 AM and 11:00 PM on May 4 show up at the same point on the category axis. It should have been called Date-scale.)
- **Automatic:** This is the default. If you select this option, you turn the issue over to Excel. If Excel finds the first number — that is, the value in A2 — formatted as Date and finds numbers in A3:A13, it treats the axis as time-scaled. In any other case — text values or numeric values *not* formatted as dates — Excel treats them all as labels on a true category axis.

What does all this have to do with forecasting? Suppose your Line chart's X axis is a true category axis. Excel charts can show you a trendline that depicts the relationship between the predictor variable and the forecast variable (see Chapter 7). Charts can also show you the R-squared value and the regression equation itself.

In a chart with a time-scaled category axis, the trendline and the regression information are based on the relationship between the predictor and the forecast variable.

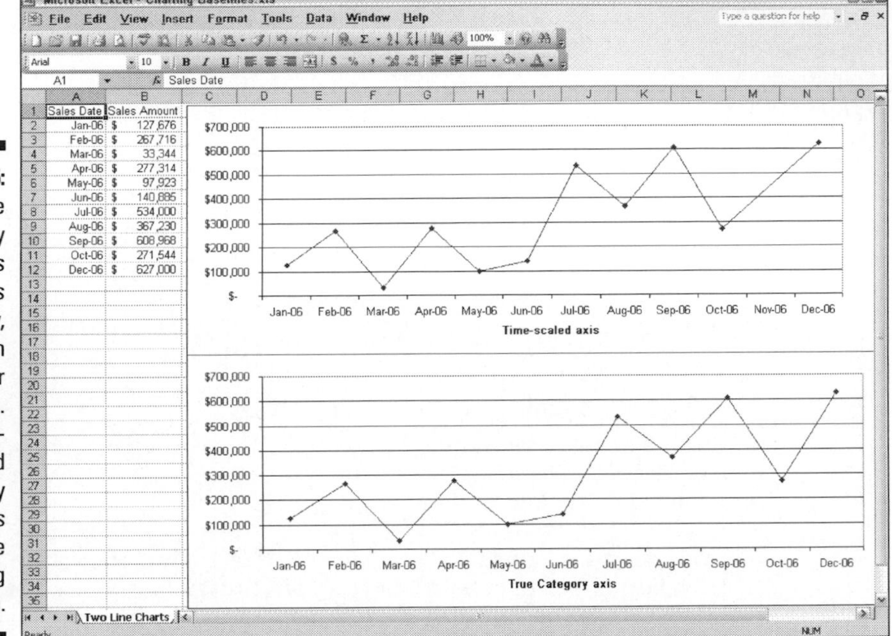

Figure 9-5: The true category axis spaces the values evenly, although November is missing. The time-scaled category axis leaves room for the missing data.

In a chart with a true category axis, Excel has to use some numeric value to represent the categories, and it uses 1, 2, 3, and so on so that it can calculate a regression. In other words, because Excel can't calculate a regression where the predictor variable is London, Paris, New York, and Boise, it would treat London as the numeral 1, Paris as the numeral 2, and so on. Figure 9-6 shows you the result of this if you have dates on the category axis, first as a time-scaled axis and second as a true category axis.

The chart with the time-scaled category axis determines the regression equation by calculating the relationship between the sales figures and the date figures (the dates, in Number format, begin with 38,718 and end with 39,052). The regression equation as you'd use it to get the forecast for January 2007 would be:

```
January 2007 Sales = 42,815.97 * 39,083 - 54,375,009
```

The chart with the true category axis determines the regression equation by calculating the relationship between the sales figures and the category numbers (that is, 1, 2, 3, . . . 11). The regression equation as you'd use it to get the forecast for January 2007 would be:

```
January 2007 Sales = 44,133.75 * 12 + 40,070.21
```

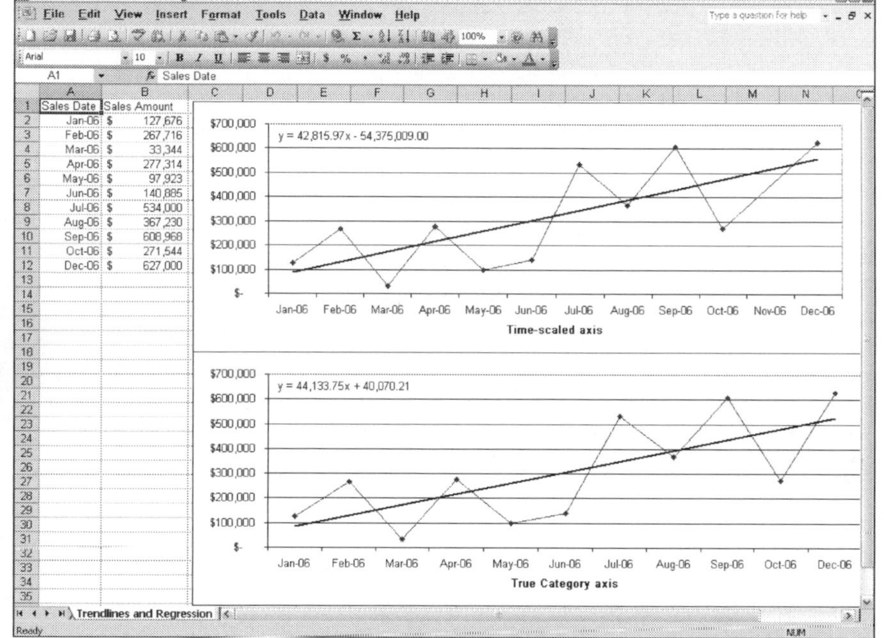

Figure 9-6: The regression equations are wildly different in the two charts.

So if you're going to make use of these equations, you'd better know whether your next predictor value is the 39,083rd day from January 1, 1900, or whether it's the 12th category ordinal number from the beginning of the series. For example, you don't want to be confusing the date values with the categories and entering in your worksheet an equation like this:

```
January 2007 Sales = 42,815.97 * 12 - 54,375,009
```

which results in a forecast of a –$53,861,217 for January 2007. If you turned that forecast in, you'd probably be reassessing your career goals soon after.

Depending on the scale of measurement, the decimal places in the coefficients may or may not be important. If they are important, you should probably get the regression equation on the worksheet with the LINEST or the Analysis ToolPak — or, you should bypass the equation and work with the TREND function instead, which will give you the forecast values without going through a lot of formulaic hand waving. (See Chapter 12 for information about these functions.)

Here's another example. There's some real seasonality going on in Figure 9-7.

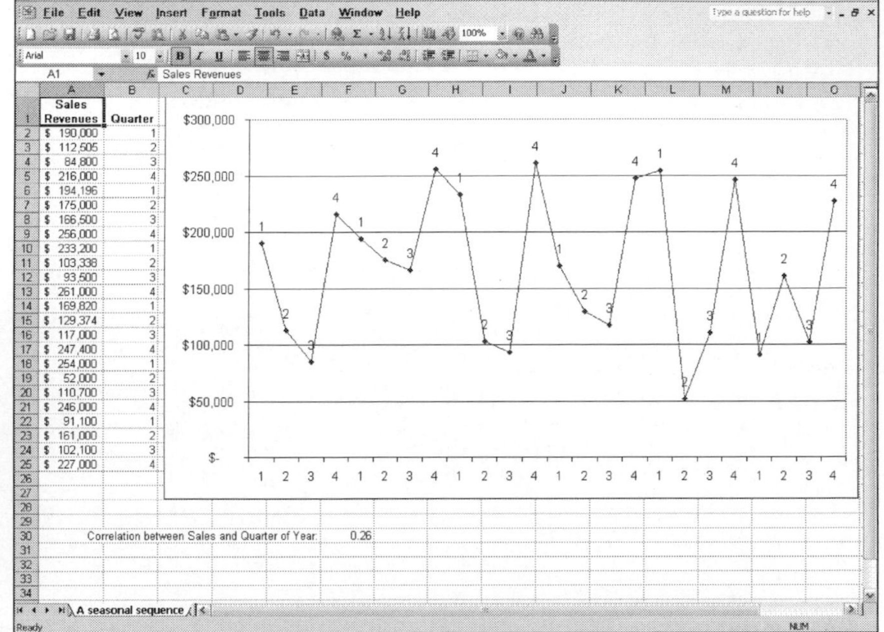

Figure 9-7: A linear correlation often obscures the seasonal regularity in a baseline.

Nearly every time the fourth quarter comes along, it has the highest sales revenue for the current year. But you wouldn't suspect such regularity in the relationship between quarter of the year and sales if all you looked at was the correlation — 0.26 is marginal at best.

But if you look at the baseline sales and quarters in a chart, the seasonality is hard to miss.

The numbers above the individual data points in the chart in Figure 9-7 are called *data labels.* In this case, each data label shows the quarter of the year that the revenue amount belongs to. There are different ways to get data labels. One is to select the data series, choose Format ⇨ Selected Data Series, select the Data Labels tab, select the Category Name check box, and click OK.

You can find information about forecasting baselines that have this sort of seasonality in Chapter 18.

Using XY (Scatter) charts

An XY (Scatter) chart has two value axes: the X axis is a value axis, as is the Y axis. (The rest of this section simplifies things by just calling them *XY charts.*) XY charts are best used when you're forecasting on some basis other than time or date. Refer to Figure 9-3 to see why Line charts are better than XY charts if you're forecasting according to some date predictor.

But if you have a different sort of predictor variable, such as size of sales force or advertising dollars, consider using an XY chart. Figure 9-8 shows an example.

XY charts help you judge the strength of a relationship between a predictor variable and a forecast variable. People often take a look at the correlation between the two variables and, if the correlation is, say, between –0.2 and 0.2 then they decide there's not much to it.

A correlation's possible values run from –1.0 to 1.0. The closer to one of those two values, the stronger the relationship. The closer to 0.0, the weaker the relationship. The R-squared value is the square of the correlation and measures how much variation in one variable is attributable to the other variable.

But look at the XY chart in Figure 9-9.

If you just looked at the correlation between number of advertisements and number of sales, you'd ignore it. A correlation of 0.17 is really too small to concern yourself with unless it's based on hundreds or thousands of cases.

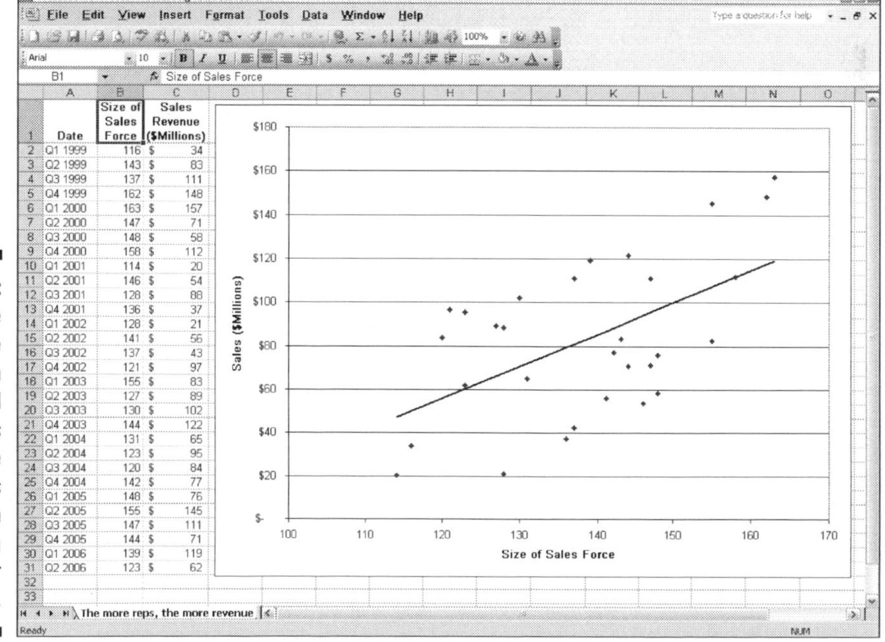

Date	Size of Sales Force	Sales Revenue ($Millions)
Q1 1999	116	$ 34
Q2 1999	143	$ 83
Q3 1999	137	$ 111
Q4 1999	162	$ 148
Q1 2000	163	$ 157
Q2 2000	147	$ 71
Q3 2000	148	$ 58
Q4 2000	158	$ 112
Q1 2001	114	$ 20
Q2 2001	146	$ 54
Q3 2001	128	$ 88
Q4 2001	136	$ 37
Q1 2002	128	$ 21
Q2 2002	141	$ 56
Q3 2002	137	$ 43
Q4 2002	121	$ 97
Q1 2003	155	$ 83
Q2 2003	127	$ 89
Q3 2003	130	$ 102
Q4 2003	144	$ 122
Q1 2004	131	$ 65
Q2 2004	123	$ 95
Q3 2004	120	$ 84
Q4 2004	142	$ 77
Q1 2005	148	$ 76
Q2 2005	155	$ 145
Q3 2005	147	$ 111
Q4 2005	144	$ 71
Q1 2006	139	$ 119
Q2 2006	123	$ 62

Figure 9-8: Here, you're more interested in how well size of sales force predicts sales than in date as a predictor variable.

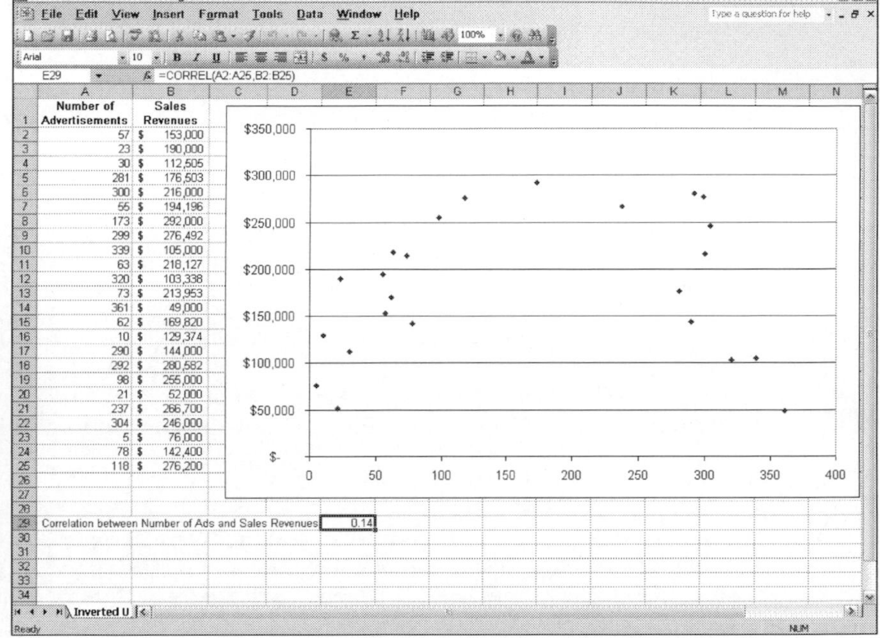

Number of Advertisements	Sales Revenues
57	$ 153,000
23	$ 190,000
30	$ 112,505
281	$ 176,503
300	$ 216,000
55	$ 194,196
173	$ 292,000
299	$ 276,492
339	$ 105,000
63	$ 218,127
320	$ 103,338
73	$ 213,953
361	$ 49,000
62	$ 169,820
10	$ 129,374
290	$ 144,000
292	$ 280,582
98	$ 255,000
21	$ 52,000
237	$ 266,700
304	$ 246,000
5	$ 76,000
78	$ 142,400
118	$ 276,200

Correlation between Number of Ads and Sales Revenues 0.14

Figure 9-9: This pattern is often termed an *inverted U function.* The name doesn't matter; going up and then back down does.

But when you look at the chart of the number of advertisements against sales, a different picture emerges. You can see that, up to a certain number of ads, sales increase fairly sharply. Then the sales flatten out and finally drop back off. This inverted U can come about if there's a relatively fixed advertising budget. Then, when the company starts buying a relatively large number of ads, the per-advertisement expense decreases, and so do things like the desirability of the placement, the size of the ad, whether or not color is used, and so on. As a result, sales decline.

So there's a useful relationship to take advantage of. But because a simple correlation assumes a linear relationship, it won't tell you what you want to know. This is only one reason that you should always chart your baselines.

Making Your Data Dance with Pivot Charts

Chapter 8 has a lot to say about how you can use Excel's PivotTable feature to summarize individual sales records in a table. The pivot table then could show you total sales revenues according to date, region, product line — any variable that you might want to use to break down the revenue results.

Since Excel 2000, an added feature has been included with the pivot table capability: a pivot chart. You can still build a pivot table, just as you always could. But now you can decide to build a pivot chart, and a pivot table comes with it like a prize in a box of Cracker Jacks. You have available all the standard chart types, from Column to Pyramid, and of course including Line and XY (Scatter).

Building a pivot chart

If you've looked at Chapter 8, you know the basics of setting up a pivot table in Excel. The process of setting up a pivot chart is the same in concept, just a little different in execution.

Why the difference? At heart, it's because a pivot table expresses the size of its data field — that is, the field that the pivot table is summarizing — with a number. For example:

- The sum of sales dollars during each month, for each product line, for each branch
- The average number of units sold of each product, in each branch, for each sales rep in that branch
- The sum of revenue, for goods separately from services, for each product line in each branch

But a chart can't show sums, averages, counts, and so on in a single cell. That's both the advantage and the disadvantage of a chart. The disadvantage: You have to reserve an entire dimension, up for Line (and other) charts, up and across for XY charts, to show the magnitude that you see in a single cell of a pivot table. The advantage: You can see how the magnitude grows, falls, rises and falls seasonally, or remains generally static over time.

Start with the baseline data laid out in a list structure, as in Figure 9-10.

Then take these steps:

1. **Select any cell in the list.**
2. **Choose Data ⇨ PivotTable and PivotChart Report.**

   The PivotTable and PivotChart Wizard appears (see Figure 9-11).
3. **Under Where Is the Data That You Want to Analyze?, choose Microsoft Office Excel List or Database.**
4. **Under What Kind of Report Do You Want to Create?, choose PivotChart Report (with PivotTable Report).**

	A	B	C	D	E
1	Month	Branch	Sales Rep	Product Line	Sales
2	Apr	NE	Allen	Laptop	$ 6,664
3	Dec	SE	Norris	Desktop	$26,212
4	Aug	SW	Morales	Desktop	$17,011
5	Mar	NW	Reynolds	Desktop	$ 6,745
6	Mar	NW	Reynolds	Laptop	$12,552
7	Aug	SW	Morales	Desktop	$12,304
8	Jun	NE	Finney	Laptop	$18,880
9	Oct	SE	Edwards	Laptop	$ 6,938
10	Jul	SW	Rodgers	Desktop	$19,261
11	Oct	SE	Edwards	Laptop	$12,311
12	Nov	SE	Anderson	Laptop	$20,055
13	Nov	SE	Anderson	Desktop	$27,544
14	Feb	NW	Smith	Laptop	$ 8,902
15	Aug	SW	Morales	Laptop	$ 6,201
16	Apr	NE	Allen	Desktop	$23,230
17	Jan	NW	Johnson	Desktop	$16,402
18	Aug	SW	Morales	Laptop	$29,314
19	Jun	NE	Finney	Desktop	$21,638
20	Mar	NW	Reynolds	Desktop	$ 8,724
21	May	NE	Roberts	Desktop	$13,608
22	Dec	SE	Norris	Desktop	$ 4,995
23	Jul	SW	Rodgers	Laptop	$19,906
24	Jan	NW	Johnson	Laptop	$ 3,858
25	Dec	SE	Norris	Laptop	$16,949
26	Feb	NW	Smith	Desktop	$ 3,136
27	Sep	SW	Timms	Laptop	$ 6,591
28	Jun	NE	Finney	Desktop	$15,374
29	Feb	NW	Smith	Desktop	$ 5,315
30	Oct	SE	Edwards	Desktop	$ 3,830
31	May	NE	Roberts	Laptop	$ 7,555
32	Mar	NW	Reynolds	Laptop	$23,846
33	Sep	SW	Timms	Desktop	$21,674
34	Nov	SE	Anderson	Desktop	$26,093
35	Jul	SW	Rodgers	Desktop	$25,567

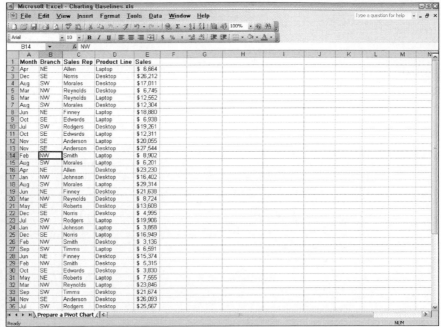

Figure 9-10: When you're preparing a pivot table or pivot chart, the order of the data in the list doesn't matter.

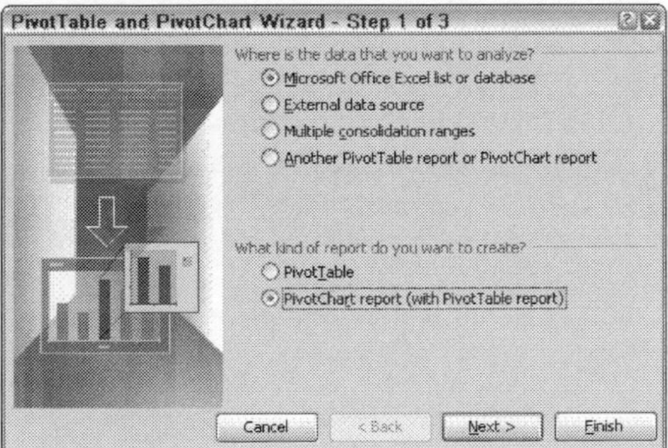

Figure 9-11: When you choose to make a pivot chart, you design the chart directly and the pivot table follows along.

5. **Click Next.**

   Step 2 of the PivotTable and PivotChart Wizard appears (see Figure 9-12).

PivotTable and PivotChart Wizard - Step 2 of 3
Where is the data that you want to use?
Range: Prepare a Pivot Chart'!$A$1:$E$49
Browse...
Cancel | < Back | Next > | Finish

Figure 9-12: This is the reason to start with a cell in your list active: Excel will select your entire list for you.

6. **Accept the range that Excel offers (unless you can see that there's something clearly wrong with it), and click Next.**

   Step 3 of the PivotTable and PivotChart Wizard appears (see Figure 9-13).

Figure 9-13: If you want to put the pivot table in a different workbook, that workbook must be open. If it is, you can choose Window on the main Excel menu to get to that other workbook.

7. **Under Where Do You Want to Put the PivotTable Report?, select whether you want the pivot table on a new or an existing worksheet, identify a starting cell if you want to use an existing worksheet, and click Finish.**

   You can put it on any worksheet you want — it doesn't have to be on the same worksheet as the underlying list.

Note: You get to say where you want the pivot table to appear. You don't have a choice about the pivot chart: Excel will put it on its own chart sheet, and not in a chart object that's embedded in a worksheet. (Refer to Figure 9-6 for an example of two embedded charts.)

After you click Finish, you see a new chart sheet rather than the worksheet with the skeleton of the pivot table on it. This is because in Step 1 of the PivotTable and PivotChart Wizard, you specified that you wanted a pivot chart.

To finish the chart that's initiated in Figure 9-14, take these steps:

1. **Click on Month in the Field List, hold down the mouse button, and drag down until your mouse pointer is over the Drop Category Fields Here, then release the mouse button.**
2. **Click on Branch in the Field List and, as you did with Month, drag it into the Drop Series Fields Here area.**

   Now you'll have a different data series in the pivot chart for each branch in your list.
3. **Click on Product Line in the Field List and drag it into the pivot chart just to the right of the Month button.**

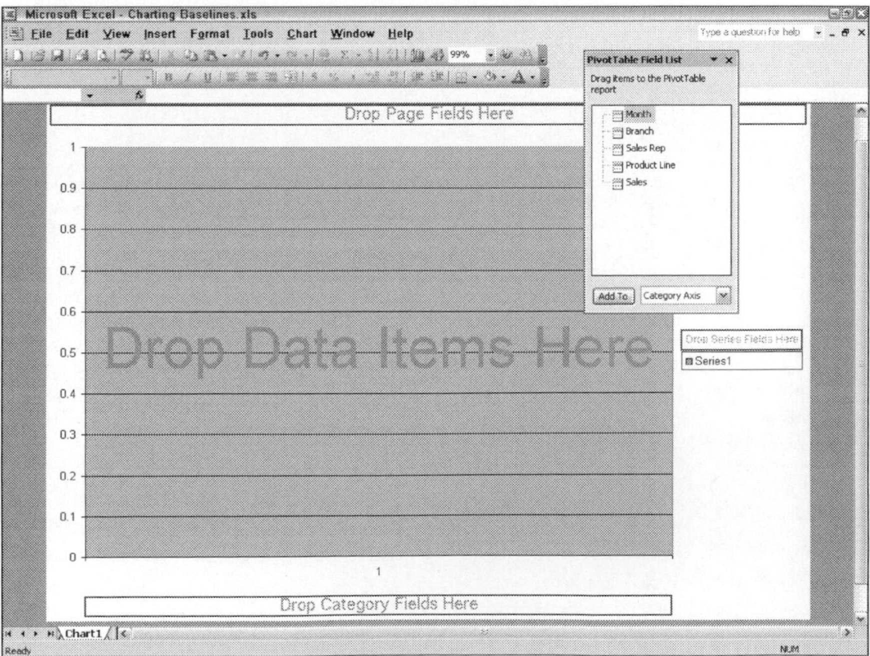

Figure 9-14: Here you can use the PivotTable Field List box to drag fields into the areas where you want them on the chart.

When you release the mouse button, you'll have established an *inner* field: Each value of Product Line will be repeated within each value of Month.

4. **Drag the Sales button from the Field List into the Drop Data Items Here area.**

   The result appears in Figure 9-15.

The pivot chart shown in Figure 9-15 is a Line chart. Unless you've taken special steps, the default pivot chart type is a Column chart. If you know that you want your pivot charts usually to be, say, Line charts, activate a chart and choose Chart ➪ Chart Type. Select the chart type and subtype you want, and then click Set As Default Chart. The next time you create a pivot chart from scratch, it will use the type and subtype you selected.

After you've created the pivot chart, if you think a different layout might make better visual sense, you can drag a field button from one area to another. For example, in Figure 9-15, you might try dragging the Branch button into the Category area along with Month, and the Product Line button from the Category area into the Series area. You might think that's an improvement (I don't), but whether or not you do, bear in mind that you *can* do so. That should be easy to bear in mind: It's why they call it a pivot chart.

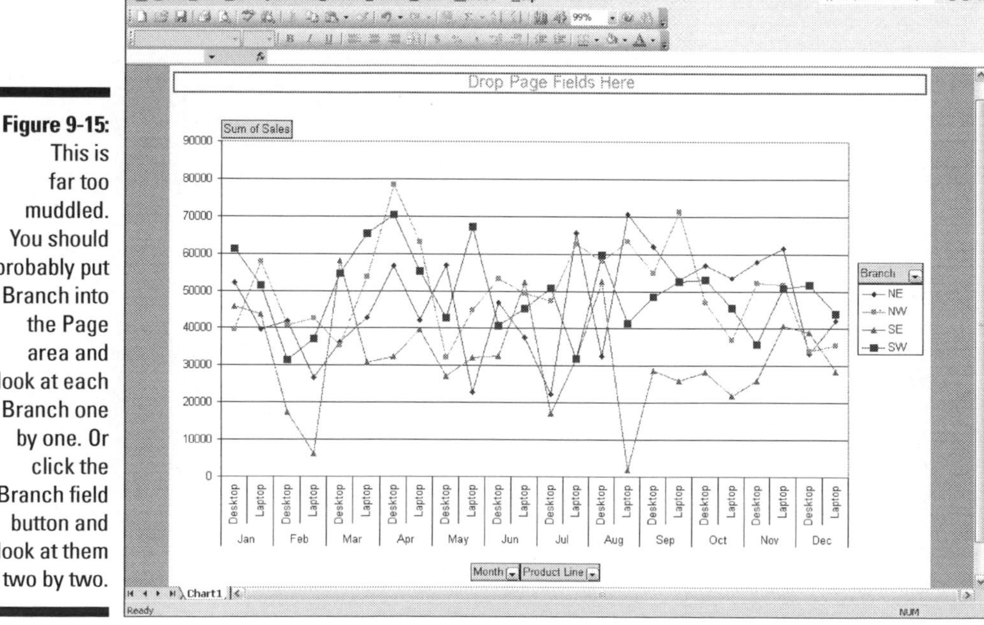

Figure 9-15: This is far too muddled. You should probably put Branch into the Page area and look at each Branch one by one. Or click the Branch field button and look at them two by two.

Take a look at the pivot table that accompanies the pivot chart. You can control where the pivot table is placed. It makes good sense to put it on the same worksheet as your list occupies, assuming you're using a list as the basis for the report, as I did in Figure 9-16.

Dealing with pivot chart annoyances

There are several frustrating aspects of pivot charts. Two of them might convince you to use a pivot table to summarize your baseline, and a conventional chart (as distinct from a pivot chart) to visually display the summaries in the pivot table.

Losing field buttons

Figure 9-17 shows a pivot chart that has no page field. Instead, it has a location where you can place a page field.

There is only one way to suppress the area reserved for a page field. Follow these steps:

1. **If the PivotTable toolbar is not visible, choose View⇨Toolbars, and select the check box next to the PivotTable menu item.**

Microsoft Excel - Charting Baselines.xls

Sum of Sales		Branch				
Month	Product Line	NE	NW	SE	SW	Grand Total
Jan	Desktop	52118.21133	39559.76915	45685.3081	61223.92499	198587.2136
	Laptop	39742.46073	57883.8754	43845.1056	51445.93387	192917.3756
Jan Total		91860.67207	97443.64455	89530.4137	112669.8589	391504.5892
Feb	Desktop	41926.37789	40703.17569	17360.73172	31330.32715	131320.6125
	Laptop	26574.74092	42514.55545	6159.051886	37247.43092	112495.7792
Feb Total		68501.11882	83217.73114	23519.78361	68577.75807	243816.3916
Mar	Desktop	36312.65933	35289.30791	58105.7048	54737.73192	184445.404
	Laptop	42836.0041	53863.01112	30873.00084	65329.82032	192901.8364
Mar Total		79148.66342	89152.31902	88978.70565	120067.5522	377347.2403
Apr	Desktop	56625.20461	78306.40344	32337.96824	70300.46327	237570.0396
	Laptop	42264.92592	63223.32703	39600.89264	55280.99578	200370.1414
Apr Total		98890.13053	141529.7305	71938.86088	125581.4591	437940.1809
May	Desktop	56958.29578	32071.75636	27066.51593	42902.48313	158999.0512
	Laptop	22697.47907	44915.05068	32225.6585	67149.40886	166987.5971
May Total		79655.77485	76986.80704	59292.17443	110051.892	325986.6483
Jun	Desktop	46841.22623	53304.23812	32519.71804	40729.27829	173394.4607
	Laptop	37563.29707	49445.83531	52504.96661	45342.62873	184856.7277
Jun Total		84404.5233	102750.0734	85024.68465	86071.90703	358251.1884
Jul	Desktop	22383.43876	47425.63445	17017.88979	50819.15515	137646.1181
	Laptop	65513.15815	62658.53125	31948.66772	31871.96081	191992.3179
Jul Total		87896.59691	110084.1657	48966.55751	82691.11595	329638.4361
Aug	Desktop	32693.92762	57993.08555	52710.03931	59717.04855	203114.101
	Laptop	70724.52844	63393.71664	1783.388128	41582.07961	177483.7128
Aug Total		103418.4561	121386.8022	54493.42744	101299.1282	380597.8138
Sep	Desktop	62068.22117	54865.45645	28764.49375	48493.51268	194191.684
	Laptop	53096.20147	71358.29673	25915.43373	52703.17089	203073.1028
Sep Total		115164.4226	126223.7532	54679.92748	101196.6836	397264.7869
Oct	Desktop	57045.10245	47019.5404	28306.45693	53096.6965	185467.7963
	Laptop	53576.95394	36829.00413	21782.05665	45655.99528	157844.01
Oct Total		110622.0564	83848.54453	50088.51357	98752.69178	343311.8063
Nov	Desktop	57876.28834	52151.34916	25927.34152	35712.13345	171667.1125
	Laptop	61570.8931	51812.24058	40711.68241	50810.79191	204905.608

Prepare a Pivot Chart

Figure 9-16: You can pivot this table by moving row and column buttons around, and the pivot chart will change in response.

2. **Select the pivot table.**
3. **Click the PivotTable menu on the PivotTable toolbar.**
4. **Click Hide PivotChart Field Buttons.**

   There's no OK button to click. As soon as you click Hide PivotChart Field Buttons, the page field area disappears. The menu command is a simple toggle, with a check mark to its left that shows whether the buttons are hidden or displayed.

Unfortunately, all the other field buttons on the pivot chart are hidden or displayed as well, and you may not want that. Figure 9-18 shows the result.

In Figure 9-18, notice that not only is the Page area gone, but also all field buttons. Those buttons are very useful for hiding or displaying certain values in the different fields. For example, Figure 9-19 shows how you hide or display the results for a sales rep by deselecting (to hide) or selecting (to show) a sales rep's check box.

But you don't have access to the field buttons if you arrange to hide the Page area.

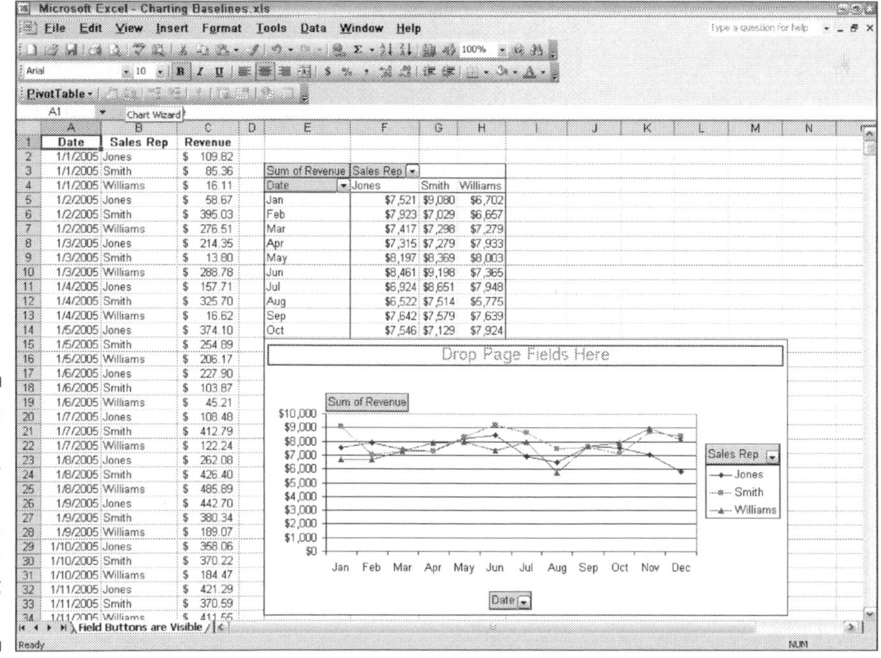

Figure 9-17: The area reserved for a page field adds no information to the pivot chart.

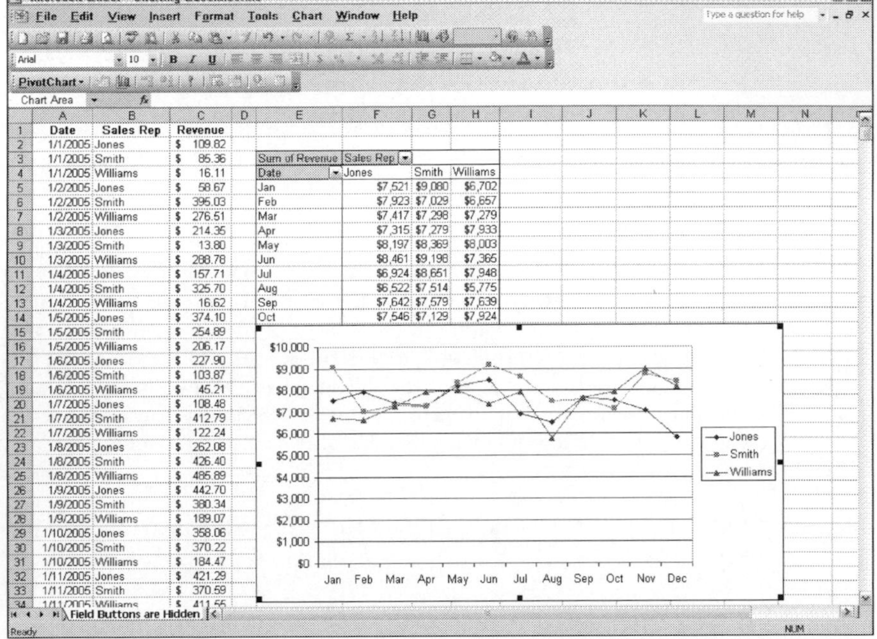

Figure 9-18: Getting rid of the field buttons and the page area leaves more room for the plot area.

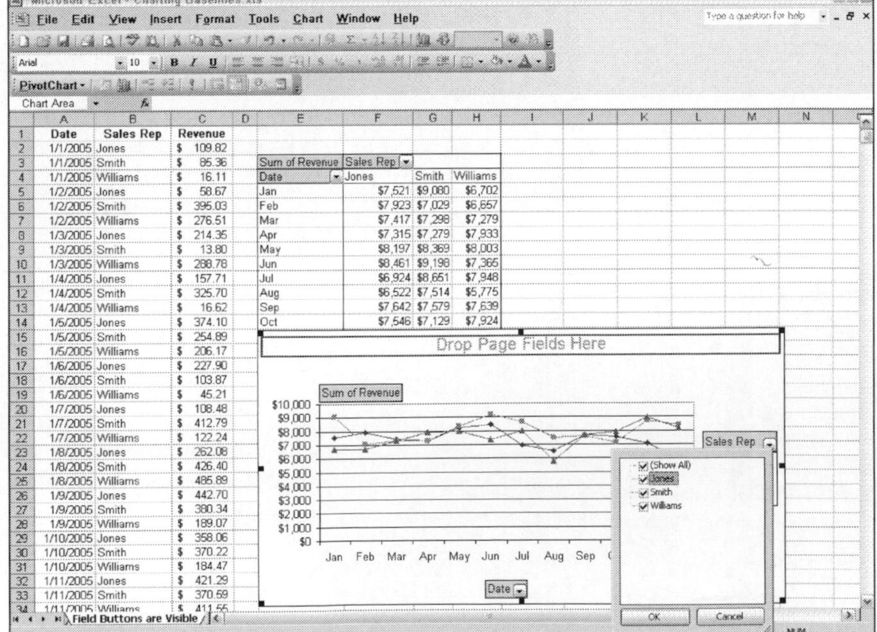

Figure 9-19: Click the drop-down arrow on a field button to see the values that are in the field.

Color me automatic

You've set up your pivot chart. It's a Line chart, with lines connecting the points in each series. You have three data series, just as shown in Figure 9-19. You overrode the automatic color for the lines and for the data markers in the third data series: the automatic color is yellow and seeing the yellow data series on the chart is difficult. So you clicked on the data series and changed the line and data marker color from yellow to green.

The chart looks a little crowded, so you use the drop-down arrow on the Sales Rep field button to hide the first data series. As soon as you've finished, the color of the third data series snaps back to yellow. You click the data series to select it and choose Format ➪ Selected Data Series. The Format Data Series dialog box, shown in Figure 9-20, pops up.

The only solution is to get your pivot chart laid out as you want it, and only then set the colors for the data series in the chart. Or use a standard chart by building the pivot table and using its row field values and its data field values to build a standard chart.

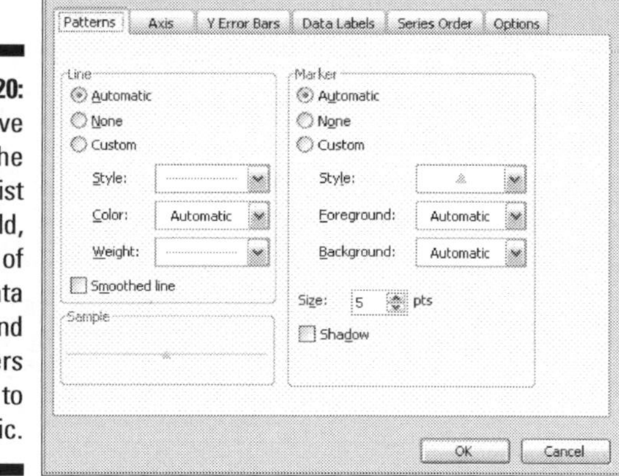

Figure 9-20: After you've changed the characteristics of a field, the color of the data lines and markers revert to Automatic.

Using Two Value Axes

There are times when you have put two data series in a chart, and they're on very different scales of measurement. One series can bury the other at the bottom of the chart.

For example, suppose your company builds and sells residential houses. You want to build a baseline of number of housing units you've sold per month, as well as the median regional price of single family detached dwellings each month. Figure 9-21 shows what that baseline might look like, along with a chart of the baseline.

The fact that one data series, Units Sold, gets no larger that 69, and the other data series, Median Regional Price, ranges from $270,569 to $275,970 means that you can't make out differences in either.

Excel charts provide a good solution with two value axes. If you run into a situation like this, follow these steps:

1. **Click on the chart to activate it.**
2. **Click on either data series to select it.**
3. **Choose Format ⇨ Selected Data Series.**
4. **Select the Axis tab and select the Secondary Axis radio button.**

   The Primary and Secondary Axis buttons are not available unless you have more than one data series in your chart.

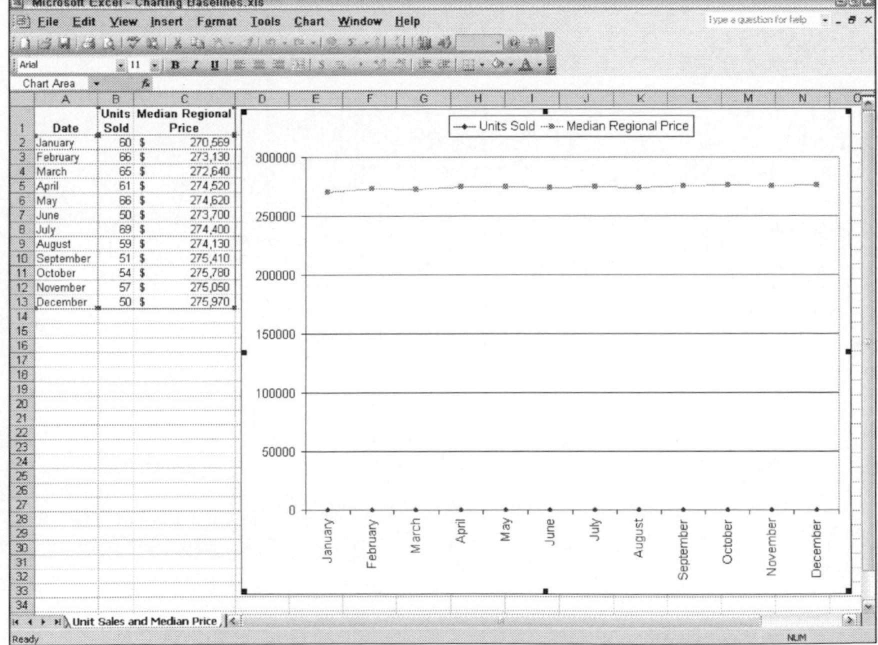

Figure 9-21: Both data series — housing units and median price — appear on the same Y axis scale.

5. **Click OK.**

   The result appears in Figure 9-22.

When you have two scales in one chart, labeling them can be helpful. After you've created the secondary scale, choose Chart ➪ Chart Options and select the Titles tab. Then supply a name for the Value (Y) Axis and the Second Value (Y) Axis.

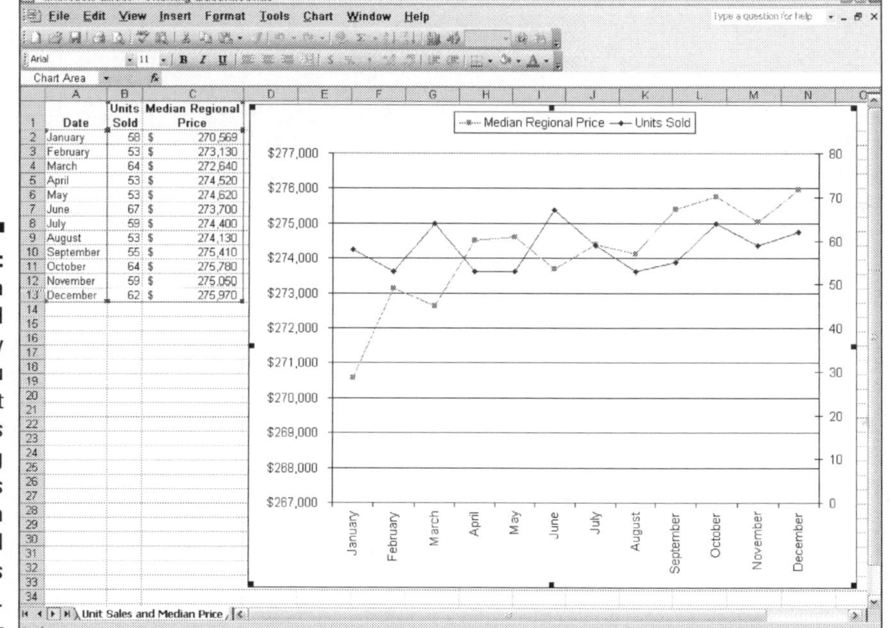

Figure 9-22: With a primary and a secondary scale, you can see that Units Sold is holding steady as Median Regional Price is rising.

Chapter 10

Forecasting with Excel's Analysis ToolPak

In This Chapter

- Getting the add-ins you need
- Working with the Moving Average, Smoothing, and Regression tools

Add-ins are collections of BASIC-like code — code that, fortunately, you never have to see. The idea behind add-ins is that they can extend Excel's reach, usually to do specialized tasks for you, such as forecasting using moving averages, exponential smoothing, and regression.

Because these tasks are not standard ones that Excel handles directly, such as inserting columns or constructing PivotTable reports, you have to make special provisions. In particular, this means installing add-ins, both onto your computer and into Excel. Installing add-ins is a straightforward process, but no one tells you how to do it. In this chapter, I remedy that situation.

The Analysis ToolPak (ATP) is an add-in, one of the few that is distributed with the retail version of Excel. It has several tools that help you do forecasting. After you've installed the ATP, you have choices. It's a tool pack, after all, so it has a bunch of tools in it, and you need to know which one to use when you're ready to make a forecast.

There are three basic methods of making quantitative forecasts: moving averages, exponential smoothing, and regression. (More-advanced methods use these three basic approaches as building blocks.) In this chapter, I give you some recommendations about how to choose between these methods to do your forecasts. There's no pat answer: Much depends on the nature of your baseline. But this chapter does offer you some guidance on what to pay attention to when you're choosing among the methods.

Installing Add-Ins

Add-ins are not at the top of the food chain at Microsoft. The tasks that add-ins perform may be important enough to automate, but they're not regarded as important enough to become a full-fledged part of the Excel application. (If add-ins did enjoy that degree of positive regard, there'd be a Data Analysis option at the bottom of Excel's Tools menu right out of the box, just like Data ➪ Sort or Data ➪ Filter.) Perhaps as a result, Microsoft doesn't include many add-ins with the retail version of Excel.

Developers other than Microsoft *do* offer lots of add-ins. A Web search returned nearly half a million pages containing the words *Excel* and *add-in.* Lots of these pages offer add-ins for sale. If you know how to code using Visual Basic for Applications and have a copy of Excel, you can create an add-in and post it for sale on a Web site. If you're looking for some sort of specialized capability that Excel doesn't offer, but that it could, check out the Web — but be prepared to get something less than what you're looking for.

First, you have to get the add-in onto your computer. Then you have to get the add-in into Excel. The following sections describe how to do that for the ATP.

Off the CD, onto the C: drive

Do a quick check, first, by making sure that the ATP isn't installed already. Start Excel and choose the Tools menu. If you see a Data Analysis item at the bottom of the Tools menu, you almost certainly have the ATP installed already. (I weasel with "almost certainly" because with add-ins you always run a certain risk that someone has installed something that isn't the ATP, but that nevertheless puts the Data Analysis item in the Tools menu.)

If you don't see the Data Analysis menu item, the add-in may still be on your computer. Choose Tools ➪ Add-Ins. If you see Analysis ToolPak in the Add-Ins Available list box, select the check box next to Analysis ToolPak and click OK. You may see a message that the Analysis ToolPak can't be found, and asking if you want to delete it from the list. If this happens, the best thing to do is to remove it from the list and reinstall it following the steps in this section.

If you think you may want to use some of the special functions in the ATP *in your own VBA code,* select both the Analysis ToolPak and the Analysis ToolPak – VBA check boxes. Otherwise, select just the Analysis ToolPak check box.

If you don't see that message, you should be okay. Check to see that you now have a Data Analysis item at the bottom of the Tools menu. If you do, you're ready to go. If you still don't find a Data Analysis, install the ATP from the CD by taking these steps:

1. **Put the CD with either Office or Excel in your CD drive.**

   If AutoRun is enabled on your computer, the setup routine will start automatically. If it doesn't start, use My Computer or Windows Explorer to find `Setup.exe` on the CD, and double-click `Setup.exe`.

   You'll see the window shown in Figure 10-1.

2. **Click the Add or Remove Features radio button, and click Next.**

   A new window appears.

3. **Click the plus sign beside the Microsoft Office Excel icon to display the items available under Excel, as shown in Figure 10-2.**

4. **In the window shown in Figure 10-2, click the plus sign beside the Add-Ins icon.**

   The available add-ins appear (see Figure 10-3).

5. **Click the down arrow beside the Analysis ToolPak icon.**

   Your choices appear in Figure 10-4.

6. **Select Run from My Computer.**

7. **I recommend that you repeat steps 4, 5, and 6 for the Solver (refer to Figure 10-3).**

   The Solver can come in handy in a number of forecasting situations, such as choosing a smoothing constant in exponential smoothing.

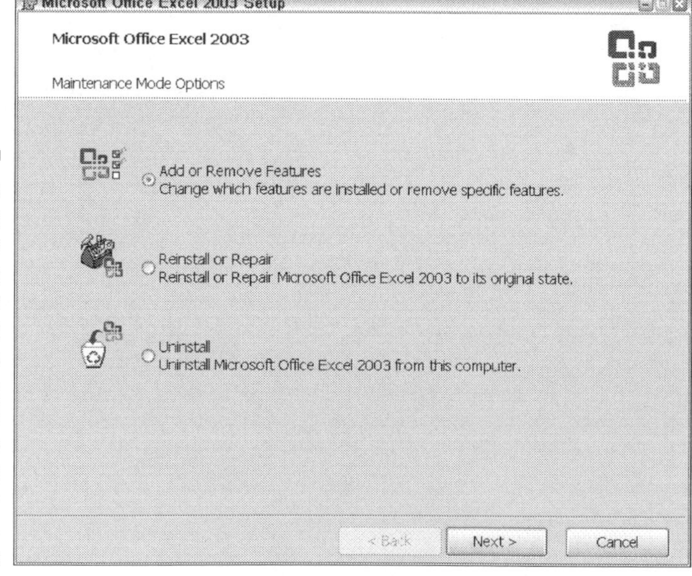

Figure 10-1: This window looks slightly different if you're installing Office, and if you're arranging a new installation.

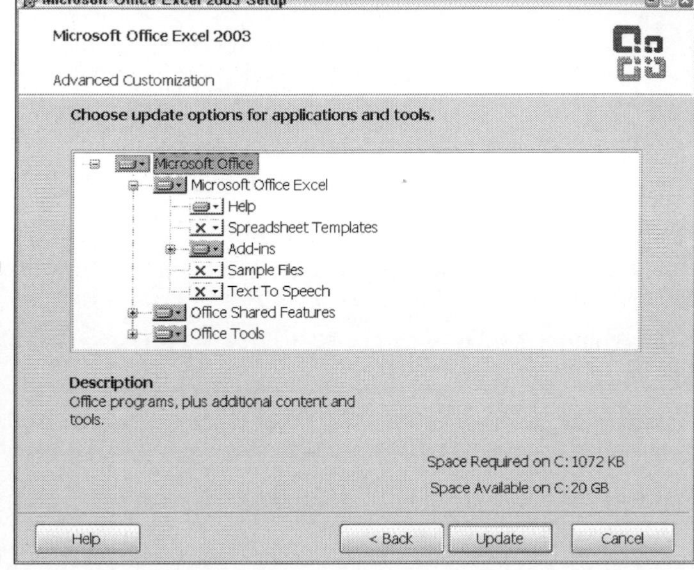

Figure 10-2: The x's mean that the feature is not currently installed on the computer.

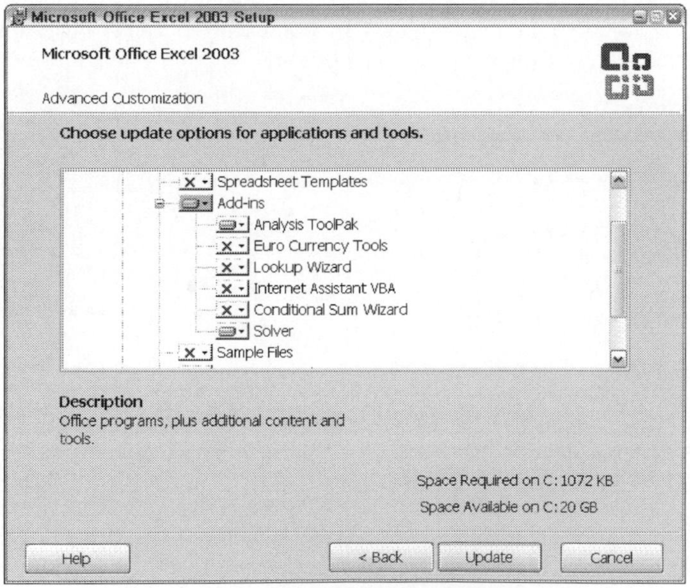

Figure 10-3: Unless you have very specific require-ments, I recommend that you install only the Analysis ToolPak and the Solver.

8. **Click Update.**

   The setup routine takes over and installs on your computer the add-ins that you've selected, where they become accessible to Excel.

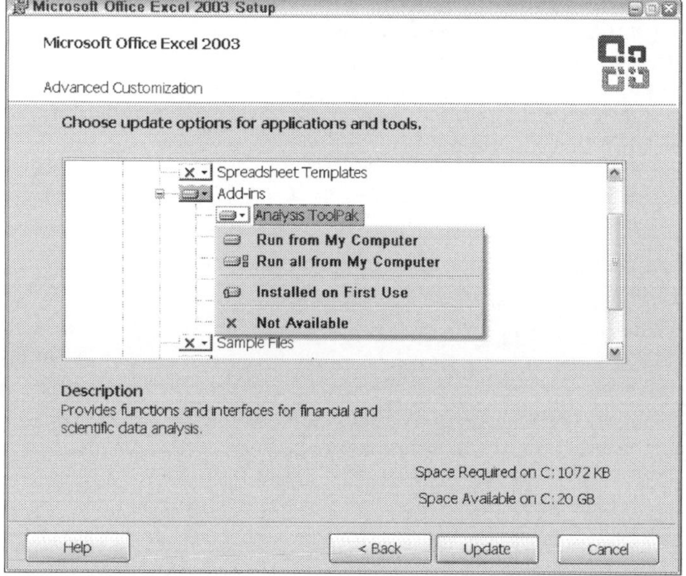

Figure 10-4: Your options for installing the Analysis ToolPak.

From the C: drive to Excel

If you didn't close Excel during the setup routine, do so now, and then start it again. This forces Excel to see if the ATP add-in is available, and if it is then Excel puts it in the Add-Ins list box. So, take these steps:

1. **Choose Tools➪Add-Ins.**

   The Add-Ins dialog box, shown in Figure 10-5, appears.

2. **Select the check box next to the Analysis ToolPak add-in.**

   Select the Analysis ToolPak – VBA add-in if you expect to use a function from the ToolPak in your VBA code. Otherwise, just select the Analysis ToolPak check box.

3. **Click OK.**

   You should now find the Data Analysis item at the bottom of the Tools menu, and Excel will load the add-in every time you start Excel, until and unless you decide to uninstall the Analysis ToolPak either from Excel or from your computer.

There are still some very old computers around, some even running Windows 95. Those older computers just aren't fast enough to make the process of installing add-ins a smooth one — it took a frustratingly long time to register the add-in. And the process of opening Excel, which required opening the installed add-in, was slowed down as well. If this is still happening to you, you have yet another reason to upgrade. If you don't want to upgrade, and you don't want to spend five minutes waiting, your best bet is to uninstall the add-ins and refer to Chapter 12.

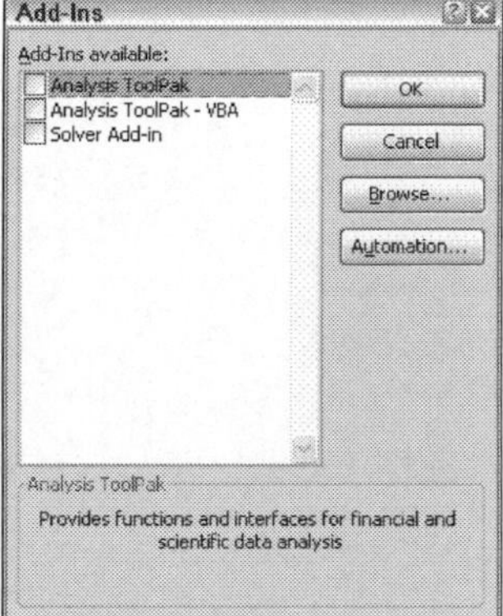

Figure 10-5: The Add-Ins dialog box.

Using Moving Averages

After you have the ATP installed and you've made it available to Excel, you can select any one of its analysis tools and run that analysis on the input data that you supply. In the world of forecasting, that means the baseline that you've gathered and structured properly on a worksheet.

The first tool you might consider — if only because it's the easiest to use and understand — is the Moving Average tool. As always with the ATP, begin by choosing Tools ⇨ Data Analysis. In the Analysis Tools list box, select Moving Average and click OK.

The Moving Average dialog box, shown in Figure 10-6, appears. You can find instructions on how to use this dialog box in Chapter 13.

Moving day: Getting from here to there

As easy as moving averages are to set up and understand, you take on an additional responsibility when you decide to forecast with them. The issue is how many time periods from your baseline you should include in each moving average.

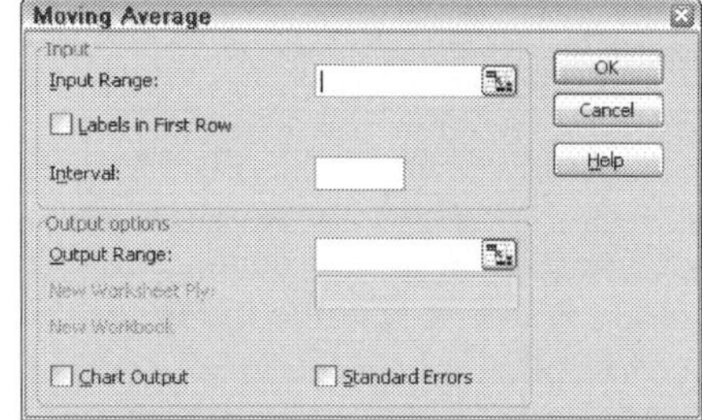

Figure 10-6: The Interval is the number of actuals from your baseline to use in each moving average.

It may go without saying, but I'll say it anyway: Use the same number of actual observations in calculating each moving average. If the first moving average that you have Excel calculate uses three periods from the baseline, then all the moving averages in your forecast use three periods.

You want to select the right number of periods:

- If you use too few, the forecasts will respond to random shocks in the baseline, when what you're after is to smooth out the random errors and focus on the real drivers of your sales results.
- If you use too many, the forecasts lag behind real, persistent changes in the level of the baseline — maybe too far for you to react effectively.

When you decide to use the Moving Average tool — or, more generally, to use moving averages regardless of whether you use the ATP or enter the formulas yourself — you're taking a position on the effect of recent baseline values versus the effect of more distant baseline values.

Suppose you have a baseline that extends from January 2005 to December 2005, and you use a three-month moving average of sales results for your forecasts. The forecast for January 2006 would be the average of the results from October, November, and December 2005. That forecast is dependent entirely on the final quarter of 2005 and is mathematically independent of the first three quarters of 2005.

What if instead you had chosen a six-month moving average? Then the forecast for January 2006 would be based on the average of July through December 2005. It would be entirely dependent on the second half of 2005, and the first half of 2005 would have no direct influence on the January 2006 forecast.

It could well be that either of these situations — or another one, such as a two-month moving average — is exactly what you want. For example, you may need your forecast to emphasize recent results. That emphasis can be especially important if you suspect that a recent event, such as a significant change in your product line, will have an effect on sales.

On the other hand, you may not want to emphasize recent sales results too much. Emphasizing recent sales results can obscure what's going on long term with your baseline. If you're not sure how much to emphasize recent results, you have a couple of good options:

- **Experiment with different numbers of time periods to make up your moving averages.** This approach is often best. A way of evaluating different moving average lengths is in Chapter 15; it's tailored for exponential smoothing, but it's easily applied to moving averages.
- **Use exponential smoothing, which uses the entire baseline to get a forecast but gives the most weight to the most recent baseline value.** Exponential smoothing gives a little less weight to the next-to-last baseline value and so on all the way back to the first baseline value, which has the least amount of influence on the next forecast. (See "Using Exponential Smoothing," later in this chapter, for more information.)

Moving averages and stationary baselines

Moving averages are well suited to *stationary baselines* (baselines whose levels do not generally increase or decrease over a long period of time). You can use moving averages with baselines that trend up or down, but you should usually detrend them first (see Chapter 17 for more information) or else use one of the more complicated moving-average models, which I don't cover in this book.

How do you tell a stationary baseline from one that is trending up or down? One way is to look at it. Figure 10-7 has an example. The baseline in Figure 10-7 certainly looks stationary. It has spikes and peaks and valleys, but overall the baseline doesn't appear to trend up or down.

The problem with just looking at the baseline is that sometimes it's not entirely clear whether it's stationary or trended. What do you think about the baseline in Figure 10-8? Looking at the chart, it's hard to say whether the baseline is stationary. It might be, but then again it might really be drifting gradually down. You can make a quick test by checking the correlation between date and revenue. (See Chapter 4 for details.)

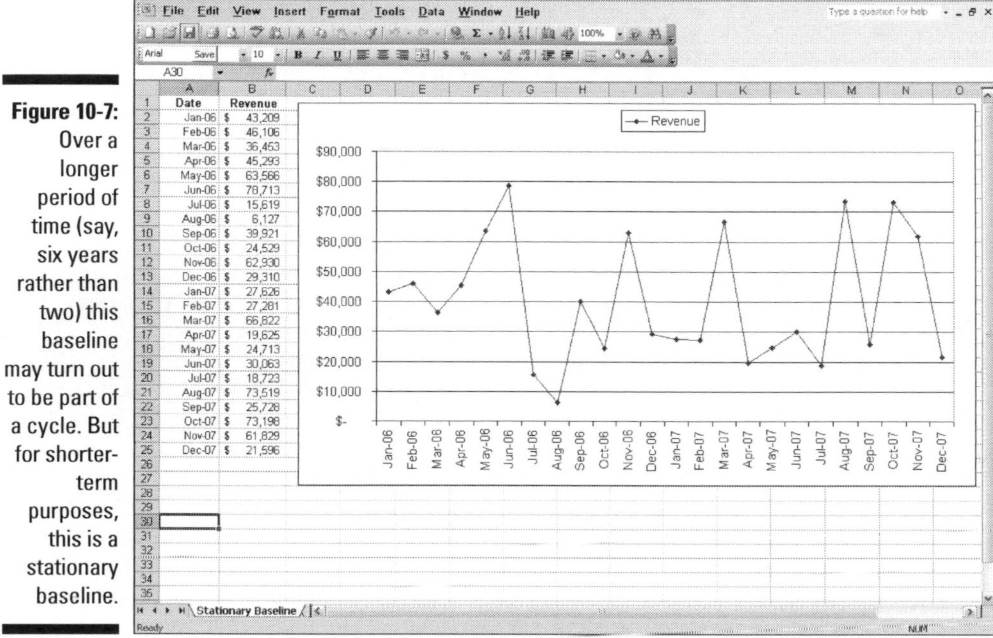

Date	Revenue
Jan-06	$ 43,209
Feb-06	$ 46,106
Mar-06	$ 36,453
Apr-06	$ 45,293
May-06	$ 63,566
Jun-06	$ 78,713
Jul-06	$ 15,619
Aug-06	$ 6,127
Sep-06	$ 39,921
Oct-06	$ 24,529
Nov-06	$ 62,930
Dec-06	$ 29,310
Jan-07	$ 27,626
Feb-07	$ 27,281
Mar-07	$ 66,822
Apr-07	$ 19,625
May-07	$ 24,713
Jun-07	$ 30,063
Jul-07	$ 18,723
Aug-07	$ 73,519
Sep-07	$ 25,728
Oct-07	$ 73,198
Nov-07	$ 61,829
Dec-07	$ 21,596

Figure 10-7: Over a longer period of time (say, six years rather than two) this baseline may turn out to be part of a cycle. But for shorter-term purposes, this is a stationary baseline.

Date	Revenue
Jan-06	$ 41,445
Feb-06	$ 71,246
Mar-06	$ 67,976
Apr-06	$ 54,419
May-06	$ 72,781
Jun-06	$ 59,110
Jul-06	$ 47,046
Aug-06	$ 34,786
Sep-06	$ 33,585
Oct-06	$ 38,856
Nov-06	$ 49,098
Dec-06	$ 33,794
Jan-07	$ 22,813
Feb-07	$ 28,390
Mar-07	$ 38,281
Apr-07	$ 45,271
May-07	$ 26,458
Jun-07	$ 30,572
Jul-07	$ 30,947
Aug-07	$ 35,609
Sep-07	$ 35,414
Oct-07	$ 56,527
Nov-07	$ 37,308
Dec-07	$ 43,562

Figure 10-8: This baseline looks as though it may be gently heading down. Adding a trendline to it can help you interpret what's going on.

Using Exponential Smoothing

The prior section on moving averages implies that you can solve the problem of how many baseline values to include in a moving average by using exponential smoothing. And that's true, as far as it goes: You don't have to make that decision, because the entire baseline is involved to one degree or another.

Take, for example, the forecast for December. It may depend 30 percent on November's actual, 20 percent on October's actual, 15 percent on September's actual, and so on all the way back to the start of the baseline. The older the actual, the less its influence on the next forecast.

But you're saddled with a new problem: How much do you want the most recent actual to influence the subsequent forecast? The best way to make this decision — at the very least, a preliminary decision — is to try different amounts of influence and see how much error each amount causes.

There's a lot packed into that last sentence. Seeing its meaning is easier in a worksheet than in words. Figure 10-9 has an example.

		Smoothing Constant					
Date	Revenue	0.3	0.4	0.5	0.6	0.7	0.8
Jan-06	$ 41,175	#N/A	#N/A	#N/A	#N/A	#N/A	#N/A
Feb-06	$ 47,504	$ 41,175	$ 41,175	$ 41,175	$ 41,175	$ 41,175	$ 41,175
Mar-06	$ 45,632	$ 43,074	$ 43,707	$ 44,340	$ 44,972	$ 45,605	$ 46,238
Apr-06	$ 59,351	$ 43,841	$ 44,477	$ 44,986	$ 45,368	$ 45,624	$ 45,753
May-06	$ 78,320	$ 48,494	$ 50,426	$ 52,168	$ 53,758	$ 55,233	$ 56,632
Jun-06	$ 98,703	$ 57,442	$ 61,584	$ 65,244	$ 68,495	$ 71,394	$ 73,983
Jul-06	$ 28,346	$ 69,820	$ 76,432	$ 81,974	$ 86,620	$ 90,511	$ 93,759
Aug-06	$ 20,000	$ 57,378	$ 57,197	$ 55,160	$ 51,656	$ 46,995	$ 41,429
Sep-06	$ 29,347	$ 46,165	$ 42,318	$ 37,580	$ 32,662	$ 28,099	$ 24,286
Oct-06	$ 20,898	$ 41,119	$ 37,130	$ 33,463	$ 30,673	$ 28,972	$ 28,335
Nov-06	$ 49,398	$ 35,053	$ 30,637	$ 27,180	$ 24,808	$ 23,320	$ 22,385
Dec-06	$ 24,830	$ 39,356	$ 38,141	$ 38,289	$ 39,562	$ 41,574	$ 43,995
Jan-07	$ 21,218	$ 34,998	$ 32,817	$ 31,560	$ 30,723	$ 29,854	$ 28,663
Feb-07	$ 21,122	$ 30,864	$ 28,177	$ 26,389	$ 25,020	$ 23,808	$ 22,707
Mar-07	$ 48,695	$ 27,942	$ 25,365	$ 23,755	$ 22,681	$ 21,928	$ 21,439
Apr-07	$ 20,000	$ 34,168	$ 34,691	$ 36,225	$ 38,290	$ 40,665	$ 43,244
May-07	$ 20,000	$ 29,917	$ 28,815	$ 28,113	$ 27,316	$ 26,200	$ 24,649
Jun-07	$ 20,901	$ 26,942	$ 25,289	$ 24,056	$ 22,926	$ 21,860	$ 20,930
Jul-07	$ 23,081	$ 25,130	$ 23,534	$ 22,479	$ 21,711	$ 21,189	$ 20,907
Aug-07	$ 70,793	$ 24,515	$ 23,353	$ 22,780	$ 22,533	$ 22,513	$ 22,646
Sep-07	$ 45,690	$ 38,398	$ 42,329	$ 46,786	$ 51,489	$ 56,309	$ 61,163
Oct-07	$ 79,861	$ 40,586	$ 43,673	$ 46,238	$ 48,010	$ 48,876	$ 48,785
Nov-07	$ 68,942	$ 52,369	$ 58,149	$ 63,050	$ 67,121	$ 70,566	$ 73,646
Dec-07	$ 34,473	$ 57,341	$ 62,466	$ 65,996	$ 68,213	$ 69,429	$ 69,883
Jan-08 Forecast:		$ 50,480	$ 51,269	$ 50,234	$ 47,969	$ 44,960	$ 41,555
Error Summary:		$ 22,999	$ 22,905	$ 22,936	$ 23,070	$ 23,295	$ 23,620

Figure 10-9: This sort of analysis is much easier to set up if you enter the formulas yourself, instead of relying on the ATP.

These components of an exponential smoothing analysis are in Figure 10-9:

- The baseline itself in cells A3:B26. (Here I'm using the more relaxed usage of the term *baseline,* to include both the actual sales results and the associated dates.)
- Several different constants, ranging from 0.3 to 0.8, in cells C2:H2.
- The constants in row 2 are used to create the forecasts in cells C4:H27. Each column from C to H contains a forecast that is based on the constant at the top of that column. You can see exactly how to create the forecasts using the constants in Chapter 15.
- The #N/A values in row 3 are due to the fact that, without earlier baseline data, you can't make a forecast for January 2006.
- The values in row 29 are measures of the overall amount of error in the forecasts. For example, there's an error associated with the forecast value in cell C5: it's the difference between the forecast in cell C5 and the actual value observed for March 2006, or $2,558.

The errors in forecasting — the differences between the forecasts and the actuals — are massaged and totaled until you wind up with a summary of the errors given a particular smoothing constant. That summary appears for each smoothing constant in C29:H29. You can also find the method for getting these summaries in Chapter 15.

One primary goal of forecasting is to minimize the errors of your forecasts: All other things being equal, the closer your forecast comes to the actual result the better. In Figure 10-9, the smallest measure of total forecast error is in cell D29: $22,905. So, you'd use the constant that created the forecasts in that column: the value in cell D2, or 0.4.

This technique is useful not only for deciding how large a constant to use, but also for deciding between using moving averages or exponential smoothing. You can calculate the error summary for both a moving average of a certain length and exponential smoothing with a given constant. Then select the approach that provides the smaller measure of forecast error.

Instead of creating a series of forecasts, as in columns C through H of Figure 10-9, you can also use the Solver to help you choose the best constant. (This is one reason I recommend, earlier in this chapter, in the "Off the CD, onto the C: drive" section, that you install the Solver add-in along with the ATP.) Although Excel's built-in Goal Seek tool is another possibility, you can establish better control using the Solver. You would have the Solver minimize the forecast error summary by selecting the optimum value of the constant for the smoothing forecast.

You can find step-by-step instructions for using the Exponential Smoothing dialog box in Chapter 15. As an overview, you start the whole process by taking these steps:

1. **Choose Tools ➪ Data Analysis.**
2. **Select Exponential Smoothing in the Analysis Tools list box.**
3. **Click OK.**

   The Exponential Smoothing dialog box, shown in Figure 10-10, appears.

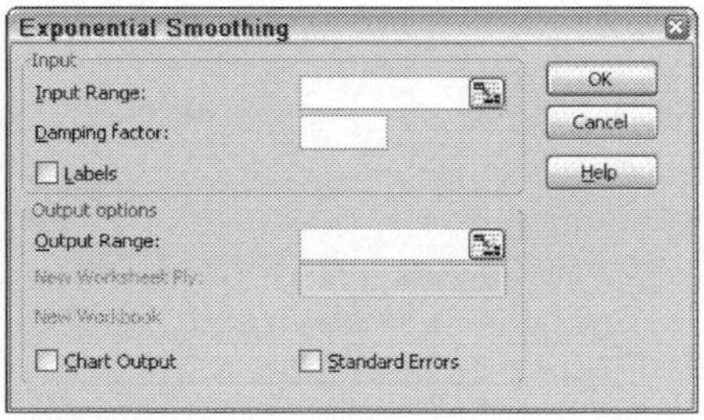

Figure 10-10: If you include a label, such as *Revenue,* at the top of the Input Range, select the Labels check box to inform Excel not to try to forecast from that label.

Here's some brief information on the controls shown in Figure 10-10:

- For the Input Range, drag through the range where you have your baseline. It should include the actual results only, in one column only. In other words, if you have an adjacent column of dates as in Figure 10-9, *don't* include it.
- The Damping Factor is 1.0 minus the smoothing constant. I know, that's irritating, but you have to make the best of it.
- In contrast to other ATP tools, Exponential Smoothing does not offer you the option of putting the output on a different worksheet, or in a different workbook, than the Input Range.
- If you want to chart the actuals and the forecasts, select the Chart Output check box. As shown in Chapter 15, though, you can do a better job of charting if you do it yourself.
- Don't bother selecting the Standard Errors check box.

Using the Regression Tool

Suppose you have one or more other variables in your baseline, along with your sales results, that you have reason to believe may be associated with those results. Neither moving averages nor exponential smoothing provides for using those other variables: Each of these approaches relies on using the forecast variable as its own predictor.

In contrast, an approach termed *regression* is designed to make use of these other variables in forecasting future values. The process of regression is not as intuitive as moving averages or exponential smoothing, and some people avoid it for this reason.

If you have additional data, at least give some thought to using it. Some things to think about:

- **Sales results are often related to the time period in which the sales were made.** That is, as your baseline moves forward in time, the sales results may improve (with a maturing product) or decline (with a mature product). If the sales results are stable over time, knowledge of the date of sale won't do you much good.
- **You need to know future values of the additional variables.** Time period is easy: You know what the next month and year are going to be. Finding out how many sales reps you'll have next month or next quarter, or how many dollars your company will put into advertising and other marketing programs, may be more difficult. If you can't get your hands on that future data in the form of plans or budgeted amounts, then you won't be able to use them to forecast sales.
- **You need a longer baseline than is absolutely necessary with moving averages or exponential smoothing.** The very mathematics of regression requires that you have more time periods in your baseline than variables in the forecast equation. Some forecasters are willing to use regression with as few as 10 periods times the number of predictor variables — so, using 3 predictors, a baseline that's at least 30 periods long. I feel much more comfortable with a baseline that has 30 time periods for each predictor variable, but I admit that baselines that long can be difficult to come by.
- **Regression does not work well with baselines that have sudden and prolonged changes in level.** Suppose your baseline chugs along at $500,000 in monthly revenue for a couple of years and then (perhaps because of a new product launch) jumps to $1,000,000 per month and stays at roughly that level. Regression has a difficult time dealing with that situation (it *can,* but the necessary management is beyond the scope I adopt here).

You can find much more detail on using regression for forecasting in Chapters 11 and 16. To get a feel for what you need to provide, a brief tour of the ATP's Regression tool is a reasonable place to start.

Suppose you have a worksheet laid out as in Figure 10-11. Here are two points to note about the layout in Figure 10-11:

- There are three variables in the baseline — Sales Results, which you want to forecast, and Date and Sales Reps, which you want to use to make the next forecast.
- You can't see them all in the figure, but there are 40 time periods in the baseline. A baseline this long is probably sufficient to support a regression analysis with two predictor variables.

To get things going, take these steps:

1. **Choose Tools ⇨ Data Analysis.**
2. **Scroll down the Analysis Tools list box and select Regression.**
3. **Click OK.**

   The Regression dialog box, shown in Figure 10-12, appears.

	A	B	C
1	Date	Sales Reps	Sales Results
2	1/1/2004	9	$ 394,111
3	2/1/2004	12	$ 486,928
4	3/3/2004	12	$ 453,364
5	4/3/2004	12	$ 410,020
6	5/4/2004	11	$ 408,268
7	6/4/2004	11	$ 414,451
8	7/5/2004	13	$ 421,922
9	8/5/2004	12	$ 418,014
10	9/5/2004	8	$ 398,349
11	10/6/2004	13	$ 431,467
12	11/6/2004	9	$ 428,235
13	12/7/2004	10	$ 459,357
14	1/7/2005	11	$ 432,037
15	2/7/2005	9	$ 441,557
16	3/10/2005	8	$ 402,219
17	4/10/2005	12	$ 416,118
18	5/11/2005	13	$ 407,462
19	6/11/2005	12	$ 475,738
20	7/12/2005	11	$ 455,049
21	8/12/2005	10	$ 471,642
22	9/12/2005	12	$ 455,037
23	10/13/2005	10	$ 483,507
24	11/13/2005	10	$ 412,324
25	12/14/2005	9	$ 445,317
26	1/14/2006	12	$ 440,194
27	2/14/2006	9	$ 482,063
28	3/17/2006	8	$ 436,424
29	4/17/2006	13	$ 419,745
30	5/18/2006	8	$ 417,446
31	6/18/2006	10	$ 491,626
32	7/19/2006	12	$ 469,181
33	8/19/2006	8	$ 499,824
34	9/19/2006	12	$ 482,901

Figure 10-11: Be sure to put your predictor variables (here, Date and Sales Reps) in contiguous ranges.

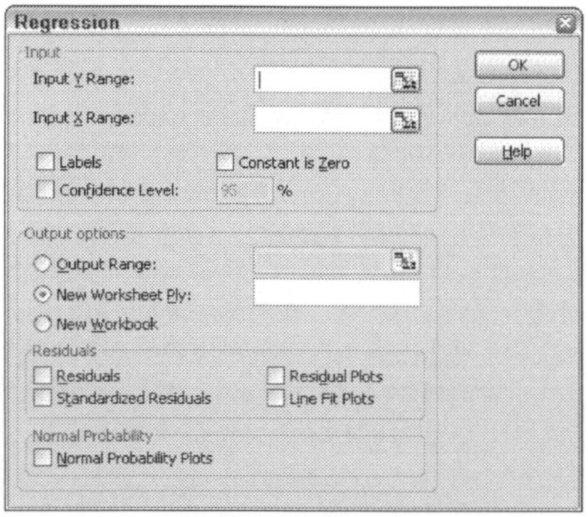

Figure 10-12: The Regression dialog box.

4. **Supply the address of a worksheet range in the Input Y Range box.**

   This range must occupy a single column. For the baseline in Figure 10-12, you'd enter **$C$1:$C$41**. (You can also just click in the Input Y Range box and drag through the range on the worksheet.)

5. **Supply the address of a worksheet range in the Input X Range box.**

   This is your predictor variables. This range need not have just one column, although it could if you have just one predictor variable.

6. **If you included the variable labels at the top of each column in the Input Range boxes, select the Labels check box.**
7. **Do *not* select the Constant Is Zero check box.**
8. **If you add a confidence level, it shows up in the output *in addition* to the default 95%.**

   If you later want to delete the level you added, you'll need to do so specifically in the Regression dialog box by clearing the check box.

9. **Choose an output option — that is, where you want the Regression tool's output to appear.**
10. **If you chose Output Range, click in the box to its right and fill in a cell address. If you chose New Workbook Ply, click in the box to its right and fill in the name for the new *ply* (an old term for a worksheet).**
11. **Click OK.**

Chapter 11 has information about the charts that you can create from this dialog box.

All you need to perform a regression forecast is a baseline with one forecast variable, such as sales revenue or units sold, and one or more predictor variables. The ATP refers to the forecast variable as the *y* variable, and you supply the worksheet range that has the baseline for the forecast variable in the Input Y Range box.

The variable that you want to use as a predictor is the *x* variable, and its worksheet address goes into the Input X Range box. Keep in mind that you can use more than one predictor variable, but if you do, the columns that the predictors occupy must be contiguous: They should be in adjacent columns, and their first and last values should be in the same rows. All variables (forecast and predictors) must have the same number of baseline periods.

This usage — referring to the forecast variable as Y — is, I'm happy to report, consistent with the syntax of the LINEST worksheet function. The LINEST function refers to known Y values as the values for the forecast variable, and to known X values as the values to use for the predictor variable(s). Bearing this in mind can be helpful when you read Chapters 12 and 16.

Chapter 11

Basing Forecasts on Regression

In This Chapter

- Knowing whether to use the Regression tool
- Getting familiar with the Regression Tool
- Avoiding common misunderstandings about the Regression tool

Regression is a standard technique in forecasting, whether sales revenues or sunspots. (And yes, meteorologists and astronomers have used regression for years in forecasting sunspots.)

This chapter introduces forecasting with regression. The idea is to get your hands on one variable (say, the price you charge for your product) that is strongly related to another variable (say, your unit sales), and then use what you know about the first variable to forecast what will happen to the second variable.

That's simple regression: One variable forecasts another. You can also make use of multiple regression, where you use more than one variable to forecast another. A typical example is to use both product price and the index of consumer confidence to forecast sales. Within limits, you can use as many predictors as you can lay your hands on — often (but not always) the more predictors you use, the more accurate your forecast.

Deciding to Use the Regression Tool

Regression sounds a lot more complicated than it really is — one of the problems is that the very word *regression* sounds intimidating. Truth to tell, regression *can* be intimidating, but more often than not it's really pretty straightforward.

Let's get a basis. You're taller now than you were when you were 5 years old. Up to a point, you can forecast a person's height if you know how old the person is. I say "up to a point" because, eventually, people quit getting taller, but, alas, not older.

Here's an example. Up to the age of 18 or so, you can predict with reasonable accuracy how tall a person is, given that you know the person's age. Even if you don't know whether the person is male or female, this equation is a pretty fair guide:

```
(0.14 * Age In Months) + 38
```

In words, multiply someone's age in months times 0.14, and add 38. This will give you a pretty fair approximation of that person's height in inches. At least until the person reaches 18 years of age.

This is what regression is all about. It's a way to develop an equation that predicts one variable (height, poppy-seed sales, sunspots, whatever) from another variable (age, poppy-seed advertising, calendar year, whatever).

The idea is to use not just one but two variables. If you were interested in forecasting height from age, you would get hold of both the height and the age of a bunch of kids. Both the heights and ages would be, in a real sense, baselines. You'd then know how tall a child was at a given age. Figure 11-1 shows a couple of baselines. Figure 11-2 shows the chart that results from the data in the baselines.

	A	B
1	Age	Height
2	210	65.5
3	210	62
4	206	68.3
5	206	69.5
6	203	66.5
7	200	71
8	197	61.5
9	197	64.8
10	196	64.5
11	194	65.3
12	193	59.8
13	193	66.3
14	193	72
15	193	67.8
16	191	62.5
17	191	65.3
18	191	63.3
19	190	66.8
20	190	56.8
21	189	64.3
22	189	67
23	189	65
24	189	66.3
25	188	67.3
26	188	63.3
27	188	71
28	188	65.8
29	186	66.5
30	186	57.8
31	186	57
32	186	63.5
33	186	66
34	185	63.3
35	185	60

Figure 11-1: Judging the relationship between age and size just by looking at the numbers is difficult.

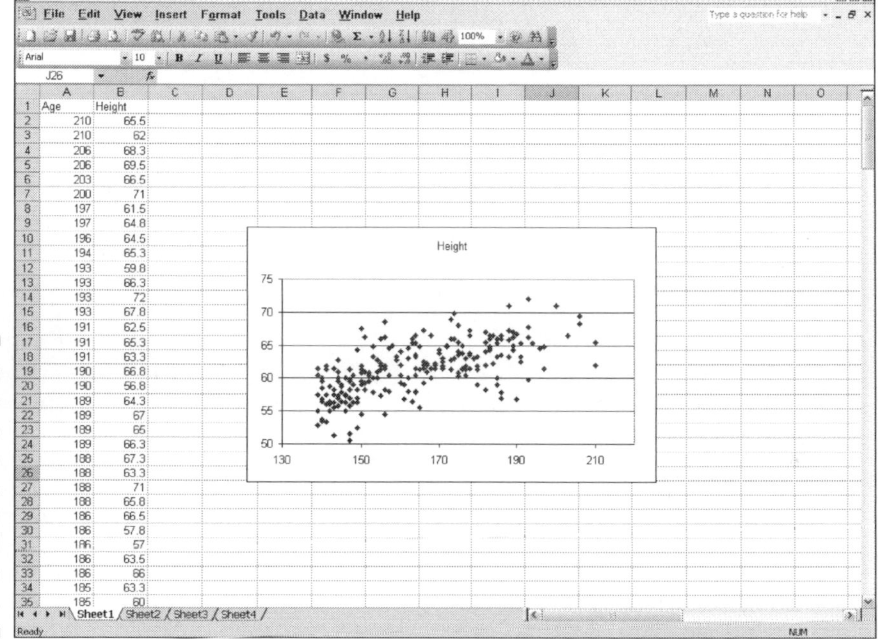

Figure 11-2: After you've got the relationship charted, telling what's going on is much easier.

Now, here's what Excel can do for you if you let it. If you haven't already installed the Analysis ToolPak on your computer and into Excel, turn to Chapter 10 for step-by-step instructions.

After you have the Analysis ToolPak installed on your computer and in Excel, you have a new menu item, Data Analysis, in the Tools menu. Choose Tools➪Data Analysis and scroll down the Analysis Tools list box until you see Regression. Select Regression and click OK. You'll see the Regression dialog box shown in Figure 11-3.

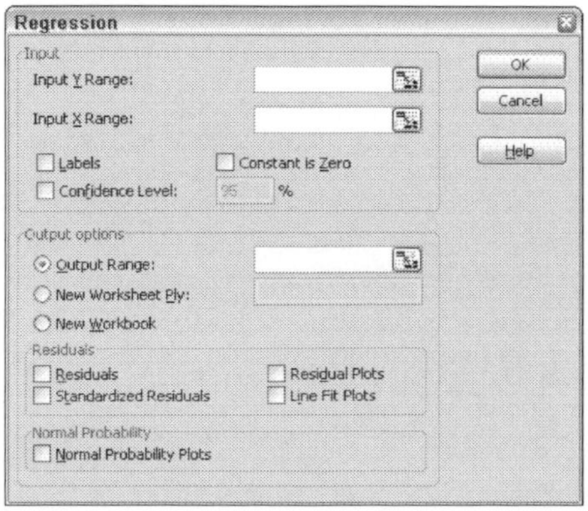

Figure 11-3: The Regression tool helps you develop a forecast without having to enter formulas.

The Regression tool gives you certain standard options for developing a forecast based on regression. You have somewhat less control over what's going on than if you entered the formulas yourself, but using the tool is certainly easier.

Adopting the Regression approach

When you're deciding whether to use regression to forecast sales, you want to keep a few things in mind.

Using related variables

In the prior section, I use a couple of variables — age and height — that are related up to the point that people stop growing. Before you consider using regression to forecast sales, you want to be sure you have one or more variables that are related to sales levels.

A good place to start is with sales drivers, such as dollars that your company spends on advertising or number of sales representatives that your company employs. If you can lay your hands on historical information for, say, advertising dollars and sales dollars, you're ready to see whether a dependable relationship exists.

You do need to be able to pair up individual values on the variables. In this example, you need to know advertising and sales dollars for January, advertising and sales dollars for February, and so on. Having an uninterrupted baseline of values is best, but if you have one or two missing months (or quarters or years, depending on how you're building your baselines), it's not a serious problem.

Later in this chapter, in "Understanding the Analysis ToolPak's Regression Tool," I show you how you can evaluate the relationship between the variables.

Using a variable you can predict

When you're preparing a sales forecast based on regression, you need to choose a variable to which you know what's going to happen. For example, suppose that you use advertising dollars to forecast sales. From looking at your baselines, you can see that a strong relationship exists between advertising and sales. And by using the Analysis ToolPak on the baselines, you can get an equation that you plug advertising dollars into in order to forecast sales.

But if you don't know how much your company is going to spend on advertising during the next time period, you can't plug that value into the equation, and you can't make a forecast. Before you spend a lot of time and energy collecting baseline data and analyzing it, make sure you're using a variable with a future you know about.

Using time periods

If your sales data show a trend over time periods, you can use those periods themselves to forecast. Figure 11-4 shows an example.

You don't need to use actual date values to create the forecast, although you can if you want. It doesn't really matter if you use, say, 1998, 1999, 2000, . . . 2005 to forecast from, or 1, 2, 3, . . . 8.

Using more than one predictor variable

So far, I've given you a look at what's called *simple regression:* using the relationship between one variable and another to forecast one of them. You can also use two or more predictor variables at once, and the Analysis ToolPak can manage that situation.

Suppose you're able to get your hands on three baselines: monthly sales dollars, monthly advertising dollars, and the number of sales reps working for you during each month. The Analysis ToolPak might report back that the equation to use to forecast a month's sales is:

$$\text{Sales} = (25 \times \text{Advertising Dollars}) + (802 \times \text{Sales Reps}) + 37{,}268$$

Month	Revenues
1	$ 56,643
2	$ 28,672
3	$ 72,425
4	$196,487
5	$ 43,430
6	$ 85,150
7	$123,233
8	$103,657
9	$ 62,086
10	$188,090
11	$223,441
12	$221,850
13	$208,672
14	$ 31,500
15	$250,028
16	$204,239
17	$193,595
18	$351,051
19	$260,425
20	$155,239
21	$185,763
22	$187,165
23	$214,788
24	$391,106
25	$202,346
26	$429,741
27	$148,911
28	$299,752
29	$226,305
30	$118,907
31	$225,471
32	$124,954
33	$374,966
34	$332,023

Figure 11-4: You know that another time period is going to come along, so you can use that to get your next sales forecast.

Here's where things can start to get a little sticky. The more predictor variables you use, the more important it is to have a good long baseline. Otherwise, your forecasts are going to dance all over the place like they're in a mosh pit. And if the number of variables you're using even comes close to the number of records in the baseline, the forecasts will become completely unreliable.

This is why I like to forecast using one month as the time period in my baseline. A month is often a useful period to forecast into ("How many widgets are we going to sell next month?"), and all you need is 4 years' worth of data to have a baseline almost 50 periods long. Just choose your predictor variables well, so you're forecasting sales using advertising or sales-rep counts or the time periods themselves, rather than using the intestines of a goat. Then a baseline of 50 will probably do just fine.

Understanding the Analysis ToolPak's Regression Tool

In this section, I show you how to forecast some sales. Figure 11-5 shows a baseline of data. Charting the data first, as shown in Figure 11-5, helps you decide whether to continue with the analysis. If you see something like a diagonal line, continuing probably makes sense. If you see something more like a circle, probably no relationship exists and you may as well take a nice long walk in the shimmering rain.

With the data laid out in this list format, you can use the Analysis ToolPak's Regression tool to help you get a forecast. Take these steps:

1. **Choose Tools ➪ Data Analysis.**
2. **Click the Regression tool in the list box and click OK.**

   The Regression tool's dialog box appears along with your data (see Figure 11-6).
3. **Click in the Input Y Range box and drag through the cells that contain the values you want to forecast.**

   Here, that's Revenues. Figure 11-6 doesn't show it all, but that range extends from B1:B51.

   In regression and, in fact, in most forecast methods, you often find the variable that's being forecast termed the *y* variable. The variables that are being used as predictors are often termed the *x* variables.

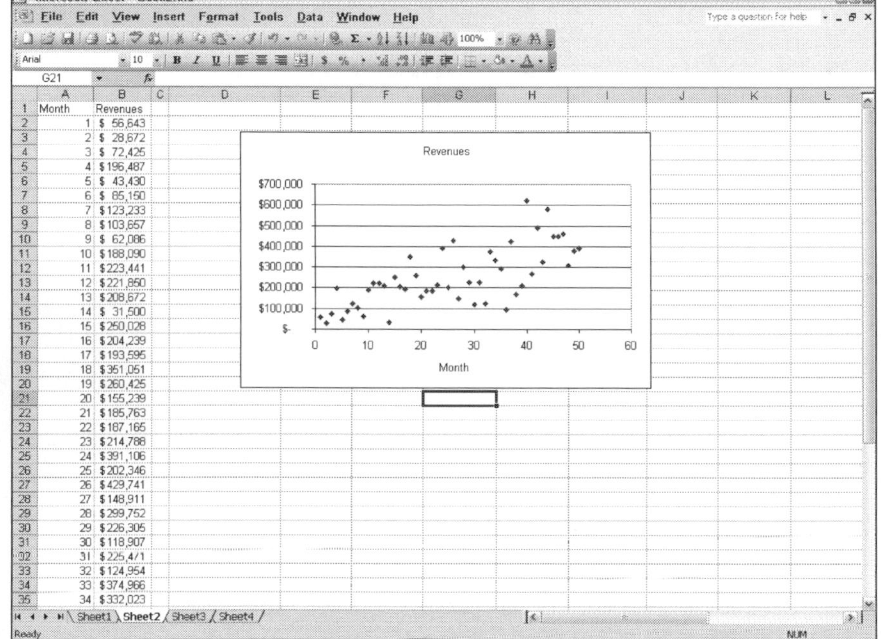

Month	Revenues
1	$ 56,643
2	$ 28,672
3	$ 72,425
4	$196,487
5	$ 43,430
6	$ 85,150
7	$123,233
8	$103,657
9	$ 62,086
10	$188,090
11	$223,441
12	$221,850
13	$208,672
14	$ 31,500
15	$250,028
16	$204,239
17	$193,595
18	$351,051
19	$260,425
20	$155,239
21	$185,763
22	$187,165
23	$214,788
24	$391,106
25	$202,346
26	$429,741
27	$148,911
28	$299,752
29	$226,305
30	$118,907
31	$225,471
32	$124,954
33	$374,966
34	$332,023

Figure 11-5: This baseline is used to forecast sales on the basis of time period.

4. **Click in the Input X Range box and drag through the cells that contain the values you want to forecast *from*.**

   Because you're forecasting using the Month number, drag through A1:A51.

   A quick way to select a range of values is to use your mouse to select all the cells in the top row, and then simultaneously press Ctrl+Shift+Down Arrow. Excel selects the range for you, but it stops when it runs into an empty cell — another good reason to avoid missing data.

5. **Because you included the variable labels in row 1 as part of the input ranges, select the Labels check box.**

   Otherwise, Excel will find nonnumeric data in the input ranges and will throw a warning message at you.

6. **If necessary, click the Output Range option button.**

   When you click any of the option buttons in the Output Option frame, Excel perversely makes the Input Y Range box active. If you're not watching what you're doing, you can easily overwrite the range address you entered as the Input Y Range with the address you want to use for your output. Not a huge deal, but it can be really annoying.

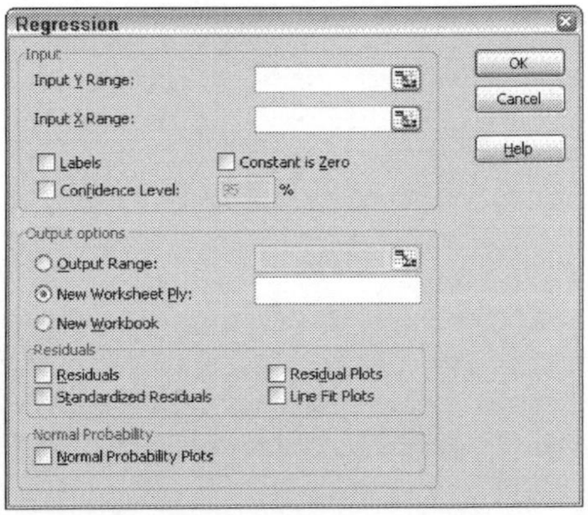

Figure 11-6: In the Regression dialog box, a *worksheet ply* is just an old term for a worksheet.

7. **When you're sure you have the Output Range box selected, click a cell where you want the output to start, and then click OK.**

   Excel creates the regression information shown in Figure 11-7.

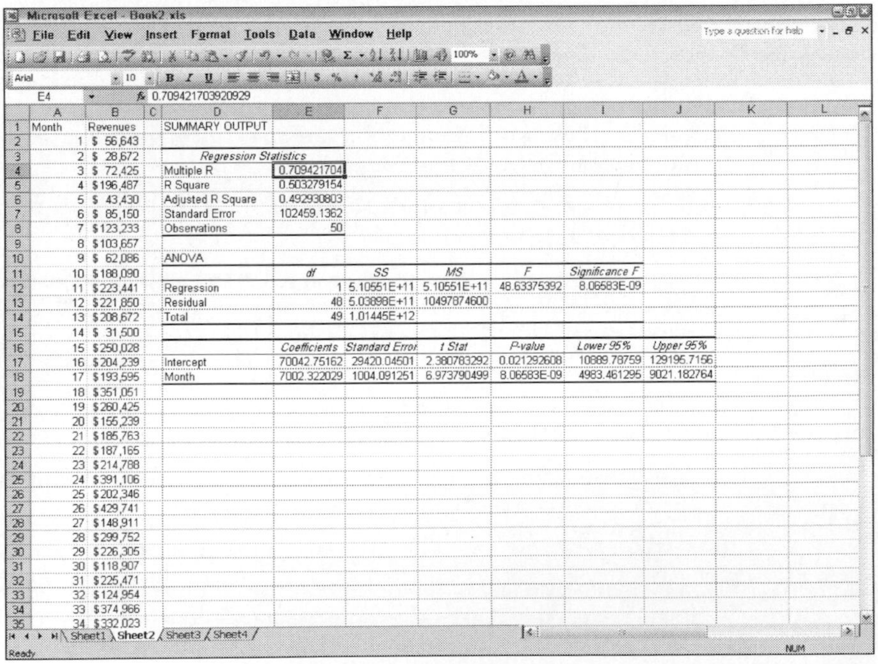

Month	Revenues
1	$ 56,643
2	$ 28,672
3	$ 72,425
4	$196,487
5	$ 43,430
6	$ 85,150
7	$123,233
8	$103,657
9	$ 62,086
10	$188,090
11	$223,441
12	$221,850
13	$208,672
14	$ 31,500
15	$250,028
16	$204,239
17	$193,595
18	$351,051
19	$260,425
20	$155,239
21	$185,763
22	$187,165
23	$214,788
24	$391,106
25	$202,346
26	$429,741
27	$148,911
28	$299,752
29	$226,305
30	$118,907
31	$225,471
32	$124,954
33	$374,966
34	$332,023

SUMMARY OUTPUT

Regression Statistics	
Multiple R	0.709421704
R Square	0.503279154
Adjusted R Square	0.492930803
Standard Error	102459.1362
Observations	50

ANOVA

	df	*SS*	*MS*	*F*	*Significance F*
Regression	1	5.10551E+11	5.10551E+11	48.63375392	8.06583E-09
Residual	48	5.03898E+11	10497874600		
Total	49	1.01445E+12			

	Coefficients	*Standard Error*	*t Stat*	*P-value*	*Lower 95%*	*Upper 95%*
Intercept	70042.75162	29420.04501	2.380783292	0.021292608	10889.78759	129195.7156
Month	7002.322029	1004.091251	6.973790499	8.06583E-09	4983.461295	9021.182764

Figure 11-7: There are only a few numbers shown here that you need to make your forecast.

I know that output looks pretty intimidating but you can ignore most of it if you want. Here are the things you want to pay attention to:

- **The number that's labeled *Multiple R:*** That's in cell E4 in Figure 11-7. The closer it is to 1.0, the stronger the relationship between the predictor variable (or variables) and the variable you want to forecast — and therefore the more confidence you can have in the forecast. The closer it is to zero, the worse the relationship and the less confidence you have. It can only run from 0.0 to 1.0, and the value of 0.709 shown in Figure 11-7 is reasonably good. In simple regression, the Multiple R is really just the correlation between the predictor and the forecast variable (although in contrast to a simple correlation, a Multiple R is always positive).
- The two numbers labeled Intercept and Month: They're in cells E17 and E18, respectively. You use them in your forecast equation. (The one in E18 is labeled *Month* only because that's the name used for that variable in the list, in cell A1.)

So, using the information you get from the Regression tool, you can round the numbers a little and write this equation:

Revenue = (7,002 × Month) + 70,043

In words, the equation says that, given these baselines, the best estimate of Revenue comes by multiplying the month number (here, 1 through 50) by 7,002 and adding 70,043.

And if you want to forecast revenue for month 51, you'd use this formula in a worksheet cell:

```
= (7002 * 51) + 70043
```

which equals 427,145 — your regression-based forecast for month 51.

Checking the forecast errors

As I keep complaining in this book, when you forecast you make errors. And regression is no different from any other approach to forecasting when it comes to errors.

Regression does use a different term, though: *residuals.* These aren't what Jerry Seinfeld gets every time his sitcom is rerun. In this sense, residuals are errors. Have another glance at the formula at the end of the prior section. Instead of putting 51 in the formula, you could put in any month number from 1 to 50, and the formula would predict the revenue for that particular month.

You could then subtract that predicted revenue amount from the actual revenue for that month — the result is a residual. Having the Regression tool chart the residuals against the month's number, shown in Figure 11-8, is useful.

You get this chart by selecting the Residual Plots check box in the Regression dialog box (refer to Figure 11-6).

The pattern of the markers in the chart is important. You'd like to see them form a shape similar to a rectangle, paralleling the chart's horizontal axis. In Figure 11-8, it's close, but I'd judge that it's not quite a rectangle: the markers tend to be closer together (vertically) on the left, in the early months, than on the right, in the later months. Sometimes you also see a shallow U shape or a rectangle that's tilted from the horizontal axis.

In these situations, your underlying data must be changed in some way before you can trust the results of the regression analysis and, thus, get a good forecast. Those changes are called *transformations;* they can get complicated, and I don't go into them in this book.

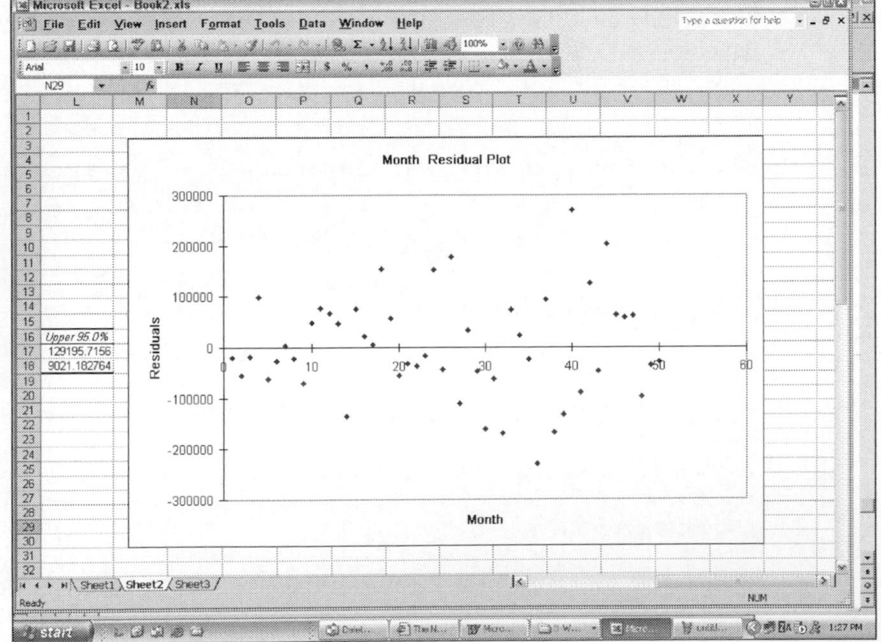

Figure 11-8: When the Regression tool creates this chart, it embeds it in the worksheet and puts it to the right of the numeric output.

Plotting your actual revenues

Another very useful chart that the Regression tool will create for you is the Line Fit Plot. Using the current example, it shows your actual sales revenues and the predicted revenues, charted against Month. You can see one in Figure 11-9.

The straight line made of dots in Figure 11-9 is called a *regression line* or *trendline.* As the Regression tool creates it, it's not very useful. I like to click on it to select it and then press Delete. Since Microsoft started including the Analysis ToolPak with Excel, it has improved Excel's charting tools. Select any marker in the chart that represents a revenue value in your baseline. Then choose Chart⇨Add Trendline. You'll see the Add Trendline dialog box, as shown in Figure 11-10.

Now click the Options tab, which looks like the one in Figure 11-11. Notice the Forecast frame, with the spinners in it. You can use the spinner to extend the trendline forward, into the future, or backward, into the past, by the number of periods that you choose using the spinner.

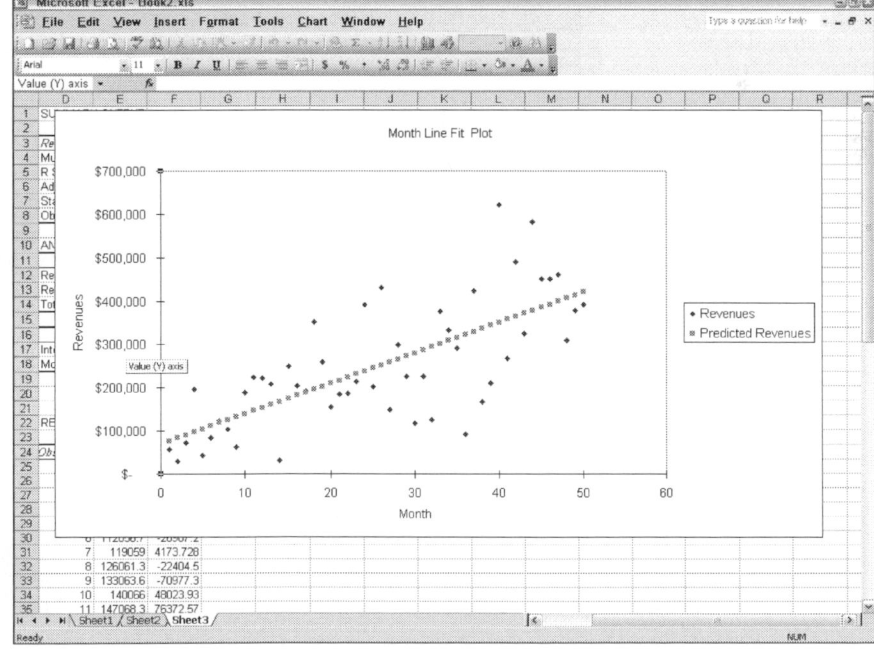

Figure 11-9: The line showing the predicted revenues is the result of applying the regression equation to each actual month number.

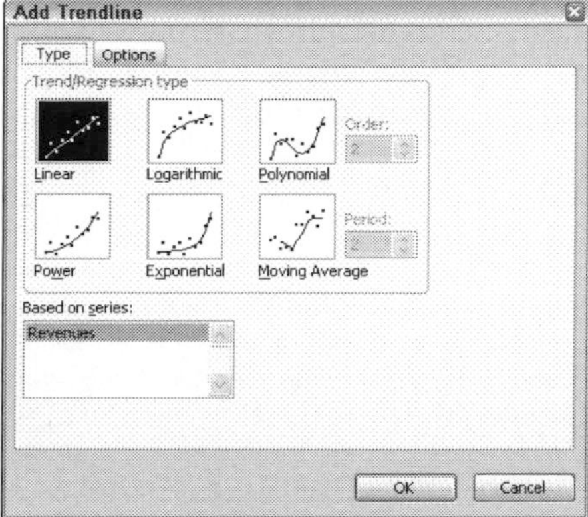

Figure 11-10: You'll usually want to choose the Linear Trendline.

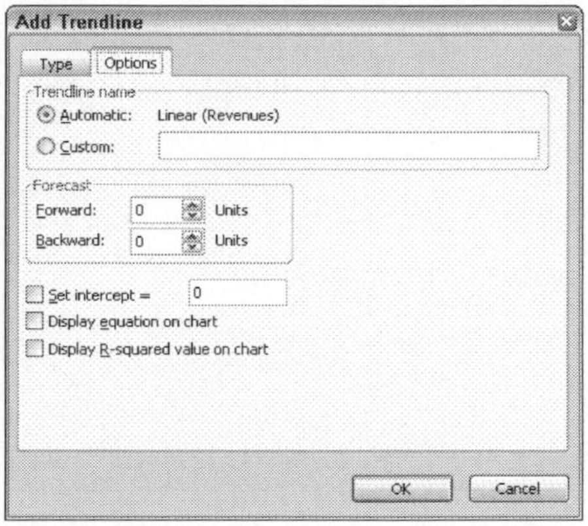

Add Trendline
Type
Options
Trendline name
Automatic: Linear (Revenues)
Custom:
Forecast
Forward: 0 Units
Backward: 0 Units
Set intercept = 0
Display equation on chart
Display R-squared value on chart
OK
Cancel

Figure 11-11: You can also display on the chart the equation that the Regression tool calculated.

The result is in Figure 11-12. The trendline is much more useful for forecasting than the line of predicted values that I deleted near the start of this section.

Understanding confidence levels

Confidence levels are closely related to probabilities expressed as percentages. At the right of Figure 11-7, you see a couple of columns with numbers that are labeled *Lower 95%* and *Upper 95%*. Notice that the Month predictor's Lower is 4963 and its Upper is 9021.

In forecasting, we often get samples of data for baselines. You might think you have a long enough baseline, but the picture might change drastically if you'd gone back another year. And the regression results — everything you see in the Regression tool's numbers — would also change.

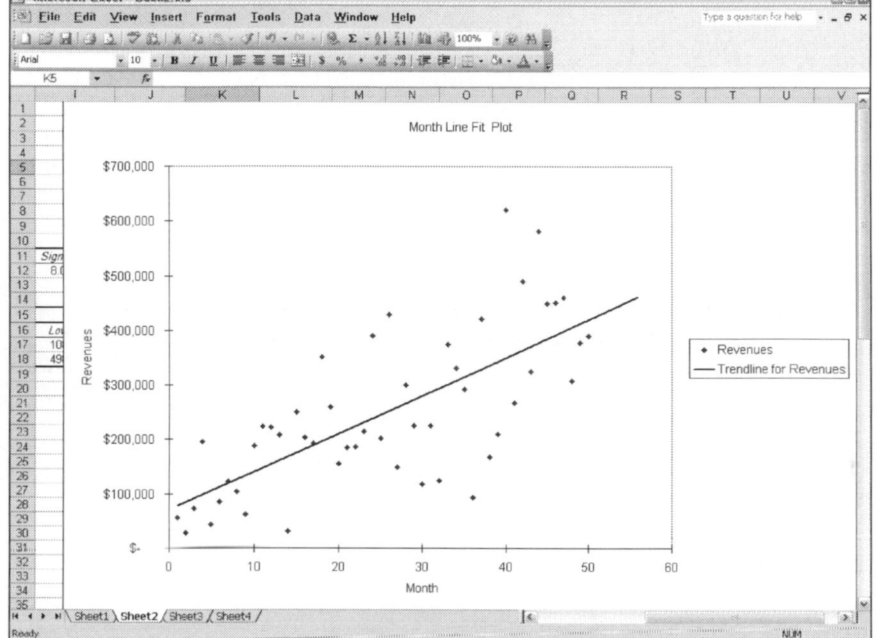

Figure 11-12: The trendline is forecasting six time periods into the future.

Suppose you had a hundred different samples of the same data, each somewhat different. Here's what the 95 percent confidence figures mean. Using the analysis shown in Figure 11-7, we believe that 95 of those 100 samples would result in a coefficient for the Month variable between 4963 and 9021.

Of course you'd never do that, but you can tell by looking at the upper and lower figures how precisely that the combination of the baseline and the regression analysis has estimated the coefficients you'll use to make your forecast.

There's nothing magic about a 95 percent confidence level. It's just a traditional level of probability that researchers have used for decades. If you select the Confidence Level check box in the Regression tool's dialog box, its associated box becomes enabled and you can enter another confidence level. That confidence level is included in the output along with the default 95 percent. In general, a lower confidence level such as 90 percent results in a narrower interval between the lower and upper figures.

Avoiding a zero constant

The Regression tool's dialog box has a check box labeled Constant Is Zero. The term *constant* is just another term for the intercept that the Regression tool includes in its output. In the equation shown at the end of the "Understanding the Analysis ToolPak's Regression Tool" section, it's the value 70043. It's called an intercept because if you extended the regression line to the vertical axis, the line would intercept that axis at 70043.

Some people who use regression know that, in reality, the intercept based on their full data set is zero, and if the Regression tool calculates a different value it's because of sampling error. So they select the Constant Is Zero check box.

In sales forecasting, that's almost certainly not the case, unless your company didn't sell anything during the first time period. The problem is that, because of the math that underlies regression, you wind up getting really screwy results. For just one example, the Multiple R, what you look at to judge the strength of the relationship between what you're forecasting and your predictors, gets inflated and you'll be misled.

You're much better off leaving the Constant Is Zero check box unchecked.

Using Multiple Regression

If you have two different predictor variables, you can often improve your forecasts. It's called *multiple regression* because you're using multiple predictor variables. This chapter gives a light once-over to that approach in the "Using more than one predictor variable" section. In this section, I show you how to use multiple regression to forecast sales using month and advertising dollars.

Suppose that, in addition to sales revenues and month number, you have advertising expenses (this is mildly unrealistic because ad expenses are often leading indicators of sales, but — as with Sunday advertising supplements — not always).

The data in Figure 11-13 is identical to earlier figures in this chapter, except that an additional column, Ad Dollars, has been added to the list and is referenced in the Regression dialog box Input X values. Running the Analysis ToolPak's Regression tool on this data requires only a slight change to the Regression dialog box so that the Input X values are found in A1:B51 (see Figure 11-14 for the resulting output).

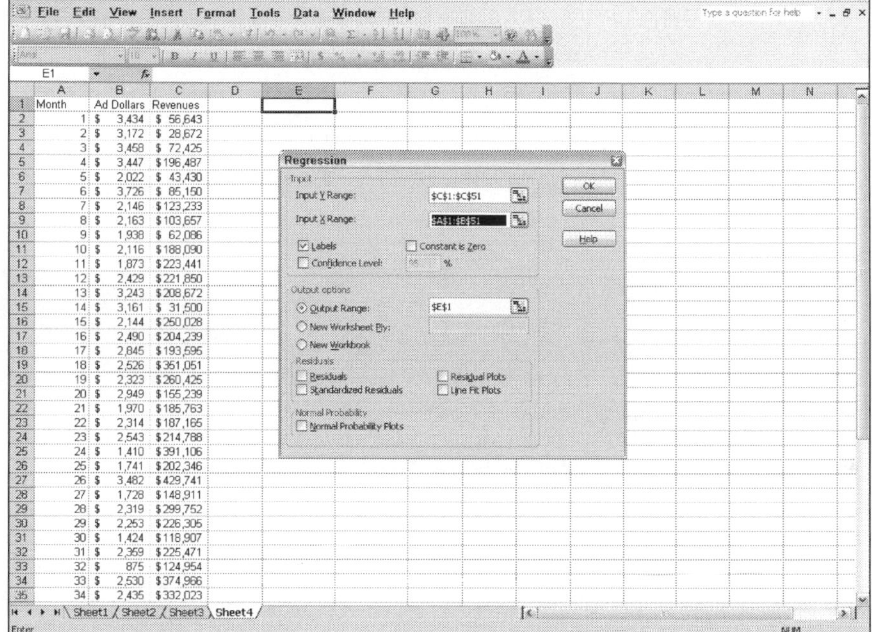

Figure 11-13: Make sure your predictor variables occupy adjacent columns. Don't lay it out as, say, Month, Sales Revenues, Ad Dollars.

Month	Ad Dollars	Revenues
1	$ 3,434	$ 56,643
2	$ 3,172	$ 28,672
3	$ 3,458	$ 72,425
4	$ 3,447	$196,487
5	$ 2,022	$ 43,430
6	$ 3,726	$ 85,150
7	$ 2,146	$123,233
8	$ 2,163	$103,657
9	$ 1,938	$ 62,086
10	$ 2,116	$188,090
11	$ 1,873	$223,441
12	$ 2,429	$221,850
13	$ 3,243	$208,672
14	$ 3,161	$ 31,500
15	$ 2,144	$250,028
16	$ 2,490	$204,239
17	$ 2,845	$193,595
18	$ 2,526	$351,051
19	$ 2,323	$260,425
20	$ 2,949	$155,239
21	$ 1,970	$185,763
22	$ 2,314	$187,165
23	$ 2,543	$214,788
24	$ 1,410	$391,106
25	$ 1,741	$202,346
26	$ 3,482	$429,741
27	$ 1,728	$148,911
28	$ 2,319	$299,752
29	$ 2,253	$226,305
30	$ 1,424	$118,907
31	$ 2,359	$225,471
32	$ 875	$124,954
33	$ 2,530	$374,966
34	$ 2,435	$332,023

SUMMARY OUTPUT

Regression Statistics	
Multiple R	0.812404282
R Square	0.660000717
Adjusted R Sq	0.645532663
Standard Error	85665.34871
Observations	50

ANOVA

	df	SS	MS	F	Significance F
Regression	2	6.69537E+11	3.35E+11	45.61779	9.766E-12
Residual	47	3.44912E+11	7.34E+09		
Total	49	1.01445E+12			

	Coefficients	Standard Error	t Stat	P-value	Lower 95%	Upper 95%
Intercept	-144708.4771	52285.72001	-2.76765	0.008051	-249893.8	-39523.18
Month	8833.890728	927.1613267	9.52789	1.49E-12	6968.6828	10699.099
Ad Dollars	73.70586482	15.83535266	4.654514	2.68E-05	41.849245	105.56248

Figure 11-14: The basic layout of the output is the same regardless of the number of predictor variables.

What's a good predictor to add to an existing equation? There are two main characteristics for a good added predictor, one having to do with the relationship between the new predictor and the forecast variable, and the other with the relationship between the new predictor and the existing predictor.

New predictor with forecast variable

A new predictor, such as Ad Dollars in this example, should bear some relationship to the value that you want to forecast — here, Sales Revenues. The correlation in this list between Ad Dollars and Sales Revenues is a small one: only 0.057. That's so close to zero (no relationship) that you may not think it worth including in the regression equation.

The Multiple R value in Figure 11-7 is 0.709. But look at the Multiple R in Figure 11-14: It's bounced all the way up to 0.812! That's quite a bounce for a predictor that correlates only 0.057 with the forecast variable. The reason lies in the next section.

New predictor with existing variable

What has happened is that Month Number has already accounted for much of the Sales Revenues. What's left are the residuals in the Sales Revenues that the "Checking the forecast errors" section covers. It turns out in this case (and in many others) that the added variable correlates well with the *residuals.* So the new predictor can explain even more about the behavior of the forecast variable than the single predictor can, and you get more of a bounce than after a presidential convention.

As we've seen, the higher the Multiple R, the better your forecast. All other things being equal, of course. If there's no fudge in your data in the first, one-predictor forecast, there better be no fudge in your second, two-predictor forecast.

By the way, you're not limited mathematically to any particular number of predictor variables, as long as you have enough observations (or a long enough baseline) to handle them. As a matter of practical fact, though, Excel limits you to 16 no matter how long your baseline is.

You're not limited to numeric predictors. For example, you could add sales region and sales branch as predictors. But to do so, you have to convert names such as Northwest Region and Snerd's Store into numeric codes. There are special ways to do this, sometimes termed *dummy coding.* I don't go into dummy coding in this book — there aren't enough pages, and you can find several more-advanced books specifically on multiple regression that cover *dummy coding.* Just keep in mind that it's both possible and feasible.

Part IV
Making Advanced Forecasts

"It's your wife Mr. Dinker. Shall I have her take a seat in the closet, or do you want to schedule a meeting in the kitchen for later this afternoon?"

In this part . . .

Here you find out how to use Excel to make more-advanced forecasts. By that, I mean forecasts that you can control more closely. For example, although the Analysis ToolPak is useful, you're largely resigned to what it tells you. But if you know how to enter the formulas yourself, you have more control over what's going on. In this part, I also show you how to account for seasonality when you forecast your sales.

Chapter 12

Entering the Formulas Yourself

In This Chapter

- Making sense of Excel formulas
- Accepting some help from Excel
- Getting familiar with array formulas
- Trying your hand at regression functions

Any worksheet program — Excel, Lotus 1-2-3, Quattro — has its own convention for indicating a formula. In Excel, you start with an equal sign. In Lotus 1-2-3, you can now start with an equal sign, but for years you had to start with an arithmetic operator like a plus sign.

This chapter starts with a brief review — or overview — of the rules for Excel formulas. As you get more and more comfortable with quantitative forecasting, you're likely to find yourself wanting to rely less on tools such as the Analysis ToolPak, and more on writing your own formulas.

Excel has hundreds of prefabricated formulas, called *functions.* A good example is the AVERAGE function. All you need to do is refer to the function in a worksheet cell and point it at a range of cells with numbers in them. The AVERAGE function adds up the values in that range of cells and divides by the number of values.

You get more information about Excel functions that are useful in forecasting in this chapter. Besides the AVERAGE function, there are some functions that are important in forecasts that use regression.

Some functions require that you array-enter them if they're to return the results you're after. This chapter goes into some detail about how to array-enter a formula, whether or not the formula contains a function.

About Excel Formulas

Formulas are at the heart of Excel, which makes it difficult to understand why 80 percent of Excel worksheets contain no formulas, only static values like

14 or *Smith* (that's what a market research study determined a few years back). Formulas, together with functions, help you summarize data with totals, analyze data with averages, find data, rearrange data, transform data — the list of things you can do with worksheet formulas is a long one.

This section recommends that, sometimes anyway, you should consider using a formula that you create yourself rather than relying on the Analysis ToolPak. But it's not an introduction to formulas. If you're comfortable with entering a formula, by all means continue. If you harbor a suspicion that I'm talking about liquid food for infants, you may want to look through *Excel 2003 For Dummies* by Greg Harvey (published by Wiley).

Doing it yourself: Why bother?

As is probably apparent by now, this book is about quantitative forecasting, and particularly quantitative sales forecasting, using Excel. Chapters 6 and 7 discuss setting up your baseline data in an Excel worksheet. With the data set up as an Excel list, you can deploy the Analysis ToolPak (ATP) and get a forecast using the Moving Average, Exponential Smoothing, or Regression tool.

So, why would you bother with entering the formulas yourself? Well, if you use formulas, you have more control over what's going on in the development of the forecast.

For example, suppose you use the ATP's Moving Average tool to develop a moving-average forecast. Although the moving averages that the tool calculates are formulas, those formulas use a constant: the length of the subset of the baseline values that are used by a given moving average — 3, for example, as in this formula:

```
=AVERAGE(A2:A4)
```

But what if you wanted to change the number of baseline values that go into each moving average — for example:

```
=AVERAGE(A2:A5)
```

where the moving average is of length 4. In that case, you'd have to go through each moving-average formula and adjust it, or you'd have to rerun the Moving Average tool. And then what if you wanted to go back to length 3?

If you wrote your own formula, you could use something like this instead:

```
=AVERAGE(OFFSET($A2,0,0,$C$1,1))
```

When you see dollar signs in a cell or range reference, as in the above formula, you know that it's an *absolute* reference. When you copy a formula into a different row or column, the cell references adjust to take account of where you copied it to. But when you use dollar signs to make a formula's cell references *absolute,* you can copy and paste it anywhere on the worksheet and the cell references will *not* adjust. *$C$1* is an absolute reference. *$A2* is a mixed reference: It will always point to column A, because of the dollar sign before the column reference. *A$2*, another mixed reference, will always point to row 2. *A2* is a relative reference, and both its row and its column will adjust, depending on where you copy and paste it to.

What's all this good for? Meet the OFFSET function. It returns a range, in this case the range that starts in cell $A2, has as many rows as whatever the number is in cell $C$1, and is one column wide.

Suppose that $C$1 contains the number 3. In that case, this formula:

```
=AVERAGE(OFFSET($A2,0,0,$C$1,1))
```

if entered in row 2, returns the address of the range of cells that you want to average: That range is in column A, in row 2, has as many rows as the number in cell $C$1, and has one column. Because $A2 is a mixed reference, you can copy the formula down into row 3, row 4 and so on, and the basis cell changes to $A3, $A4 and so on. This approach is useful because you can change the number of cells in each average by simply changing the number in cell C1.

Here I walk you through the formula, repeated here for convenience, and assuming that it's been entered in cell B2:

```
=AVERAGE(OFFSET($A2,0,0,$C$1,1))
```

- It refers to cell $A2. That's the basis cell, the one that anchors the range of cells that we're after so we can average them. In this example, it would be smart for $A2 to be the first value in the baseline.
- It makes $A2 a mixed reference. The dollar sign anchors it to column A: You can copy the formula to, say, cell Q5 and it will still use a cell in column A (specifically, it will use A5 as a basis cell). But because no dollar sign is anchoring the row, if you copy and paste the formula from B2 to, say, F20, the reference to $A2 will change to $A20.
- The two zeros used in the function mean that the range that OFFSET returns begins in $A2. That is, the range will begin zero rows and zero columns away from $A2. If the formula instead were this one:

  ```
  =AVERAGE(OFFSET($A2,1,0,$C$1,1))
  ```

  then the range that OFFSET returns would begin one row below $A2, and

  ```
  =AVERAGE(OFFSET($A2,0,1,$C$1,1))
  ```

would cause OFFSET to return a range that begins one column right of $A2 — that is, B2.

- Whatever numeric value you enter in $C$1 controls how many rows are in the range that OFFSET returns.
- The range will be one column wide.
- By surrounding the OFFSET function with the AVERAGE function, you get the average of the values in the range that OFFSET returns.

So, if the number 4 were in $C$1, the OFFSET function would return the range A2:A5. Figure 12-1 shows how this works in practice. (Bear with me: I get into what INDIRECT is, and how StartRow is used, very shortly.)

In Figure 12-1, you can tell the number of values that are averaged to create each moving average by looking at cell C1, which contains 3. Three values are averaged for each moving average.

If you want to get a look at the moving-average series with a moving-average length of 4, all you do is change the value in C1 from 3 to 4 (see Figure 12-2).

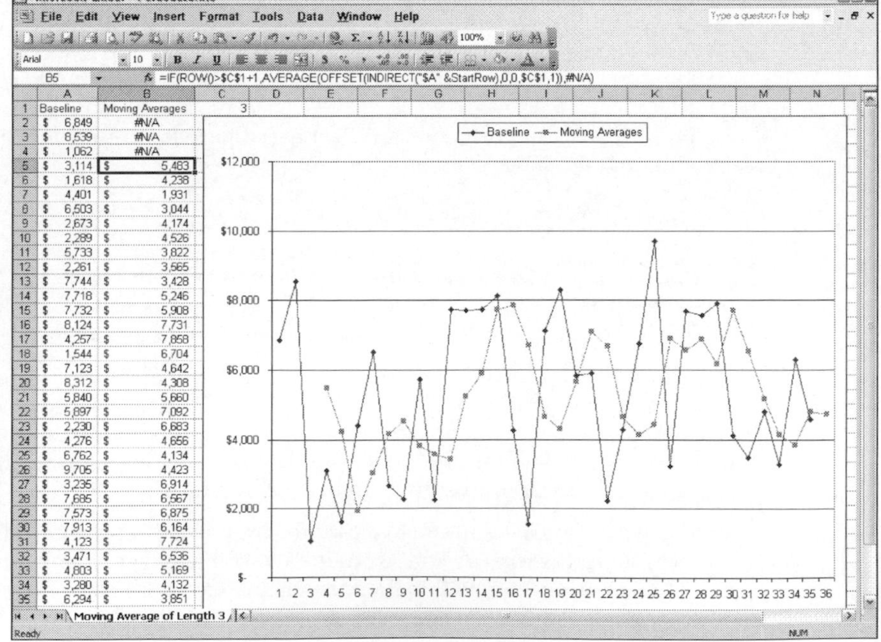

	A	B	C
1	Baseline	Moving Averages	3
2	$ 6,849	#N/A	
3	$ 8,539	#N/A	
4	$ 1,062	#N/A	
5	$ 3,114	$ 5,483	
6	$ 1,618	$ 4,238	
7	$ 4,401	$ 1,931	
8	$ 6,503	$ 3,044	
9	$ 2,673	$ 4,174	
10	$ 2,289	$ 4,526	
11	$ 5,733	$ 3,822	
12	$ 2,261	$ 3,565	
13	$ 7,744	$ 3,428	
14	$ 7,718	$ 5,246	
15	$ 7,732	$ 5,908	
16	$ 8,124	$ 7,731	
17	$ 4,257	$ 7,858	
18	$ 1,544	$ 6,704	
19	$ 7,123	$ 4,642	
20	$ 8,312	$ 4,308	
21	$ 5,840	$ 5,660	
22	$ 5,897	$ 7,092	
23	$ 2,230	$ 6,683	
24	$ 4,276	$ 4,656	
25	$ 6,762	$ 4,134	
26	$ 9,705	$ 4,423	
27	$ 3,235	$ 6,914	
28	$ 7,685	$ 6,567	
29	$ 7,573	$ 6,875	
30	$ 7,913	$ 6,164	
31	$ 4,123	$ 7,724	
32	$ 3,471	$ 6,536	
33	$ 4,803	$ 5,169	
34	$ 3,280	$ 4,132	
35	$ 6,294	$ 3,851	

Figure 12-1: This is one way to change the length of the baseline section that goes into each moving average.

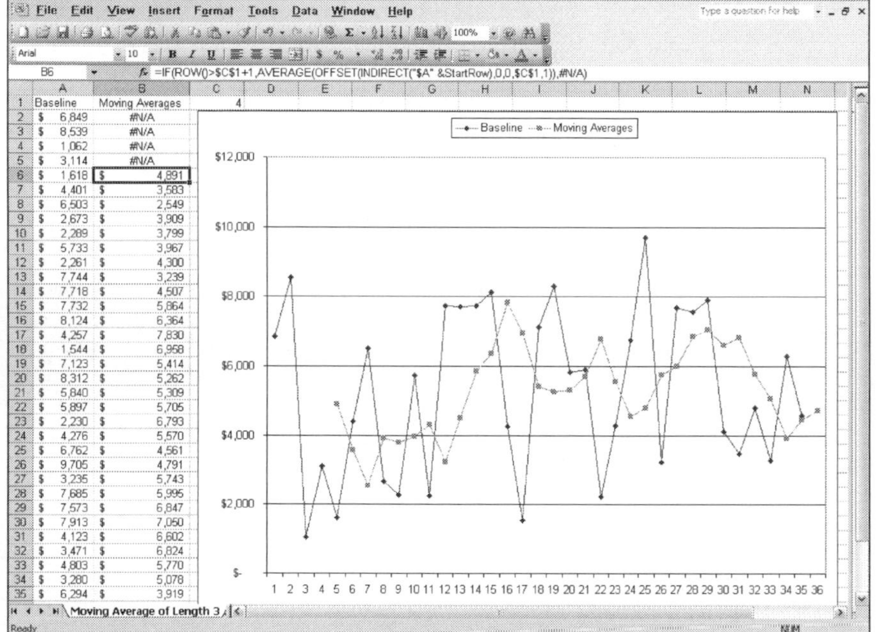

Figure 12-2: Changing just one number, in C1, is a lot easier than rerunning the Moving Average tool.

Although the basic idea is the same, the formula actually used in column B of Figures 12-1 and 12-2 is somewhat more complicated than the one we've been discussing. That's because we want to make the starting point of the moving-average series in the chart depend on the length we want to use for the moving average. Here's the formula:

```
=IF(ROW()>$C$1+1,AVERAGE(OFFSET(INDIRECT("$A"
        &StartRow),0,0,$C$1,1)),#N/A)
```

It's best to take something like this in small doses, and to work inside out:

- There's a defined name in the workbook, StartRow. It's defined as:

  ```
  =ROW()-$C$1
  ```

  Wherever you enter that formula, it will return the number of the row where you entered it minus the value in cell C1. This tells Excel how far up to look to find the baseline's starting value for the moving average. If 3 is in C1 and you enter the formula in B15, then it returns 15 – 3 = 12. The current moving average should average baseline values beginning in row 12.

- In Excel, if you define a name such as StartRow to refer to a formula, as here, you can use the name rather than the formula, as in this segment of the complete formula:

  ```
  INDIRECT("$A"&StartRow)
  ```

  Let's continue to assume that StartRow returns 12, given the value in C1 and the row where you enter this formula. Then using the INDIRECT function results in a cell address — in this case, that's A12. (You define a name in Excel by choosing Insert ➪ Name ➪ Define. Type the name in the Names in Workbook box, and the formula in the Refers To box.)

- Expanding and simplifying the segment a little further, you've got this segment of the formula:

  ```
  OFFSET(A12,0,0,$C$1,1)
  ```

  In other words, return the range that's zero rows and zero columns from cell A12. Give that range as many rows as the number in $C$1 — which you're assuming is 3 — and one column.

- Get the average of the values in that range:

  ```
  AVERAGE(A12,0,0,3,1)
  ```

  or:

  ```
  AVERAGE(A12:A14)
  ```

- Finally, the full formula (taking into account the simplifications you've already made:

  ```
  =IF(ROW()>$C$1+1,AVERAGE(A12:A14),#N/A)
  ```

  and simplifying further:

  ```
  =IF(ROW()>4,AVERAGE(A12:A14),#N/A)
  ```

  In words, you're telling the formula to look at the number of the row where you're entering the formula. If that number is greater than 4, return the average of the values in A12:A14 — that is, the current moving average. Otherwise, return the Excel error value `#N/A`.

A couple of issues are wrapped up in that formula. One is that you'll get a `#REF!` error if you put this formula in rows 1, 2, 3, or 4, because it will start referring to cells A0, A–1, and so on (these last references are just for illustration — there's no such thing as *row zero* or *row –1*. Excel would actually show you the `#REF!` error value). Instead, you use the IF function to make sure that the formula hasn't been entered too far up on the worksheet. If it has, return `#N/A`.

The other issue is the use of `#N/A`. That keeps those cells out of the chart and ensures that the series of moving-average values are in the correct rows vis-à-vis the baseline. See Chapter 13 for information about how the baseline values and the forecast values should line up so that your forecast will be for the correct period, and so that the baseline and forecast will chart correctly.

There are at least three other reasons to consider entering your own formulas rather than relying on the ATP.

Until they get it right

Some ATP tools don't get the analysis right, and the Moving Average tool is one of them. Not to beat a dead horse, but the ATP's Moving Average tool doesn't correctly chart the forecasts against the actuals in the baseline. The way that the ATP lines up the forecast values against the baseline values, it treats the actual value for the current period as part of the forecast for that period.

Another problem with the ATP is the standard errors that the Exponential Smoothing tool returns. You can find more information about this in Chapter 15.

In words: if you're looking for a moving-average forecast of length 3 for July, you want that forecast to average the baseline for April, May, and June. But the ATP's Moving Average tool forecasts July by averaging May, June, and July, and that's clearly wrong. If you're going to include July in the forecast for July, then you have to wait for July's actual. In that case, what's the point of forecasting July? You avoid this tail-chasing by calculating and placing the moving averages yourself.

Static electricity

Every tool in the ATP other than Moving Average and Exponential Smoothing puts static values on your worksheet. (Before I wrote this book, I hadn't counted and checked every ATP tool to see whether it returns formulas or values. I was a little surprised that, of the three tools this book discusses, two of them are the only two tools in the ATP that return formulas.)

Formulas are usually better than static results: With formulas, you can change the inputs and the results will recalculate. Using a tool that returns static results means that you have to rerun the analysis when your inputs change, or when the next period's actuals become available.

Managing the layout

Using your own formulas, you can lay out the worksheet however you want, and recalculate with new inputs without disturbing the layout. With the ATP, though, if you have new inputs and you're using a tool that returns static values, you'll need both to rerun the tool and then move the results around again to get the layout the way you want it.

Getting the syntax right

Functions like the ones used in the last section (such as AVERAGE and OFFSET) soothe a lot of headaches on your behalf. All you have to do is supply the right values, or point them at the right cells, and they'll take care of the rest.

But sometimes you have to be careful to supply those values and cells in a particular order, and sometimes you don't. If you're using the SUM function, for example, you need to tell it which values to total, or which cells contain the values you want it to total, but order doesn't matter. You could use this:

```
=SUM(5,4,3,2,1)
```

or, equivalently, this:

```
=SUM(1,2,3,4,5)
```

Or, if you want to get the sum of several cells (and that's really the way to do it, instead of putting constants inside the parentheses), you could use this:

```
=SUM(A1,B2,C3,D4,E5)
```

or, equivalently, this:

```
=SUM(E5,C3,A1,B2,D4)
```

But other functions are persnickety about the order of the numbers and cell addresses that you supply them. Returning to OFFSET, consider that

```
=OFFSET(A1,1,0,1,2)
```

returns the range A2:B2. But just swapping the order of the first two numbers and of the second two numbers,

```
=OFFSET(A1,0,1,2,1)
```

returns the range B1:B2.

By the way, the values inside the parentheses following the name of a function are called its *arguments.* The arguments just give the function the information it needs to operate properly.

An Excel function cannot handle more than 30 arguments. So if you want to get the sum of 31 individual numbers, you're out of luck. Excel won't react properly if you enter `=SUM(1,2,3,4 . . . 31)`. But — and it's a big but — Excel treats a range of cells as just one argument. So if you had the number 1 in cell A1, the number 2 in cell A2, and so on down to the number 31 in cell A31, this would work just fine:

```
=SUM(A1:A31)
```

Using Insert Function

Without years of experience (and even *with* them), keeping the necessary order of a function's arguments in mind is difficult. Fortunately, you don't have to. Use Insert Function by clicking the f_x button, just to the left of the Formula Bar. When you do, two things happen:

- The Formula Bar gets itself ready to accept a formula and put it in the active cell. (Notice in Figure 12-3 that both the Formula Bar and cell B3 now contain equal signs.)
- The Insert Function dialog box appears.

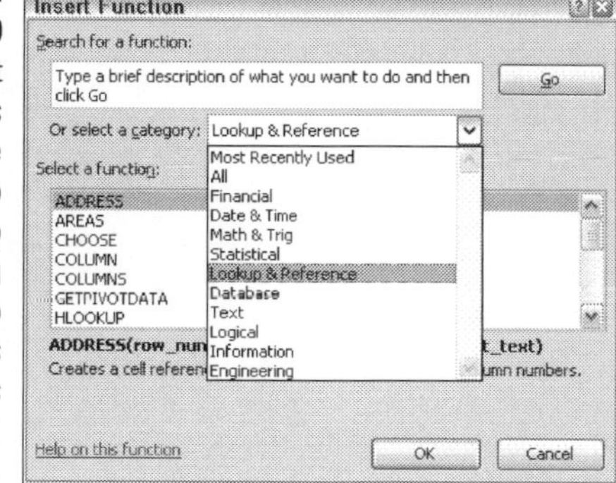

Figure 12-3: Over 200 worksheet functions are available to you, so breaking them up into categories makes pretty good sense.

Suppose you want to enter the OFFSET function on your worksheet, and you'd like to use the Insert Function button to help you out with OFFSET's arguments. After you've clicked the Insert Function button to open its dialog box, there are four ways to get that assistance:

- Choose All in the Select a Category list box. Scroll down the Select a Function list box until you find OFFSET, select it, and then click OK.
- You may know from experience that OFFSET belongs to the Lookup and Reference category. So, select Lookup and Reference in the Select a Category list box, scroll down the Select a Function list box, select OFFSET, and click OK. The virtue of starting by selecting Lookup and Reference first is that, in this case, you have only 18 Lookup and Reference functions to deal with in the Select a Function list box, rather than over 200.
- If you used the OFFSET function recently (at least, recently as far as Excel is concerned), you may start by choosing Most Recently Used from the Select a Category list box. Excel puts the ten functions that

you most recently used in the Select a Function list box — so, you may not have to scroll at all. Select OFFSET and click OK.

- If you're really in the dark (you don't know the function's category, you don't know its name, and it doesn't show up when you choose the Most Recently Used category), you can try typing a question in the Search for a Function box and click Go. Because you're relying on finding a keyword in the function's description, this is the least reliable way to locate a particular function. But sometimes it's all you've got.

When you can't find what you're looking for using Insert Function, try Google or Google Groups. Enter some pertinent words in Google's search box. If you're using Google Groups, use this to restrict the groups that Google searches:

Microsoft.Public.Excel.WorksheetFunctions

After you've selected a category, the Select a Function list box adjusts its entries (all the available functions, all the functions that belong to a smaller category such as Lookup and Reference, or the ten most recently used), as shown in Figure 12-4.

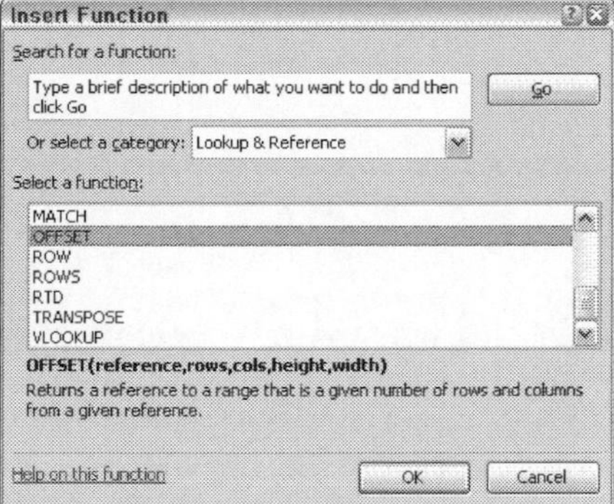

Figure 12-4: Clicking a function causes the names of its arguments and its purpose to appear in the Insert Function dialog box.

The category that a function belongs to is a little arbitrary. For example, Excel puts the TRANSPOSE function into the Lookup and Reference category. This isn't unreasonable, because TRANSPOSE puts a horizontal range of cells (such as A1:E1) into a vertical range (such as F1:F5) — or vice versa, and so it sort of belongs to Lookup and Reference. Putting it there is a bit of a stretch, though, because TRANSPOSE neither looks something up nor provides a reference, as COLUMN does. I'd expect to find it in the Math and Trig category (TRANSPOSE is used in matrix algebra) or conceivably in the Statistical category (it's used in regression analysis). The point is that if you don't find what you're looking for in one category, try another possible category, or go back to the All category.

I've been a little coy about the number of functions that are available in Excel, because it depends. If you haven't installed the ATP, you have 235 functions available to you. The ATP adds some functions, though, and it's both possible and feasible for you to write your own functions if you're hip to Visual Basic. If you install the ATP, you have an additional 103 functions available, largely in the areas of imaginary numbers and coupons (you use the coupon functions when you're analyzing securities, not in the express checkout line — at least, not when you're ahead of me, you don't).

After you've selected the OFFSET function and you've clicked OK, you see the Function Arguments dialog box, shown in Figure 12-5.

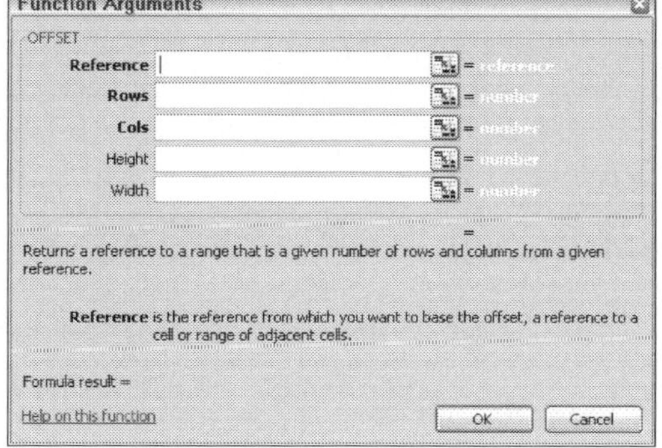

Figure 12-5: The Function Arguments dialog box shows the names of the arguments that the function in boldface.

Now that you're at the Function Arguments dialog box, a lot of problems resolve themselves. The dialog box shows you the name of each argument; it gives you those names in the order that the function expects them to come. In each box, you just put the value you want, or first click in the box you want to use next, and then click a worksheet cell that contains that value.

It's hard to see on the printed page, but to the right of each argument box is a label that shows what kind of information you're expected to provide. In Figure 12-5, the Reference argument is expected to be a worksheet address (to the right of the box is the word *Reference* in a white font on a light-gray background). The rest of the arguments to OFFSET are all *Number.*

If you see *Reference* next to an argument box, you'll need to enter a cell or range address in the box. If you see *Number* or *Text,* you can enter a numeric or a text value, or you can enter a cell reference that contains the value you want to use for that argument.

As soon as you've entered the final required argument, the result of the function appears in the dialog box to the right of *Formula result =*.

There's a difference between an Excel formula and an Excel function. *Formula* is a more inclusive term. It might contain a function all by itself:

```
=OFFSET(A1,5,3,10,1)
```

or fixed values only (this is pretty rare in a well-designed worksheet):

```
=96/12
```

or a combination of a function with fixed values:

```
=RAND()*1000
```

Function refers to the function itself, with its arguments. For example, you could refer to

```
=OFFSET(A1,5,3,10,1)
```

as either a function or a formula. But

```
=96/12
```

is not a function.

As the Function Arguments dialog box implies, you can get to detailed Help on the function by clicking the Help on This Function hyperlink in the dialog box's lower-left corner.

There's a button at the right end of each argument box. It's called a *collapse dialog* button. If you click it, the dialog box collapses and shows only the argument box whose button you clicked. This gives you more room on the worksheet (see Figure 12-6).

You don't really need that button, though. You can always click the dialog box's title bar and drag it out of the way if it's hiding cells that you want to click in.

You can enter the address of a range of cells that are on a different worksheet. Just click that worksheet's tab to activate it and drag through the cells you want. However, if the tab isn't visible — perhaps because you have so many worksheets that there isn't room to show all the tabs — you'll have to arrange to make it visible before you start this whole process by clicking the Insert Function button. One way to make the hidden worksheet tab visible is to choose Edit ➪ Move or Copy Sheet.

Assuming you want the monthly sales results for the sales rep named Johnson, using the OFFSET function, Figure 12-7 shows how the Function Arguments dialog box would look after you filled in the argument boxes.

Microsoft Excel - Forecasts.xls

File Edit View Insert Format Tools Data Window Help

OFFSET =OFFSET()

	A	B	C	D	E	F	G	H	I	J	K	
1	Sales Rep	January Sales	February Sales	March Sales	April Sales	May Sales	June Sales	July Sales	August Sales	September Sales	October Sales	Novem
2	Brown	$ 2,530	$ 20,206	$ 8,981	$ 8,432	$ 1,580	$ 36,059	$ 25,359	$ 29,356	$ 18,316	$ 3,644	$
3	Buzzi	$ 13,827	$ 21,658	$ 49,395	$ 15,243	$ 20,346	$ 44,424	$ 30,093	$ 5,423	$ 47,766	$ 40,116	$
4	Gibson	$ 22,315	$ 47,026	$ 40,290	$ 44,640	$ 17,371	$ 11,335	$ 6,489	$ 14,542	$ 11,651	$ 29,720	$
5	Hawn	$ 29,516	$ 21,882	$ 13,121	$ 33,854	$ 47,785	$ 20,604	$ 18,590	$ 15,302	$ 22,023	$ 45,236	$
6	Johnson	$ 3,056	$ 7,5	[illegible]	[illegible]	[illegible]	[illegible]	[illegible]	626	$ 25,335	$ 5,352	$
7	Martin	$ 35,447	$ 32,9						727	$ 44,560	$ 45,386	$
8	Owens	$ 42,257	$ 48,9						600	$ 33,908	$ 40,471	$
9	Rowan	$ 15,954	$ 10,452	$ 8,640	$ 15,101	$ 33,477	$ 33,566	$ 46,620	$ 45,191	$ 3,674	$ 39,683	$
10	Tomlin	$ 21,278	$ 20,658	$ 46,013	$ 6,274	$ 47,573	$ 4,669	$ 24,149	$ 25,598	$ 15,678	$ 48,397	$
11	Worley	$ 6,548	$ 27,012	$ 18,657	$ 46,065	$ 40,667	$ 37,166	$ 24,273	$ 18,219	$ 11,861	$ 5,038	$
14	FSET()											

Function Arguments

Sales Results

Figure 12-6: Click the button again to restore the Function Arguments dialog box.

If you omit the third and fourth arguments from the OFFSET function, it defaults to the number of rows and columns in your selection. So, given that you've selected 1 row and 12 columns in Figure 12-7, that's how many OFFSET returns.

Now, you click OK in the Function Arguments dialog box, to get the result shown in Figure 12-8.

A couple of things to bear in mind if you're using Insert Function to put a function in several cells at once, as shown in Figure12-3 through Figure 12-8:

- Begin by selecting all the cells you want the function to occupy. In Figure 12-8, that's B14:M14. There are 12 months, preceded by the sales rep's name, and M is the 13th column from column A.
- When you're ready to click OK on the Function Arguments dialog box, first press Ctrl and continue pressing it as you click OK. This signals Excel that the function is to occupy all the selected cells. You do this directly on the worksheet if you're not using Insert Function. Select a range of cells, enter a formula, and finish with Ctrl+Enter rather than just Enter. (This is different from array formulas, which often also occupy multiple cells, which you enter with Ctrl+Shift+Enter. See "Understanding Array Formulas.")

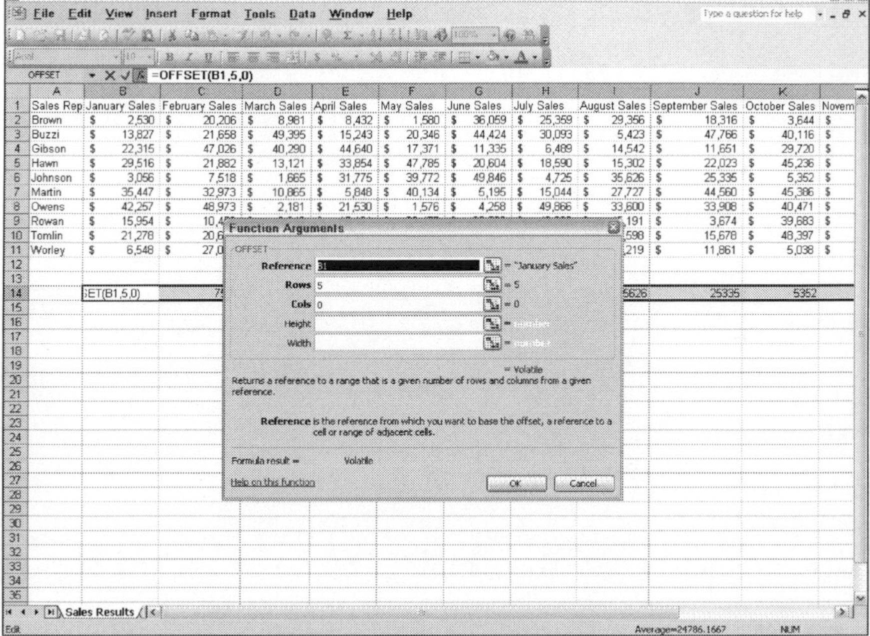

Figure 12-7: Notice that the arguments appear in the correct order in the Formula Bar.

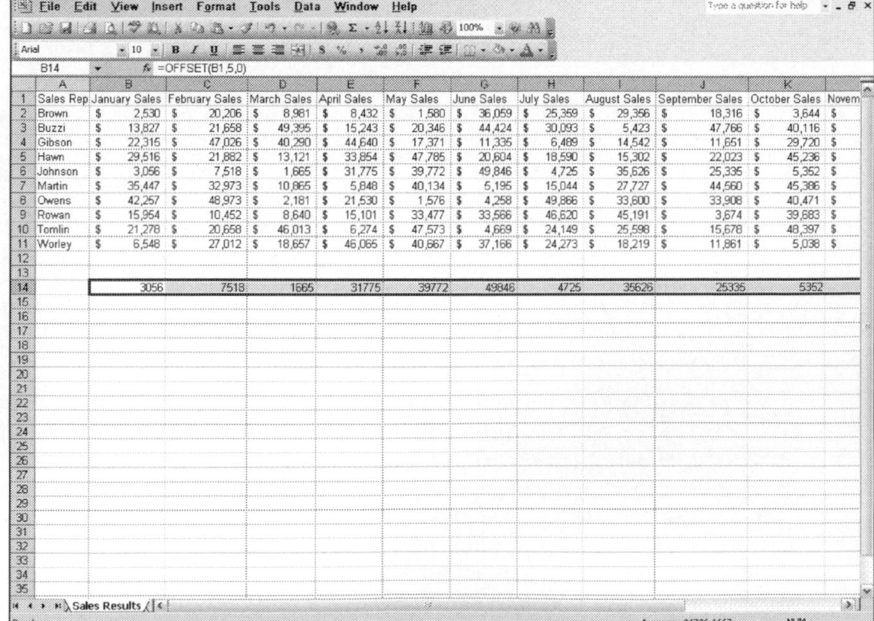

Figure 12-8: A function that picks up existing values and shows them elsewhere, such as OFFSET or INDEX, doesn't carry the source formats along with the values.

Understanding Array Formulas

You can use array formulas to get a lot of unusual results, such as:

- Reversing the order of the letters in a word or phrase (so that *Washington* becomes *notgnihsaW*).
- Using that reversed order of letters to separate out, say, a last name from a full name. Suppose you have a list of sales reps with their full names in column A, and you want to sort the list by last name. A fairly complicated array formula will strip the last names out of the list and put them in an adjacent column, which you can then sort along with the original list.
- Finding out if two different sets of data have duplicate values.
- Combining the functions SMALL and ROW to sort a range of values into a new range

"Understanding Array Formulas" is without doubt the most arrogant heading I've ever written. I've been using Excel for roughly 15 years and I still don't fully understand array formulas, so how can I expect myself to explain them in one section of a chapter? But I do know when I should *use* an array formula.

An overbroad and oversimplified guide is that you use an array formula rather than a regular formula when:

- You're using a function that you *must* array-enter.
- You're using a function that doesn't normally expect to get an array of worksheet cells as an argument. (For example, the IF function doesn't normally expect to get an array of worksheet cells as its condition, but that structure can be very useful if you have multiple conditions.)
- You're manipulating two different arrays of worksheet cells. (For example, multiplying B2:B5 by C2:C5 so as to get four different multiplications in D2:D5).

As I just indicated, some functions, such as TRANSPOSE, *require* you to array-enter them; if you don't, you won't get the result you're after, and you may even get an error value instead. Of special interest to forecasting are the functions LINEST and TREND, particularly if you're entering the formulas yourself rather than relying on the ATP's Regression tool. Further, TREND makes for an easy forecast of values if all you're interested in is the forecast and not at all in the regression equation, or the statistical analysis itself.

Choosing the range for the array formula

One reason that array formulas can require some specialized knowledge is that you need to select the range that the results will occupy before you enter the array formula. Suppose you want to transpose the range B1:F1 in Figure 12-9.

You want to transpose B1:F1 into B3:B7, and one good way is to use the TRANSPOSE function. But you need to know that transposing a range of, say, one row and five columns results in a range that occupies five rows and one column.

Another way is to copy B1:F1, select B3, choose Edit ⇨ Paste Special, select the Transpose check box, and click OK. But this pastes B1:F1 into B3:B7 as values, not as a formula. So if you later change a value in B1:F1, that change won't be reflected in B3:B7.

Transposing data comes up a *lot* in forums and newsgroups that involve Excel. The question usually comes up when someone has a worksheet that contains a moderately large table of values, and someone wants to use it in a formal report. The problem is that the original table doesn't work well in a report — but if it were turned 90 degrees it would be perfect. For example, the original list might put sales reps' names in one column and monthly sales in adjacent columns. You'd like to present it to your corporate management team the other way around: Sales reps' names in one row and monthly sales in subsequent rows. The Excel glitterati generally recommend using the TRANSPOSE function.

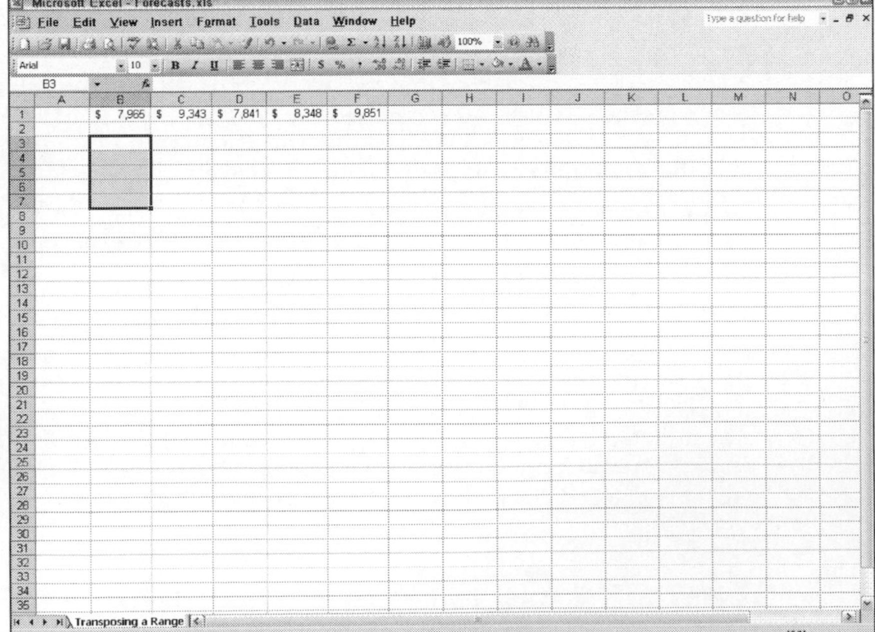

Figure 12-9: The range B1:F1 has the same number of columns as B3:B7 has rows.

So you need to know that TRANSPOSE will put the values in B1:F1 into a one-column-by-five-row range, and you need to start by selecting a range with those dimensions. Then, array-enter the TRANSPOSE function with the argument B1:F1:

```
=TRANSPOSE(B1:F1)
```

How do you array-enter a function or formula? Use the three-finger salute. No, not Ctrl+Alt+Delete. I mean the three-finger salute à la Excel (see the following section).

Excel's three-finger salute: Ctrl+Shift+Enter

You indicate to Excel that you want your formula treated as an array formula by a special keyboard sequence: Ctrl+Shift+Enter. In words, after you've typed the formula, hold down Ctrl and Shift at the same time, and while you're still holding them down, press Enter. Then release all three keys.

You would also use Ctrl+Shift+Enter if you've used Insert Function to build the function's argument list. After entering the arguments, you would hold down Ctrl and Shift, and then either press Enter or click OK in the Function Arguments dialog box.

See Figure 12-10 for the result of the example begun in Figure 12-9.

Select a range with the correct dimensions before you array-enter your formula. This comes up a lot in forums and newsgroups: "I array-entered a function. The Help documents say I'm supposed to see values in several cells, but I see a value in just one cell. What's going on?" And the answer, inevitably and invariably, is "Start by selecting the correct *range* of cells, not just a single cell."

Recognizing array formulas

Occasionally, you find yourself dealing with an Excel workbook that you didn't create. It might have array formulas in it, and if you're going to understand what the worksheet does and how it does it, then you're going to have to recognize that a formula *is* an array formula.

An array formula has a special appearance in the Formula Bar: it's surrounded by curly brackets, like this:

```
{=TRANSPOSE(B1:F1)}
```

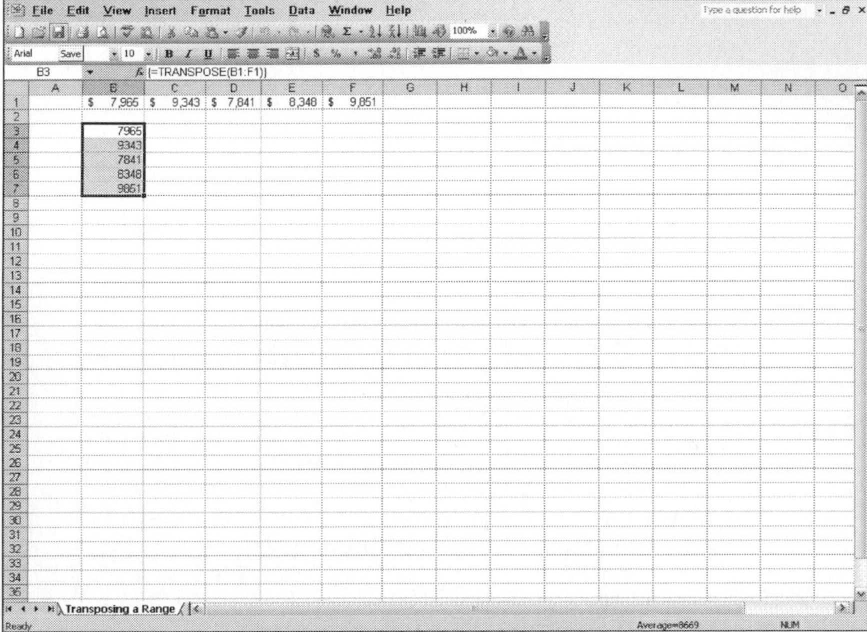

Figure 12-10: Using Ctrl+Shift+Enter is the only way to get the result in B3:B7 by means of the TRANSPOSE function.

You won't see the curly brackets in the worksheet cells that contain the array formula, not even if you choose Tools ➪ Options, select the View tab, and select the Formulas check box.

And bear this in mind: When you *enter* an array formula, you shouldn't type the curly brackets yourself. Leave that up to Excel. If you type the curly brackets yourself, Excel treats the formula as text — and I can't think why you'd want that to happen.

A special problem with array formulas

Array formulas pose a special problem that, therefore, requires special handling. It's an all-or-none issue.

Changing part of an array formula

You can't.

I wanted to let this section go with that warning, but my editor said I should give you some more information.

Suppose you've entered an array formula in A1:A5, and you later decide that you don't need to see the value in A5. So you select A5 and press the Delete key, or you try to type another formula or value into it. Excel won't let you. You'll get the terse, even testy, error message, `You cannot change part of an array.`

You'll also get that message if you enter either a regular formula or an array formula in a range of cells that overlaps part of an existing array formula.

Resistance is futile

But you don't need to let yourself be bullied by Excel — you're the one who's in control here. Here's the fastest way around the `You cannot change part of an array` problem. Continuing the example started in the prior section:

1. **Select the entire range that's occupied by the array formula.**

   In this example, that's A1:A5. You'll see the formula in the Formula Bar.

2. **Select the equal sign in the Formula Bar by dragging across it.**
3. **Press the Delete key.**

   You should now see the formula, minus the equal sign, in the Formula Bar.

4. **Press Ctrl+Shift+Enter.**

   This enters the formula in the selected range as text values only.

5. **Select A5 and press the Delete key.**
6. **Select A1:A4, reenter the equal sign, and press Ctrl+Shift+Enter.**

   Now your array formula occupies A1:A4 and A5 is free for you to use in some other way.

Using the Regression Functions

When you decide that you want to use formulas with functions that calculate a regression equation and related statistics, you're usually thinking of using LINEST and TREND. If you have just one predictor variable, you can also use SLOPE to get the best regression coefficient and INTERCEPT for the constant to use with your predictor variable (you use just Enter, not Ctrl+Shift+Enter, to enter SLOPE and INTERCEPT).

Using the LINEST function

The LINEST function shows you the following information:

- **The coefficient that you use to multiply by the predictor variable to get the best regression estimate of the forecast variable.**

- **The standard error of each coefficient:** You can use this information to decide whether to include a predictor variable in the regression equation.
- **The R-squared value:** This value ranges from 0.0 to 1.0. The closer it is to 1.0, the more accurate the regression equation is as an approach to forecasting the data you handed off to LINEST. You can interpret the R-squared value as the percent of the variation in the forecast variable that you can attribute to the predictor variable or variables.
- **The standard error of estimate:** This is the standard deviation of the residuals — that is, the differences between the actual values in the baseline and the values predicted by the regression equation. The smaller the standard error of estimate, the better the forecast.
- **The F-ratio, the degrees of freedom, the regression sum of squares, and the residual sum of squares:** If your last statistics course was a while back, or if you haven't heard of these statistics, don't worry about it. You don't need them to do forecasting. If you have heard of them, you already know what they're about — it's not like they come up in casual conversation.

Figure 12-11 shows both the LINEST function, array-entered, and the results of the ATP's Regression tool. Both are used on the same data set, in A1:B41.

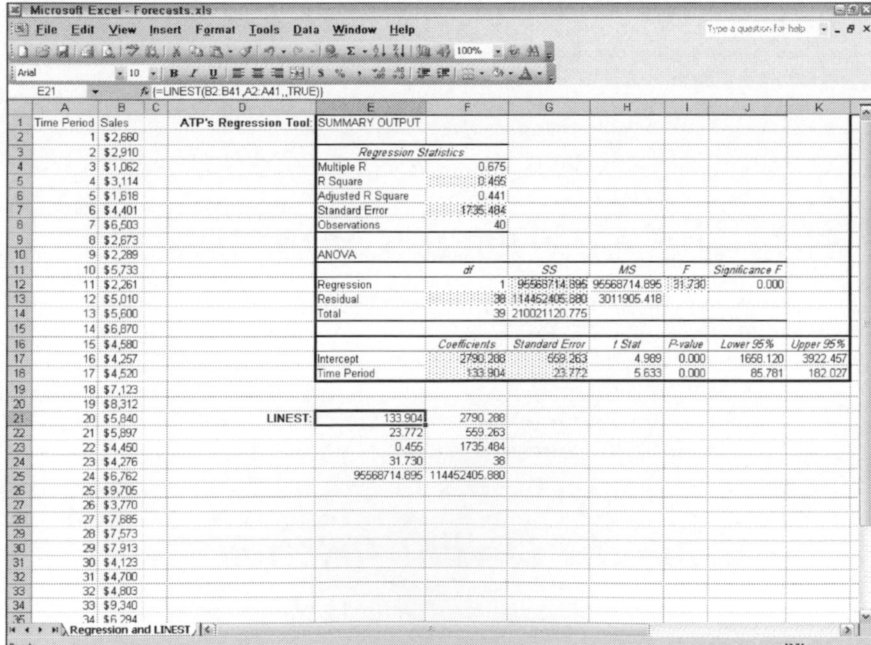

	A	B	C	D	E	F	G	H	I	J	K
1	Time Period	Sales		ATP's Regression Tool:	SUMMARY OUTPUT						
2	1	$2,660									
3	2	$2,910			*Regression Statistics*						
4	3	$1,062			Multiple R	0.675					
5	4	$3,114			R Square	0.455					
6	5	$1,618			Adjusted R Square	0.441					
7	6	$4,401			Standard Error	1735.484					
8	7	$6,503			Observations	40					
9	8	$2,673									
10	9	$2,289			ANOVA						
11	10	$5,733				*df*	*SS*	*MS*	*F*	*Significance F*	
12	11	$2,261			Regression	1	95568714.895	95568714.895	31.730	0.000	
13	12	$5,010			Residual	38	114452405.880	3011905.418			
14	13	$5,600			Total	39	210021120.775				
15	14	$6,870									
16	15	$4,580				*Coefficients*	*Standard Error*	*t Stat*	*P-value*	*Lower 95%*	*Upper 95%*
17	16	$4,257			Intercept	2790.288	559.263	4.989	0.000	1658.120	3922.457
18	17	$4,520			Time Period	133.904	23.772	5.633	0.000	85.781	182.027
19	18	$7,123									
20	19	$8,312									
21	20	$5,840		LINEST:	133.904	2790.288					
22	21	$5,897			23.772	559.263					
23	22	$4,450			0.455	1735.484					
24	23	$4,276			31.730	38					
25	24	$6,762			95568714.895	114452405.880					
26	25	$9,705									
27	26	$3,770									
28	27	$7,685									
29	28	$7,573									
30	29	$7,913									
31	30	$4,123									
32	31	$4,700									
33	32	$4,803									
34	33	$9,340									
35	34	$6,294									

Figure 12-11: All the statistics returned by LINEST show up in the ATP's output.

In this case, you would enter LINEST by following these steps:

1. **Select a range that's two columns wide and five rows high.**
2. **Type** =LINEST(B2:B41,A2:A41,,TRUE) **into the Formula Bar or use Insert Function to let it guide you.**

   Notice that you don't include row 1, because LINEST can't handle text labels.
3. **Array-enter the formula using Ctrl+Shift+Enter.**

You may want to have another look at that LINEST syntax, whether you enter it directly or use Insert Function to help you follow the trail of breadcrumbs:

- The first argument, B2:B41, is where Excel looks to find the baseline values of the forecast variable — in this case, Sales.
- The second argument, A2:A41, is where Excel looks to find the baseline values of the predictor variable — in this case, Time Period.
- The third argument is left blank — notice the consecutive commas among the arguments. If it's blank, or if you set it to TRUE, LINEST calculates the value of the intercept (or *constant*) normally. This tells you the value of Sales at the time period zero: where the regression line intercepts the vertical axis on a chart. If the third argument is 0, or if you set it to FALSE, LINEST forces the regression line to intercept the vertical axis at its zero point. See Chapter 11 for more information and for why this is seldom a good idea.
- The fourth argument, TRUE, tells Excel whether to calculate the third through fifth rows of its output: the R-squared value, the standard error of estimate, and so on. If TRUE, Excel calculates those statistics and displays them if you started by selecting a range with five rows. If you enter FALSE, Excel does not calculate the additional statistics. You lose nothing by setting the argument to TRUE, and you can gain considerably by evaluating the size of the R-squared value.

See Chapter 11 for information on how to use the ATP's Regression tool to get the results shown in Figure 12-11.

In Figure 12-11, the Regression tool's output in the range E1:K18 contains some shaded cells. These shaded cells contain values that are provided by using the LINEST function, shown in the range E21:F25. In particular:

- The coefficients to use in making a forecast are found in F17 and F18 (ATP) and in E21:F21 (LINEST). So the regression equation is:

  ```
  Forecast for Time Period 2 = 2790.288 + 133.904 *
  2
  Forecast for Time Period 2 = 3058.1
  ```

In words, the forecast for any time period that you get by using regression on this baseline is the intercept, 2790.288 plus the result of multiplying the coefficient for Time Period by the actual value for that time period. By the way, the Regression tool calls the intercept a coefficient, to keep it in the same column as the actual coefficients and, thus, to make for a neater table of statistics. But it's not really a coefficient; it's an intercept (some people call it the *constant*).

- The R-squared value for the regression equation is found in F5 (ATP) and E23 (LINEST).
- The standard errors for the coefficients and intercept are found in G17:G18 (ATP) and in E22:F22 (LINEST).
- The standard error of estimate is found in F7 (ATP) and F23 (LINEST).
- The sums of squares are found in G12:G13 (ATP) and E25:F25 (LINEST). The degrees of freedom are found in F13 (ATP) and F24 (LINEST). The F-ratio is found in I12 (ATP) and E24 (LINEST).

Clearly, you get a lot more information with the ATP than with LINEST. You can get all that additional information by using other Excel worksheet functions. For example:

- TDIST to get the P-value
- The ratio of the coefficient or intercept to its standard error to get the t Stat
- Dividing the sums of squares by the degrees of freedom to get the mean square (MS)

But I'm not sure why you'd want all this other stuff if your intent is to forecast. To make a forecast, you need the R-squared value to decide whether regression is a good tool to use on your baseline, and the intercept and coefficient(s) to actually make the forecast.

Selecting the right range of cells

If you want to use LINEST to get the really important stuff for forecasting, you need to be aware of how many rows and how many columns to select before you enter the LINEST formula.

- The R-squared value shows up in the third row of LINEST's results. So the range of cells you select before array-entering the LINEST function should have at least three rows (and no more than five — subsequent rows in the range that you select will just show the error value `#N/A`).

- The range that you select for the LINEST function should have as many columns as you have predictor variables, plus 1. LINEST returns a coefficient for each predictor variable, plus the intercept.

So if you're using two predictor variables, you should select a range with three columns and at least three rows (at most, five rows).

Getting the statistics right

Figure 12-12 shows an example with two predictor variables, again analyzed using both the ATP Regression tool and the LINEST function.

The location of the key forecasting statistics is similar to the single predictor situation shown in the "Using the LINEST Function" section, earlier in this chapter. One difference is that the ATP's output has an additional row, and the LINEST output has an additional column, because you're now using not one but two predictor variables.

Figure 12-12 hints at an extremely annoying aspect of LINEST — really, it's one of only a few annoyances in this function, but it can be a major one. Compare the order of the coefficients in LINEST to the order of the predictor variables in the baseline. For example:

- The value in G22 (returned by LINEST) is the same as the value in F17 (returned by the ATP). It is the intercept for the regression equation: LINEST always puts the intercept in the first row, final column of the range it occupies. (This assumes that you started out by selecting a range with the proper number of columns.) No problem so far.
- The value in F22 (LINEST) is the same as the value in F18 (ATP). It is the coefficient for Size of Sales Force.
- The value in E22 (LINEST) is the same as the value in F19 (ATP). It is the coefficient for Time Period.

So LINEST puts the coefficient for Time Period in column E and for Size of Sales Force in column F. In the LINEST results, Time Period comes before Sales Force. But in the baseline, Sales Force comes before Time Period: Sales Force in column A, Time Period in column B. LINEST reverses the order of the predictor variables.

This means that if you're going to use the LINEST results in an equation that returns the predicted values, you have to remember to get the right coefficient aligned with the right column in the baseline. Figure 12-13 shows how you might do that.

Microsoft Excel - Forecasts.xls

E22 {=LINEST(C2:C41,A2:B41,,TRUE)}

	A	B	C	D	E	F	G	H	I	J	K
1	Size of Sales Force	Time Period	Sales	ATP's Regression	SUMMARY OUTPUT						
2	89	1	$ 2,660	Tool:							
3	21	2	$ 2,910		*Regression Statistics*						
4	25	3	$ 1,062		Multiple R	0.711					
5	21	4	$ 3,114		R Square	0.506					
6	46	5	$ 1,618		Adjusted R Square	0.479					
7	93	6	$ 4,401		Standard Error	1674.986					
8	92	7	$ 6,503		Observations	40					
9	74	8	$ 2,673								
10	86	9	$ 2,289		ANOVA						
11	47	10	$ 5,733			*df*	*SS*	*MS*	*F*	*ignificance F*	
12	3	11	$ 2,261		Regression	2	106214670.399	53107335.199	18.929	0.000	
13	62	12	$ 5,010		Residual	37	103806450.376	2805579.740			
14	2	13	$ 5,600		Total	39	210021120.775				
15	22	14	$ 6,870								
16	70	15	$ 4,580			*Coefficients*	*Standard Error*	*t Stat*	*P-value*	*Lower 95%*	*Upper 95*
17	23	16	$ 4,257		Intercept	1801.890	740.813	2.432	0.020	300.860	3302.92
18	1	17	$ 4,520		Size of Sales Force	19.027	9.768	1.948	0.059	-0.764	38.81
19	93	18	$ 7,123		Time Period	133.042	22.947	5.798	0.000	86.547	179.53
20	63	19	$ 8,312								
21	71	20	$ 5,840								
22	56	21	$ 5,897	LINEST:	133.042	19.027	1801.890				
23	45	22	$ 4,450		22.947	9.768	740.813				
24	69	23	$ 4,276		0.506	1674.986	#N/A				
25	82	24	$ 6,762		18.929	37	#N/A				
26	81	25	$ 9,705		106214670.399	103806450.376	#N/A				
27	94	26	$ 3,770								
28	55	27	$ 7,685								
29	44	28	$ 7,573								
30	44	29	$ 7,913								
31	47	30	$ 4,123								
32	19	31	$ 4,700								
33	23	32	$ 4,803								
34	80	33	$ 9,340								
35	68	34	$ 6,294								

Mult. Regression - ATP & LINEST

Figure 12-12: Notice that LINEST's arguments specify that the predictor variables, Size of Sales Force and Time Period, occupy columns A and B. Multiple predictors result in multiple regression.

Microsoft Excel - Forecasts.xls

E2 =$J$3+$I$3*A2+$H$3*B2

	A	B	C	D	E	F	G	H	I	J
1	Size of Sales Force	Time Period	Sales		Forecast			**Time Period**	**Size of Sales Force**	**Intercept**
2	89	1	$ 2,660		3106.604			**Coefficient**	**Coefficient**	
3	21	2	$ 2,910		2437.086		LINEST:	**153.817**	**12.108**	**1875.186**
4	25	3	$ 1,062		2639.335			36.301	15.246	1065.183
5	21	4	$ 3,114		2744.72			0.420	1711.055	#N/A
6	46	5	$ 1,618		3201.234			9.765	27	#N/A
7	93	6	$ 4,401		3924.122			57179301.955	79048190.045	#N/A
8	92	7	$ 6,503		4065.831					
9	74	8	$ 2,673		4001.706					
10	86	9	$ 2,289		4300.818					
11	47	10	$ 5,733		3982.428					
12	40	11	$ 2,261		4051.49					
13	62	12	$ 5,010		4471.681					
14	52	13	$ 5,600		4504.419					
15	42	14	$ 6,870		4537.158					
16	70	15	$ 4,580		5029.995					
17	63	16	$ 4,257		5099.057					
18	51	17	$ 4,520		5107.58					
19	68	18	$ 7,123		5467.231					
20	63	19	$ 8,312		5560.509					
21	71	20	$ 5,840		5811.189					
22	56	21	$ 5,897		5783.388					
23	45	22	$ 4,450		5804.019					
24	69	23	$ 4,276		6248.425					
25	82	24	$ 6,762		6559.644					
26	81	25	$ 9,705		6701.354					
27	94	26	$ 3,770		7012.573					
28	55	27	$ 7,685		6694.183					
29	44	28	$ 7,573		6714.814					
30	44	29	$ 7,913		6868.631					
31	47	30	$ 4,123		7058.772					

Forecasting with LINEST

Figure 12-13: You'll have to do it yourself, but labeling the columns of the LINEST results according to which predictor variables they represent is a good idea.

The formula in cell E2 in Figure 12-13 multiplies a predictor value in column A by a coefficient in column I, and a predictor value in column B by the coefficient in column H. This formula, copied down through cell E31, untangles the snarl introduced by the order in which LINEST returns coefficients.

I've developed my own multiple-regression functions for Excel, using Visual Basic for Applications. I am now telling you that there is no sound reason to reverse the worksheet order of the predictor variables in LINEST's results. Following the algorithms and the matrix algebra results in coefficients the order of which matches the order of the predictor variables in the baseline.

This is a good illustration of the reason that you need to make sure you've got it right before you put a feature such as a function into a widely distributed application. By now (several Excel versions after including LINEST in Excel), Microsoft wouldn't dare correct the order of the coefficients. Doing so would screw up too many customer worksheets that assume the coefficients are coming out backward.

Using the TREND function

An easier way to get forecasts from regression — easier than using LINEST — is the TREND function. The trade-off is that you don't see the R-squared value, the coefficients, and the intercept. But of course there's nothing to stop you from using both LINEST and TREND.

As with LINEST, you must array-enter the TREND function (see Figure 12-14 for an example).

TREND is much easier to use for forecasting than LINEST. To get the forecast values in Figure 12-14, follow these steps:

1. **Select the range E2:E31.**
2. **Type** =TREND(C2:C31,A2:B31) **into the Formula Bar.**
3. **Press Ctrl+Shift+Enter.**

What about forecasting the next time period, the one you don't yet have actuals for? As usual, you'll need information about the next period's values on your predictors. In the current example, you need to know (or have a good estimate of) the company's sales force next month. The next period's value for Time Period is just the next value in the baseline — here, 31.

Figure 12-15 shows these new values and how you use the TREND function to forecast the next period's sales.

Microsoft Excel - Forecasts.xls

E2 {=TREND(C2:C31,A2:B31)}

Size of Sales Force	Time Period	Sales		Forecast
89	1	$2,660		$ 3,107
21	2	$2,910		$ 2,437
25	3	$1,062		$ 2,639
21	4	$3,114		$ 2,745
46	5	$1,618		$ 3,201
93	6	$4,401		$ 3,924
92	7	$6,503		$ 4,066
74	8	$2,673		$ 4,002
86	9	$2,289		$ 4,301
47	10	$5,733		$ 3,982
40	11	$2,261		$ 4,051
62	12	$5,010		$ 4,472
52	13	$5,600		$ 4,504
42	14	$6,870		$ 4,537
70	15	$4,580		$ 5,030
63	16	$4,257		$ 5,099
51	17	$4,520		$ 5,108
68	18	$7,123		$ 5,467
63	19	$8,312		$ 5,561
71	20	$5,840		$ 5,811
56	21	$5,897		$ 5,783
45	22	$4,450		$ 5,804
69	23	$4,276		$ 6,248
82	24	$6,762		$ 6,560
81	25	$9,705		$ 6,701
94	26	$3,770		$ 7,013
55	27	$7,685		$ 6,694
44	28	$7,573		$ 6,715
44	29	$7,913		$ 6,869
47	30	$4,123		$ 7,059

Forecasting with TREND

Figure 12-14: The TREND forecast is identical to the forecast based on LINEST.

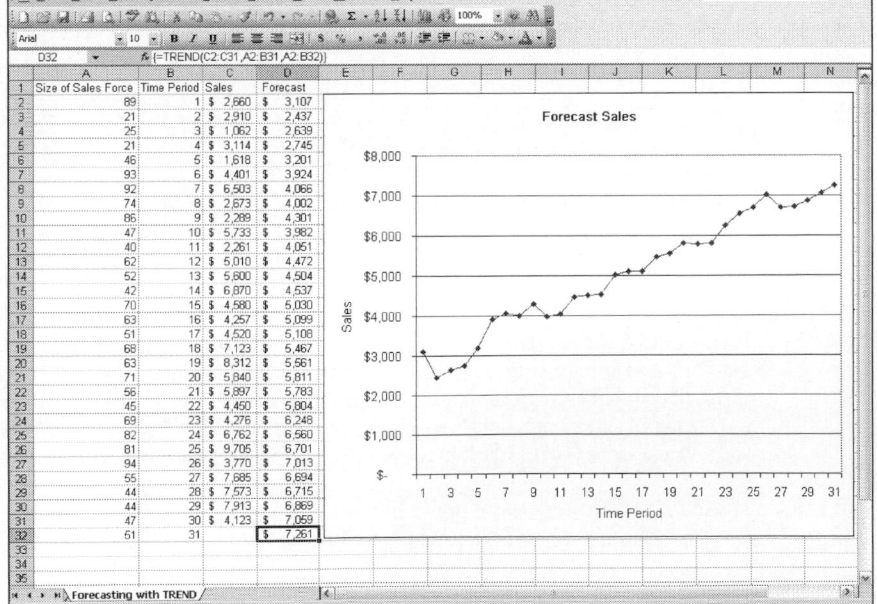

Microsoft Excel - Forecasts.xls

D32 {=TREND(C2:C31,A2:B31,A2:B32)}

Size of Sales Force	Time Period	Sales	Forecast
89	1	$ 2,660	$ 3,107
21	2	$ 2,910	$ 2,437
25	3	$ 1,062	$ 2,639
21	4	$ 3,114	$ 2,745
46	5	$ 1,618	$ 3,201
93	6	$ 4,401	$ 3,924
92	7	$ 6,503	$ 4,066
74	8	$ 2,673	$ 4,002
86	9	$ 2,289	$ 4,301
47	10	$ 5,733	$ 3,982
40	11	$ 2,261	$ 4,051
62	12	$ 5,010	$ 4,472
52	13	$ 5,600	$ 4,504
42	14	$ 6,870	$ 4,537
70	15	$ 4,580	$ 5,030
63	16	$ 4,257	$ 5,099
51	17	$ 4,520	$ 5,108
68	18	$ 7,123	$ 5,467
63	19	$ 8,312	$ 5,561
71	20	$ 5,840	$ 5,811
56	21	$ 5,897	$ 5,783
45	22	$ 4,450	$ 5,804
69	23	$ 4,276	$ 6,248
82	24	$ 6,762	$ 6,560
81	25	$ 9,705	$ 6,701
94	26	$ 3,770	$ 7,013
55	27	$ 7,685	$ 6,694
44	28	$ 7,573	$ 6,715
44	29	$ 7,913	$ 6,869
47	30	$ 4,123	$ 7,059
51	31		$ 7,261

Forecasting with TREND

Figure 12-15: The chart's X axis is labeled Time Period, but the forecast is based on both Time Period and Size of Sales Force.

In Figure 12-15, the array formula in D2:D32 is:

```
=TREND(C2:C31,A2:B31,A2:B32)
```

This form of the TREND function has three arguments. (***Remember:*** When used in a function as here, a cell range is an argument to the function.)

- **C2:C31:** This range of values, the actual sales, is what Excel terms the *known_y's.* The letter *y* is often used to represent the predicted variable in a regression analysis.
- **A2:B31:** This range of values, the actual Size of Sales Force and the actual Time Period, is what Excel terms the *known_x's.* The letter *x* means the predictor variable (or, as in this case, variables) in a regression analysis.
- **A2:B32:** Excel terms this range of values the *new_x's.* Despite the name, it includes both the existing predictor values in A2:B31 (the known_x's) and the predictor variables that you expect for the next, as-yet-unobserved time period. These are in A32:B32. Time Period is easy, but you need special knowledge to determine what the size of the sales force will be next time period.

So these are the steps to use TREND to get a forecast for the upcoming time period:

1. **Determine that period's values on the predictor variables.**
2. **Enter the predictor variables' values for the new period in the next row, under the existing predictor variables' values.**

   In Figure 12-15, you'd enter those in A32:B32.
3. **Select the cells that will contain the forecast values, including the one for the upcoming period.**

   In Figure 12-15, that's D2:D32.
4. **Type** =TREND(C2:C31,A2:B31,A2:B32)**.**
5. **Array-enter the formula by pressing Ctrl+Shift+Enter.**

Another worksheet function, FORECAST, also predicts the next value in a baseline. Like TREND, it uses known_y's, known_x's and new_x's. But FORECAST can handle only one predictor variable, whereas TREND can handle multiple predictor variables. To keep things straight and relatively simple, I recommend that you decide to always use one or the other — and I also think that the one you choose should be TREND.

Chapter 13

Using Moving Averages

In This Chapter

- Deciding on a length
- Figuring out how many baseline values to use
- Charting your moving-average trendline

When you decide to look at a baseline's moving-average values — whether to get a better idea of the baseline's behavior or to make a forecast — the number of values you choose to put into each average has consequences, if not necessarily truth. For example, the more values in an average, the smaller the number of averages.

And your choice has an effect on how smooth or rough the moving averages are. Generally, the fewer the data points you include in a moving average, the more it will jump around, and the faster it will react to changes in the baseline. The greater the number of data points, the smoother it becomes and the slower it will react.

Excel's Analysis ToolPak has a Moving Averages tool that you can use to put the averages into a chart, along with the original baseline. In this chapter, I show you how to use that.

Choosing the Length of the Moving Average

If you've worked with moving averages before, you may think them too basic to discuss in a book about a topic as grand as forecasting. The humble moving average?

No. Although the basic idea of moving averages is simple and intuitive, they play a starring role in some pretty complicated forecasts. These complex forecasts that combine autoregression with moving averages — and more often than not the moving-average part is the diva and the autoregression part is just the spear carrier. (Actually, if you take those two components far enough, you find that they're the same thing, but I don't take things that far here.)

So if you're going to forecast sales or anything else, it's worth your while to take moving averages seriously. Two concepts are useful when you're considering moving averages: signal and noise.

Signaling: Left turn coming up?

A baseline that isn't completely random has what's termed *signal.* Signal is the true, credible part of the baseline, whether it's headed up or down or holding steady; whether it's moving up and down with the seasons or with a regional business cycle.

If only you could get your hands on that signal, you'd have your best estimate of what's going to happen next.

Think of what comes out of the speakers when your car begins to get within range of a radio station. As you start to hear the station, you hear a lot of static, but you can faintly hear the signal, which is trying to get you to buy Cloying Munchies if you're on AM.

As you get closer to the source of the transmission, you hear more of the announcer and less of the static, and finally you're close enough that you can't hear the static any longer, just a nice clear signal that, if you've got the FM tuned to NPR, asks you for more money.

It's similar with baselines, especially sales revenues and, to a lesser degree, units sold. The signal in the baseline is the result of all sorts of different influences, among them:

- The size of, and the experience and skill in, the sales force
- The increasing or decreasing desirability of the product, often due to its technology, its novelty, or its appearance
- Its price, relative to that of the competition
- Money spent on marketing, advertising in particular
- Changes in social attitudes — for example, toward smoking and drinking

Fortunately, you don't have to identify all the influences on sales, list them, measure them, and then forecast them so as to get a forecast of what you're really after, which is sales revenues and units. All the influences combine in the signal and if you can get a reliable forecast of that signal, you've slain the Uncertainty Dragon and a bonus check will surely be yours.

So, how do you identify that signal? The idea is that over time, some special and unpredictable events — the *noise,* or the discrepancy between the signal and the actual results — averages out. Some unwelcome noisy event that pulls your actual revenues below the signal in June can be compensated for by other, welcome noisy events in July and August.

And moving averages take advantage of this. If you're getting a three-month moving average, those noisy events (the hit you take in June, the good luck in July and August) tend to average out, and the average for any given three months provides a better estimate of the signal than do the monthlies.

A little less noise, please

Moving averages try to get the noise to cancel itself out in the baseline, and in that way to emphasize the signal. Where does the noise come from? There are many more sources of noise than of signal. Every one of your customers, every one of your sales reps, your production facilities, your distribution channel, possibly your customers' customers, is a source of noise that drags your actual results from the signal.

Suppose you're calculating a moving average that includes two months. Your first moving average might include January and February. The unseen and unseeable signal in those two months — the result of a conspiracy among the sales force, the product, the pricing, and so on — is $100 million for January and $110 million for February. But the noise steers the actual results off signal:

- In February there's a bad flu outbreak that knocks out several of your sales reps as well as some buyers who normally purchase from the reps who are still standing.
- In December, a customer with a January-to-December fiscal year makes a large end-of-year purchase, to get the cost into its current fiscal year. Your company recognizes the revenue in January, which artificially swells the results for that month.
- One of your competition's big customers gets upset by a price increase, starts shopping around, and decides it likes your pricing structure better, even though your product line isn't quite as sexy. Yes, Virginia, there is a bluebird, and up bounce your January revenues.
- A moderate earthquake hits your San Andreas assembly and kitting site, disrupting production for a couple weeks during last year's first quarter. You can't fulfill existing orders on time and January revenues fall in consequence.

Notice that neither you nor your company can predict or control any of these events — perhaps apart from questioning the advisability of locating a production facility next to an earthquake fault line. And that's the definition of *noise* — or, if you prefer, residuals or error. Its long-term expected value is zero. Figure 13-1 shows an example of how this works, in theory at least.

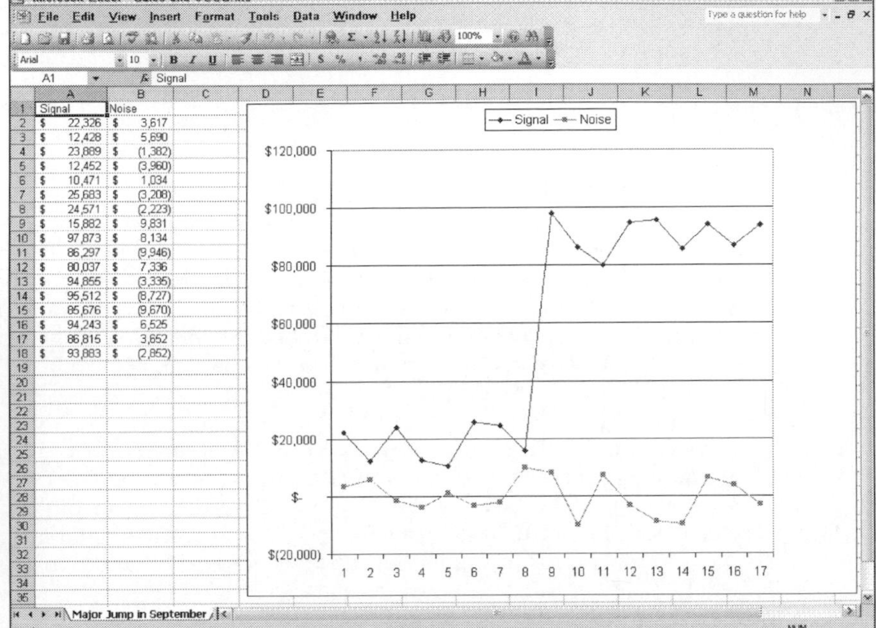

Figure 13-1: This is what you'd like to see, if you could see it. You never *know* the exact value of the signal or the noise.

This is one reason it's a good idea to look at a chart of residuals. Unlike the ATP's Regression tool, neither the Moving Average tool nor the Exponential Smoothing tool calculates residuals, and therefore cannot chart them. See "Charting residuals," later in this chapter, for the steps to take to create a residuals chart from a moving-average analysis.

In Figure 13-1, you see what you never see in practice: the true values of the signal and the noise. The best you can really do is:

- Calculate a moving average using your actual results.
- Treat the moving average as if it were the signal — this is the whole point behind getting moving averages, after all: to estimate the signal as best you can.
- Treat the difference between the actuals and the moving average as if it were the noise.

As several other chapters in this book mention, the difference between the forecast and the actual is the error, or the residual. Noise is just a more-generalized term.

You like to see noise in the baseline like that shown in Figure 13-2. The chart shows that it forms a horizontal data series. And, in cell B20, you can see that its average value is $30. In the context of actuals that are in the tens and even hundreds of thousands of dollars, $30 is effectively zero.

Figure 13-2 shows how the signal and the noise combine to form the actuals.

Again, you never really see the signal, you just do your best to estimate it with your forecast formula. So my regrettable lack of omniscience led me to make up the signal and the actuals (and, by subtraction, the noise) shown in Figures 13-1 and 13-2. Figure 13-3 shows a more realistic situation.

Why doesn't the chart shown in Figure 13-3 look quite the same as the chart in Figure 13-2? Because Figure 13-2 is a fantasy: It acts as though you can know what the signal is. You can't ever know that. You can only estimate it — here, by using moving averages — and this example comes reasonably close.

The big discrepancy is at the ninth data point. The actual and the signal are very close in Figure 13-2, but the actual and the moving average are a ways apart in Figure 13-3. That's because the moving averages in Figure 13-3 take the prior two actuals into account, and they drag the estimate down to $54,651 rather than the Figure 13-2 value of $97,873.

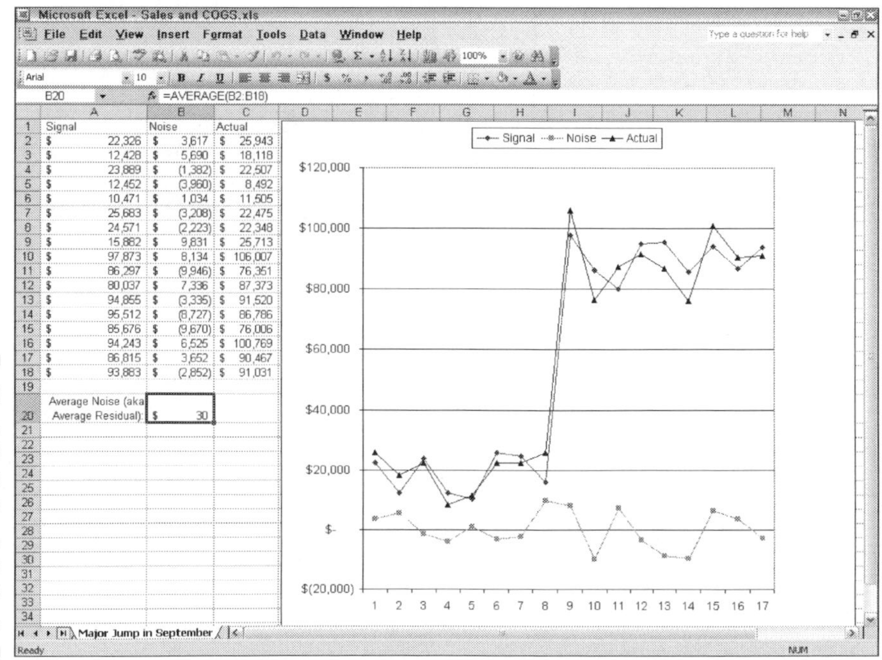

Figure 13-2: In this case, the actuals track the signal very closely, because the errors are so small.

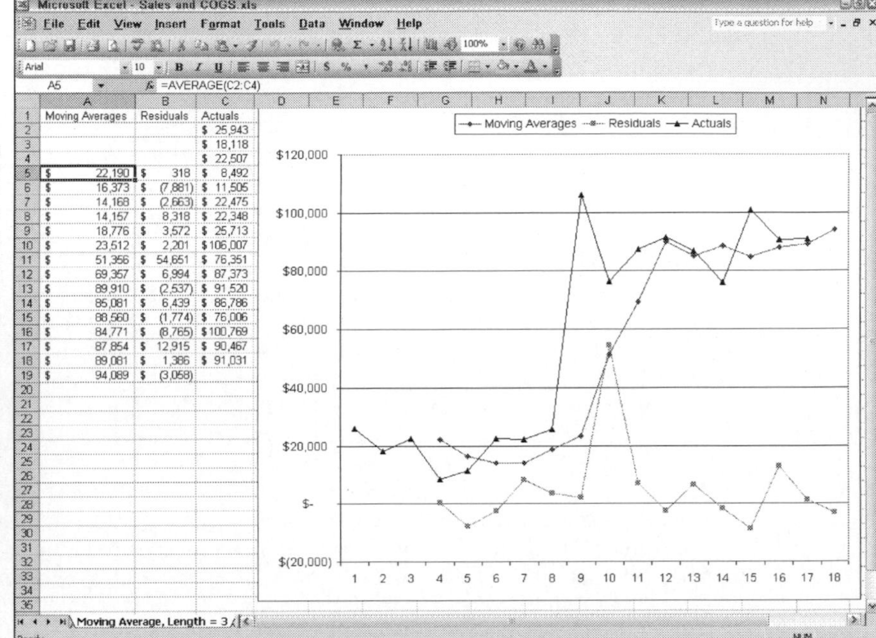

	Moving Averages	Residuals	Actuals
2			$ 25,943
3			$ 18,118
4			$ 22,507
5	$ 22,190	$ 318	$ 8,492
6	$ 16,373	$ (7,881)	$ 11,505
7	$ 14,168	$ (2,663)	$ 22,475
8	$ 14,157	$ 8,318	$ 22,348
9	$ 18,776	$ 3,572	$ 25,713
10	$ 23,512	$ 2,201	$ 106,007
11	$ 51,356	$ 54,651	$ 76,351
12	$ 69,357	$ 6,994	$ 87,373
13	$ 89,910	$ (2,537)	$ 91,520
14	$ 85,081	$ 6,439	$ 86,786
15	$ 88,560	$ (1,774)	$ 76,006
16	$ 84,771	$ (8,765)	$ 100,769
17	$ 87,854	$ 12,915	$ 90,467
18	$ 89,081	$ 1,386	$ 91,031
19	$ 94,089	$ (3,058)	

Figure 13-3: Here, the chart *estimates* the signal by way of moving averages, and calculates the errors by subtracting the moving average from the actual.

Stepping it up

The actuals in Figures 13-1 through 13-3 show a phenomenon that moving averages (and also exponential smoothing) lend themselves well to. Notice the big jump in the value of the baseline at the ninth data point. In the terminology of forecasting, this is called a *random shock.* (In some contexts, this is called a *step function.*) Although the term *random shock* may make you think of Janet Leigh in a shower stall, it actually means a change in the level of a baseline that persists over time. That's what you see in Figure 13-3, starting at the ninth time period.

A good example of a random shock is a purchase to inventory. Perhaps your Product Management group has an opportunity to buy a large supply of materials or finished goods at a discounted unit price. The group does so, and now — if you maintain your current selling price, your company's profit margin per unit will increase. You could even discount your selling price a little, and as long as the discount you offer is less than the discount you obtained, you'll still increase your profit margin.

But there are costs involved in that decision. There's the time cost of money, for one thing. For another, there are additional carrying costs, costs that might continue for as long as you maintain that additional inventory, depending on how you warehouse. Your sales force may need quite some time to sell down that inventory.

And that's a characteristic of random shocks: They tend to persist. Not always — some sudden increases or decreases in the level of a baseline die out rapidly, but more often they die out gently or persist for quite some time. In Figure 13-3, you see how a moving average tracks against a random shock; see Figure 13-4 for an example of why you'd want to use moving averages rather than regression for your forecast.

The best fit you can get using regression on this baseline has an R-squared value of 0.26. That means you can associate only about one fourth of the variability in the inventory costs with the time period.

And even that's misleading. Both before and after the random shock, the inventory costs are declining. But the math underlying the regression equation takes account of the sudden increase at the ninth time period, and that outweighs the declines starting at period 1 and at period 10. Linear regression analyses *always* returns a straight line — that's why they're called *linear.*

This is not to say that you can't do what's called *curvilinear* regression using Excel. You can. You just need to build an exponential component into your predictor variables. In a multiple regression context, for example, it might be right to predict using both the number of the time period (1, 2, 3, . . . 50) and the square of the number of the time period (1, 4, 9, . . . 2,500). That's just an example, one of thousands of possible examples. There's no special reason to use the square (or the cube, for that matter) of a time period's number as a predictor.

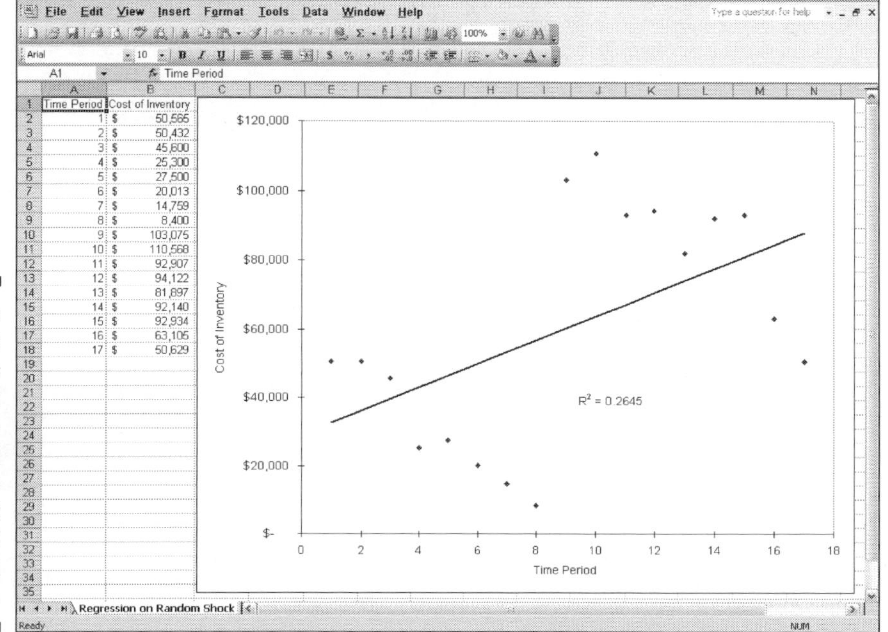

Figure 13-4: A regression forecast is seldom a good choice for a baseline that has experienced a random shock.

Remember to chart your data early during the forecasting process. There's a lot that a chart will reveal easily that a glassy-eyed stare at a bunch of numbers will hide. And if you see a random shock like the one this section talks about, remember to think about using a moving-average (or an exponential-smoothing) forecast model.

Reacting Quickly versus Modeling Noise

Figuring out how many actual baseline values to include in a moving average isn't easy. Some students of statistics ask similar questions when they ask their professor in Statistics 101, "How big a sample should I take?" And the prof, who as yet has no information at all about the study that the student wants to do, and who wants to dismiss the class and go have a beer, says "Thirty. Your sample size should be 30."

A ridiculous answer, of course, but you'd be surprised at how many people who've taken a couple of statistics courses believe that the minimum size for a sample is 30 observations.

There's a silly reason for that criterion. When you're building a frequency distribution and find that it's beginning to resemble a normal curve, you find that the curve begins to get steeper than 45 degrees by the time that you've got around 30 data points in the distribution. You need to know quite a bit about the variables you're analyzing before you can estimate the right sample size.

But I digress. The point is that you can't just pull a number — 2, 3, 4, 5, whatever — out of the air and decide that's how many baseline values will go into each moving average. Oh, that's an overstatement: Of course you can do exactly that, if you want. But you shouldn't. You need to know more first.

Choosing a number of baseline values is a balancing act. You're trying to achieve the right mix of reacting to changes in the level of the baseline (also called *tracking*) and letting errors average out (also called *smoothing*).

Getting a smoother picture

The number of baseline values you put in each moving average affects how fast the moving average reacts to changes in the baseline. The fewer the baseline values in each moving average, the faster it reacts. Of course, there are two extremes:

- **The smallest number of values in a moving average is 1.** Then the moving average reacts extremely fast — in fact, it's identical to the baseline. Every moving average of length 1 has one value from the baseline in it.

- **The largest number of values in a moving average is all the values in the baseline.** Then you'll have only one moving average, and you can't get any smoother than that. But it makes for an unwieldy forecast, and it has little more to tell you than does the single-value moving average.

Figure 13-5 shows visually how this works.

Look first at the chart that shows the baseline and the moving averages of length 2. It tracks quite closely to the baseline. It reacts quickly to changes — look particularly at period 10, when the baseline and the moving average are separated by about $10,500.

The chart with moving averages of length 3 has a smoother moving-average line than the length 2 moving-average line. Smoothness itself is not the goal; coming closer to the signal *is.* Although you can't know for certain what a line depicting the signal would look like, you do know that a length 3 moving average gives random noise more of a chance to cancel out than does a length 2 moving average.

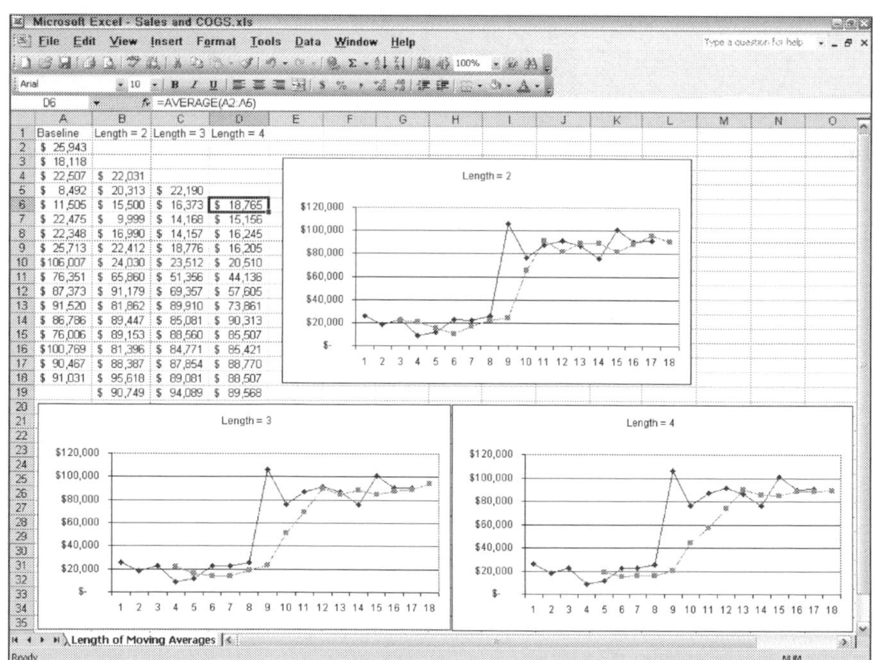

	A	B	C	D
1	Baseline	Length = 2	Length = 3	Length = 4
2	$ 25,943			
3	$ 18,118			
4	$ 22,507	$ 22,031		
5	$ 8,492	$ 20,313	$ 22,190	
6	$ 11,505	$ 15,500	$ 16,373	$ 18,765
7	$ 22,475	$ 9,999	$ 14,168	$ 15,156
8	$ 22,348	$ 16,990	$ 14,157	$ 16,245
9	$ 25,713	$ 22,412	$ 18,776	$ 16,205
10	$106,007	$ 24,030	$ 23,512	$ 20,510
11	$ 76,351	$ 65,860	$ 51,356	$ 44,136
12	$ 87,373	$ 91,179	$ 69,357	$ 57,605
13	$ 91,520	$ 81,862	$ 89,910	$ 73,861
14	$ 86,786	$ 89,447	$ 85,081	$ 90,313
15	$ 76,006	$ 89,153	$ 88,560	$ 85,507
16	$100,769	$ 81,396	$ 84,771	$ 85,421
17	$ 90,467	$ 88,387	$ 87,854	$ 88,770
18	$ 91,031	$ 95,618	$ 89,081	$ 88,507
19		$ 90,749	$ 94,089	$ 89,568

Figure 13-5: The fewer the values in a moving average, the faster it tracks.

Also in the Length = 3 chart, notice period 10. Here, the baseline and the moving average are separated by almost $25,000. The difference between the two charts is that the moving averages with a length of 2 react faster:

- When the length is 2, only two values go into the average. At the tenth time period, that means $25,713 and $106,007, or $65,860.
- When the length is 3, there are three values in the average: $22,348, $25,713 and $106,007, or $51,356.

So putting a third value in the moving average, one that is relatively small, pulls that moving average down away from the baseline at point 10. This is why the more baseline data points you put in a moving average, the slower it reacts to changes in the baseline. You're putting more data points that precede the change in the baseline into the moving average. This slows the reaction time down, and at the same time smoothes the moving-average line.

Finally, look at the Length = 4 chart. The line of moving averages reacts even more slowly to changes in the baseline. At the benchmark I've been using, point 10 on the chart, the difference between the baseline and the associated moving average is $32,215, compared to about $25,000 at length 3, and about $10,500 at length 2. It's the smoothest of the three moving-average lines, and the slowest to react to changes in the baseline.

Calculating and charting moving averages

I've left a few points implicit so far, and it's time to make them explicit. They have to do with which baseline values to put in a moving average, and how to line up a list's values to make the chart as clear as possible.

Using an equal number of points

It may seem obvious, but a lot of people get it wrong: Each moving average must have the same number of baseline points as every other. If one takes the average of two baseline points, the rest of them must do the same. If one moving average involves three baseline points, so must all the others.

Which values go into the forecast?

A moving-average forecast for a given time period involves the *previous* time periods. So, for a moving average of length 3, the forecast for April includes January, February, and March; for May, it includes February, March, and April. This makes good sense, of course. It's illogical for May's moving average to include May's baseline — when it comes time to calculate May's moving average, you would already know May's actual.

Where does the forecast go on the worksheet?

The forecast — the moving average — is in the row immediately following the final baseline data point that the average uses. In other words, it's in the same row as the time period that it forecasts. That sounds trivial, of course, but its effect is to extend the column of moving averages one row past the final baseline figure. That's your forecast for the period you haven't seen yet.

You lose averages at the start of the moving average

In Figure 13-5, notice that the more baseline data points go into a moving average, the more moving averages you lose at the start of the series. In a moving average of length 4, you "lose" the first four periods in the moving-average series.

You can't calculate the first four moving averages if you're using Length = 4. Suppose in Figure 13-5 that you wanted to put a moving average in cell D5. That would be the average of the values in A1:A4. But you can't include the text value "Baseline" in the average; Excel just ignores it, and gives you the average of the values in A2:A4. This is equivalent to putting a different number of values in different moving averages — which is breaking the rules.

So, in a length 4 moving average, you start in the same row as the fifth baseline value. In a length 3, you start in the baseline's fourth row, and in a length 2 you start in the baseline's third row.

Using the Analysis ToolPak to Get Moving Averages

The ATP is a handy way to get a moving average quickly. You can also get a chart of the baseline and the moving average. It has a serious downside, though. As you'll see, it doesn't chart the moving averages correctly.

Using the ATP's Moving Average tool

With the Analysis ToolPak installed in Excel, and a baseline on the active worksheet, follow these steps:

1. **Choose Tools ➪ Data Analysis.**

   The Data Analysis dialog box appears.

2. **Scroll down the Analysis Tools list box (if necessary) until you find the Moving Average tool, and then click on it.**

3. **Click OK.**

   The Moving Average dialog box appears (see Figure 13-6).

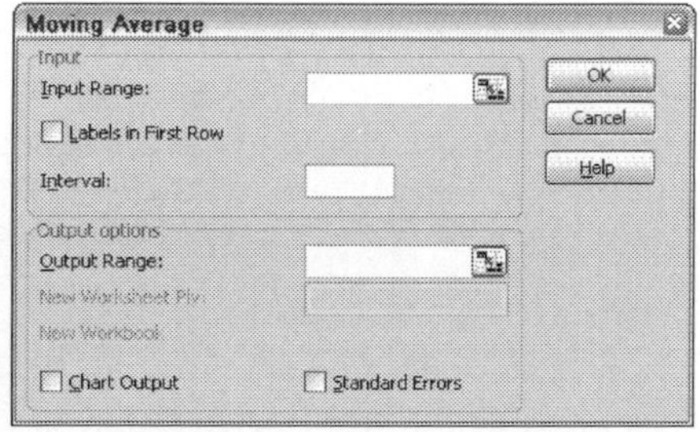

Figure 13-6: Although you can see them, the New Worksheet Ply and New Workbook options are disabled in the Moving Average dialog box.

4. **If necessary, click in the Input Range box and drag through your baseline.**

   If you've used an Excel list structure so that your baseline has a variable name in a cell at its top, include that also. In Figure 13-6, that's cell A1.

5. **If you included a variable name in the input range, select the Labels in First Row check box.**

6. **If you want a moving average of length 3, enter** 3 **as the interval.**

   The Moving Average tool refers to the number of baseline data points in a moving average as the *interval.*

7. **Click in the Output Range box.**

   You're in luck. The Moving Average tool doesn't ask you to choose among three output locations. Therefore, it does not unexpectedly snap you back to the Input Range box as soon as you've made your choice, as it does with Regression and Exponential Smoothing — and others, such as Correlation.

8. **With the cursor still in the Output Range box (here's where things start to get strange), click in the cell where you want the moving average series to begin.**

9. **Select the Chart Output check box and click OK.**

   The Moving Average tool takes over, calculates the moving averages, and charts both the baseline and the moving averages (see Figure 13-7). (I've adjusted the size of the chart so it's easier to see what's going on.

Notice that in Figure 13-7, the Moving Range tool has aligned the first moving average on the chart with the *third* baseline observation, rather than, correctly, with the fourth. Was that my fault? Shouldn't I have started the output range one row farther down, in $B$3? Well, that would have helped a little, as shown in Figure 13-8.

I entered the formulas to calculate the moving ranges by hand, in column B. It didn't take much time at all: I typed one formula:

```
=AVERAGE(A2:A4)
```

in cell B5 and autofilled it down through B19.

Here's how to save time by autofilling. In this case, after entering the formula in B5, I selected B5 and moved my mouse pointer over the cell's lower-right corner. The pointer changed from a cross to crosshairs. I pressed and held down the left mouse button, dragged into B19, and released the mouse button. That sequence copied the formula from B5 and pasted it into B6:B19, adjusting the addresses in the formula accordingly.

Notice first that I moved the output range down one row in the Moving Range dialog box; instead of having it start in the second row, it starts in the third. So, on the worksheet, the calculated moving ranges align properly with the baseline. Not so in the chart. Regardless of where you tell the Moving Range tool to start the output, it aligns the moving range on the chart one row too high. With an interval of 3, the tool should have associated the first moving range value on the chart with the fourth baseline value.

What the Moving Range dialog box calls an *interval* is what most forecasters — and this book — call a *length,* as in "a moving range of length 3."

So if you're going to use the ATP's Moving Average tool to create the moving averages on the worksheet, and the chart of the baseline and the moving averages, you need to open the chart and click on the data series that represents the moving averages. You see something like this in the Formula Bar, immediately above the column headers:

```
=SERIES("Forecast",,'Moving Average Via ATP'!$C$3:$C$19,2)
```

Change $C$3 to $C$2 so that the moving averages on the chart start one row higher than called for by the Moving Average tool. Now the baseline and the moving averages will line up correctly on the chart.

If you select the Standard Errors check box, you get a different standard error for each moving average. I don't subscribe to the notion that each moving average has a different standard error, so I don't ever select this check box when I'm seriously making a moving average forecast.

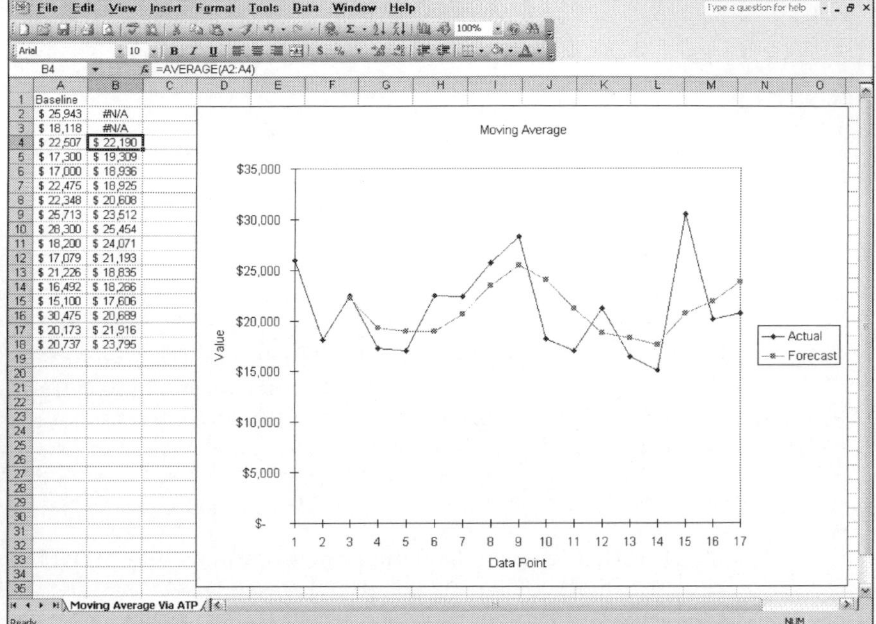

Figure 13-7: I chose an interval of 3 (that is, a moving average of length 3) and an output range starting in $B$2 for this analysis.

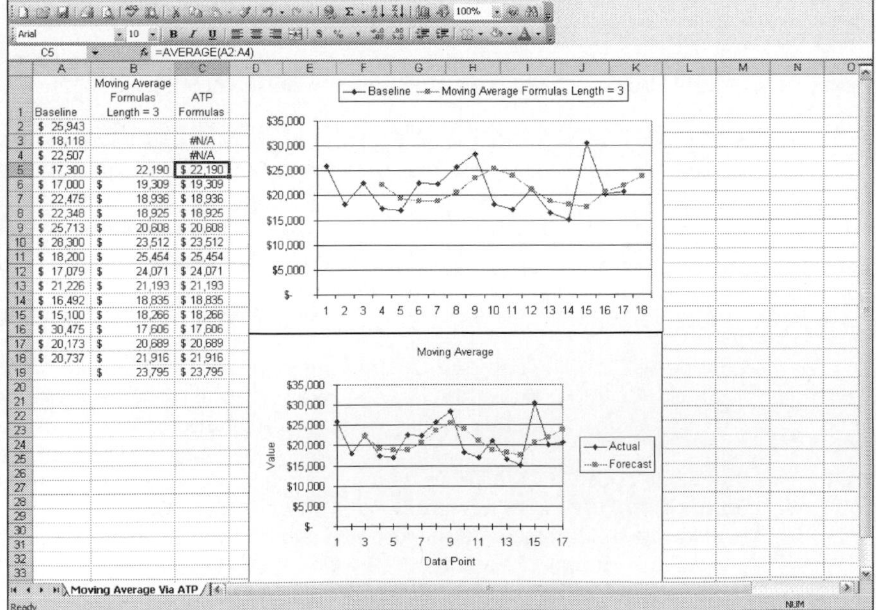

Figure 13-8: The upper chart was created by using the keyboard and the mouse; the lower chart was created by the ATP's Moving Average tool.

If you want, you can avoid the ATP entirely and still get moving averages into a chart. After you've charted your baseline, follow these steps:

1. **Click the chart to select it.**
2. **Click the charted baseline to select it.**
3. **Choose Chart ➪ Add Trendline.**

   The Add Trendline dialog box appears.
4. **If necessary, select the Type tab.**
5. **On the Type tab, click the depiction of the Moving Average trendline.**
6. **The Add Trendline, in contrast to the ATP, terms the length of the moving average as a *period*. Use the spinner to set the length to however many periods you want to include in each moving average.**
7. **Click OK.**

If you now click the Options tab in the Add Trendline dialog box, you see that the Moving Average tool doesn't give you the opportunity to forecast beyond the end of the baseline by means of a trendline. Furthermore, the trendline gives you no actual values on the worksheet — they can be handy in doing further analysis. But the Moving Average trendline can be a handy way to get a quick peek at the moving averages that would result from your baseline.

Charting residuals

Charting the residuals from a moving average analysis is always a good idea if you think you're going to adopt the moving-average approach, and if you're reasonably happy (or at least not repulsed by) the results of choosing a particular length for your moving averages.

Figure 13-9 shows a chart of residuals.

The chart doesn't reveal any particular pattern to the residuals. They're distributed fairly evenly above and below their mean, which is quite close to zero given that the baseline is measured in the 10,000s.

You get the chart by taking the following steps:

1. **With the baseline and the moving averages themselves in place, subtract a baseline value from an associated moving-average value.**

   In Figure 13-9, for example, the formula in cell C5 is:

   ```
   =B5 - A5
   ```
2. **Autofill the formula down to the final row of the baseline.**

These subtractions are the residuals — the error in your forecast when compared to the actual, which eventually becomes available.

3. **Create a Line chart based on those residuals and examine it for any regularity in the residuals — a sine wave, for example, or a straight line with up or down trend.**

   If you find regularity, you might want to consider a different forecasting approach, or a transformation of your baseline such as first differencing. (*First differencing* involves taking the difference between consecutive values in your baseline and analyzing those differences rather than the original values. Chapters 14 and 17 have lots of information on the differencing process.)

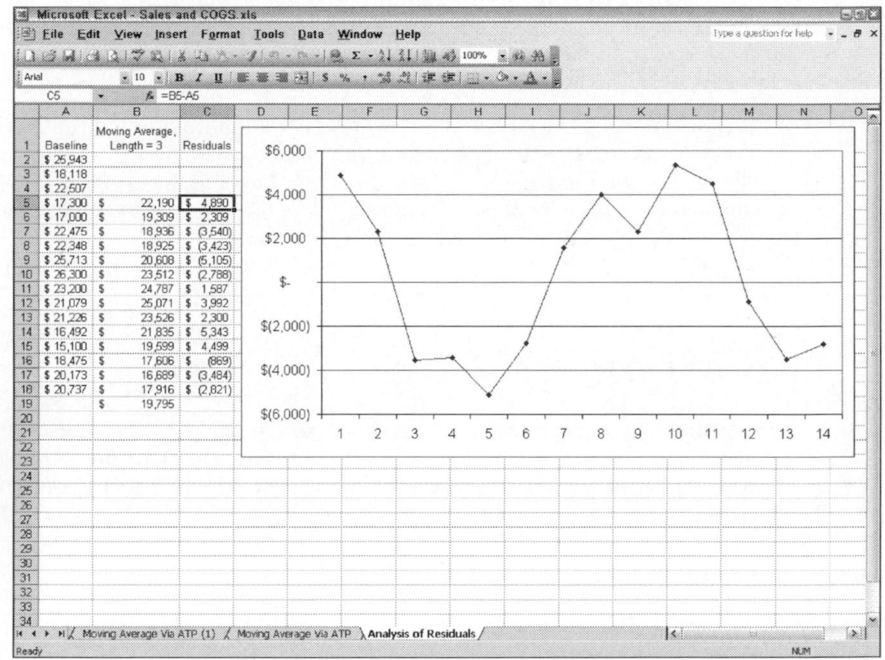

Figure 13-9: The chart is of the residual values in column C.

Chapter 14

Evaluating a Moving Average

In This Chapter

- Knowing when two items correlate
- Making sense of autocorrelation

For all their simplicity and intuitive appeal, moving averages have baggage. One of the problems comes with a short baseline (it's amazing how many forecasting problems a long baseline solves). Even if you choose to include only two actuals in each moving average, you lose two observations from your forecasts. Choosing a shorter or smaller length for the averages is a balancing act between tracking and smoothing, but it's also a choice of how much data you're willing to part with.

In forecasting, the notion of correlation is usually connected to regression forecasts, because correlations are the building blocks of any regression analysis. But moving averages and exponential smoothing also have to do with correlation, a special kind called *autocorrelation.* Before you can think sensibly about autocorrelation, though, you need to get a basis by looking at garden-variety correlation, and you find that basis in this chapter.

With correlation as background, the third major section in this chapter goes into autocorrelation: how it can get in the way of a good moving-average forecast, how to calculate and diagnose it, and how to make it go away and leave your forecast alone.

Losing Early Averages

One of the problems with forecasting by means of moving averages is that you lose the opportunity to make early forecasts. The reason, when you think about how moving-average forecasts work, is really pretty clear.

A forecast based on a moving average is the average of two or more *prior* time periods. So a moving average of length 2 is the average of the two prior observations, whether the observations are sales results or traffic accidents. Using a moving average of length 2, the average sales revenue for March would be January revenue plus February revenue, divided by two.

If you're going to average two results to forecast the next one, you can't get a forecast for the second period. There's no result from time zero to average with the first result. The same is true with a moving average of length 3: The first forecast you can get is for the fourth period.

The word *forecast* doesn't necessarily mean a future value that hasn't yet been observed. It also means a value that's forecast for a period in the past. You might get the average of January, February, and March to forecast April, even though you're into the next December and you've known about April for eight months now.

This sort of thing is easier to see on a chart. Figure 14-1 has an example.

In Figure 14-1, the first legitimate moving average is in cell C7. It's the average of the actual revenues shown in cells B4:B6. The earlier attempts at calculating moving averages are:

- **Cell C6:** As you can see from the formula, this is the average of the values in cells B3:B5. But the value in B3 is text. The AVERAGE function ignores text values, so C6 shows the average of B4:B5. The average of two months of revenue isn't *wrong* so much as *different* from the later moving averages, and comparing them directly is misleading.
- **Cell C5:** This formula attempts to get the average of B2:B4. There are two text values in those cells, which AVERAGE ignores, so it just returns the "average" of the first month of revenue.
- **Cell C4:** By now I've run out of numbers, and when AVERAGE has no numbers to work with it returns `#DIV/0!`, which is an error value. It informs you that, with no numbers to average, Excel has tried to divide a sum by zero. This is a mathematical error, of course, not a problem with moving averages as such.

The main point is that you lose as many forecasts from the start of your baseline as you have actual values that contribute to a moving average. The same is not true of the end of the baseline, because you're not usually running out of prior actuals.

You can run out of prior actuals, though, if your baseline is too short for the length of the moving average. A baseline with two actuals in it can't support a moving average of length 3. Wait for more data to come in before you start forecasting.

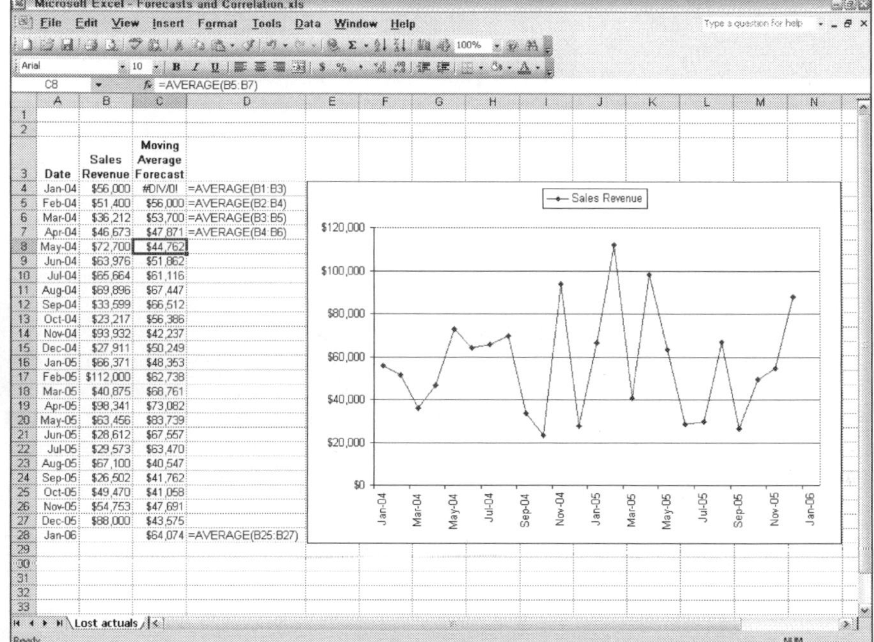

Figure 14-1: You could get an additional legitimate forecast in cell C6 by shifting to two-period averages.

You can improve things a little if you switch to a smaller number of periods per moving average. In this case, you could choose two periods rather than three, and that would get you one extra forecast at the start. But then the forecasts might start to track the noise as much as the signal. In general, the fewer the periods that comprise a moving average, the more closely the moving average tracks the actuals and fails to smooth out the noise in the baseline.

Understanding Correlation

Correlation is a fundamental part of forecasting. You can do forecasting without knowing the first thing about correlation, but you handicap yourself if you don't bother. Correlations are key to understanding regression forecasts, and they play an important part in diagnosing how well your forecasts work. Better yet, they're not really tough to understand.

Do me a favor: At least scan this chapter's material on correlation. If you decide it's not for you, no problem — you can still do your forecasting, even if you don't have all the available tools at hand.

When did they start going together?

You want to get your virtual hands on two variables. Let's start by assuming those variables are people's height and weight. Now, you know just from general life experience that the taller a person is, the more the person tends to weigh. It's not anything like one for one — people don't automatically weigh 2½ pounds more for every additional inch taller they are. But there is a strong tendency for height and weight to go together. Like teenagers spending time together, it's not easy to keep them apart.

Suppose you decide to do some research. You stand on a street corner in the business district of a large metropolitan area and stop people who are walking by. You engage each person in conversation and while you've got him distracted, you get his height with a tape measure. Then you ask him how much he weighs. Some tell you, and you note down the height and weight. (Some of them cold-cock you and walk away, and that's why you have some missing data.)

After you collect data on about 50 people, you head back to your office and put the data in an Excel worksheet. It looks like the one in Figure 14-2.

Microsoft Excel - Forecasts and Correlation.xls

Person	Height (inches)	Weight (pounds)
1	78	184
2	61	173
3	56	148
4	68	189
5	54	142
6	55	158
7	62	162
8	49	131
9	73	190
10	50	143
11	57	160
12	72	168
13	54	163
14	66	154
15	60	169
16	73	186
17	77	177
18	49	149
19	66	183
20	70	172
21	66	185
22	64	180
23	61	178
24	66	175
25	68	185
26	68	166
27	73	190
28	54	135
29	69	170
30	56	154
31	67	182
32	65	150

Height and weight

Figure 14-2: You can't tell just by looking at the numbers that there's a fairly strong relationship between height and weight.

So far, it's just a jumble of numbers. When a numeric jumble gets in your face, the first thing to do is chart it, like I've done in Figure 14-3.

Each point in the chart represents a different person you conned into letting you get a height and weight measurement. If you pick out one point and look over to the vertical axis, you can see what that person's height is. And if you look down from that point to the horizontal axis, you can see what the weight is.

Now the jumble is starting to resolve into some patterns:

- The points on the chart that are higher up the vertical axis also tend to be farther along the horizontal axis.
- The points describe a sort of cigar shape, running from the lower left to the upper right.
- The points do *not* lie directly on a straight line, but you can imagine one running through the middle of the cigar, as in Figure 14-4. Or you can draw it: Click the charted data series and choose Chart ➪ Add Trendline.

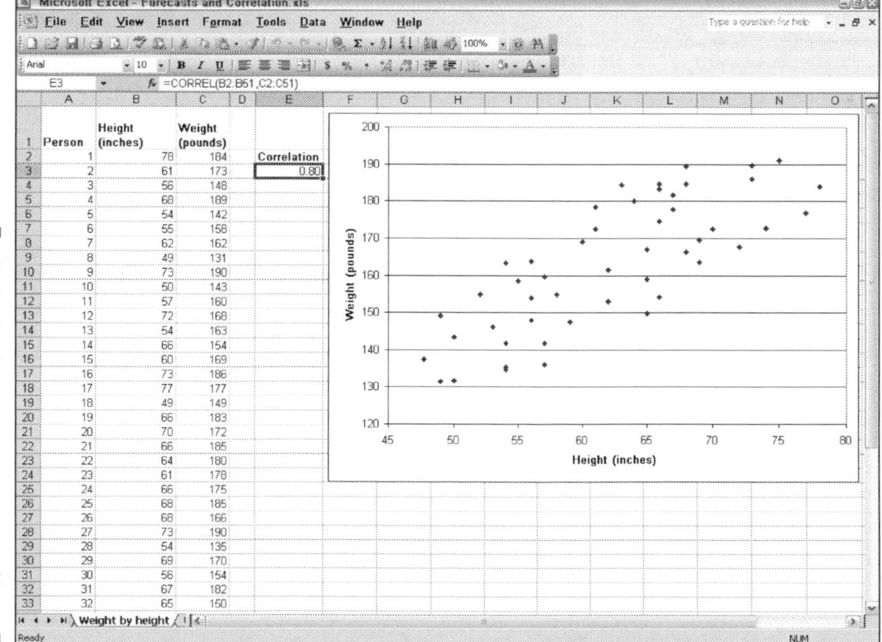

	Person	Height (inches)	Weight (pounds)
2	1	78	184
3	2	61	173
4	3	56	148
5	4	68	189
6	5	54	142
7	6	55	158
8	7	62	162
9	8	49	131
10	9	73	190
11	10	50	143
12	11	57	160
13	12	72	168
14	13	54	163
15	14	66	154
16	15	60	169
17	16	73	186
18	17	77	177
19	18	49	149
20	19	66	183
21	20	70	172
22	21	66	185
23	22	64	180
24	23	61	178
25	24	66	175
26	25	68	185
27	26	68	166
28	27	73	190
29	28	54	135
30	29	69	170
31	30	56	154
32	31	67	182
33	32	65	150

Figure 14-3: It can clutter up the chart, but some find it useful to add vertical gridlines by choosing Chart ➪ Chart Options.

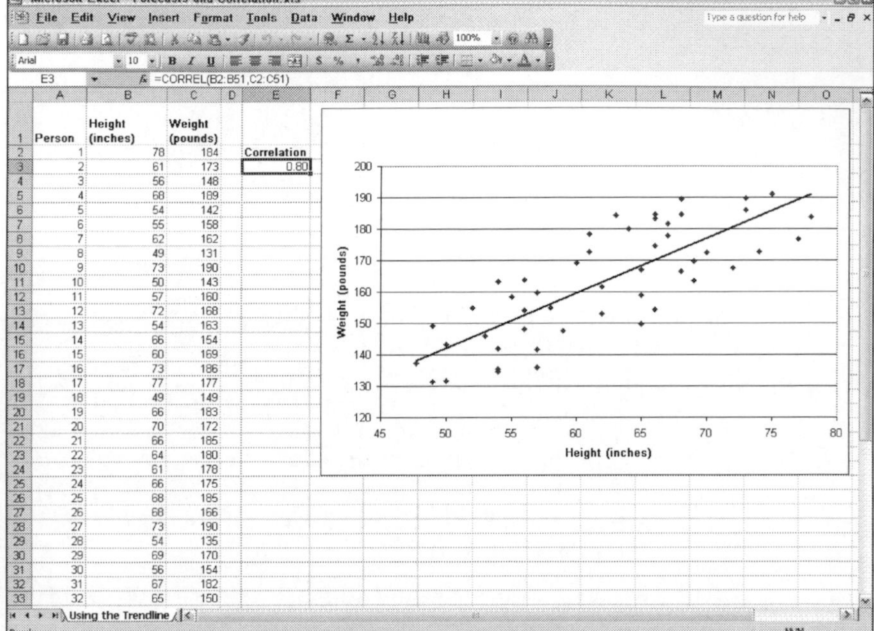

Person	Height (inches)	Weight (pounds)
1	78	184
2	61	173
3	56	148
4	68	189
5	54	142
6	55	158
7	62	162
8	49	131
9	73	190
10	50	143
11	57	160
12	72	168
13	54	163
14	66	154
15	60	169
16	73	186
17	77	177
18	49	149
19	66	183
20	70	172
21	66	185
22	64	180
23	61	178
24	66	175
25	68	185
26	68	166
27	73	190
28	54	135
29	69	170
30	56	154
31	67	182
32	65	150

Figure 14-4: Lower left to upper right means a positive, or *direct,* correlation.

You can make some statements about the relationship between two variables:

- The closer those points come to lying on the imaginary straight line, the stronger the relationship between the two variables.
- You can express the strength of the relationship with a number. It turns out that, because of the way it's calculated, the number must be between –1 and +1. That number is called the *correlation coefficient.*
- If the correlation coefficient is positive, like 0.6, then the imaginary straight line runs from the lower left to the upper right. If the correlation coefficient is negative, then the line runs from the upper left to the lower right.
- The closer the correlation coefficient is to +1.0 or –1.0, the stronger the relationship. The closer it is to zero, the weaker the relationship.

Suppose you analyzed the golf scores of 100 golfers, whose skill levels range from beginner to expert. You could put them on a chart, just like height and weight, with, say, their scores on the vertical axis and their years of golfing experience on the horizontal axis (see Figure 14-5).

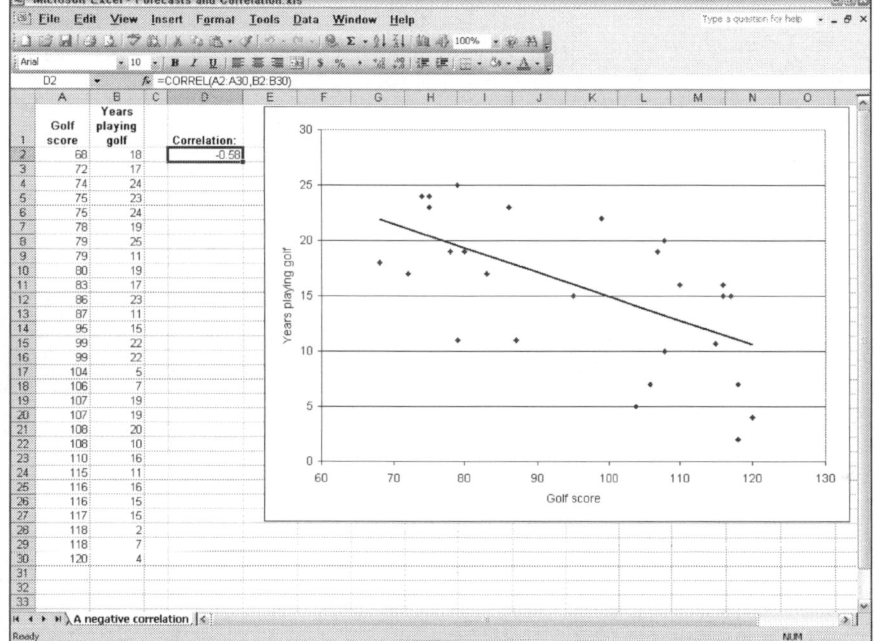

Figure 14-5: Upper left to lower right means a negative, or *inverse,* correlation.

So you see that the more the years of experience playing golf, the lower the golf score. The fact that the correlation is negative has nothing to do with the *strength* of the relationship — just with its direction.

Using Excel, you can calculate the correlation coefficient between two variables very easily. Just use the CORREL function, with two ranges of data values as its arguments. In Figure 14-5, the formula used in cell D2 is:

```
=CORREL(A2:A30,B2:B30)
```

Charting correlated data

When you use Excel to chart correlated data, it's almost always best to use an XY (Scatter) chart.

For simplicity, I refer to this as an XY chart. Excel uses the term *Scatter* in the name because earlier applications — and this goes back to mainframe days — referred to this kind of chart as a *scatter chart* or *scattergram.* Now if you'll excuse me for a moment, I need to change my spats.

The main reason that an XY chart is best is that, if you're working with correlations, you're automatically working with variables that are entirely numeric. Height and weight are both numeric variables. Golf score and years of experience are both numeric variables.

When you chart them, you want a chart that has a numeric horizontal (or X) axis, and a numeric vertical (or Y) axis. Other chart types don't offer this arrangement. For example, a Column chart assumes that categories (such as make of car or political affiliation) are on its horizontal axis, and numbers (such as number of cars sold or number of registered voters) are on its vertical axis.

The problem with putting numeric values on a category axis is that Excel doesn't reflect the magnitude of the difference between numbers in their spacing on the axis. So, the numbers 2, 4, and 8 would show up with equal distances between them on a category axis. But the difference between 2 and 4 is 2, and the difference between 4 and 8 is 4. Only a numeric axis can represent those differences accurately, and only an XY chart has two numeric axes to handle your two numeric variables.

There are other reasons to use an XY chart for two numeric variables. Among them:

- Trendlines are calculated and drawn accurately.
- R-squared values and regression equations are based on the proper values.
- You get some play between the vertical axis and the leftmost data point, and between the horizontal axis and the bottommost data point. This improves your visualization of the relationship between the two variables.

Understanding Autocorrelation

Autocorrelation is a specific kind of correlation that's comes up frequently in forecasting. You interpret it just as you would standard correlation — as the strength of the relationship between two variables. The difference is that you're correlating one set of values with a different set of values *of the same variable.*

The previous section discusses the relationship between height and weight: how taller people tend to weigh more, and how shorter people tend to weigh less. When you're considering autocorrelation, you think in slightly different terms. You think of how earlier values in the baseline are related to later values in the baseline.

With height and weight, you're looking at how Smith's height relates to Smith's weight and how Anderson's height relates to Anderson's weight, and so on.

With autocorrelation and sales forecasting, you're looking at how January's revenue relates to February's revenue, how February's revenue relates to March's revenue, and so on.

This sort of effect is not limited to a month-to-month relationship. It can and does apply to weekly, quarterly, and annual measures.

Frequently, an earlier time period's value carries forward into a later period. Suppose your company spifs a particular product line for a month. (*Spif* is short for Special Product Incentive Fund, or Sales Performance Incentive Formula, or something else, depending on whose commission plan you're reading). The spif might take the form of a bonus, over the normal commission, for sales of that product during May. The effect of that spif sometimes carries forward into June, July, and August, or even longer.

A one-month spif on that vital automobile option, undercoating, can have effects on revenue in subsequent months, for a number of reasons — among them:

- As the sales reps concentrate on selling undercoating, they gain more experience in drawing customers' attention to undercoating's undisputed effects on the longevity of the vehicle.
- Satisfied customers refer their friends to the company's dealerships, and these new customers all ask for undercoating.
- Some, perhaps most, of the sales may be in the form of leases. If the company recognizes revenue only as it receives monthly payments, then the additional revenue due to the spif will carry forward through the life of each lease.

Different situations bring about different reasons that one time period's results can persist through later time periods. If you're selling a political candidate rather than undercoating, there can be a real bandwagon effect. The higher a candidate rises in the polls, the more coverage provided by the media, the more the name recognition, and the higher the candidate rises in the polls — until, of course, the candidate concludes a concession speech with a primal scream.

Why should you concern yourself with autocorrelation? There are a several reasons, depending on the approach you're using. Two of the more important:

- **Autocorrelation usually means that the errors are correlated.** That is, the difference between the forecast value and the actual value for one period is related to the difference for another period. If you're using regression (rather than moving averages or exponential smoothing), this violates one of the assumptions that form the basis of a regression forecast: independence of errors.

- **If you're using moving averages or exponential smoothing, autocorrelation (whether positive or negative) often causes your forecasts to be too high when the actuals are low, and too low when the actuals are high.**

In either case, the answer is often taking the first differences. You can find more information on taking differences in Chapter 17, but briefly:

- You take first differences by calculating the difference between one actual value and a previous value, usually but not always the immediately prior value.
- With the autocorrelation removed by using the first differences, you're okay to go ahead and make your forecasts using those differences. You still have to account for the differencing in the forecasts — Chapter 17 shows you how to do that.

The first differences in Figure 14-6 are calculated by subtracting the previous value from an actual value. For example, you get the difference in cell C3, –$17,000, by subtracting B2 from B3.

The autocorrelation in the differenced series, 0.04, is shown in cell D2. This correlation coefficient is very close to zero. (You'll see how to calculate an autocorrelation later in this chapter, in the section unimaginatively titled "Calculating autocorrelation.") That indicates that you've removed the autocorrelation in the series by taking first differences. And there's no special regularity in the chart of the first differences — regularity can still occur when first differencing was not enough to dispose of the autocorrelation.

Compared to the original baseline in B2:B25 of Figure 14-6, the first differences in C3:C25 are what you want as the basis for your forecast. But there are two drawbacks to using first differences:

- **You lose the data for one time period.** Notice the #N/A value in cell C2 of Figure 14-6. When you take first differences, you always wind up with one time period fewer than in the original baseline. With a good, long baseline — say, 20 time periods, just as a rule of thumb and with no statistical theory to back it up — the loss is trivial.
- **At first it's not intuitively clear what first differences represent, much less the forecasts of first differences.** Don't worry about it: It takes some time and experience to get a feel for what's going on. And when you've undifferenced the data (you'll see how later in this section) you're back to the original scale and back on more comfortable ground.

Figure 14-7 illustrates another autocorrelated series. When you calculate an autocorrelation on the first differences, you generally find that the correlation coefficient is near zero. Figure 14-7 shows an example of the small amount of autocorrelation in a set of first differences.

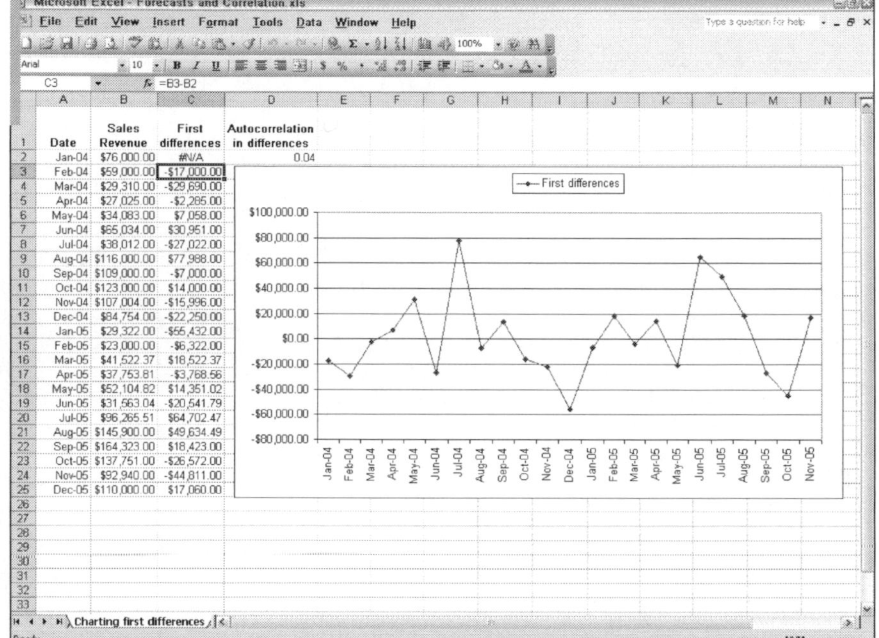

Date	Sales Revenue	First differences	Autocorrelation in differences
Jan-04	$76,000.00	#N/A	0.04
Feb-04	$59,000.00	-$17,000.00	
Mar-04	$29,310.00	-$29,690.00	
Apr-04	$27,025.00	-$2,285.00	
May-04	$34,083.00	$7,058.00	
Jun-04	$65,034.00	$30,951.00	
Jul-04	$38,012.00	-$27,022.00	
Aug-04	$116,000.00	$77,988.00	
Sep-04	$109,000.00	-$7,000.00	
Oct-04	$123,000.00	$14,000.00	
Nov-04	$107,004.00	-$15,996.00	
Dec-04	$84,754.00	-$22,250.00	
Jan-05	$29,322.00	-$55,432.00	
Feb-05	$23,000.00	-$6,322.00	
Mar-05	$41,522.37	$18,522.37	
Apr-05	$37,753.81	-$3,768.56	
May-05	$52,104.82	$14,351.02	
Jun-05	$31,563.04	-$20,541.79	
Jul-05	$96,265.51	$64,702.47	
Aug-05	$145,900.00	$49,634.49	
Sep-05	$164,323.00	$18,423.00	
Oct-05	$137,751.00	-$26,572.00	
Nov-05	$92,940.00	-$44,811.00	
Dec-05	$110,000.00	$17,060.00	

Figure 14-6: No indication that the first differences are anything but independent of one another.

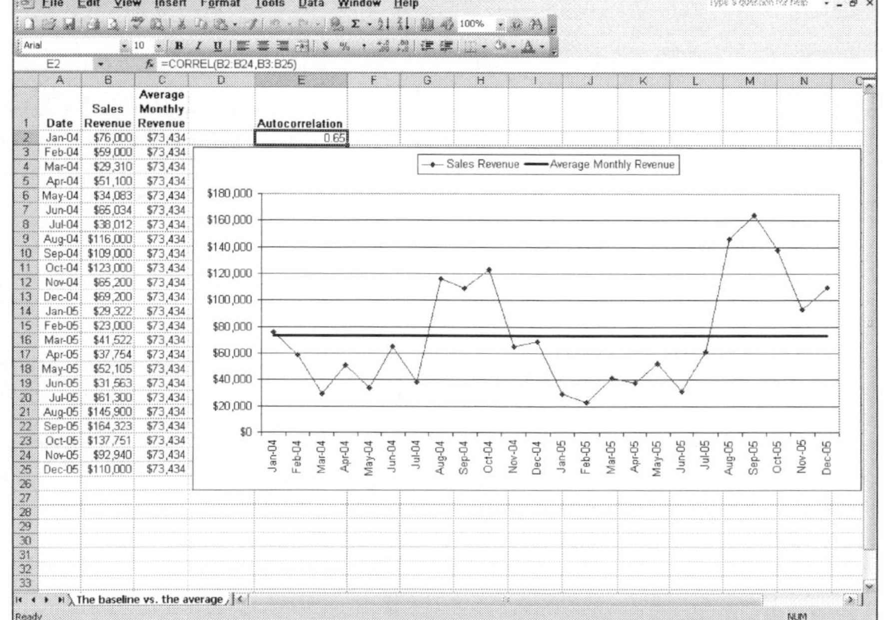

Date	Sales Revenue	Average Monthly Revenue	Autocorrelation
Jan-04	$76,000	$73,434	0.65
Feb-04	$59,000	$73,434	
Mar-04	$29,310	$73,434	
Apr-04	$51,100	$73,434	
May-04	$34,083	$73,434	
Jun-04	$65,034	$73,434	
Jul-04	$38,012	$73,434	
Aug-04	$116,000	$73,434	
Sep-04	$109,000	$73,434	
Oct-04	$123,000	$73,434	
Nov-04	$65,200	$73,434	
Dec-04	$69,200	$73,434	
Jan-05	$29,322	$73,434	
Feb-05	$23,000	$73,434	
Mar-05	$41,522	$73,434	
Apr-05	$37,754	$73,434	
May-05	$52,105	$73,434	
Jun-05	$31,563	$73,434	
Jul-05	$61,300	$73,434	
Aug-05	$145,900	$73,434	
Sep-05	$164,323	$73,434	
Oct-05	$137,751	$73,434	
Nov-05	$92,940	$73,434	
Dec-05	$110,000	$73,434	

Figure 14-7: Positive autocorrelations drift, as shown here. Negative autocorrelations bounce up and down.

The baseline shown, and charted, in Figure 14-7 is typical of positive autocorrelations. The data drift below the average value for several periods, and then spend some periods above the average, and so on. This pattern can represent a *cycle,* but not usually a *seasonal* baseline.

A cycle is different from a seasonal pattern because it often covers more than one year, and because the high and low points do not follow a regular schedule. A cycle such as the business cycle often spans several years, but you expect a seasonal pattern to repeat each year. A cycle might reach a high point in 2008, and then bottom out in 2009, only to climb gradually to another high point in 2014. But the sales of flip-flops peak every summer and crash every winter.

Figure 14-8 shows the forecasts that you get for the baseline in Figure 14-7, and they're charted along with the actuals. This forecast uses exponential smoothing rather than moving averages, to show autocorrelation in a different context. The chart also shows the average value of the actuals in the baseline.

There are 23 time periods that have both an actual and a forecast. In 19 of those 23 periods:

- The forecasts are higher than the actuals when the actuals are below the average.
- The forecasts are lower than the actuals when the actuals are higher than the average.

As mentioned earlier in this chapter, this pattern is typical of baselines with positively autocorrelated values. Because you want your forecasts to be as accurate as you can make them, you'd like to get rid of this source of errors.

You can see the average of the actuals in the chart in Figure 14-8, but you can't see their values on the worksheet. Nevertheless, they're on the worksheet. To avoid cluttering things up even worse than they are, I make the averages invisible. I select the range of cells that contains the average values (for what it's worth, that's C2:C26) and choose Format ➪ Cells, select the Number tab, and choose Custom from the Category list box. In the Type box, I enter ;; (that's two consecutive semicolons). When I click OK, the average values vanish, although the formulas stay put.

You can make the autocorrelation go away by taking first differences. Figure 14-9 illustrates the process, which is really a pretty simple one.

1. **Clear the forecasts from column C that were shown in Figure 14-8 (the fastest way is to click the letter C at the top, to select the column, and press the Delete key).**

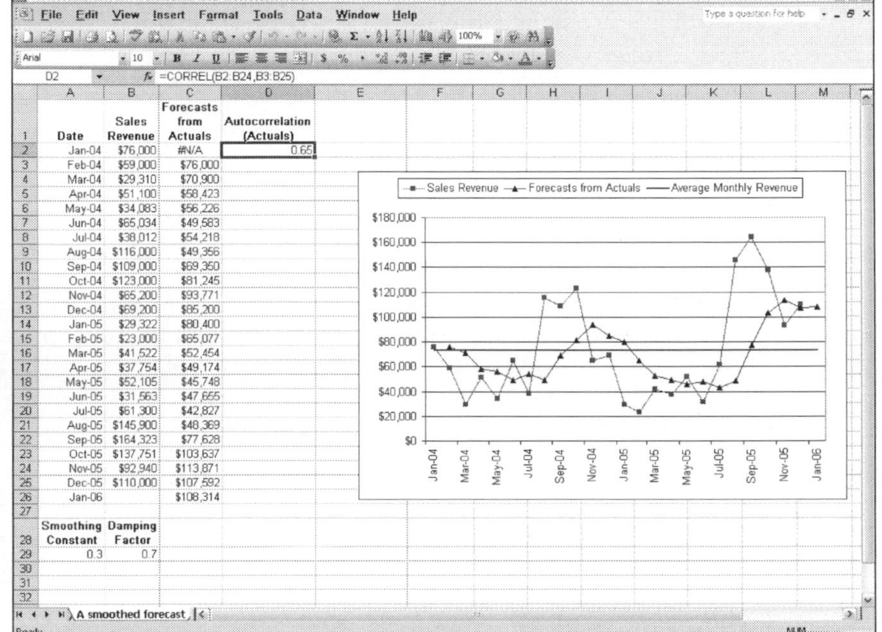

	A	B	C	D
1	Date	Sales Revenue	Forecasts from Actuals	Autocorrelation (Actuals)
2	Jan-04	$76,000	#N/A	0.65
3	Feb-04	$59,000	$76,000	
4	Mar-04	$29,310	$70,900	
5	Apr-04	$51,100	$58,423	
6	May-04	$34,083	$56,226	
7	Jun-04	$65,034	$49,583	
8	Jul-04	$38,012	$54,218	
9	Aug-04	$116,000	$49,356	
10	Sep-04	$109,000	$69,350	
11	Oct-04	$123,000	$81,245	
12	Nov-04	$65,200	$93,771	
13	Dec-04	$69,200	$85,200	
14	Jan-05	$29,322	$80,400	
15	Feb-05	$23,000	$65,077	
16	Mar-05	$41,522	$52,454	
17	Apr-05	$37,754	$49,174	
18	May-05	$52,105	$45,748	
19	Jun-05	$31,563	$47,655	
20	Jul-05	$61,300	$42,827	
21	Aug-05	$145,900	$48,369	
22	Sep-05	$164,323	$77,628	
23	Oct-05	$137,751	$103,637	
24	Nov-05	$92,940	$113,871	
25	Dec-05	$110,000	$107,592	
26	Jan-06		$108,314	
27				
28	Smoothing Constant	Damping Factor		
29	0.3	0.7		

Figure 14-8: The forecast is heavily smoothed because of the relatively small smoothing constant.

2. **Select cell C3, and enter** =B3-B2, **either by typing the whole thing or by selecting the cells with your mouse.**
3. **If necessary, select cell C3 again.**
4. **Choose Edit ⇨ Copy.**
5. **Select the range C4:C25.**
6. **Choose Edit ⇨ Paste.**

   You now have the series of first differences in column C, and you can use those first differences to make your forecasts. First, though, you should check to make sure that first differencing really did remove the autocorrelation.

That check is shown in cell E2 of Figure 14-9. The autocorrelation in the first differences is –0.10, which is small enough to be negligible. (You can see the formula for the autocorrelation in the Formula Bar.)

Step 3 in the preceding list says to select cell C3 again if necessary. The reason that it might be necessary has to do with how Excel reacts when you press the Enter button. If you choose Tools ⇨ Options and select the Edit tab, you'll see a Move Selection After Enter check box. If that check box is selected, Excel reacts to the Enter key by changing the selection. The default direction is down (by one cell), but you can use the Direction drop-down list to choose Right, Up, or Left. If you clear the check box, Excel doesn't change the selection cell when you press Enter. Finally, if you click the Enter button (the button with the green checkmark left of the Formula Bar, which appears when you're editing a cell), the selection doesn't change. And if you want, you can press Ctrl+Enter to prevent the selection from changing.

You're ready to make a forecast based on first differences. That's shown in Figure 14-10.

In Figure 14-10, the forecast differences appear in the range D4:D26. They were created by using exponential smoothing. The smoothing constant is in cell A29 and the damping factor is in cell B29. The formulas in D4:D26 use those addresses rather than constant numbers, so you can easily change the smoothing constant if you want to see the result.

The forecast differences, those shown in D4:D26 of Figure 14-11, are just that: forecasts of the differences between the actuals. In each cell in the range D5:D26, we forecast what the difference between two specific actuals would be, if the prior forecast had been more accurate — this is the basic idea that underlies exponential smoothing. (As the first forecast, D4 is calculated differently from D5:D26.)

Microsoft Excel - Forecasts and Correlation.xls

E2 =CORREL(C3:C24,C4:C25)

	A	B	C	D	E
1	Date	Sales Revenue		Autocorrelation (Actuals)	Autocorrelation (First Differences)
2	Jan-04	$76,000		0.65	-0.10
3	Feb-04	$59,000	-$17,000		
4	Mar-04	$29,310	-$29,690		
5	Apr-04	$51,100	$21,790		
6	May-04	$34,083	-$17,017		
7	Jun-04	$65,034	$30,951		
8	Jul-04	$38,012	-$27,022		
9	Aug-04	$116,000	$77,988		
10	Sep-04	$109,000	-$7,000		
11	Oct-04	$123,000	$14,000		
12	Nov-04	$65,200	-$57,800		
13	Dec-04	$69,200	$4,000		
14	Jan-05	$29,322	-$39,878		
15	Feb-05	$23,000	-$6,322		
16	Mar-05	$41,522	$18,522		
17	Apr-05	$37,754	-$3,769		
18	May-05	$52,105	$14,351		
19	Jun-05	$31,563	-$20,542		
20	Jul-05	$61,300	$29,737		
21	Aug-05	$145,900	$84,600		
22	Sep-05	$164,323	$18,423		
23	Oct-05	$137,751	-$26,572		
24	Nov-05	$92,940	-$44,811		
25	Dec-05	$110,000	$17,060		
26	Jan-06				
27					
28	Smoothing Constant	Damping Factor			
29	0.3	0.7			

Removing the autocorrelation

Figure 14-9: Taking first differences usually makes a baseline stationary.

Date	Sales Revenue		Forecasts from Differences
Jan-04	$76,000		
Feb-04	$59,000	-$17,000	#N/A
Mar-04	$29,310	-$29,690	-$17,000
Apr-04	$51,100	$21,790	-$20,807
May-04	$34,083	-$17,017	-$8,028
Jun-04	$65,034	$30,951	-$10,725
Jul-04	$38,012	-$27,022	$1,778
Aug-04	$116,000	$77,988	-$6,862
Sep-04	$109,000	-$7,000	$18,593
Oct-04	$123,000	$14,000	$10,915
Nov-04	$65,200	-$57,800	$11,841
Dec-04	$69,200	$4,000	-$9,052
Jan-05	$29,322	-$39,878	-$5,136
Feb-05	$23,000	-$6,322	-$15,559
Mar-05	$41,522	$18,522	-$12,788
Apr-05	$37,754	-$3,769	-$3,395
May-05	$52,105	$14,351	-$3,507
Jun-05	$31,563	-$20,542	$1,851
Jul-05	$61,300	$29,737	-$4,867
Aug-05	$145,900	$84,600	$5,514
Sep-05	$164,323	$18,423	$29,240
Oct-05	$137,751	-$26,572	$25,995
Nov-05	$92,940	-$44,811	$10,225
Dec-05	$110,000	$17,060	-$6,286
Jan-06			$718
Smoothing Constant	Damping Factor		
0.3	0.7		

Figure 14-10: You lose one forecast due to differencing, and another due to smoothing.

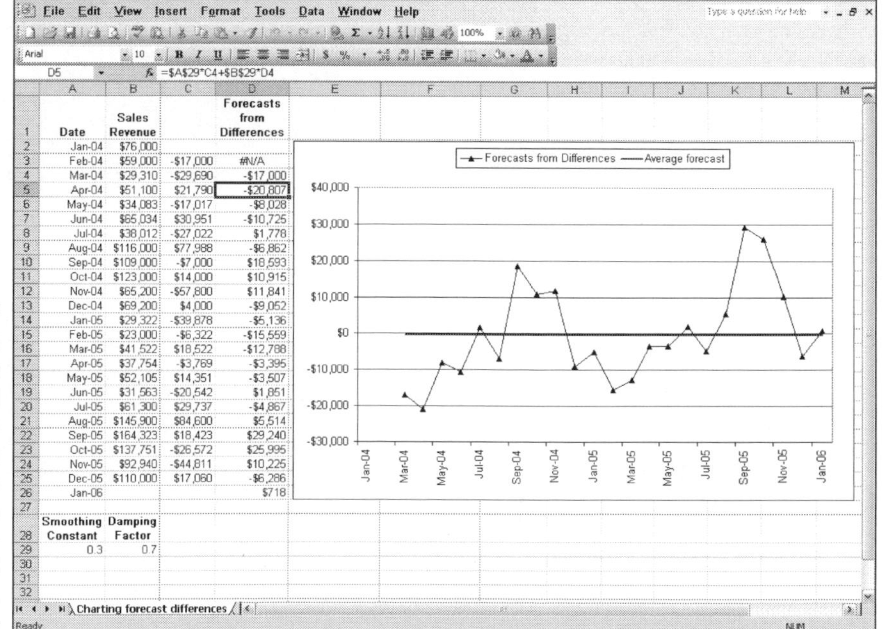

Figure 14-11: The drifts below and above the mean are much shorter than in the original baseline.

Finally, you're ready to integrate the forecast differences back into the original actuals. (***Note:*** It's called *integration* but we're *not* talking calculus here, I promise.) This last step, along with a chart of the results, is shown in Figure 14-12.

You do the integration by adding the forecast difference to the associated actual value that preceded it. So, to get the first integrated forecast of $42,000 in cell E4, you would enter **=B3+D4** and copy and paste it down through E5:E26. Create the chart by following these steps:

1. **Select A3:B26, and release the mouse button.**
2. **Hold down the Ctrl key and select E3:E26.**

   You should now see two ranges highlighted, one in columns A and B and one in column E.
3. **Click the Chart Wizard button on the main toolbar, or choose Insert ➪ Chart.**
4. **Step through the Chart Wizard, choosing whatever options you want.**

   Because the horizontal axis will represent the values in A3:A26, the time period dates, a Line chart is a good choice.

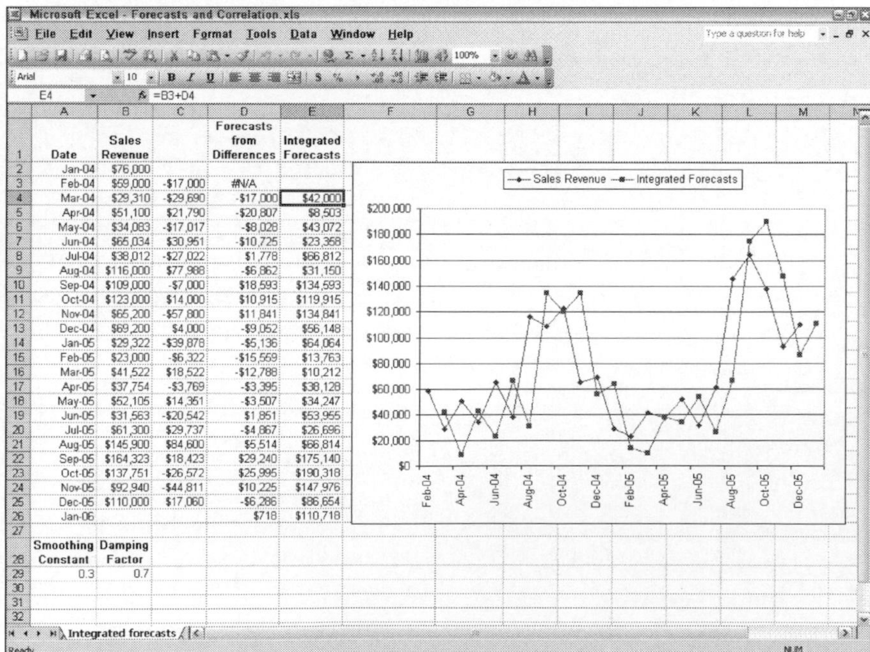

Date	Sales Revenue		Forecasts from Differences	Integrated Forecasts
Jan-04	$76,000			
Feb-04	$59,000	-$17,000	#N/A	
Mar-04	$29,310	-$29,690	-$17,000	$42,000
Apr-04	$51,100	$21,790	-$20,807	$8,503
May-04	$34,083	-$17,017	-$8,028	$43,072
Jun-04	$65,034	$30,951	-$10,725	$23,358
Jul-04	$38,012	-$27,022	$1,778	$66,812
Aug-04	$116,000	$77,988	-$6,862	$31,150
Sep-04	$109,000	-$7,000	$18,593	$134,593
Oct-04	$123,000	$14,000	$10,915	$119,915
Nov-04	$65,200	-$57,800	$11,841	$134,841
Dec-04	$69,200	$4,000	-$9,052	$56,148
Jan-05	$29,322	-$39,878	-$5,136	$64,064
Feb-05	$23,000	-$6,322	-$15,559	$13,763
Mar-05	$41,522	$18,522	-$12,788	$10,212
Apr-05	$37,754	-$3,769	-$3,395	$38,128
May-05	$52,105	$14,351	-$3,507	$34,247
Jun-05	$31,563	-$20,542	$1,851	$53,955
Jul-05	$61,300	$29,737	-$4,867	$26,696
Aug-05	$145,900	$84,600	$5,514	$66,814
Sep-05	$164,323	$18,423	$29,240	$175,140
Oct-05	$137,751	-$26,572	$25,995	$190,318
Nov-05	$92,940	-$44,811	$10,225	$147,976
Dec-05	$110,000	$17,060	-$6,286	$86,654
Jan-06			$718	$110,718

Smoothing Constant	Damping Factor
0.3	0.7

Figure 14-12: The integrated forecasts still show some lag but do not over- and underestimate as much as the forecasts based directly on the actuals.

Notice in Figure 14-12 that the forecasts track the actuals much better than they do in Figure 14-8, where the forecasts are based on the actuals, with all that autocorrelation.

Steps 1 and 2 advised you to select one range (in columns A and B) and then hold down Ctrl and select a third range (in column E). Whether you're selecting ranges or individual cells, this is the way to get a *multiple selection* in Excel. A multiple selection is two or more cells or ranges that are *not* contiguous — and here, the range E3:E26 is not contiguous to A3:B26, because columns C and D are in between. If you want to select a range of contiguous cells (such as A3:B26), click A3, hold down Shift, and then click B26. Using Shift means that, in this example, all cells between A3 and B26 are selected — so it's not a multiple selection.

One more thing (I feel like I'm wearing a rumpled raincoat, holding a stinky stogie, and holding one hand over my head with my forefinger extended): Although this example used exponential smoothing to create the forecasts in Figures 14-8 and 14-12, you'd get roughly the same outcome if you used moving averages or regression.

I say "roughly the same" because moving averages, exponential smoothing, and regression always produce forecasts that are at least slightly different from one another. The point is that moving averages and regression can react to autocorrelation in ways that can mislead you. In particular, if you're using regression, you'd often want to difference the series so that the forecast *errors* (the differences between the forecasts and the actuals) are independent of one another.

Calculating autocorrelation

Figure 14-13 shows an example of calculating an autocorrelation coefficient.

The autocorrelation of 0.69 shown in Figure 14-13 is between the values in cells B2:B24 and the values in cells B3:B25. The formula in cell E3 is:

```
=CORREL(B2:B24,B3:B25)
```

Notice the similarity between this formula and the one used in Figure 14-5:

```
=CORREL(A2:A30,B2:B30)
```

In each case, you're using the CORREL function to calculate a correlation between two different worksheet ranges. The only real difference between the two formulas is that in the case of autocorrelation, you're getting the correlation between the first through the 23rd values, and the second through the 24th values of the same variable.

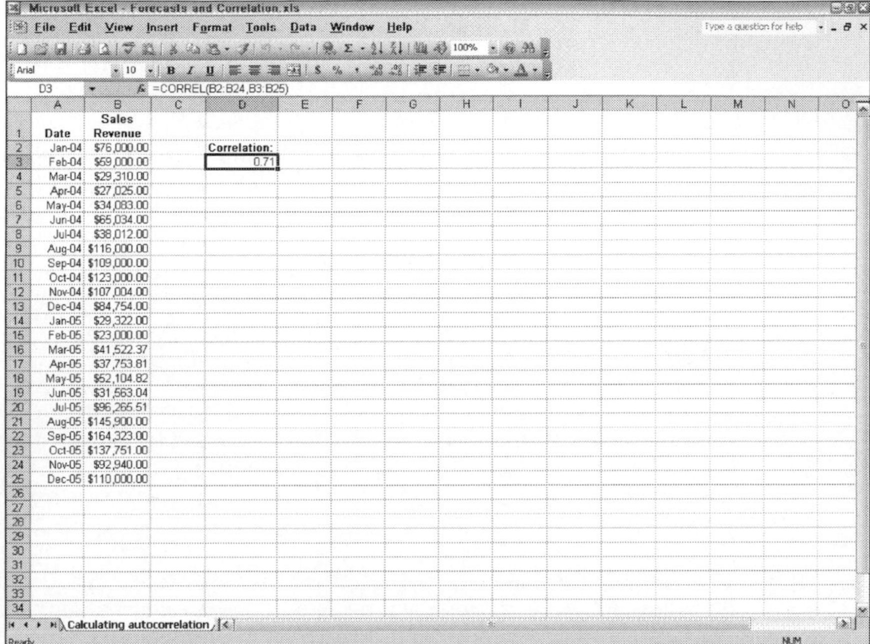

	A	B
1	Date	Sales Revenue
2	Jan-04	$76,000.00
3	Feb-04	$59,000.00
4	Mar-04	$29,310.00
5	Apr-04	$27,025.00
6	May-04	$34,083.00
7	Jun-04	$65,034.00
8	Jul-04	$38,012.00
9	Aug-04	$116,000.00
10	Sep-04	$109,000.00
11	Oct-04	$123,000.00
12	Nov-04	$107,004.00
13	Dec-04	$84,754.00
14	Jan-05	$29,322.00
15	Feb-05	$23,000.00
16	Mar-05	$41,522.37
17	Apr-05	$37,753.81
18	May-05	$52,104.82
19	Jun-05	$31,563.04
20	Jul-05	$96,265.51
21	Aug-05	$145,900.00
22	Sep-05	$164,323.00
23	Oct-05	$137,751.00
24	Nov-05	$92,940.00
25	Dec-05	$110,000.00

Figure 14-13: The CORREL function can handle overlapping ranges.

It can be easier to see what's going on by splitting the baseline into two different ranges. This is done in Figure 14-14. The correlation of 0.71 in cell G3 of Figure 14-14 is the same as in cell E3 of Figure 14-13. This isn't surprising, because the values in the ranges in each figure are identical. The only unfamiliar aspect in Figure 14-13 is that the two ranges overlap.

Diagnosing autocorrelation

Earlier in this chapter, I imply that if the autocorrelation in a baseline is 0.65, you should take first differences to remove the autocorrelation. A little later, I said that the autocorrelation of the first differences was negligible if it was as small as –0.10. So, that begs the question, "How small is negligible?"

Chapters 4 and 17 describe tests that help you decide whether a correlation is real or phantom. Here's another test that you'll probably find quicker to carry out than the others. Take these steps:

1. **Copy the baseline you're going to forecast from (whether it's the actuals or the first differences you've taken from the actuals) and, for convenience, paste it into a new worksheet.**

   Let the paste start in, say, cell A1.

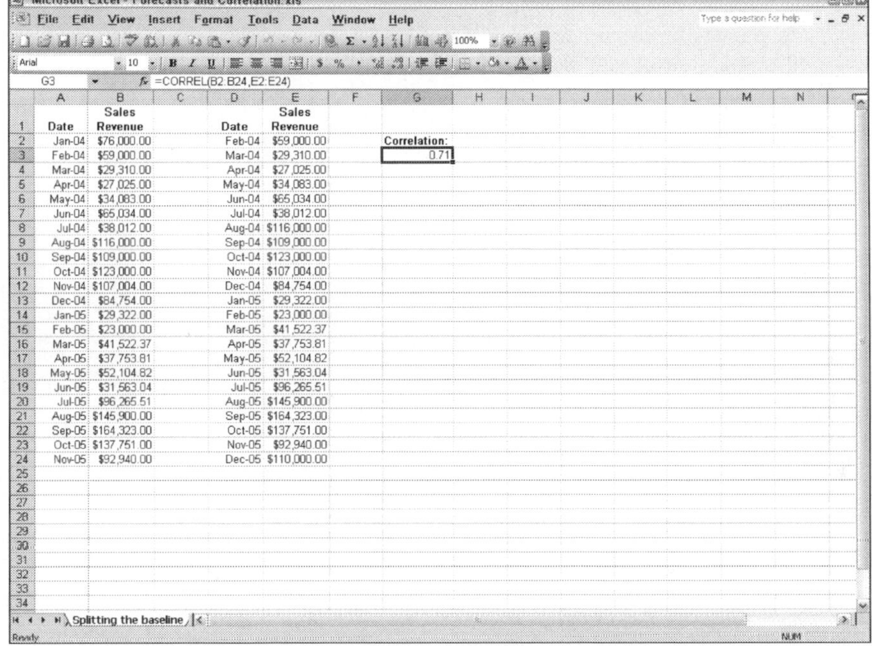

Figure 14-14: The values in column E start with the value in B3.

2. **Select cell B1 and paste again.**

   You now have identical values in columns A and B of the new worksheet. Suppose that these values are in A1:A48 and B1:B48.

3. **Choose Tools➪Data Analysis, and select Regression in the Analysis Tools list box.**

   The Regression dialog box, shown in Figure 14-15, appears.

4. **In the Regression dialog box, click in the Input Y Range box and drag through B2:B48.**

5. **Click in the Input X Range box and drag through A1:A47.**

   The Regression tool will not allow these two ranges to overlap on the worksheet, which is why this list asks you to create two separate ranges in columns A and B.

6. **Click the Output Range option button.**

7. **Make sure that the Output Range address box has the focus rather than the Input Y Range box.**

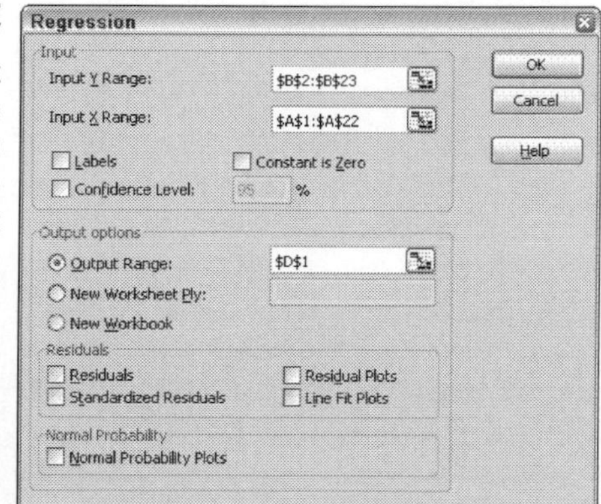

Figure 14-15: The Input Y Range box can take the focus when you click the Output Range button, which can cause you to lose the address in the Input Y Range box.

8. **Click in a worksheet cell that has blank cells below it and to its right.**
9. **Click OK.**

   The results look something like those in Figure 14-16.

The cell to focus on is the one labeled *Significance of F.* As you've set up the regression analysis, that cell tells you the statistical significance of the correlation between cells A1:A47 and B2:B48 — which is, in fact, the autocorrelation between A1:A47 and A2:A48.

The higher the value labeled *Significance of F,* the less likely it is that the autocorrelation is real. (Sorry about that: Statements of statistical significance are usually bassackwards.) In Figure 14-16, the significance level is a touch over 0.65. This means that you would have gotten an autocorrelation as large as –0.10 about 65 percent of the time, even if there were no real autocorrelation in the data at all. So you can assume that the autocorrelation in the baseline actuals has been removed by the first differencing.

Suppose that the autocorrelation was 0.65 and the resulting significance level was, say, 0.05. This would mean that only 5 percent of the time would you see an autocorrelation as large as 0.65, if the real autocorrelation were zero. So in that case you should assume that the autocorrelation is real.

Microsoft Excel - Forecasts and Correlation.xls

I12 0.65139899814662

	A	B	C	D	E	F	G	H	I
1	-$17,000	-$17,000		SUMMARY OUTPUT					
2	-$29,690	-$29,690							
3	$21,790	$21,790		*Regression Statistics*					
4	-$17,017	-$17,017		Multiple R	0.102032				
5	$30,951	$30,951		R Square	0.010411				
6	-$27,022	-$27,022		Adjusted R Square	-0.03907				
7	$77,988	$77,988		Standard Error	36553.52				
8	-$7,000	-$7,000		Observations	22				
9	$14,000	$14,000							
10	-$57,800	-$57,800		ANOVA					
11	$4,000	$4,000			*df*	*SS*	*MS*	*F*	*Significance F*
12	-$39,878	-$39,878		Regression	1	281129241.3	281129241.3	0.210401	0.65
13	-$6,322	-$6,322		Residual	20	26723196910	1336159845		
14	$18,522	$18,522		Total	21	27004326151			
15	-$3,769	-$3,769							
16	$14,351	$14,351							
17	-$20,542	-$20,542							
18	$29,737	$29,737							
19	$84,600	$84,600							
20	$18,423	$18,423							
21	-$26,572	-$26,572							
22	-$44,811	-$44,811							
23	$17,060	$17,060							

An insignificant result

Figure 14-16: Look to the Significance of F to determine whether you should treat the autocorrelation as real.

What's a "real" autocorrelation? The values that you're testing are usually samples from a much longer baseline. Perhaps the baseline *could* go back to, say January 1920, and you don't have the time, patience, or resources to retrieve all those values. If you did, you could calculate the real autocorrelation, the one based on the full population of values, rather than just a sample from that population. What you're doing with the significance test is checking the likelihood that you'd get an autocorrelation as large as –0.10, or 0.65, in your sample if the autocorrelation in the population were zero.

Chapter 15

Smoothing: How You Profit from Your Mistakes

In This Chapter

- Familiarizing yourself with smoothing
- Working with the Exponential Smoothing tool
- Deciding on a smoothing constant
- Dealing with smoothing problems

Smoothing, in this case *exponential* smoothing, is a kind of modified moving average. Don't let the name put you off. You won't have to deal with any exponents (or, for that matter, proponents, deponents, opponents, or components). It's a simple idea, tricked out — as so many simple ideas are — with a fancy name. The idea is to correct a prior forecast and use that correction in making the next forecast. That's pretty straightforward, no?

The Analysis ToolPak (ATP) does exponential smoothing on your behalf. The Exponential Smoothing tool is one of the two in the ATP that returns a formula, so if your input data changes, the forecasts will update automatically. But you want a bit more control over the formulas than the ATP gives you, and this chapter shows you how to get that control.

Exponential smoothing uses something called — here's another bit of jargon — a *smoothing constant.* It helps determine the amount of the error in an earlier forecast to use in making the next one.

After you've chosen, even just for the time being, a smoothing constant, you've automatically chosen a *damping factor* — yet another piece of jargon. I wouldn't even bring it up here except that the ATP's Exponential Smoothing tool uses that term.

The point to take away from this prolog is that, when you get past the snooty terminology, exponential smoothing is no more difficult than moving averages.

Correcting Errors: The Idea Behind Smoothing

You don't *have* to get a handle on the idea behind exponential smoothing. But it doesn't take much time or effort, and it can help you understand what's going on when you make your forecast. Plus, if you're ever asked to explain a forecast, you don't want to have to say, "We used Excel's Analysis ToolPak. It took care of making the actual forecasts. It's really convenient." That doesn't exactly add to your credibility.

Much better is something like, "We used exponential smoothing. It's a standard forecasting technique. We could have used moving averages, but in this case, we would have lost too much of the baseline. We could have used regression, but exponential smoothing gave us better results. Using the error in the last forecast to fine-tune the current forecast — and that's the basic idea behind exponential smoothing — improved the accuracy of our forecasts. Now, if we can return to the chart. . . ."

Adjusting the forecast

Believe it or not, forecasts are usually wrong. Most often, if they're created rationally, the forecasts are not off by too much, but they *are* off.

You'd love to go back and adjust your forecast for, say, January after the actual results came in. You'd take your forecast of 26,000 units sold, compare it to the actual of 25,437 units sold, and adjust your forecast down by 563 units. You'd look like a wizard.

Unfortunately, most of us don't own tall pointy hats with stars and moons on them. But although you can't pretend that you made that adjustment before you saw the actuals, you can still use it. You can use it on the next forecast.

Suppose that a baseline of sales revenue has been gradually trending up. Some months the sales are up a good bit, some months they're down some, but when you chart the baseline, you can tell that the general trend is up. On the basis of that general trend, you make a forecast for June. Your May actuals were $510,545, and you forecast $519,827 for June. When the next set of actuals comes in, you find that the revenue for June was $516,188.

Of course, you'd like to take some of your rosy forecast back, but you can't. Management has already seen it, they've seen the actuals, and they've noticed the difference. Fortunately, you've prepared them emotionally for this sort of thing and you know they won't jump your case — not as long as they know that you've noticed it too and will take it into account in your next forecast.

And you will, if you're using exponential smoothing. In effect, here's what you'll do:

1. **Decide how much weight you want to give to the error in the June forecast.**

   That will be somewhere between 0 percent and 100 percent. Suppose you choose 30 percent.

2. **Multiply that weight times the error.**

   The error for June was $516,188 – $519,827, or $(3,639). Thirty percent of $(3,639) is $(1,091.70), which is the weighted error.

3. **Add the weighted error to the prior forecast.**

At this point the error is a negative number. This is because your forecast was too high and you subtract the forecast from the actual to get the error. The effect of adding June's negative weighted error to June's forecast is to pull the forecast for July down.

The result would be:

July Forecast = June Forecast + 0.3 (June Actual – June Forecast)

July Forecast = $519,827 + [0.3 × $(3,639)]

July Forecast = $518,735.30

You wish you could have done that for June, because it would have made your June forecast closer to the June actual. But it's not too late to build it into the July forecast.

Keep in mind a few things about the exponential smoothing approach:

- **It helps your forecasts start reacting quickly when a baseline is starting to turn up or to turn down.** In fact, it starts as quickly as the very next period. If things start ticking down in June, your July forecast will reflect that, same as it would reflect an uptick.
- **Your choice in the matter, after you've decided to use exponential smoothing, is limited to *how much* you'll react to the previous error.** In this example, you made that choice when you decided to give 30 percent weight to the error in the prior forecast.
- **That 30 percent (equivalently, 0.3) weight is the smoothing constant.** The smoothing constant is required to be between 0.0 and 1.0, inclusive.

Figure 15-1 shows an example of forecasting with exponential smoothing.

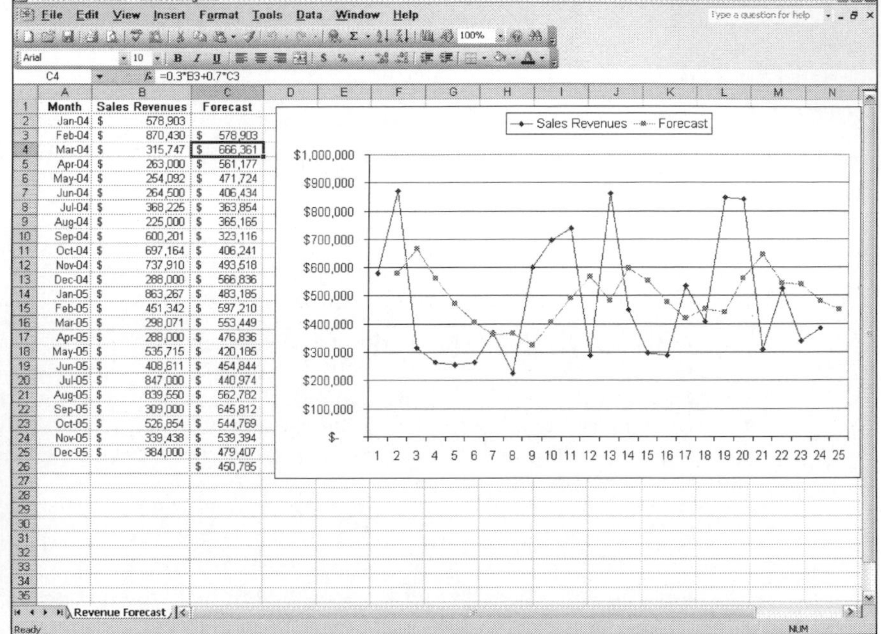

Figure 15-1: The forecasts in column C were created by Excel's Exponential Smoothing tool.

There's a more convenient form of the equation than we've looked at so far, and you'll see it more frequently than any other form. In cell C4 of Figure 15-1, it's

```
=0.3*B3+0.7*C3
```

That is, the smoothing constant times the prior actual, plus the damping factor times the prior forecast. This form is convenient to copy and paste down the worksheet, but it doesn't tell you what's really going on — not, at least, in an intuitive sense. For that, see the following section.

Why they call it "exponential smoothing"

You can safely skip this section and still use exponential smoothing as an approach to forecasting. But if you're interested, read on.

Make these assumptions:

- You're working with a baseline built with monthly data.
- The baseline starts in April.
- The smoothing constant you're using is 0.3.

Then the forecast for July would be:

July forecast = 0.3 × June actual + 0.7 × June forecast

What's the June forecast? It's

June forecast = 0.3 × May actual + 0.7 × May forecast

Here, the smoothing constant is 0.3 and the damping factor is, therefore, 0.7.

The smoothing constant and the damping factor always add up to 1.0. If you know one of them, you know the other.

Expanding the equation

In the July forecast, if you remove the June forecast figure and replace it with the *formula* for the June forecast, you get:

July forecast = 0.3 × June actual + 0.7 × (0.3 × May actual + 0.7 × May forecast)

The May forecast is:

0.3 × April actual + 0.7 × April forecast

Now, because the baseline begins in April, you can't go back to March and forecast a value for April, so you take the April actual to be the April forecast. This is standard operating procedure for forecasting. When you get back to the start of a baseline looking for a forecast of the baseline's first value, you use the actual value instead. (There's no earlier value available to forecast from.)

So, substituting the April actual for the April forecast, you have:

July forecast = 0.3 × June actual + 0.7 × (0.3 × May actual + 0.7 × [0.3 × April actual + 0.7 × April actual])

Or:

July forecast = 0.3 × June actual + 0.7 × (0.3 × May actual + 0.7 × [1.0 × April actual])

Or:

July forecast = 0.3 × June actual + 0.7 × (0.3 × May actual + 0.7 × April actual)

Or:

July forecast = 0.3 × June actual + 0.7 × 0.3 × May actual + 0.7^2 × April actual

Making sense of the equations

I think I can actually see your eyes glazing over. But bear with me just a little further. See the final term in the last equation? It has an exponent in it: The value 0.7 is squared. If the baseline had been longer, the equation would have had the term $0.7^3 \times$ March actual, or the term $0.7^4 \times$ February actual, and so on.

And that's why it's called exponential smoothing. The farther back you go toward the start of the baseline, the larger the exponent for the damping factor. And because you're raising a fraction (in this example, that's 0.7) to higher and higher powers, the contribution made by older actuals gets smaller and smaller ($0.7^2 = 0.49$, $0.7^3 = 0.34$, $0.7^4 = 0.24$, and so on).

Intuitively, this is how things should be. The farther away a baseline value is from the present day, the smaller you expect its lingering influence to be.

One more thing: Any number raised to the power of zero is, by definition 1.0, and any number raised to the first power is the number itself. So you could write that last equation for the July forecast as:

> July forecast = $0.7^0 \times 0.3 \times$ June actual + $0.7^1 \times 0.3 \times$ May actual + $0.7^2 \times$ April actual

Now this looks a little more consistent. The damping factor of 0.7 and its exponent are actually in each term, but they're superfluous in the early terms, as follows:

- The exponent is zero in the first term, so both the exponent and the damping factor drop out ($0.7^0 = 1$).
- The exponent is 1 in the second term, so the damping factor is raised to the first power. But any number raised to the first power is the number itself, so the exponent itself doesn't need to appear in the equation.
- The final term in this form of the forecasting equation does not make use of the smoothing constant.

Fooling around with the smoothing constant

Perhaps the idea of fooling around with a smoothing constant has never occurred to you — it sounds like something your brother-in-law may have gotten arrested for. But it's a useful exercise anyway.

Chapter 13 talks some about the effect of longer and shorter lengths in a baseline that contribute to a moving average. Other things being equal, these statements are true:

- The more baseline periods that go into a moving average, the more slowly the moving average reacts to changes in the baseline, and the smoother the series of forecasts. Also, there are fewer forecasts you can make because you lose some periods at the start of the baseline.
- The fewer baseline periods that go into a moving average, the more quickly the moving average reacts to — or *tracks* — changes in the baseline, and the more closely the forecasts come to the baseline values themselves. Also, you lose fewer periods at the start of the baseline.

You can see the same effect in exponential smoothing, but because of the smoothing constant and the damping factor, the effect is somewhat different from moving averages. Apropos, here are another couple of truths about exponential smoothing:

- The higher the smoothing constant, the more quickly the forecast tracks the baseline.
- The lower the smoothing constant, the slower the tracking — and therefore the smoother the forecast series tends to appear.

Notice what happens to the equation at the smoothing constant's extremes of 1.0 and 0.0:

> July forecast = Smoothing Constant × June actual + Damping Factor × June forecast
>
> July forecast = 1.0 × June actual + 0.0 × June forecast

So with a smoothing constant of 1.0, the forecasts track the actuals precisely, just one period late. The closer the smoothing constant is to 1.0, the closer the tracking.

On the other hand:

> July forecast = 0.0 × June actual + 1.0 × June forecast

In this case, the only actual that comes into play is the first one in the baseline. Because the baseline's first value is also taken to be its forecast value, all forecasts are equal to the first value in the baseline.

Figures 15-2 and 15-3 show how this works. As a practical matter, the forecasts in Figure 15-2 are useless because they're nothing more than the actuals, delayed a month. Figure 15-3's forecasts are useless because they're nothing more than January 2004's actual, projected forward 23 months.

So, in practice, you should never have use for either 0.0 or 1.0 as a smoothing constant. But seeing what happens when you use those values helps you remember what happens when you use a smaller or a larger smoothing constant.

For a more realistic view, take a look at Figure 15-4. It's another version of Figure 15-1, but there the smoothing constant was 0.3 (and, therefore, the damping factor was 0.7). Figure 15-4 reverses them: The smoothing constant is 0.7 and the damping factor is 0.3.

In Figure 15-4, where the smoothing constant is 0.7, the forecasts track the actuals much more closely than they do in Figure 15-1, where the smoothing constant is 0.3. The issue once again is tracking versus smoothing. The closer the forecasts track the actuals, the more that noise enters the picture and the more that noise obscures the signal. The more smoothing there is in the forecasts, the more slowly the forecasts react to fundamental, lingering changes in the baseline — therefore, the longer it may take you to decide something important has occurred.

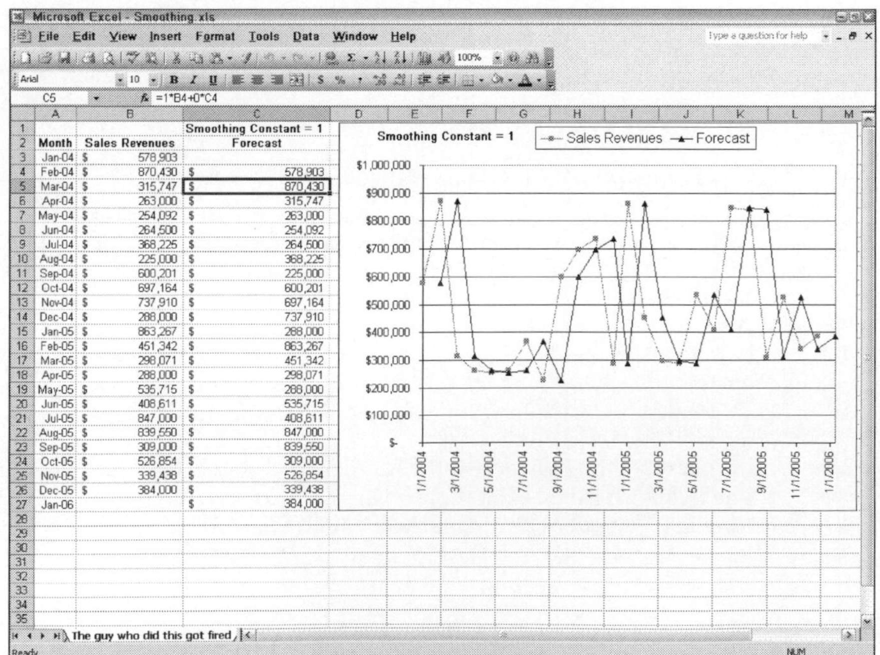

Month	Sales Revenues	Smoothing Constant = 1 Forecast
Jan-04	$ 578,903	
Feb-04	$ 870,430	$ 578,903
Mar-04	$ 315,747	$ 870,430
Apr-04	$ 263,000	$ 315,747
May-04	$ 254,092	$ 263,000
Jun-04	$ 264,500	$ 254,092
Jul-04	$ 368,225	$ 264,500
Aug-04	$ 225,000	$ 368,225
Sep-04	$ 600,201	$ 225,000
Oct-04	$ 697,164	$ 600,201
Nov-04	$ 737,910	$ 697,164
Dec-04	$ 288,000	$ 737,910
Jan-05	$ 863,267	$ 288,000
Feb-05	$ 451,342	$ 863,267
Mar-05	$ 298,071	$ 451,342
Apr-05	$ 288,000	$ 298,071
May-05	$ 535,715	$ 288,000
Jun-05	$ 408,611	$ 535,715
Jul-05	$ 847,000	$ 408,611
Aug-05	$ 839,550	$ 847,000
Sep-05	$ 309,000	$ 839,550
Oct-05	$ 526,854	$ 309,000
Nov-05	$ 339,438	$ 526,854
Dec-05	$ 384,000	$ 339,438
Jan-06		$ 384,000

Figure 15-2: Perfect (but noisy) tracking.

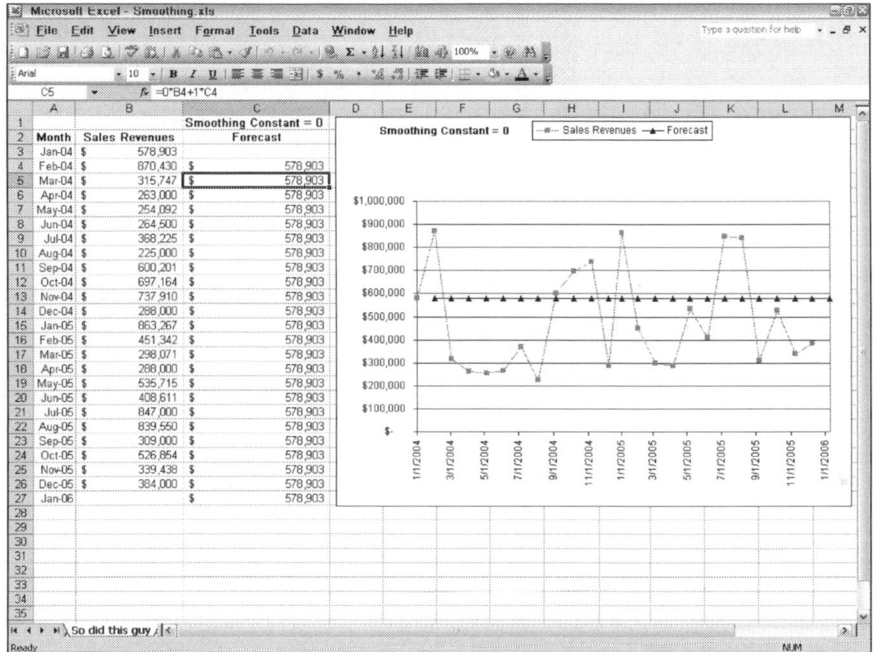

Month	Sales Revenues	Smoothing Constant = 0 Forecast
Jan-04	$ 578,903	
Feb-04	$ 870,430	$ 578,903
Mar-04	$ 315,747	$ 578,903
Apr-04	$ 263,000	$ 578,903
May-04	$ 254,092	$ 578,903
Jun-04	$ 264,500	$ 578,903
Jul-04	$ 368,225	$ 578,903
Aug-04	$ 225,000	$ 578,903
Sep-04	$ 600,201	$ 578,903
Oct-04	$ 697,164	$ 578,903
Nov-04	$ 737,910	$ 578,903
Dec-04	$ 288,000	$ 578,903
Jan-05	$ 863,267	$ 578,903
Feb-05	$ 451,342	$ 578,903
Mar-05	$ 298,071	$ 578,903
Apr-05	$ 288,000	$ 578,903
May-05	$ 535,715	$ 578,903
Jun-05	$ 408,611	$ 578,903
Jul-05	$ 847,000	$ 578,903
Aug-05	$ 839,550	$ 578,903
Sep-05	$ 309,000	$ 578,903
Oct-05	$ 526,854	$ 578,903
Nov-05	$ 339,438	$ 578,903
Dec-05	$ 384,000	$ 578,903
Jan-06		$ 578,903

Figure 15-3: Perfect (but information-free) smoothing.

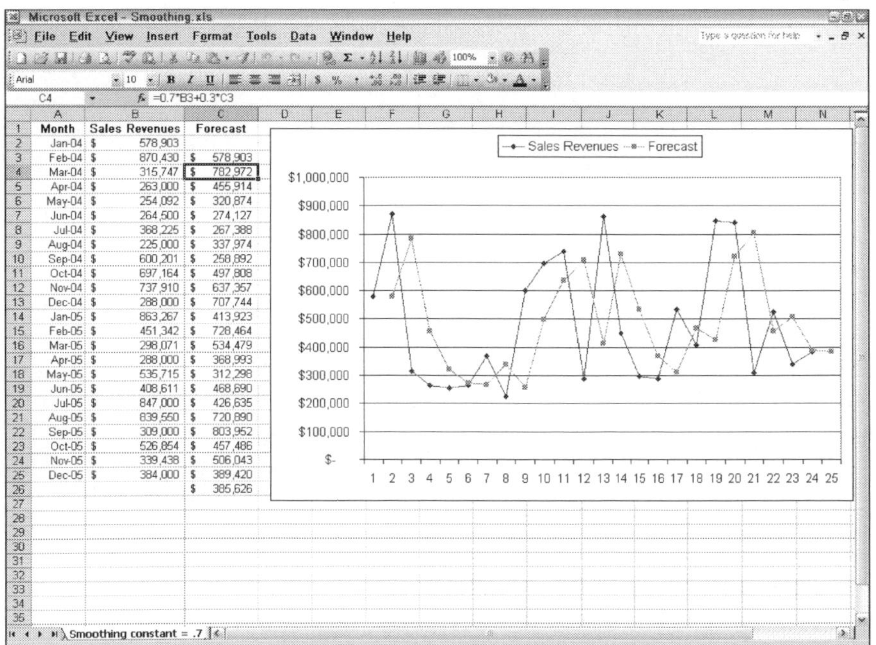

Month	Sales Revenues	Forecast
Jan-04	$ 578,903	
Feb-04	$ 870,430	$ 578,903
Mar-04	$ 315,747	$ 782,972
Apr-04	$ 263,000	$ 455,914
May-04	$ 254,092	$ 320,874
Jun-04	$ 264,500	$ 274,127
Jul-04	$ 368,225	$ 267,388
Aug-04	$ 225,000	$ 337,974
Sep-04	$ 600,201	$ 258,892
Oct-04	$ 697,164	$ 497,808
Nov-04	$ 737,910	$ 637,357
Dec-04	$ 288,000	$ 707,744
Jan-05	$ 863,267	$ 413,923
Feb-05	$ 451,342	$ 728,464
Mar-05	$ 298,071	$ 534,479
Apr-05	$ 288,000	$ 368,993
May-05	$ 535,715	$ 312,298
Jun-05	$ 408,611	$ 468,690
Jul-05	$ 847,000	$ 426,635
Aug-05	$ 839,550	$ 720,890
Sep-05	$ 309,000	$ 803,952
Oct-05	$ 526,854	$ 457,486
Nov-05	$ 339,438	$ 506,043
Dec-05	$ 384,000	$ 389,420
		$ 385,626

Figure 15-4: Notice that the forecasts are more volatile than in Figure 15-1.

Using the Smoothing Tool's Formula

Chapter 10 gives a brief overview of using the Analysis ToolPak (ATP) to make a forecast by means of its Exponential Smoothing tool. This section recaps that process and shows you how to tinker with the forecasts after the basic spadework has been done.

Getting a forecast from the Exponential Smoothing tool

Figure 15-5 shows a baseline you may start with.

Here are the steps to add to this baseline a series of forecasts using the ATP's Exponential Smoothing tool:

1. **Make sure the ATP is installed in Excel.**

   See Chapter 7 for installation information.

Month	Units Sold
Jan-04	$ 283,827
Feb-04	$ 423,000
Mar-04	$ 252,807
Apr-04	$ 66,557
May-04	$ 191,595
Jun-04	$ 112,950
Jul-04	$ 480,000
Aug-04	$ 447,000
Sep-04	$ 239,079
Oct-04	$ 464,860
Nov-04	$ 336,000
Dec-04	$ 232,940
Jan-05	$ 284,959
Feb-05	$ 437,854
Mar-05	$ 171,704
Apr-05	$ 33,832
May-05	$ 229,253
Jun-05	$ 87,895
Jul-05	$ 289,019
Aug-05	$ 87,000
Sep-05	$ 213,257
Oct-05	$ 63,524
Nov-05	$ 305,242
Dec-05	$ 153,337

Figure 15-5: You don't need the date information, but having it there lets you verify the sales figures.

2. **If necessary, activate the worksheet that contains the baseline.**
3. **Choose Tools ➪ Data Analysis.**

   The Data Analysis dialog box opens.
4. **In the Data Analysis dialog box, click on Exponential Smoothing in the list box, and click OK.**
5. **Click in the Input Range box, and drag through B1:B25 on the worksheet.**
6. **Click in the Damping Factor box and enter** 0.7.

   This corresponds to a smoothing constant of 0.3.
7. **Because your input range included cell B1, which names the baseline in B2:B25, select the Labels check box.**
8. **Click in the Output Range box, and then click in the cell where you want the output to begin.**

   On the worksheet shown in Figure 15-5, that would be C2 — it would not be C1. The Exponential Smoothing tool does not provide a label for its forecasts, so the first output value would be put in C1, one row higher than the first value in the baseline.

   Figure 15-6 shows how the dialog box appears just before you click OK.

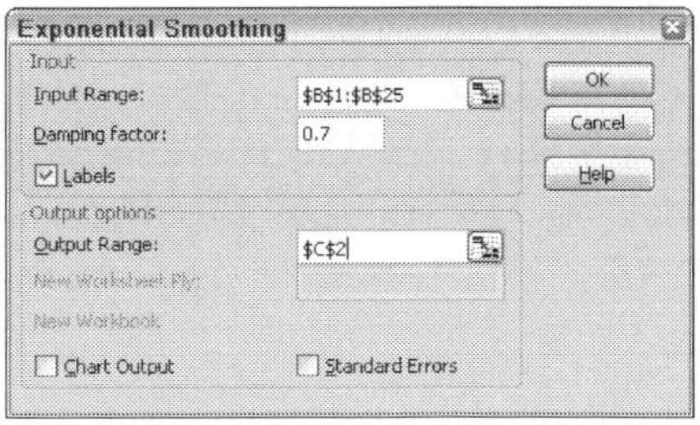

Figure 15-6: This example continues by putting the forecasts into a new chart, so don't bother to select the Chart Output check box.

9. **Click OK.**
10. **Type the label** Forecasts **in cell C1.**

    You'll find the results of using the Exponential Smoothing tool in column C of Figure 15-7.

One problem with the Exponential Smoothing tool is that it doesn't automatically give you the forecast for the period following the baseline's last period — and that's what you're most interested in. So, to get that value, take these steps:

1. **Using the layout in Figure 15-7, select cell C25.**

   More generally, select the bottommost cell that the Exponential Smoothing tool returned.

2. **Move your mouse pointer over the bottom-right corner of that cell until the pointer changes to a crosshair.**

3. **Press and hold down the left mouse button, drag down one row, and release the mouse button.**

   Steps 1 through 3 get you a forecast for the next time period. All that's left is to put the forecasts into the chart.

4. **Using the layout in Figure 15-7, select the range B1:C26.**

   More generally, select the cell that contains the label for your baseline field; in Figure 15-7, that's B1.

	A	B	C
1	Month	Units Sold	
2	Jan-04	$ 283,827	#N/A
3	Feb-04	$ 423,000	$ 283,827
4	Mar-04	$ 252,807	325578.9
5	Apr-04	$ 66,557	303747.33
6	May-04	$ 191,595	232590.231
7	Jun-04	$ 112,950	220291.6617
8	Jul-04	$ 480,000	188089.1632
9	Aug-04	$ 447,000	275662.4142
10	Sep-04	$ 239,079	327063.69
11	Oct-04	$ 464,860	300668.283
12	Nov-04	$ 336,000	349925.7981
13	Dec-04	$ 232,940	345748.0587
14	Jan-05	$ 284,959	311905.6411
15	Feb-05	$ 437,854	303821.6487
16	Mar-05	$ 171,704	344031.3541
17	Apr-05	$ 33,832	292333.1479
18	May-05	$ 229,253	214782.8035
19	Jun-05	$ 87,895	219123.8625
20	Jul-05	$ 289,019	179755.2037
21	Aug-05	$ 87,000	212534.3426
22	Sep-05	$ 213,257	174874.0398
23	Oct-05	$ 63,524	186388.9279
24	Nov-05	$ 305,242	149529.4495
25	Dec-05	$ 153,337	196243.2147

Figure 15-7: The Exponential Smoothing tool does not apply formats (here, currency) in the input range to its output range.

5. **Hold down the Shift key and click in the cell with the forecast you created manually in steps 1 through 1.**

   In Figure 15-7, that's C26.

6. **Click the Chart button (or choose Insert ⇨ Chart), choose Line chart, and click Finish.**

Change the chart formatting however you want. In Figure 15-8, I made the chart larger by dragging its corner handles, I set the font size to 11 for all text in the chart, moved the legend to the top, and formatted the Plot area to have no pattern.

When you're using the ATP's Exponential Smoothing tool, you need to think in terms of a damping factor, because the tool insists on it. Specifying a damping factor and getting the smoothing constant by subtracting the damping factor from 1.0 isn't unreasonable, but it is unusual.

Don't try putting the damping factor in a worksheet cell and then referencing the cell in the Exponential Smoothing dialog box's Damping Factor box. That box won't accept a cell address. If you want to take that tack — and I recommend you do so (see the next section) — you have to do it after the tool has created the forecast.

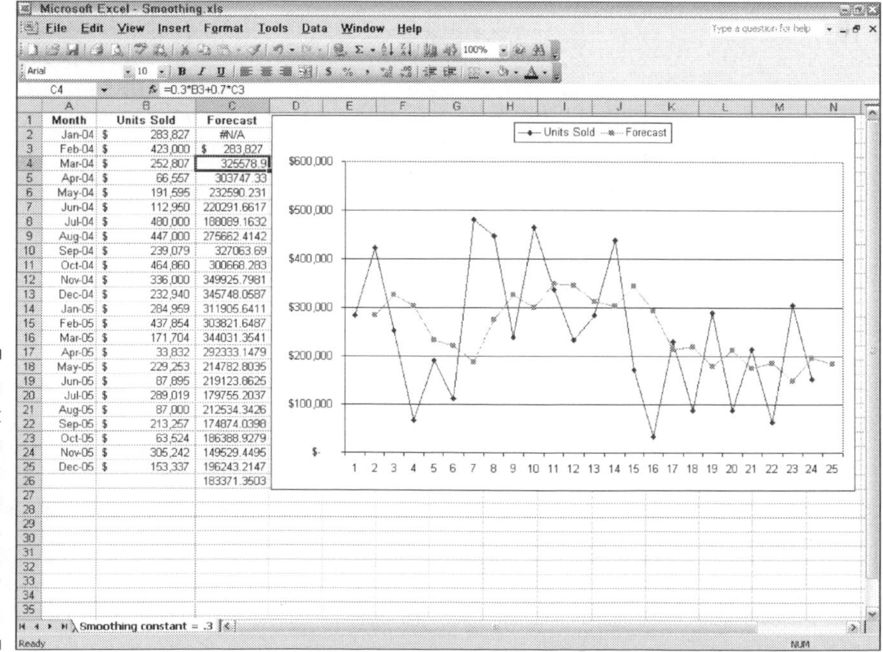

Figure 15-8: A cell that contains either a blank value or an #N/A value will not appear in the chart.

Modifying the smoothing constant

After the Exponential Smoothing tool has given you a series of forecasts, you're in a position to change the forecasts by tinkering with the value of the smoothing constant. The formulas for the forecasts follow the form mentioned at the end of the "Adjusting the forecast" section, early in this chapter. The formulas for the forecasts in C4:C6 of Figure 15-8 are

```
=0.3*B3+0.7*C3
=0.3*B4+0.7*C4
=0.3*B5+0.7*C5
```

This is good news and bad news. The good news is that you have formulas to work with, not static values like these:

```
325578.9
303747.3
232590.2
```

which are the results of the formulas in C4:C6.

The bad news is that the formulas contain constants, 0.3 and 0.7, which you can't easily change. You can turn that bad news into good news by taking these steps, using the worksheet in Figure 15-8 as a basis:

1. **In cell B28, enter** =1 - A28.

   It doesn't matter where you enter it, as long as it's in some blank cell so that you're not overwriting anything important.

2. **In cell A28, enter** 0.3.

3. **If necessary, format A28:B28 to the Number format, with two decimals: Select A28:B28, choose Format ➪ Cells, select the Number tab, choose Number from the list box, set the spinner to 2, and click OK.**

4. **Select cell C4.**

   In the Formula Bar, you'll see its formula:

   ```
   =0.3*B3+0.7*C3
   ```

5. **Click in the Formula Bar, change the 0.3 in the formula to $A$28, change the 0.7 in the formula to $B$28, and press Enter or click the Enter button.**

   The formula should now be:

   ```
   =$A$28*B3+$B$28*C3
   ```

6. **If necessary, select cell C4 again. Then move your mouse pointer over its lower-right corner until the pointer changes to a crosshair. Press and hold the left mouse button, and drag down through C26, and release the mouse button.**

Be sure to include the dollar signs in Step 5. If you don't, the references will be relative, and when you do the autofill in Step 6, the subsequent references point to different cells, your Unit Sales forecasts go to zero, and here you are with no Get Out of Zero Free card.

The effects of steps 1 through 6 are to:

- Put the values for the smoothing constant and the damping factor explicitly on the worksheet.
- Make the forecast formulas in column C refer to the smoothing constant and damping factor in A28:B28.

Now you can change the smoothing constant in A28. When you do, the damping factor in B28 changes accordingly. And when they've changed, so do the forecasts in column C that depend on those two values. Furthermore, the chart updates.

Figure 15-9 shows the result of changing the smoothing constant in A28 from 0.3 to 0.5.

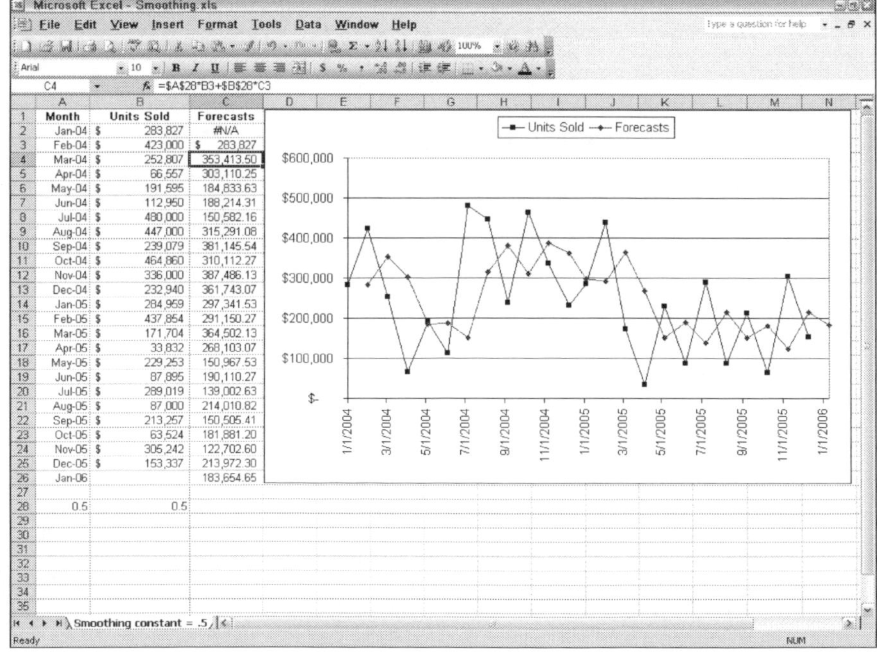

C4 =$A$28*B3+$B$28*C3

	Month	Units Sold	Forecasts
1	Month	Units Sold	Forecasts
2	Jan-04	$ 283,827	#N/A
3	Feb-04	$ 423,000	$ 283,827
4	Mar-04	$ 252,807	353,413.50
5	Apr-04	$ 66,557	303,110.25
6	May-04	$ 191,595	184,833.63
7	Jun-04	$ 112,950	188,214.31
8	Jul-04	$ 480,000	150,582.16
9	Aug-04	$ 447,000	315,291.08
10	Sep-04	$ 239,079	381,145.54
11	Oct-04	$ 464,860	310,112.27
12	Nov-04	$ 336,000	387,486.13
13	Dec-04	$ 232,940	361,743.07
14	Jan-05	$ 284,959	297,341.53
15	Feb-05	$ 437,854	291,150.27
16	Mar-05	$ 171,704	364,502.13
17	Apr-05	$ 33,832	268,103.07
18	May-05	$ 229,253	150,967.53
19	Jun-05	$ 87,895	190,110.27
20	Jul-05	$ 289,019	139,002.63
21	Aug-05	$ 87,000	214,010.82
22	Sep-05	$ 213,257	150,505.41
23	Oct-05	$ 63,524	181,881.20
24	Nov-05	$ 305,242	122,702.60
25	Dec-05	$ 153,337	213,972.30
26	Jan-06		183,654.65
27			
28	0.5	0.5	

Figure 15-9: A smoothing constant of 0.5 tracks the baseline more closely than a smoothing constant of 0.3.

Comparing Figures 15-8 and 15-9, you can see that Figure 15-8's forecasts chart a little smoother than do Figure 15-9's. The other side of that coin is that Figure 15-9's forecasts respond a little faster to changes in the baseline than do Figure 15-8's. You can experiment with different values of the smoothing constant to see what effect they have on the charted forecasts.

Experimenting with different smoothing constants is a good way to get familiar with the relationship between the constants, the forecast, and the appearance of the forecasts when they're charted with the baseline actuals. But when it comes time to settle on a smoothing constant for your forecasts, there's nothing like running the numbers.

Finding the Smoothing Constant

Perhaps the best way to decide on a value for the smoothing constant is to use a yardstick of some sort to compare the results you get using different constants. Probably the standard method is to minimize the forecast errors you get with different constants.

The forecast error, or just *error,* is the difference between the forecast for a given period and the actual for the same period.

Developing the yardstick

Figure 15-10 shows a baseline, a smoothing constant, and a damping factor, the forecasts created by the ATP's Exponential Smoothing tool, and the forecast errors obtained by subtracting the forecasts from the actuals.

Here's an overview of what's coming next: You're going to enter a formula that tells you how much error there is in all of your forecasts. After you have that formula, you'll use either trial and error (or a very short VBA procedure) to tell you the best value of the smoothing constant to *minimize* that error. That's your yardstick.

The formula starts with the Excel worksheet function SUMXMY2, an unfriendly looking function that means this:

SUM: Sum the results

X: A range of values on the worksheet

M: Minus

Y: Another range of values on the worksheet

2: Squared

So, `SUMXMY2(B3:B23,C3:C23)` means this:

1. **Subtract the values in C3:C23 from those in B3:B23 (that is, get B3 – C3, B4 – C4, and so on).**

   The results are the errors in your forecasts, the differences between the forecast for a period and its actual result. This is the XMY part of the function.

2. **Square the results.**

   This is the XMY2 part of the function.

3. **Get the sum of the squares.**

   This is the SUM part of the function.

Microsoft Excel - Smoothing.xls

D4 =B4-C4

	A	B	C	D	E	F	G	H
1	Month	Units Sold	Forecasts	Forecast Errors				
2	Jan-06	3029	#N/A			Smoothing Constant	Damping Factor	Total
3	Feb-06	2825	3029.0	-204.0		0.10	0.90	1
4	Mar-06	3746	3008.6	737.4				
5	Apr-06	3945	3082.3	862.7				
6	May-06	3007	3168.6	-161.6				
7	Jun-06	3309	3152.4	156.6				
8	Jul-06	3404	3168.1	235.9				
9	Aug-06	3933	3191.7	741.3				
10	Sep-06	3883	3265.8	617.2				
11	Oct-06	4042	3327.5	714.5				
12	Nov-06	3934	3399.0	535.0				
13	Dec-06	3231	3452.5	-221.5				
14	Jan-07	3434	3430.3	3.7				
15	Feb-07	3564	3430.7	133.3				
16	Mar-07	3396	3444.0	-48.0				
17	Apr-07	3471	3439.2	31.8				
18	May-07	3940	3442.4	497.6				
19	Jun-07	3488	3492.2	-4.2				
20	Jul-07	3745	3491.8	253.2				
21	Aug-07	3088	3517.1	-429.1				
22	Sep-07	2862	3474.2	-612.2				
23	Oct-07	3609	3413.0	196.0				
24			3432.6					

Choosing a smoothing constant

Figure 15-10: At this point, you have no idea whether a smoothing constant of 0.1 is good, bad, or indifferent.

The idea behind squaring the differences is to get them to all be positive values. If you used just the simple differences, some would be positive and some would be negative, and these tend to cancel one another out. You could use the sum of the absolute value of the differences, but using the squares magnifies the effect of large errors. This is a good thing when you're trying to find the best smoothing constant.

Now, divide `SUMXMY2(B3:B23,C3:C23)` by the number of forecasts:

```
SUMXMY2(B3:B23,C3:C23)/COUNT(B3:B23)
```

The COUNT function gives you the number of numeric values in a range. In effect, you're getting the average squared error in your forecasts.

Finally, take the square root of the average squared error:

```
=SQRT(SUMXMY2(B3:B23,C3:C23)/COUNT(B3:B23))
```

In Figure 15-11, the result appears in cell G6. It's the value on the yardstick that tells you how good your forecasts are. The larger the value, the greater the errors, the worse the forecasts.

Microsoft Excel - Smoothing.xls

G6 =SQRT(SUMXMY2(B3:B23,C3:C23)/COUNT(B3:B23))

	A	B	C	D	E	F	G	H
1	Month	Units Sold	Forecasts	Forecast Errors				
2	Jan-06	3029	#N/A			Smoothing Constant	Damping Factor	Total
3	Feb-06	2825	3029.0	-204.0		0.10	0.90	1
4	Mar-06	3746	3008.6	737.4				
5	Apr-06	3945	3082.3	862.7				
6	May-06	3007	3168.6	-161.6			444.1	
7	Jun-06	3309	3152.4	156.6				
8	Jul-06	3404	3168.1	235.9				
9	Aug-06	3933	3191.7	741.3				
10	Sep-06	3883	3265.8	617.2				
11	Oct-06	4042	3327.5	714.5				
12	Nov-06	3934	3399.0	535.0				
13	Dec-06	3231	3452.5	-221.5				
14	Jan-07	3434	3430.3	3.7				
15	Feb-07	3564	3430.7	133.3				
16	Mar-07	3396	3444.0	-48.0				
17	Apr-07	3471	3439.2	31.8				
18	May-07	3940	3442.4	497.6				
19	Jun-07	3488	3492.2	-4.2				
20	Jul-07	3745	3491.8	253.2				
21	Aug-07	3088	3517.1	-429.1				
22	Sep-07	2862	3474.2	-612.2				
23	Oct-07	3609	3413.0	196.0				
24			3432.6					

Figure 15-11: Start and end your formula with rows that have both a baseline actual and a forecast — here, that's row 3 and row 23.

The result of taking the square root is called the *square root of the mean squared error* (call it *root mean square* for short). It has lots of applications in statistical analysis, but I let it go at that for forecasting purposes.

Next, the idea is to find the smoothing constant that *minimizes* the root mean square (that is, the constant that will make the forecast value in your baseline — and, you hope, for the next and as-yet-unknown actual value — as accurate as possible).

Minimizing the square root of the mean square error

Suppose you put your smoothing constant and damping factor on the worksheet, as in A30 and B30 in Figure 15-10, and point your forecast formulas at those cells. For example, in cell C4 of Figure 15-10:

```
=$A$30*B3+$B$30*C3
```

Now you can change the smoothing constant; the damping factor recalculates accordingly, and so do your forecasts. With the formula for the root mean square on the worksheet (cell G6 in Figure 15-11), you can try different values for the smoothing constant and find the one that minimizes the root mean square value on the yardstick.

Your task isn't too difficult. It's usually enough to try smoothing constants between 0.1 and 0.9, noting the resulting root mean square error each time.

Here's a short Visual Basic for Applications (VBA) procedure that will help you zero in on the best smoothing constant for this baseline, the one that results in the smallest root mean square.

```
Sub Minimize_Smoothing_Constant()
Dim i As Single, RowNumber As Integer
RowNumber = 12
With ActiveSheet
    For i = 0.1 To 1 Step 0.1
         .Cells(3, 6) = i
         .Cells(RowNumber, 6) = i
         .Cells(RowNumber, 7) =.Cells(6, 7)
         RowNumber = RowNumber + 1
    Next i
End With
End Sub
```

Here's a walk through this code. If you're not familiar with VBA, the following will give you an idea of just how easy it is to use. Plus, this will show in a very concrete way how you can find the best smoothing constant, given your baseline data:

- The `Sub` statement just names the procedure. You can refer to its name, `Minimize_Smoothing_Constant`, in several different ways. One of them is shown in the list of numbered steps near the end of this section.
- The `Dim` statement names the variables that the procedure uses. It says that `i` can take on decimal values (`single` means *single precision* and defines a decimal variable), and `RowNumber` is an integer.
- `RowNumber` is set to begin at the number 12. This means that the first row of results is written in row 12.
- A `With` block starts. In this case, anything in the block that begins with a dot (such as `.Cells`) is taken to belong to the `ActiveSheet`.
- A loop starts. The keyword `For` says, "Here begins a loop." A loop is just a sequence of statements that repeats some number of times. Here, the statements repeat as `i` goes from 0.1 to 1, in increments, or *steps,* of 0.1. So i will equal 0.1, and then 0.2, and then 0.3, and so on until it gets to 1.

You can get even more precision in this sort of analysis by making the increments even smaller, such as 0.05 rather than 0.1.

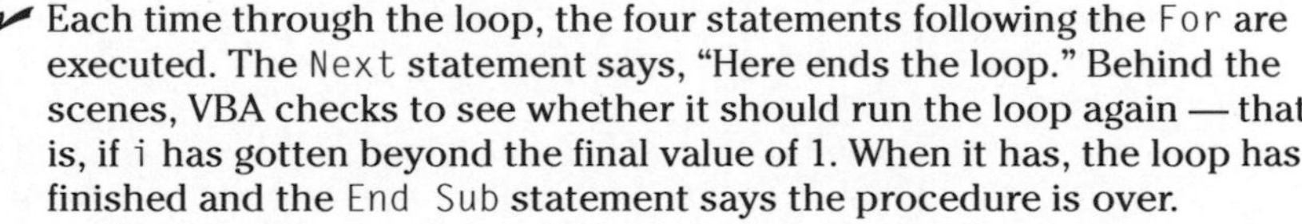

- Each time through the loop, the four statements following the `For` are executed. The `Next` statement says, "Here ends the loop." Behind the scenes, VBA checks to see whether it should run the loop again — that is, if `i` has gotten beyond the final value of 1. When it has, the loop has finished and the `End Sub` statement says the procedure is over.

The statements inside the loop do the following:

- `.Cells(3, 6) = i`: The current value of `i` is written to the active worksheet, in the third row and the sixth column (that is, cell F3). This is the key statement. It sets the smoothing constant to the current value of `i` (0.1, 0.2, 0.3 . . . 0.9). When it does, all the forecasts in C3:C24 recalculate, as does the value of the root mean square in G6. Note that the `ActiveSheet` used in the `With` statement is taken to "own" cell F3.
- `ActiveSheet.Cells(RowNumber, 6) = i.Cells(RowNumber, 6) = i`: The value of `i` is written to the sixth column of the active worksheet, in the row identified by `RowNumber`. `RowNumber` starts out with a value of 12, so the first time through the loop, the current value of `i` is written in cell F12. `RowNumber` will be incremented by 1 each time through the loop, so later loops will write the information further down the worksheet.
- `ActiveSheet.Cells(RowNumber, 7) = ActiveSheet.Cells(6, 7).Cells(RowNumber, 7) = .Cells(6, 7)`: The current value of the root mean square is in column G, row 6 — which corresponds to `Cells(6, 7)`. This statement picks up that value and writes it to the row identified by `RowNumber`, in column 7 (or G) — right next to the current value of `i`.

- `RowNumber = RowNumber + 1`: `RowNumber` is incremented by 1. The next time through the loop, the value of `i` and the current value of the root mean square are written the next row down. The `With` block is ended and so is the subroutine.

To run this code, follow these steps:

1. **With Excel active, choose Tools ⇨ Macro ⇨ Visual Basic Editor.**
2. **Choose Insert ⇨ Module.**
3. **Type the subroutine shown earlier into the new module.**

   When you're through, the Visual Basic Editor should resemble Figure 15-12 (the actual appearance depends on which windows are open).
4. **Choose File ⇨ Close and Return to Microsoft Excel.**
5. **Activate a worksheet that contains data laid out as in Figure 15-13.**

   In particular, make sure that you have a Root Mean Square Error formula in cell G6:

   ```
   =SQRT(SUMXMY2(B3:B23,C3:C23)/COUNT(B3:B23))
   ```
6. **Choose Tools ⇨ Macro ⇨ Macros.**

   The Macro dialog box, shown in Figure 15-12, appears.

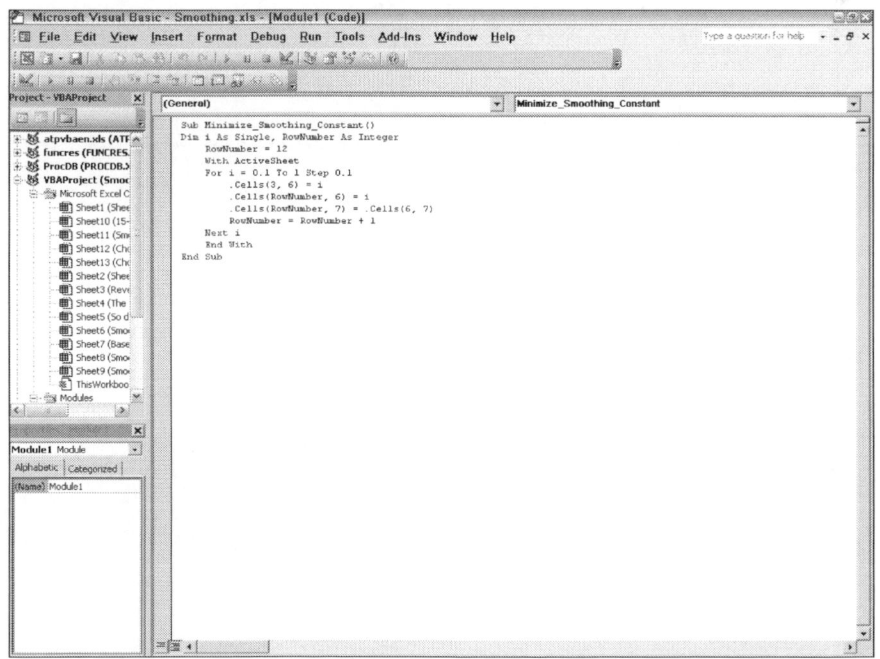

Figure 15-12: The Visual Basic Editor.

7. **Make sure that the subroutine named** `Minimize_Smoothing_Constant` **is selected, and Click Run.**

   The macro will execute and put the different values for the smoothing constant in F12:F20, and the corresponding values of the root mean square in G12:G20.

   The results appear in Figure 15-13.

By looking at the root mean squares in G12:G20, you can see that it's minimized when the smoothing is 0.3. So you can enter 0.3 into cell F3 and know that you've chosen the constant that minimizes the amount of error in your forecasts (see Figure 15-14).

If you're familiar with the Solver, another add-in that comes with Excel, it might occur to you to use the Solver to find the optimum value of the smoothing constant — that strategy often works well. You would tell the Solver to minimize the value of the root mean square, by changing the smoothing constant, and specifying criteria that the smoothing constant must be between 0 and 1. I have a mild preference for the VBA approach, because I can better see what's going on.

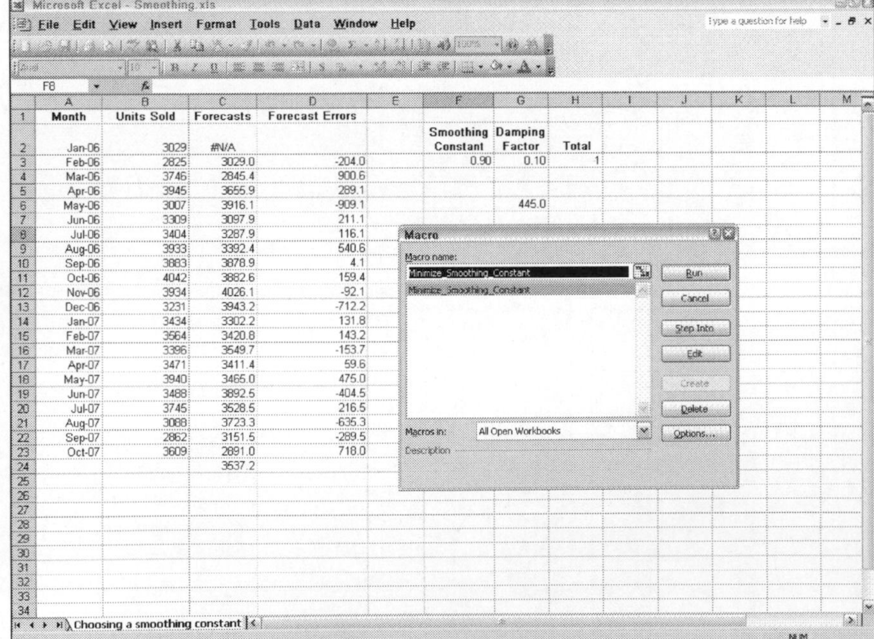

Figure 15-13: You can walk through your code, statement by statement, if you click Step Into rather than Run.

Microsoft Excel - Smoothing.xls

G6 =SQRT(SUMXMY2(B3:B23,C3:C23)/COUNT(B3:B23))

	A	B	C	D	E	F	G	H
1	Date	Units Sold	Forecast	Error				
2	Jan-06	3029	#N/A			Smoothing Constant	Damping Factor	Total
3	Feb-06	2825	3029.0	-204.0		0.90	0.10	1
4	Mar-06	3746	2845.4	900.6				
5	Apr-06	3945	3655.9	289.1				
6	May-06	3007	3916.1	-909.1		Square root of Mean Square Error:	445.0	
7	Jun-06	3309	3097.9	211.1				
8	Jul-06	3404	3287.9	116.1				
9	Aug-06	3933	3392.4	540.6				
10	Sep-06	3883	3878.9	4.1				
11	Oct-06	4042	3882.6	159.4		Smoothing Constant Values		
12	Nov-06	3934	4026.1	-92.1		0.1	444.1	
13	Dec-06	3231	3943.2	-712.2		0.2	415.2	
14	Jan-07	3434	3302.2	131.8		0.3	408.5	
15	Feb-07	3564	3420.8	143.2		0.4	409.7	
16	Mar-07	3396	3549.7	-153.7		0.5	414.4	
17	Apr-07	3471	3411.4	59.6		0.6	420.7	
18	May-07	3940	3465.0	475.0		0.7	428.0	
19	Jun-07	3488	3892.5	-404.5		0.8	436.1	
20	Jul-07	3745	3528.5	216.5		0.9	445.0	
21	Aug-07	3088	3723.3	-635.3				
22	Sep-07	2862	3151.5	-289.5				
23	Oct-07	3609	2891.0	718.0				
24			3537.2					

Choosing a smoothing constant

Figure 15-14: You can use the information in cells F12:G20 to select the best value for the smoothing constant.

Problems with Exponential Smoothing

Nothing's perfect, least of all a forecasting technique and the way that it's implemented in an application like Excel. Two of the problems with exponential smoothing aren't really too terrible. I give you the scoop in the following sections.

Losing an observation at the start

You've probably noticed that the first value that the ATP's Exponential Smoothing tool returns is #N/A, or Not Available. That's because there's no observation prior to the first one on which you can base a forecast of the first time period.

And the first forecast you make is the actual value of the first time period. That's because subsequent forecasts are a combination of the prior actual and the prior forecast. But there's no forecast for the first time period, and the best you can do is to use the first period's actual.

This is better than the periods you lose with moving averages, where you lose one, two, or more time periods at the start, depending on how many actuals go into your moving averages.

Actually, a technique called *backcasting* can take you back prior to the first time period — kind of like asking what preceded the Big Bang. I don't cover it here, but if you really get into forecasting you should know that it exists so you can look into it.

The ATP's standard errors: They're wrong

The Exponential Smoothing tool in the ATP has an option to output standard errors. Here's an example of the formulas it returns:

```
=SQRT(SUMXMY2(A2:A4,C2:C4)/3)
```

Look familiar? It's very similar to the formula developed earlier in this chapter for the root mean square. The only real difference is that it restricts itself to three baseline values and their corresponding forecast values.

There's nothing in statistical or forecasting theory that holds that standard errors should be based on three values. Furthermore, the notion that different parts of the baseline have different standard errors is one on which there is no good consensus.

I don't know what happened to the Exponential Smoothing tool here. My best guess is that a developer was trying to add a Standard Errors capability to the tool, got it to work to his satisfaction in the three-value case, and forgot to generalize it later.

Regardless of the reason that the Standard Errors tool is there, or that it's formulated as it is, my recommendation is that you not bother with it.

Chapter 16

Fine-Tuning a Regression Forecast

In This Chapter

- Making use of multiple regression
- Charting your regression trendline
- Looking at your regression forecasts

Other chapters, particularly Chapter 11, look at using regression to forecast one variable, such as sales revenue, from a predictor variable, such as time period or number of sales reps. This sort of analysis is sometimes termed *simple regression.* Forecasting one variable from more than one predictor is possible and sometimes useful. You may try forecasting sales revenue from *both* time period and number of sales reps. This approach is termed *multiple regression* and this chapter shows you how to do it in Excel.

Perhaps the most valuable aspect of Excel charts to come along since the charts themselves were introduced is the trendline. Using the trendline, you can, in one step, display the relationship between your predictor variables and your forecast variable. The trendline can be linear or nonlinear, or it can represent a moving average. The trendline can visually inform you about the direction and strength of the relationship of the predictors to the forecast. You can also choose whether to show underlying information such as the R-squared value and the regression equation itself.

Taking a number that's produced by a computer with no salt at all is tempting. Take it with a grain or even two. Apart from the usual warnings such as the venerable "garbage in, garbage out," there are other pitfalls waiting for you. You'll save yourself some grief if you evaluate your forecasts before you buy into them, so it's just as well that there are some tools available in Excel to help you do your evaluation.

Doing Multiple Regression

Multiple regression is a way of using more than one predictor variable to forecast another variable, such as sales revenues. It can make your forecasts more accurate, but you have to know how to get your computer (in this case, that means Excel running on your PC) to do what's called *multiple regression.* Not only do you have to know how to do it, you need to know how to interpret its results. The rest of this chapter shows you how.

Using more than one predictor

How can you use more than one predictor at a time to forecast some other variable? Here's where multiple regression comes in. It combines, say, two predictor variables to form a new variable.

Suppose you were interested in forecasting the weight of men between their infancy and their 18th birthdays. You may have, in an Excel worksheet, information on 30 men, conveniently including their weight, height, and age. If you direct Excel's attention to those three variables in just the right way, Excel's regression functions will do the following:

- Combine height and age into a new variable.
- Calculate that new variable so that it's the best possible predictor of young men's weight, given the information you made available to Excel.

For example, regression might calculate that new variable like this:

New Variable = -20.34 + (3.92 × Age) + (2.21 × Height)

Regression would choose the factors for age and height (3.92 and 2.21, respectively) so that the new variable has the highest correlation with weight that is possible, given the data in your worksheet. The ATP's Regression tool itself doesn't show you this new variable — although you could create it easily enough with your data on age and height, in combination with the factors that regression figures out. Or, with less effort, you could use Excel's TREND function to display the new variable.

The new variable is actually the forecast values for weight: Forecast by multiplying a person's age by its factor, the person's height by its factor, and adding the results together. Then it's on to the next person to forecast *his* weight. Figure 16-1 shows this process in some detail.

Figure 16-1 shows you the situation that this section discusses: forecasting weight, given knowledge of age and height. (I know you're not interested in forecasting weight, but using these variables makes the discussion easier to follow. I move on to sales forecasts with regression in "Interpreting the coefficients and their standard errors.")

The basic data is in Figure 16-1 in columns A, B, and C. The TREND function is in column E: It shows the forecasts of weight, given age and height. Another way of saying that is that column E contains the combination of age and height that has the highest correlation with actual weight.

Microsoft Excel - Chapter 16.xls

E2 {=TREND(C2:C25,A2:B25)}

Height (inches)	Age (years)	Weight (pounds)		Trend forecast
71	16	220		199.0
56	7	115		130.6
60	9	125		147.3
40	5	120		87.5
72	17	202		205.1
58	8	137		138.9
48	7	122		113.0
35	3	60		68.6
71	16	215		199.0
33	3	48		64.2
59	8	107		141.1
49	6	142		111.2
52	9	132		129.6
52	7	130		121.8
65	13	146		174.0
31	3	44		59.8
68	17	184		196.3
59	9	118		145.1
45	6	134		102.4
70	14	210		188.9
69	12	190		178.9
64	10	168		160.0
59	7	145		137.2
64	17	173		187.4

Figure 16-1: You have to array-enter the TREND formula just as you do LINEST, with Ctrl+Shift+Enter.

If all you were interested in were the forecasts, you might stop there. And that would be understandable, because it's the forecasts you're after. But you haven't gone far enough yet. Looking at some of the other information from a regression analysis is important. This other information will tell you such things as:

- Whether it's even worth forecasting weight from age and height
- Whether you should use both age and height, or whether one or the other would be enough
- How useful the regression equation is likely to be if you use it with a different set of inputs

This is important stuff, because it helps you decide whether and how to use the regression equation, whether you should look for some predictors other than age and height, how stable the equation is, and so on. A more complete analysis — one that shows more than just the forecast values — is shown in Figure 16-2.

Figure 16-2 shows how the LINEST function gives you some of the information you need to interpret a multiple regression. Here are the steps you take to get the LINEST function on the worksheet. The steps assume that you have the data laid out as in Figure 16-2. If your data is in different columns or rows, just change the addresses used in steps 1 and 2 accordingly.

Microsoft Excel - Chapter 16.xls

E2 {=LINEST(C2:C25,A2:B25,,TRUE)}

	A	B	C	D	E	F	G
1	Height (inches)	Age (years)	Weight (pounds)				
2	31	3	44		3.92	2.21	-20.34
3	33	3	48		2.09	0.78	27.54
4	35	3	60		0.84	20.60	#N/A
5	40	5	120		53.80	21	#N/A
6	45	6	134		45652.15	8910.44	#N/A
7	48	7	122				
8	49	6	142				
9	52	7	130				
10	52	9	132				
11	56	7	115				
12	58	8	137				
13	59	8	107				
14	59	9	118				
15	59	7	145				
16	60	9	125				
17	64	17	173				
18	64	10	168				
19	65	13	146				
20	68	17	184				
21	69	12	190				
22	70	14	210				
23	71	16	215				
24	71	16	220				
25	72	17	202				

Coefficients from LINEST

Figure 16-2: The curly brackets around the formula show you that it's been array-entered.

1. **Count the number of predictor variables, and add 1.**

   In Figure 16-2, there are two predictor variables (height and age), so you get 3.

2. **Select a range of cells — blank ones, unless you have some cells with data you don't care about — that has five rows and as many columns as the number you got in Step 1.**

   In this example, then, you'd select a range of cells five rows high and three columns wide; Figure 16-2 uses E2:G6.

3. **Type** =LINEST(C2:C25,A2:B25,,TRUE), **but *don't* press Enter yet.**

4. **Press Ctrl+Shift+Enter.**

   This *array-enters* the formula. LINEST is one of the Excel functions that you must array-enter so as to get the right results.

If, as here, you're array-entering a formula that will occupy a range of cells, begin by selecting the full range. Excel doesn't figure out the dimensions of the range and fill them in on your behalf. As terrific an application as Excel is, there are a few areas in which it can be remarkably obtuse, and this is one of them.

Here's what LINEST shows you:

- The first row always has what are called the *coefficients* and the *intercept.* These are the numbers you use along with your actuals to create your forecasts. In Figure 16-2, they're in cells E2:G2.
- The second row always has the *standard errors* of the coefficients and the intercept. These help you decide whether to pay attention to a variable when you're creating a forecast. In Figure 16-2, they're in cells E3:G3.
- The third through the fifth rows have useful information only in the first and the second columns. The remaining columns always show the error value #N/A in the third, fourth, and fifth rows. In Figure 16-2, that useful information is in cells E4:F6.

What is that useful information? Here's an overview. And I do mean overview. (Even intermediate statistics texts have entire chapters devoted to each one of these topics.)

Squaring R

In the third row, first column of the LINEST results you'll find the R-squared value. This is the square of the correlation coefficient between the actuals and the forecasts. In Figure 16-2, it's the square of the correlation between the values in C2:C25 (the actuals) and the values in A2:B25 (the forecasts). In this case, the R-squared value is 0.84.

The R-squared value is actually a percentage. It tells you what percent of the variation — the *spread* — in the forecast variable that you can attribute to the predictor variables. In this example, you can attribute 84 percent of the actual weight to the combination of age and height. So, higher weights are associated with higher combinations of age and height; lower weights with lower combinations of age and height.

If that sounds to you suspiciously like the meaning of a correlation, you're right. R-squared is called that R-squared because it's the square of the correlation coefficient (the correlation coefficient is often called *r*, in lower case, for short while the multiple correlation is always *R*, in upper case).

The higher the R-squared, the better the job your predictor variables are doing as forecasters. Because it's a squared number, R-squared can never be negative. And because the maximum value of a correlation coefficient is 1.0, R-squared itself can never be greater than 1.0.

So, in the LINEST results, look for the value of R-squared in LINEST's third row, first column. The closer the number you see there is to 1.0, the better your forecast. The closer to 0.0, the worse.

Nobody's perfect . . .

And neither is LINEST. The value in LINEST's third row, second column is the *standard error of estimate,* and it helps you understand how much error is involved in the forecasts you make using LINEST.

In Figure 16-2, the standard error of estimate is found in cell F4, and it's about 20.6. If you go up and down by two standard errors from any forecast, you'll bracket that forecast within two numbers, and you can be 95 percent confident that an actual observation will be between those two numbers.

For example, suppose you wanted to forecast the weight of a young male whose age was 13 years and whose height was 64 inches. The equation that LINEST returns in Figure 16-2 would forecast this:

$$-20.34 + (3.92 \times \text{Age}) + (2.21 \times \text{Height}) = \text{Forecast Weight}$$

$$-20.34 + (3.92 \times 13) + (2.21 \times 64) = 171.8$$

Chapter 12 discusses the fact that LINEST displays the coefficients in the *reverse* order that they appear on the worksheet. That's why you use 3.92 for Age and 2.21 for Height, even though the values for Height come first and Age second, and the coefficient's the other way around.

Now, the standard error of estimate in this case is 20.6. So if you were to make this forecast, you could be 95 percent confident that the actual weight would be between 130.6 and 213.0:

$$171.8 - 2 \times 20.6 = 130.6$$

$$171.8 + 2 \times 20.6 = 213.0$$

People often misinterpret the phrase "95 percent confident." It doesn't mean that the probability is 95 percent that the actual value lies between the lower limit of 130.6 and the upper limit of 213.0. That probability is either 0.0 (it doesn't lie within those limits) or 1.0 (it does). But if you got these measurements on thousands of young males and ran LINEST on them, 95 percent of those people would have an actual weight within two standard errors of their forecast weight.

As you may guess, the larger the R-squared value (a measure of the accuracy of the forecast), the smaller the standard error of estimate (a measure of the inaccuracy of the forecast).

The other LINEST statistics

Rows 4 and 5, columns 1 and 2 of the LINEST results are fairly esoteric, and unless you feel comfortable with intermediate-level statistical analysis, I suggest that you ignore them. They're the building blocks for further analyses that tell you whether you can regard the results as "statistically significant."

There are probably three categories of interest in this sort of thing:

- **Low interest:** You should just skip this stuff and use the TREND function to get your forecasts.
- **Moderate interest:** You should use the Analysis ToolPak to get the information about your regression equation. It does those further analyses for you. See Chapter 11 for information on interpreting the results you get from the Analysis ToolPak's Regression tool.
- **High interest:** This is the Glutton for Punishment category. If you're deranged enough to want to know the details, check out the following list:
    - **The F ratio:** The F ratio divides the mean square (regression) by the mean square (residual). The F ratio is in the fourth row, first column of LINEST's results. If you use Excel's FDIST function along with the F ratio, the number of predictor variables, and the residual degrees of freedom (see the next item), you can determine the statistical significance of the regression. This is the same as testing whether R-squared is significantly different from zero.
    - **Residual degrees of freedom:** The degrees of freedom (or *df*) is found in LINEST'S fourth row, second column. It tells you what to divide by to convert the residual sum of squares to a residual mean square. It also tells you the third argument to FDIST.
    - **Regression sum of squares:** The sum of squares (or *SS*) regression is in LINEST's fifth row, first column. Divide it by the number of predictor variables to get the mean square regression.
    - **Residual sum of squares:** The SS residual is in LINEST's fifth row, second column. Divide it by the residual degrees of freedom to get the mean square residual. Divide the mean square regression by the mean square residual to get the F ratio.

The thinking person's approach to multiple regression

The previous section mentions the Regression tool in the Analysis ToolPak (ATP) as a middle-of-the-road approach to getting a regression forecast. It provides you with most of the LINEST results that you'd want, both to generate forecasts and to diagnose how well your regression equation does at forecasting. So, if you decide to use the ATP, you haven't decided to ignore its results completely.

At the same time, you've decided that you don't want to gin up all these diagnostics yourself, basing them on the LINEST results. You could do so, that's true, but it's the sort of thing only a purist would do, and the result is something only a mother would love.

Chapter 11 gives you an overview of the parts of the Regression tool's output that are the really critical ones to examine before you go public with a forecast. Here's a review, along with a *really* brief overview of each:

- **Multiple R:** This is, redundantly, the square root of R-squared. You can look at either to judge the accuracy of the regression equation. If you're more comfortable thinking in terms of correlation coefficients, look at the Multiple R.
- **Intercept and coefficients:** These are the numbers you apply to the values of the predictors that you have in hand, in order to get the best forecast that's available to you.
- **Confidence levels:** These bracket the intercept and coefficients, giving you a sense of how much they might jump around if you got other samples of the predictor variables and the forecast variable.
- **Residual plot:** Look at this chart to see whether you've got something funny going on with the error values.
- **Line fit plot:** This chart plots the actual and the forecast values against the predictor's values. It's less useful in a multiple regression situation than with a single predictor, because as the chart is designed it can't handle more than one predictor at once.

The incredible shrinking R-squared

Figure 16-3 shows an example of the output, based on the same Age, Height, and Weight data that I've been showing you.

The Adjusted R-squared appears in cell F6 of Figure 16-3. Another term for Adjusted R-squared is the Shrinkage Estimator, and it has nothing to do with *Seinfeld.* Nevertheless, if you're forecasting sales, you're going to want to pay attention to it.

Suppose you get data on another sample of men and use the intercept and coefficients that you got in *this* sample in the new sample. In other words, you could take the values in cells F17 through F19 of Figure 16-3 and use them on the age and height of the men in your new sample, to forecast their weight.

Then you could find the correlation of these new forecasts with the new actuals. (This is what the Multiple R in Figure 16-3 is giving you: the correlation between the forecasts and the actuals in your original sample.)

The new Multiple R will almost always be smaller than the original Multiple R — that is, it *shrinks.* The reasons for this are a little arcane, but they have to do with some capitalization on chance in the original sample. Why should you be concerned with this? There are a couple of good reasons.

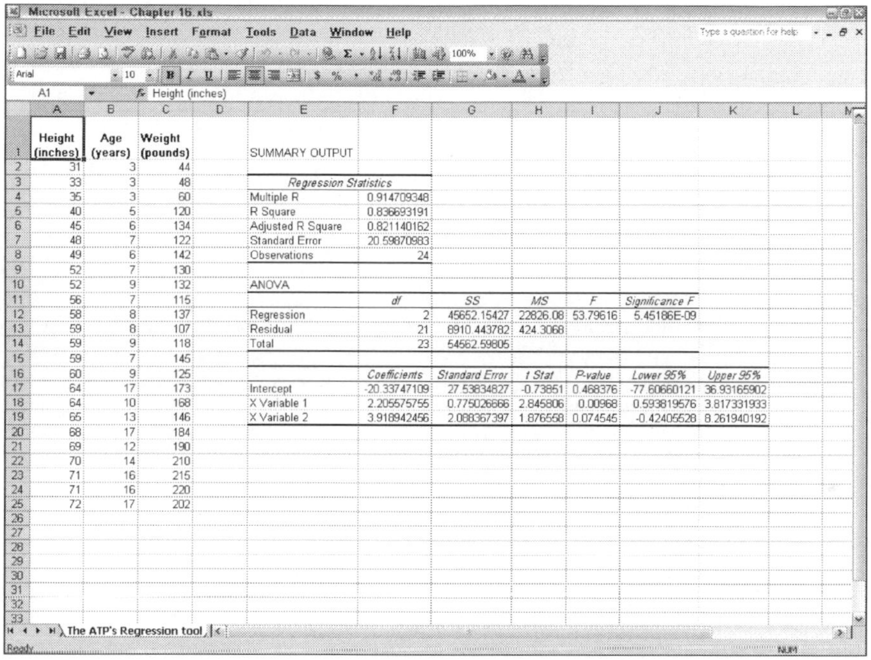

Microsoft Excel - Chapter 16.xls

Height (inches)	Age (years)	Weight (pounds)
31	3	44
33	3	48
35	3	60
40	5	120
45	6	134
48	7	122
49	6	142
52	7	130
52	9	132
56	7	115
58	8	137
59	8	107
59	9	118
59	7	145
60	9	125
64	17	173
64	10	168
65	13	146
68	17	184
69	12	190
70	14	210
71	16	215
71	16	220
72	17	202

SUMMARY OUTPUT

Regression Statistics	
Multiple R	0.914709348
R Square	0.836693191
Adjusted R Square	0.821140162
Standard Error	20.59870983
Observations	24

ANOVA

	df	*SS*	*MS*	*F*	*Significance F*
Regression	2	45652.15427	22826.08	53.79616	5.45186E-09
Residual	21	8910.443782	424.3068		
Total	23	54562.59805			

	Coefficients	*Standard Error*	*t Stat*	*P-value*	*Lower 95%*	*Upper 95%*
Intercept	-20.33747109	27.53834827	-0.73851	0.468376	-77.60660121	36.93165902
X Variable 1	2.205575755	0.775026666	2.845806	0.00968	0.593819576	3.817331933
X Variable 2	3.918942456	2.088367397	1.876558	0.074545	-0.42405528	8.261940192

The ATP's Regression tool

Figure 16-3: You get a lot more bang for your buck by using the Regression tool than from the LINEST function, but it has some drawbacks too.

In sales forecasting, you constantly have new data coming in. Shortly after you make your July forecast, or your second-quarter forecast, the actuals come in and it's time to make a forecast for August, or for the third quarter. Of course, you want to compare those new actuals with the prior period's forecasts.

If you pay attention to the Adjusted R-squared, you have a sort of worst-case estimate of how much the accuracy of the regression forecast could drop. Only one new period is coming in, not a substitution of an entirely new set of data. If the Adjusted R-squared is still acceptable to you, you can feel reasonably comfortable that your forecasts will continue to be reasonably accurate.

The other important reason to pay attention to the Adjusted R-squared is that it's sensitive to the relationship between the number of observations in the baseline and the number of predictor variables in the equation. Here's the formula:

$$\text{Adjusted R-squared} = 1 - [(1 - \text{R-squared}) \times ([N - 1] \div [N - K - 1])]$$

where N is the number of observations and K is the number of predictor variables in the analysis.

To see how the formula works out with sales data, see Figure 16-4. In Figure 16-4, I've deployed the ATP's Regression tool on a data set that shows revenues, dollars spent on advertising, size of sales force, and the discount offered to customers (the discounts were based on the need to reduce inventory). The Regression tool's output appears in the range F1:L20.

Applying the formula for the Adjusted R-squared in cell G23, you get 0.56, just as reported by the Regression tool in cell G6. Adding more predictors to the equation causes the Adjusted R-squared to drop quickly, all the way to 0.46 with six predictors, as shown in cell G26.

Now, bear in mind that this is an "other things being equal" analysis. For example, if one of the variables you add to the regression analysis has a perfect 1.0 correlation with sales revenues, then the R-squared value would jump to 1.0, making a liar of both the Adjusted R-squared and me. But first go find a variable that predicts sales revenues perfectly, and *then* write me.

Counting noses

The Regression tool's output also shows the number of observations — in a forecasting context, that's the number of records in the baseline — that went into the regression analysis. In Figure 16-4, you'll find that in cell G8. It can come in handy if you're figuring Adjusted R-squared values. Notice that the equations for Adjusted R-squared in the range G23:G26 all rely on G8 to provide the count of observations.

Microsoft Excel - Chapter 16.xls

File Edit View Insert Format Tools Data Window Help

G23 =1-(1-$G$5)*(($G$8-1)/($G$8-F$23-1))

	A	B	C	D	F	G	H	I	J	K	L
1	Revenues ($000)	Advertising Dollars	Sales Force	Discount %	SUMMARY OUTPUT						
2	$ 1,519	$ 344	5	17%							
3	$ 3,955	$ 534	11	27%	*Regression Statistics*						
4	$ 4,340	$ 3,834	14	26%	Multiple R	0.79					
5	$ 8,413	$ 2,798	54	37%	R Square	0.63					
6	$ 371	$ 795	11	5%	Adjusted R Square	0.56					
7	$ 706	$ 3,534	13	1%	Standard Error	1801.87					
8	$ 255	$ 2,143	21	12%	Observations	20					
9	$ 762	$ 1,518	38	1%							
10	$ 6,758	$ 207	25	33%	ANOVA						
11	$ 352	$ 289	5	38%		*df*	*SS*	*MS*	*F*	*Significance F*	
12	$ 429	$ 1,022	30	17%	Regression	3	88308601.1	29436200.4	9.1	0.001	
13	$ 3,068	$ 5,195	56	4%	Residual	16	51947971.9	3246748.2			
14	$ 5,775	$ 5,489	27	35%	Total	19	140256573.0				
15	$ 3,664	$ 7,093	21	1%							
16	$ 497	$ 405	10	1%		*Coefficients*	*Standard Error*	*t Stat*	*P-value*	*Lower 95%*	*Upper 95%*
17	$ 592	$ 627	4	14%	Intercept	-1227.58	957.7	-1.3	0.22	-3257.8	802.60
18	$ 5,937	$ 3,736	36	33%	Ad Dollars	0.42	0.2	1.9	0.07	0.0	0.88
19	$ 3,007	$ 560	32	24%	Sales Force	34.74	25.3	1.4	0.19	-18.9	88.35
20	$ 4,974	$ 924	56	26%	Discount %	13983.36	3119.9	4.5	0.00	7369.4	20597.33
21	$ 7,616	$ 1,282	3	31%							
22					Number of Predictors	Adjusted R Square					
23					3	0.56	=1-(1-$G$5)*(($G$8-1)/($G$8-F23-1))				
24					4	0.53	=1-(1-$G$5)*(($G$8-1)/($G$8-F24-1))				
25					5	0.50	=1-(1-$G$5)*(($G$8-1)/($G$8-F25-1))				
26					6	0.46	=1-(1-$G$5)*(($G$8-1)/($G$8-F26-1))				
27											
28											
29											
30											
31											
32											
33											

Shrinking the R Square

Ready NUM

Figure 16-4: The SUMMARY OUTPUT table contains static values, not formulas, so you have to rerun the Regression tool if your inputs change.

Degrees of freedom

Two values are of interest: the degrees of freedom for the regression and the degrees of freedom for the residual. Getting a good grasp on the *why* of degrees of freedom can take quite a bit of study and head-scratching. For now, let it go at knowing that you divide the sums of squares in H12:H13 by their respective degrees of freedom to get the mean square.

Mean squares

A *mean square* (MS) is just another term for a variance. You divide the MS for the regression by the MS for the residual. The result is the F ratio.

The F ratio

The F ratio is what you actually test to help you decide whether the regression is significant: more precisely, whether the R-squared value is significantly different from zero. This chapter touches on the issue in "The other LINEST statistics."

Significance of F

The discussion of LINEST earlier in the chapter mentions how to use the FDIST function, along with the F ratio and the degrees of freedom, to determine how confident you can be that the true R-squared is greater than zero. The ATP's Regression tool does that for you. In Figure 16-4, you can find the significance level in cell K12. The smaller the significance level (and 0.001 is quite small), the more confident you can be that you have a statistically significant regression.

That may sound important, and perhaps it is. But all it really means is that the true R-squared, the one you would calculate if you had access to all possible baseline observations, is not zero.

All these esoteric statistics, the SS and the df and the MS, for the regression and for the residual, and the F ratio, are shown by the ATP's regression tool as a matter of convention. Since Sir Ronald Fisher invented the Analysis of Variance (or, as it's labeled in cell F10 of Figure 16-4, *ANOVA*), it's been traditional to show all these values in an ANOVA table. The ATP is just following convention. It's nice to know these numbers, but only the Significance of F (if even that) is necessary for the evaluation and use of the regression equation.

Interpreting the coefficients and their standard errors

The final section of the Regression tool's output concerns the intercept and the coefficients that you use to make your forecast. In Figure 16-4, you'll find the intercept in cell G17 and the coefficients in cells G18:G20.

Even though it's found in a column labeled *Coefficients,* the Intercept is not a coefficient. It's just a number that you add into the regression equation as a scaling adjustment. The coefficients are the numbers by which you multiply your predictor variables.

The standard errors that are associated with the coefficients and the intercept help you gauge whether they really belong in the equation. These standard errors are used much like the standard error of estimate, which I discuss in the "Nobody's perfect" section, earlier in the chapter. Adding two standard errors to the coefficient and subtracting two standard errors from the coefficient, then seeing if the resulting range spans zero, is typical. Plus and minus two standard errors is a bracket — a span of values. You could also construct a bracket defined by plus and minus *three* standard errors. Figure 16-5 shows how this works with the sales data in Figure 16-4.

All those columns in the range C2:I6 are telling you the same thing: Only the Discount variable is reliably related to sales revenues — at least, in the data set that the regression was calculated on.

Microsoft Excel - Chapter 16.xls

F10 =D10+2*E3

	Coefficients	*Standard Error*	*t Stat*	*P-value*	*Lower 95%*	*Upper 95%*
Intercept	-1227.58	957.7	-1.3	0.22	-3257.8	802.60
Ad Dollars	0.42	0.2	1.9	0.07	0.0	0.88
Sales Force	34.74	25.3	1.4	0.19	-18.9	88.35
Discount %	13983.36	3119.9	4.5	0.00	7369.4	20597.33

Predictor	**Coefficient**	**Coefficient minus 2 Standard Errors**	**Coefficient plus 2 Standard Errors**	**Spans Zero?**
Intercept	-1227.58	-3142.92	687.77	Yes
Ad Dollars	0.42	-0.02	0.85	Yes
Sales Force	34.74	-15.84	85.32	Yes
Discount %	13983.36	7743.49	20223.23	No

Using 2 standard errors

Figure 16-5: If a coefficient's bracket spans zero, you need to deal with the possibility that it really *is* zero.

In particular, if you add and subtract two standard errors from the intercept and the coefficients, each of the resulting brackets spans zero, except for Discount. That means you can't depend on it that the true population coefficients *aren't* zero. And if you use a zero coefficient in the equation, then the equation changes from this:

Revenue = –1227.58 + (0.42 × Ad $) + (34.74 × Sales Force) + (13983.36 × Discount)

to this:

Revenue = 0 + (0 × Ad $) + (0 × Sales Force) + (13983.36 × Discount)

That is, the intercept, Advertising Dollars, and Sales Force drop out of the equation because you don't have reason to believe that the true coefficients and the true intercept are nonzero.

Chapter 4 mentions that one of the goals of the regression approach to forecasting is *parsimony:* The fewer the predictor variables, the better. On that principle, if you can get rid of Advertising Dollars and the size of the Sales Force and still have a good forecast, that's good. At the very least, you save the time and cost of collecting the information on those predictor variables each month or quarter. And thinking back to what this chapter has to say about the Adjusted R-squared and shrinkage, restricting the number of predictor variables may be a good idea anyway.

Figure 16-6 shows you another way to look at things. In fact, the remainder of this section shows you how you can use the information in the Regression tool's output to demonstrate whether a coefficient is to be trusted (it's significantly different from zero) or not (it's not significantly different from zero). So far, I've given you a brief look at brackets by using standard errors. Next I show you t statistics and confidence intervals. They should all come to the same conclusions. If they don't, you should take a closer look at what they're telling you.

A statistic called Student's t helps you assess the statistical significance of the difference of a number from zero. In this situation, it's calculated by dividing the number (the intercept or the coefficient) by its standard error. This has been done in F10:F13 of Figure 16-6, and you can tell that the results are identical to the t statistics that the Regression tool returns (E3:E6 in Figure 16-6).

The Regression tool also tests the statistical significance of the t statistic, and the results are shown in F3:F6. You interpret these results in the same way as you do the Significance of F. (See the "Significance of F" section earlier.)

H10 =TDIST(ABS(G10),20-1,2)

	Coefficients	Standard Error	t Stat	P-value	Lower 95%	Upper 95%
Intercept	-1227.58	957.7	-1.3	0.22	-3257.8	802.60
Ad Dollars	0.42	0.2	1.9	0.07	0.0	0.88
Sales Force	34.74	25.3	1.4	0.19	-18.9	88.35
Discount %	13983.36	3119.9	4.5	0.00	7369.4	20597.33

Predictor	Coefficient	Standard Error	Coefficient over Standard Error	t statistic	TDIST	TDIST formula
Intercept	-1227.58	957.67	-1.28	-1.3	0.22	=TDIST(ABS(G10),20-1,2)
Ad Dollars	0.42	0.22	1.93	1.9	0.07	=TDIST(ABS(G11),20-1,2)
Sales Force	34.74	25.29	1.37	1.4	0.19	=TDIST(ABS(G12),20-1,2)
Discount %	13983.36	3119.94	4.48	4.5	0.00	=TDIST(ABS(G13),20-1,2)

Figure 16-6: Compare the values labeled *P-value* (in cell G2) with the values under TDIST.

In the case of the intercept and the coefficients for Advertising Dollars and Sales Force, the p-values reported by the Regression tool are not below the level of 0.05 that has traditionally been taken as the criterion for statistical significance. The Discount predictor variable, however, has a p-value smaller than 0.05, and so this analysis says that it is significantly greater than zero.

The *smaller* the p-value (or, in the ANOVA table, the Significance of F), the *more* significant the number being tested.

These p-values have also been calculated in the range H10:H13 by using Excel's TDIST function. Notice that the p-values are identical to those returned by the Regression tool.

Excel's TDIST function cannot cope with a negative t statistic. If you use the TDIST function, you should always use it in conjunction with Excel's ABS function, which returns the absolute value of a number. (The absolute value is always positive: the absolute value of –2.6 is +2.6.) If you don't use the ABS function, as shown in cells I10:I13 of Figure 16-6, TDIST will return the `#NUM!` error value if the first argument is negative.

So, this t statistic analysis has the same outcome as the brackets-spanning-zero analysis: You're in good shape, using Discount to predict these sales revenues, but there's no argument for using the other variables.

Finally, consider the information you get from the Regression tool's confidence interval analysis (see Figure 16-7).

As you may expect from the earlier analyses, the intercept, the Advertising Dollars and the Sales Force predictors have brackets that span zero: The upper 95 percent is in each case greater than zero, and the lower 95 percent is below zero (see cells H3:I5 in Figure 16-7). So you can't reject the possibility that the true population coefficients (and the intercept) are in fact zero. This once again leads you to believe that the best forecast is based on the Discount predictor alone.

The difference between the upper/lower 95 percent brackets and the brackets that were created with +/- two standard errors is that the former are based on a t value of 2.1, rather than an even 2.0. The reasons for this are a little complicated, but they have to do with the fact that the sample size used in developing this regression is limited, rather than very large, as would be the case if you could lay your hands on the entire population of predictor values.

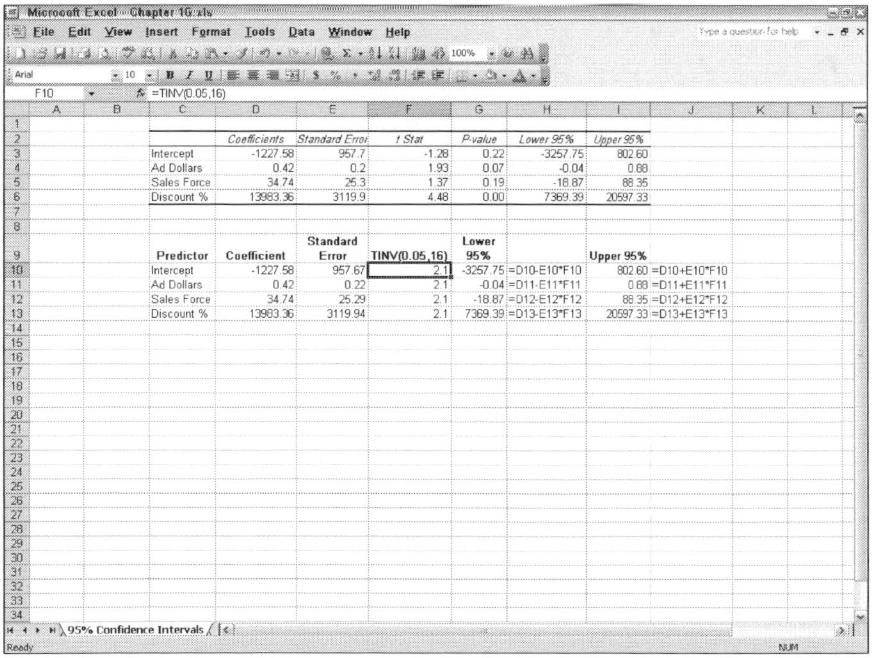

Microsoft Excel - Chapter 16.xls

F10 =TINV(0.05,16)

	Coefficients	Standard Error	t Stat	P-value	Lower 95%	Upper 95%
Intercept	-1227.58	957.7	-1.28	0.22	-3257.75	802.60
Ad Dollars	0.42	0.2	1.93	0.07	-0.04	0.88
Sales Force	34.74	25.3	1.37	0.19	-18.87	88.35
Discount %	13983.36	3119.9	4.48	0.00	7369.39	20597.33

Predictor	Coefficient	Standard Error	TINV(0.05,16)	Lower 95%		Upper 95%	
Intercept	-1227.58	957.67	2.1	-3257.75	=D10-E10*F10	802.60	=D10+E10*F10
Ad Dollars	0.42	0.22	2.1	-0.04	=D11-E11*F11	0.88	=D11+E11*F11
Sales Force	34.74	25.29	2.1	-18.87	=D12-E12*F12	88.35	=D12+E12*F12
Discount %	13983.36	3119.94	2.1	7369.39	=D13-E13*F13	20597.33	=D13+E13*F13

95% Confidence Intervals

Figure 16-7: Using Student's t statistic to create 95 percent intervals.

So, you can calculate the upper and lower 95 percent values using the value returned by TINV, as shown in F10:F13 of Figure 16-7. With 0.05 as the first argument (which is 1 – 0.95; if you wanted a 90 percent value, you'd use 0.10 rather than 0.05) and the number of degrees of freedom as the second argument, you get a value of 2.1. Multiplying 2.1 times the standard error and adding the result to the coefficient or intercept, you get the upper 95 percent values. You get the lower 95 percent values by subtracting rather than adding.

In this example, all three methods point to the same conclusion: Use Discount as your predictor variable; regression will calculate a new intercept for you. There are some close cases in which the methods do not agree (although the t-statistic method and the 95 percent bracket method will nearly always point to the same conclusion). When they don't agree, your best bet is to get more data: Either dig farther back into the past, or wait for some more actuals to come in. More data often brings a fuzzy outcome into focus.

And bear in mind that the formulas shown or implied in Figures 16-5 through 16-7 give you a way to let the analyses update if you change your input values. This is the main reason that, in the long run, I prefer to use my own formulas instead of relying on the static values provided by the ATP.

Getting a Regression Trendline into a Chart

Looking at your regression forecast on a chart is almost always helpful so that you can visually compare your baseline, what's already happened, with what regression has forecast is going to happen next. This is the role of trendlines, and this chapter shows you how to get them.

It's never, ever a good idea to just accept a computer-generated forecast (or any sort of analysis, for that matter) at face value. You need to look at some of the underlying statistics to judge whether the forecast is sense or nonsense. In the previous section, I show you how to use statistics that Excel reports back to you so as to make that kind of judgment.

But numbers don't tell the whole story. Figure 16-8 shows a situation in which the number alone would lead you astray, but looking at the data in a chart would put you straight again.

There's a clear relationship between the number of sales reps and the sales revenue. Up to a point, the more reps you have, the greater the revenues.

Beyond 16 reps, though, the revenues actually start to fall. This can happen for several reasons, among them:

- Territories are defined both geographically and by national accounts. In these cases, Jamie's national account might well have a presence in Jim's geographical territory. Without double commissions, this situation leads to competition *within* the sales office, and not of the good sort.
- The sales territory can support up to, but not more than, a given number of sales reps.
- A third variable, such as a product line that is losing market share, prompts management to throw more reps at the territory, instead of studying the marketability of the product itself.

The correlation coefficient, also discussed in Chapter 14, is a *linear* statistic. In other words, it assumes that the two variables you hand off to it have a linear, straight-line relationship with each other — something such as a person's height and weight. The relationship need not be perfect, but in general the higher one variable, the higher the other variable.

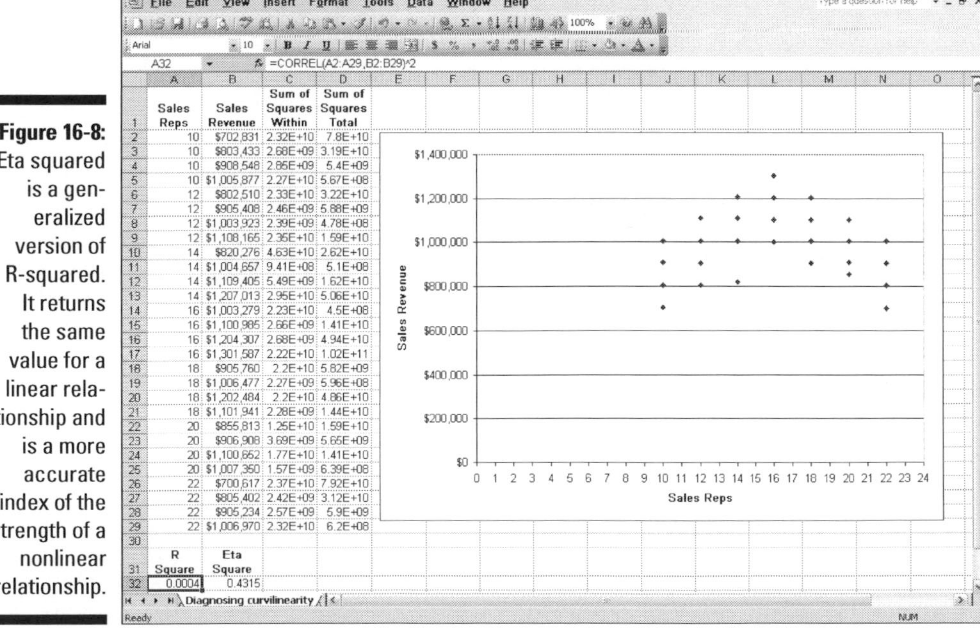

	Sales Reps	Sales Revenue	Sum of Squares Within	Sum of Squares Total
2	10	$702,831	2.32E+10	7.8E+10
3	10	$803,433	2.68E+09	3.19E+10
4	10	$908,548	2.85E+09	5.4E+09
5	10	$1,005,877	2.27E+10	5.67E+08
6	12	$802,510	2.33E+10	3.22E+10
7	12	$905,408	2.46E+09	5.88E+09
8	12	$1,003,923	2.39E+09	4.78E+08
9	12	$1,108,165	2.35E+10	1.59E+10
10	14	$820,276	4.63E+10	2.62E+10
11	14	$1,004,657	9.41E+08	5.1E+08
12	14	$1,109,405	5.49E+09	1.62E+10
13	14	$1,207,013	2.95E+10	5.06E+10
14	16	$1,003,279	2.23E+10	4.5E+08
15	16	$1,100,985	2.66E+09	1.41E+10
16	16	$1,204,307	2.68E+09	4.94E+10
17	16	$1,301,587	2.22E+10	1.02E+11
18	18	$905,760	2.2E+10	5.82E+09
19	18	$1,006,477	2.27E+09	5.96E+08
20	18	$1,202,484	2.2E+10	4.86E+10
21	18	$1,101,941	2.28E+09	1.44E+10
22	20	$855,813	1.25E+10	1.59E+10
23	20	$906,908	3.69E+09	5.65E+09
24	20	$1,100,652	1.77E+10	1.41E+10
25	20	$1,007,350	1.57E+09	6.39E+08
26	22	$700,617	2.37E+10	7.92E+10
27	22	$805,402	2.42E+09	3.12E+10
28	22	$905,234	2.57E+09	5.9E+09
29	22	$1,006,970	2.32E+10	6.2E+08
30				
31	R Square	Eta Square		
32	0.0004	0.4315		

Figure 16-8: Eta squared is a generalized version of R-squared. It returns the same value for a linear relationship and is a more accurate index of the strength of a nonlinear relationship.

The relationship can work the other way around, such as that between frequency of car accidents and driver's age in years (up to age 30, say). The older the driver, the fewer the accidents. This would result in a negative correlation but can nevertheless be a strong one.

In Figure 16-8, the R-squared between sales reps and sales revenues appears in cell A32. You can see that it is, in effect, zero. But the nonlinear relationship, measured by a statistic called *Eta Squared* or the *correlation ratio,* in cell B32, agrees with the chart: Both suggest strongly that there is a dependable relationship between number of sales reps and the amount of sales revenue — just not a linear one.

Cell A32 in Figure 16-8 shows R-squared as the square of CORREL. If you find yourself calculating R-squared frequently (as I do) you may find it more convenient to use Excel's RSQ function, which calculates R-squared directly. In this case, you would use `=RSQ(A2:A29,B2:B29)`.

Another way of looking at things is to dispense with the numeric analysis and just look at the chart. The linear trendline puts you in a position to evaluate how well a linear analysis fits the data (see Figure 16-9).

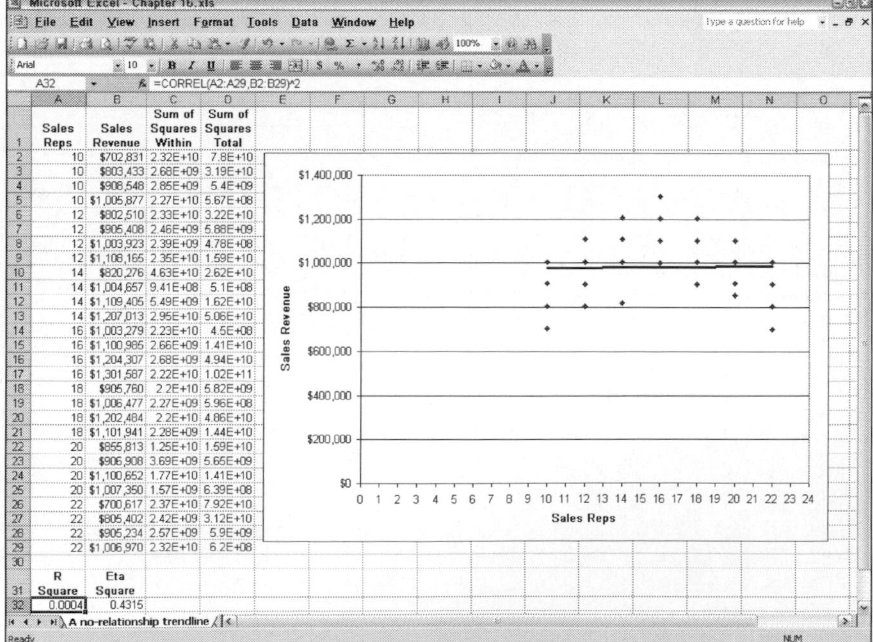

	A	B	C	D
1	Sales Reps	Sales Revenue	Sum of Squares Within	Sum of Squares Total
2	10	$702,831	2.32E+10	7.8E+10
3	10	$803,433	2.68E+09	3.19E+10
4	10	$908,548	2.85E+09	5.4E+09
5	10	$1,005,877	2.27E+10	5.67E+08
6	12	$802,510	2.33E+10	3.22E+10
7	12	$905,408	2.46E+09	5.88E+09
8	12	$1,003,923	2.39E+09	4.78E+08
9	12	$1,108,165	2.35E+10	1.59E+10
10	14	$820,276	4.63E+10	2.62E+10
11	14	$1,004,657	9.41E+08	5.1E+08
12	14	$1,109,405	5.49E+09	1.62E+10
13	14	$1,207,013	2.95E+10	5.06E+10
14	16	$1,003,279	2.23E+10	4.5E+08
15	16	$1,100,985	2.66E+09	1.41E+10
16	16	$1,204,307	2.68E+09	4.94E+10
17	16	$1,301,587	2.22E+10	1.02E+11
18	18	$905,760	2.2E+10	5.82E+09
19	18	$1,006,477	2.27E+09	5.96E+08
20	18	$1,202,484	2.2E+10	4.86E+10
21	18	$1,101,941	2.28E+09	1.44E+10
22	20	$855,813	1.25E+10	1.59E+10
23	20	$906,908	3.69E+09	5.65E+09
24	20	$1,100,652	1.77E+10	1.41E+10
25	20	$1,007,350	1.57E+09	6.39E+08
26	22	$700,617	2.37E+10	7.92E+10
27	22	$805,402	2.42E+09	3.12E+10
28	22	$905,234	2.57E+09	5.9E+09
29	22	$1,006,970	2.32E+10	6.2E+08
30				
31	R Square	Eta Square		
32	0.0004	0.4315		

Figure 16-9: This is an extreme example, used to make a point. You could tell you've got a nonlinear situation even without the trendline.

You get the trendline by following these steps:

1. **Click the chart to activate it.**

   Notice that the Chart menu appears on the main menu bar.

2. **Choose Chart ➪ Add Trendline.**

   The Add Trendline dialog box, shown in Figure 16-10, appears.

3. **Click the Linear Trend/Regression type. If you want to stop at this point, click OK.**

Figure 16-10: You can easily over-model a baseline by using nonlinear trendlines. You need a really good reason to do so — usually a statistical test called "goodness of fit" (strange but true).

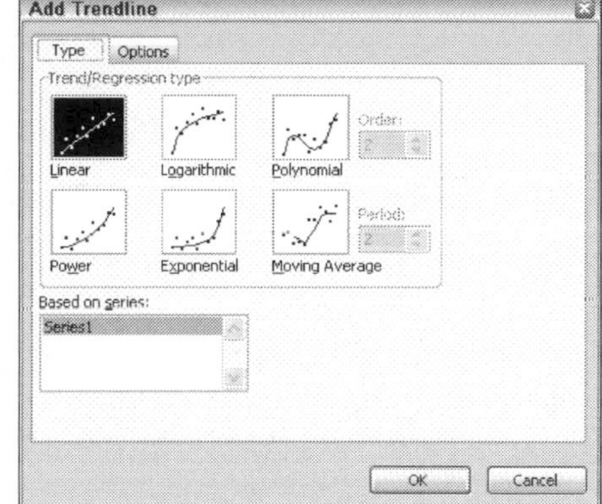

Notice in Figure 16-9 that the trendline is virtually horizontal.

If you have more than one data series in a chart, first select the data series for which you want the trendline, in Step 1 in the preceding list.

Two conditions are usually found when there's a strong correlation between two variables: The trendline's slope is close to 45 degrees from the horizontal, *and* the charted data points lie close to the trendline. The very mathematics of correlation bring this about.

If you know when you call for the trendline in the first place that you'll want this additional information, you can continue from here in Step 3 in the preceding list.

If you want more information about the relationship, follow these steps:

1. **Click on the trendline to make it active.**
2. **Choose Format ⇨ Selected Trendline.**

   The Format Trendline dialog box appears.
3. **Select the Options tab, shown in Figure 16-11.**

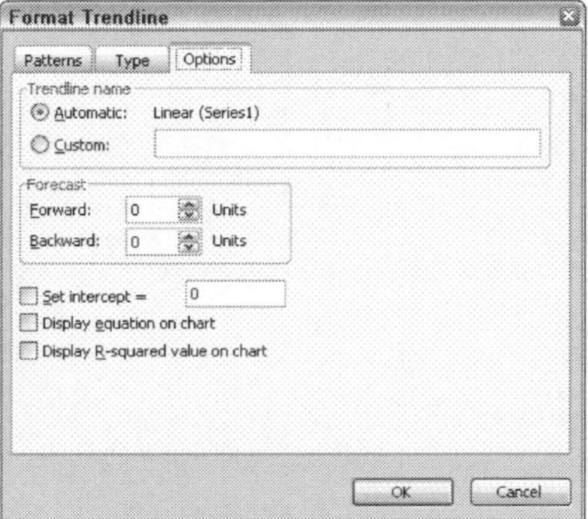

Figure 16-11: If you have more than one data series to name, switch back to the Type tab to select a different series.

The options that are available to you are as follows:

- You can give the trendline a more descriptive name than its default. This is useful primarily if you're including a legend on the chart, where you can display the name you've chosen. Click the Custom radio button and type the name into the text box.
- If you've chosen any type of trendline other than Moving Average, you can extend the forecast forward, into the future, or backward, into the past. Click the up arrow on one of the spinners to increase the number of periods to forecast, and the down arrow to reduce the number of periods.
- You can set the intercept to a particular value. Select the Set Intercept = check box and type a value in the box.
- You can display the equation on the chart. Select the associated check box.
- You can display the R-squared value on the chart. Again, select the associated check box. (This is the same thing that the ATP terms R square: the proportion of variability in the forecast variable that's attributable to the predictor variables.)

And here's some additional information about the intercept, the trendline equation, and the R-squared value:

- Setting the intercept manually is not recommended. Beginning analysts find that they can increase the R-squared by setting the intercept to, say, zero. But they're looking at a quirk in the mathematics of regression. If your data set really does have a zero intercept, the analysis will put the intercept either at zero or close enough.
- You can move the equation and the R-squared around on the chart, to get them out of the way of other elements such as gridlines. Click on it and drag it wherever you want.
- You can adjust the number of decimals and the font size of both the equation and the R-squared value. Click on it and choose Format ⇨ Selected Data Labels. Use the Font tab to adjust the font size, and the Number tab to adjust the number of decimals. Or you can click the Increase or Decrease Decimals buttons on Excel's Formatting toolbar.

Some people try to forecast values by using the equation that optionally accompanies the trendline. This is a mistake. The intercept and the coefficients almost certainly do not display enough decimals, it's too easy to make a typing error when you transcribe the numbers to the worksheet, and it's a waste of your time. Use LINEST instead to get the intercept and coefficients directly on the worksheet, or use TREND to bypass the equation completely and get the forecast values in one step. See Chapter 12 for information on using the TREND function.

Evaluating Regression Forecasts

When you make a regression forecast, you should look out for some problems beyond those mentioned in other chapters, such as independence of errors. Two of the more important problems that can arise concern autoregression and using two trended series.

Using autoregression

The topic of autoregression has come up in several other chapters in this book. Briefly, when you use autoregression, you use one set of values in your baseline to predict another set of values in the same baseline. It's a lot easier to see autoregression than to read about it, so have a look at Figure 16-12.

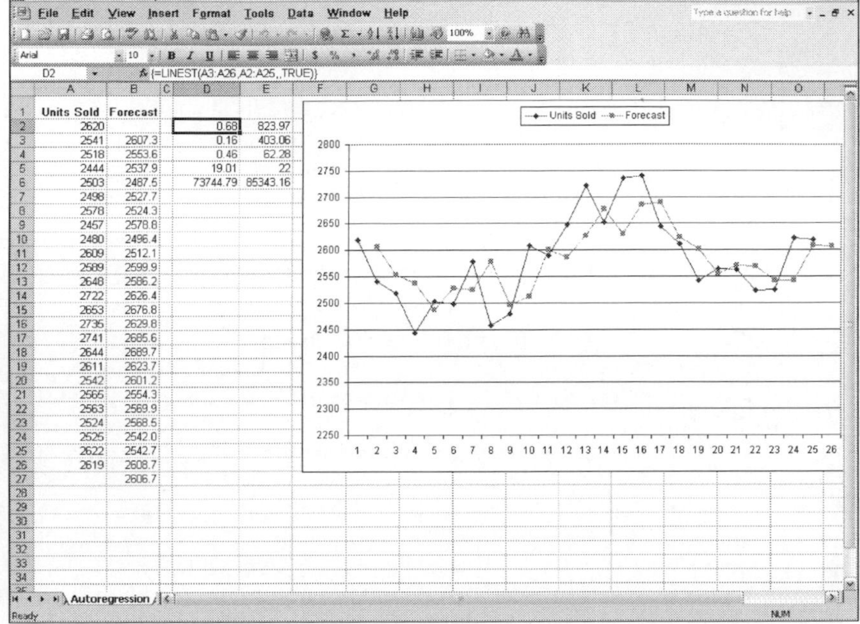

Figure 16-12: Notice that LINEST names A3:A26 first, because those cells represent the *y* variable, the one that is forecast. This conforms to LINEST syntax.

In Figure 16-12, the LINEST formula (in cells D2:E6) uses the values in A2:A25 as the predictor variable, and the values one row down, A3:A26, as the forecast variable. In effect, what you're asking LINEST to do is to forecast each value in the baseline from the prior value. In words, you're saying, "Please forecast the second value in the series from the first value, given what I know about the relationship between A2:A25 and A3:A26."

In one way at least, autoregression is similar to exponential smoothing: It uses a prior period's value to help forecast the next period's value.

One of the differences, though, between autoregression and exponential smoothing is that exponential smoothing always uses the prior actual in the baseline to help forecast the next period. In autoregression, you may want to forecast using not the prior time period's value, but the value that's two or even three periods back.

Using the LINEST equation in Figure 16-12, you can get the forecasts shown in column B from the coefficients. For example, the value in cell B3 is obtained by this formula:

```
=$E$2+$D$2*A2
```

That is, add the intercept to the product of the coefficient and the prior period's actual. Copy and paste this formula down through B27 to get the remaining forecasts.

But two issues remain. One is that you want to work with a stationary baseline; otherwise, if the baseline is trended, you could easily get some spurious results. The other is that you don't know how far back to look for your predictor value: One period? Two? Three or more? In Figure 16-12, you look one period back. But to answer those two questions for other data sets, you need to look at a couple of charts.

You can go to `www.dummies.com/go/excelsffd` and download an Excel workbook named Correlogram.xls that contains VBA code that will analyze your baseline and tell you first whether it's stationary, and second how far back you should go in your baseline to create your LINEST formula (or, equivalently, your TREND formula).

When you open the workbook, named Correlograms.xls, you get a new menu item in the Data menu. That item is labeled Correlograms. Put your baseline on Sheet1 of the workbook, and choose Data ➪ Correlograms. A dialog box named Correlograms appears, with a reference edit box labeled Input Range for Time Series where you can enter the range that your baseline occupies. When you click OK in the dialog box, a new workbook opens with two charts: an ACF chart and a PACF chart.

ACF stands for autocorrelation function, and *PACF* stands for partial autocorrelation function. Don't worry about the terms; you don't need them. What you do need is to look at the charts. Figure 16-13 shows the ACF chart for the data in Figure 16-12.

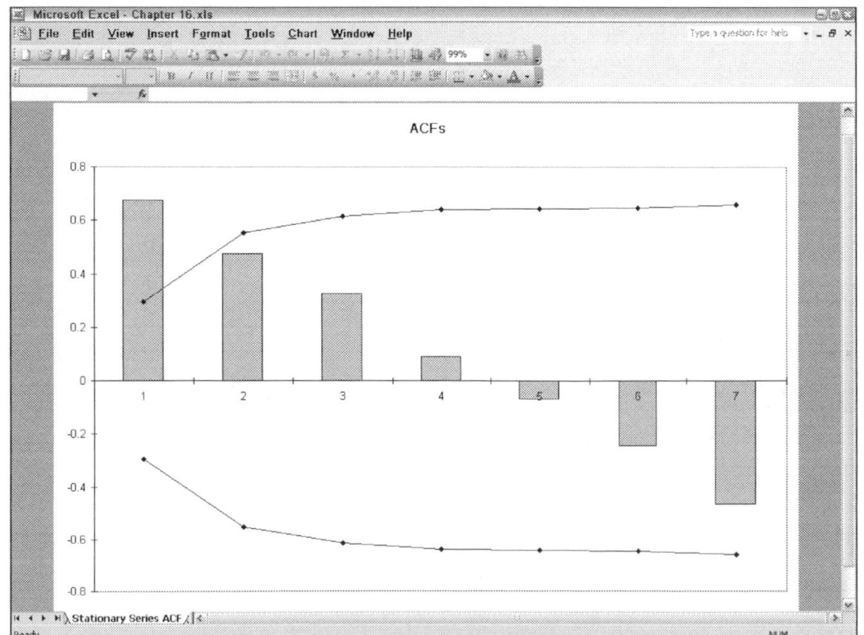

Figure 16-13: The size of the column represents the size of the autocorrelation.

ACF charts — one type of *correlogram* — show the autocorrelations between a series of observations and other observations from the same data set that are one period back, two periods back, three periods back, and so on. In a stationary data series, you expect to see these correlations drop quickly to zero and below, as they do in Figure 16-13.

The lines in Figure 16-13 (which are curved in an ACF chart and straight in a PACF chart) show the statistical significance limit: You can consider an ACF or a PACF that extends beyond that limit to be statistically significant — that is, a reliable finding.

If you create an ACF chart that does *not* show this pattern, in which the size of the correlations decays rapidly, then you do not have a stationary baseline and you should detrend it by taking first differences and, if necessary, second differences (it's rare that you need to go beyond first differences; see Chapter 14 for more information).

Figure 16-14 shows the PACF chart. This is a good guide to how *far* back you need to go in creating your autoregression analysis. In this case, the first PACF spikes above the significance limit (the lines at +/– 0.4) but none of the others do. This indicates that you need go back only one time period to develop your forecast equation: That is, the LINEST formula would involve A2:A25 forecasting A3:A26, just as in Figure 16-12.

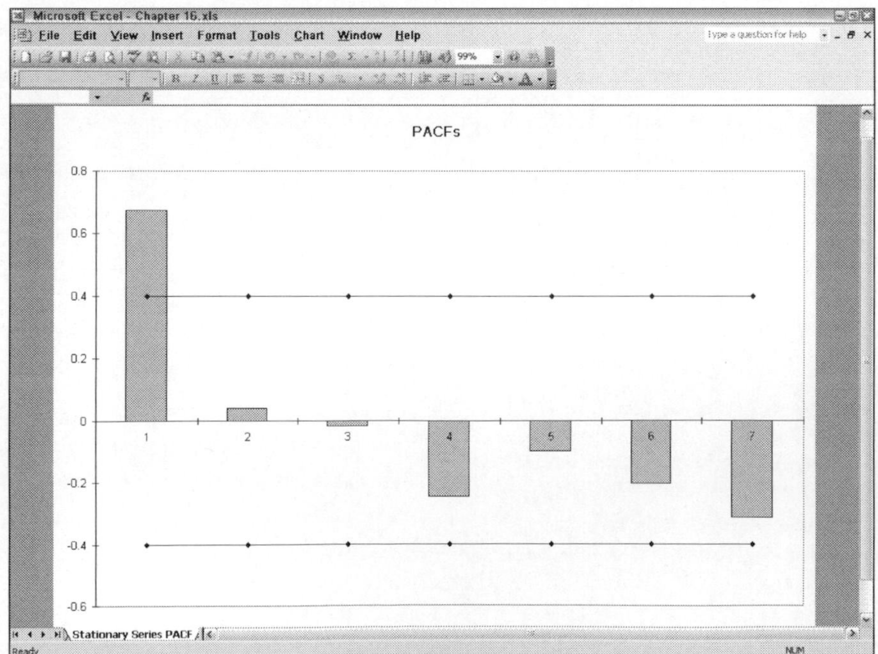

Figure 16-14: A stationary series usually has only a single spike in the PACFs.

However, if the second PACF were to spike, you would go back two periods and use A2:A24 to forecast A4:A26 (two periods back) as well as A3:A25 to forecast A4:A26 (one period back).

Regressing one trend onto another

If the phrase "causation and correlation" sounds familiar, it's probably because at some point you've read about the difference between the two. Suppose that some sociologist studies the relationship in 100 communities between the number of books in the public libraries and the number of residents of those communities who go on to careers in rocket science.

The sociologist finds a strong and positive relationship between those two variables — number of books and number of rocket scientists. Does this mean that if a community increases the number of books in a community's libraries, the number of the community's high school graduates who go on to college and medical school will also increase?

Of course not. There's no causation here, just correlation. Probably there's another variable (or cluster of variables) behind the sociologist's finding. Communities with a higher per-capita income spend more on community resources such as libraries. And families who live in those communities have more personal resources available to support their children's higher education.

But if you had some way of increasing the per-capita income of a community, you might well see an increase in both the number of books in the libraries and the number of students going on to higher education. That's the gold standard for deciding that causation exists: Apply a treatment to one randomly constituted group, withhold it from another, and look for a difference between the two groups.

The same effect can occur when you use regression to investigate the relationship between a variable that you want to forecast and some other variable that might be related to it. Suppose you have sales results that have been trending up for the last ten years. You notice that, over the same period of time, your company has been offering more and more product lines.

It's possible to conclude that you can increase sales by increasing the number of product lines, particularly if there's some real perceived differentiation among the products. But it ain't necessarily so. For one thing, two things that both grow as time goes by are a company's breadth of product line and its sales — the product line, because companies have to keep up with changing technologies; the sales, because, in the long run, companies either grow or die.

The issue here is that both sales and breadth of product line change in response to time, not to one another. A third variable, the passage of time, is at work here, just as per-capita income works on both a community's number of books and its number of post-graduate students.

The solution is to detrend both series first, and then see if you can get a useful regression equation from the detrended series. There are various ways of detrending (such as changing a variable to a rate like per-capita income), but a convenient one is to take first differences (see Chapter 17).

Chapter 17

Managing Trends

In This Chapter

- Understanding when to remove the trend from a baseline
- Keeping your baseline from jumping around
- Putting the pieces of a baseline back together

Sometimes you'll decide that you'd prefer to use a single-variable forecast method — for example, one of the two single-variable methods that this book discusses: moving averages and exponential smoothing. If you're going to do that — and there are some pretty good reasons to go that direction, including improved accuracy and seasonality in the baseline — you should first check to see if the baseline has a trend. As several other chapters discuss, a trend is the tendency in a baseline to move up or down (not both) over time. Both moving averages and exponential smoothing behave better in baselines that don't have a trend.

One good way to remove a trend from a baseline is called *differencing.* If you use differencing, you subtract one value in the baseline from a subsequent value. Doing that subtraction has some consequences for the values you use to forecast from. The decision to use differencing isn't a slam-dunk, though — some trade-offs are involved.

If you use differencing, you apply your forecast method to the differences. After you've got your forecast, you still have to put it back into the original baseline's scale. This is called *integrating,* and this chapter shows you how to do it.

Knowing Why You May Want to Remove the Trend from a Baseline

You can remove trend from a baseline in several ways, and this chapter takes a look at them in the "Getting a Baseline to Stand Still" section. First, though, you need to know more about why you may want to remove a trend from a baseline, and something about ways to diagnose whether a trend is really present in a baseline.

Understanding why trend is a problem

Some forecasters have argued that removing the trend from a baseline before doing any forecasting was almost always best. They cited three reasons:

- Because forecast equations using regression were more difficult to calculate than other methods, you needed a pretty good reason to use regression instead of another, simpler approach.
- Regression makes a number of assumptions about the data that other approaches don't make. So you have to test those assumptions on your data to decide whether you can even *use* regression with a clear conscience.
- There's always autocorrelation, often substantial, in a trended series. For various reasons, discussed in Chapters 2, 4, 14, and 16, autocorrelation can present a problem. There's some autocorrelation in a baseline from which the trend has been removed, but usually less — often much less — than in a baseline that has trend.

The first objection — mathematical complexity — has gone away in the intervening years. If you have a PC and Excel, you can perform a regression analysis in a minute or so — less if you type fast, more if you don't.

The second objection is thornier. There are several assumptions that should be tested before using the results of a regression analysis. I won't go into them in detail here, but just so you have a general idea:

- The average of the errors (also known as *residuals*) is zero. In other words, if you took the difference between each actual value and its associated forecast value (that is, the error in the forecast) and averaged them, you'd get an average value of zero, or very close to zero.
- The errors are normally distributed. That is, if you graphed the frequency of ranges of error values, you'd see a normal distribution or "bell curve."

- The variability of the errors is the same for each value of the predictor variable. If your predictor variable is time period, this assumption is not an issue: You have one observation for each value of the predictor, so there's no variability. But suppose you're using a predictor, such as unit price, that might have multiple forecast values for each value of unit price. Then if you charted the forecast errors against unit price, the spread of those errors on the vertical axis should look to be about the same for each unit price.
- The errors are not autocorrelated. That is, if you calculated the correlation between, say, errors 1 through 49 and errors 2 through 50, the correlation would not be significantly different from zero.

Formal descriptions of how to test each of these assumptions is beyond the scope of this book. You can get an idea of whether some assumption has been violated by graphing errors against time periods. Excel's Analysis ToolPak does this for you if you ask it to (it's just a matter of filling a check box — see Chapter 11 for more information).

Beyond the assumptions, there's the issue of the number of values in your baseline compared to the number of predictor variables that you may want to use in a regression forecast. You can use more than one.

As to autocorrelation, if you're concerned about its magnitude, keep in mind that a baseline from which the trend has been removed will tend to have less autocorrelation than the original baseline.

What does all this have to do with getting a baseline to stand still? Well, suppose you can't get your data to behave so you're confident that you've met all the assumptions made by the regression method. In that case, you're probably better off using one of the other methods, among them moving averages and exponential smoothing, that don't make such restrictive assumptions about the baseline. And if you're going to do that, you should remove the trend from the forecast variable's baseline. That means you'll transform it from one that's headed up or down over time to one that's roughly horizontal over time. And that's easier than you may suppose. A good place to start is in an upcoming section, "Subtracting one value from the next value."

Diagnosing a trend

Chapter 4 goes into some detail about diagnosing whether a trend exists in a baseline. Sometimes you can tell easily by eyeballing a chart of the baseline, but sometimes it's close, whether a trend is there or not. In that case, you want to use a numeric test to help you decide.

Chapter 4 describes what's called a *parametric test,* one that helps you decide whether the correlation between the forecast variable and the predictor variable is real or just random chance. Why the term *parametric?*

Here's a brief detour into a couple of statistical concepts — don't worry, no Greek symbols here, no obscure math. Just two definitions that help explain the concept:

- **Population:** A *population* is everyone or everything that you can characterize in some way. The population of Oklahoma is everyone who lives in Oklahoma. The population of your sales revenues is all the sales that your company has ever made. Some populations you may be able to observe and make calculations on — for example, the total sales revenues your company has ever made.

  Some populations you can't observe, at least as a practical matter. You're just not in a position, for example, to calculate the average age of every Oklahoma resident. But that average age exists, even if you can't measure it. It's called a *parameter.* Any numeric summary, such as an average or a total or a correlation, that involves all the members of a population is a parameter.

- **Sample:** A *sample* is a subset of a population. Not necessarily a random sample, although a random sample is usually better — nonrandom samples can mislead you. Samples have numeric summaries, too — averages and totals and correlations. But when you calculate these summaries by using a sample, you refer to them as *statistics* rather than parameters.

So, what's a parametric test? It's a test that tries to estimate the value of a population parameter when all the information you have is the sample statistic. You might estimate the average age of all Oklahomans by using the average age of the sample you took. The test comes into it when you use both the sample average and the amount of variability in the individual ages to compare them to a theoretical distribution such as the normal, "bell curve." It's called a parametric test because you're trying to make an inference about a parameter from a statistic.

There are other kinds of tests, *nonparametric* tests, that have one good aspect (simplicity) and one aspect that's kind of moot: They don't make a bunch of assumptions that parametric tests do. If you're going to test for trend, you can't go far wrong using the Sign Test. It's simple, and although it's not as sensitive a test as the one described in Chapter 4, it's still a good guide to whether a baseline has a trend.

Figure 17-1 shows an example of the Sign Test. In Figure 17-1, the figures shown in cells D24:D30 are calculated with these formulas:

- D24 contains the number of positive first differences in column B. It's calculated with this formula:

  ```
  =COUNTIF(B3:B21,">0")
  ```

  In words, the formula looks at B3:B21, and if a value in that range is positive, then the function counts that value — otherwise, it ignores the value. Then it takes the values in the range all together to give you a count of the number of positive figures in B3:B21.

- D25 contains the number of nonzero first differences. First differences that equal zero can come about if your baseline contains two consecutive values that equal one another. You get that figure with this array formula:

  ```
  =COUNTIF(B3:B21,"<>0")
  ```

  This is another instance of an array formula — notice the curly brackets. This time the formula is counting the number of nonzero first differences in B3:B21, not simply the number of positive values.

- D26 contains half the number of nonzero first differences:

  ```
  =D25/2
  ```

- D27 contains the standard deviation of the number of nonzero first differences. For the purposes of the Sign Test, this is:

  ```
  =SQRT(D25/4)
  ```

- D29 contains the Sign Test value itself:

  ```
  =(D24-D26)/D27
  ```

- D30 contains the critical value that is compared to the Sign Test value. If the absolute value of the Sign Test is greater than the value in D30, you decide that the baseline has trend. Otherwise, you decide it doesn't. The absolute value of a number is always positive. The absolute value of 31.2 is 31.2; the absolute value of –31.2 is 31.2. Cell D30 contains:

  ```
  =NORMSINV(0.975)
  ```

  where 0.975 is 1 – 0.025. I decide I can live with the probability of making a bad decision about the presence of trend in the baseline 5 percent of the time. I divide 5 percent (0.05) by 2 and get 0.025, and then subtract that from 1.0.

In this case, the Sign Test's absolute value, 0.23, is less than the critical value of 1.96. So, despite the fact that the baseline is rising during four of the final six points, the Sign Test regards the baseline as a stationary one.

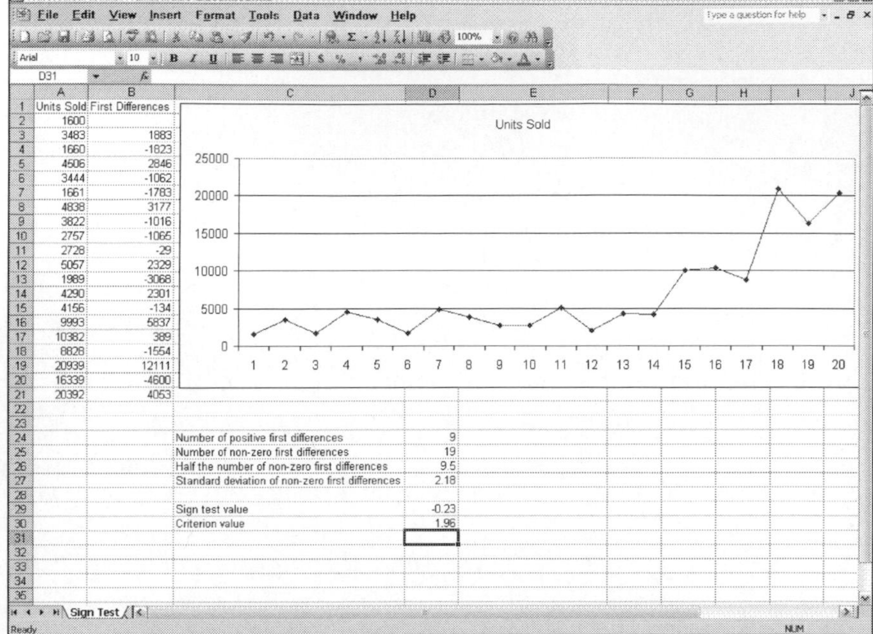

Figure 17-1: An example of a non-parametric test for trend in a baseline.

Getting a Baseline to Stand Still

When you have a baseline that has a trend, whether up or down, you can decide to leave the trend in place. If you make that decision, you've decided to use regression as your forecast method.

And that may very well be the right choice. It's very often the case that a regression-based forecast is more accurate than alternatives such as exponential smoothing or moving averages.

Subtracting one value from the next value

There is a method called *first differencing* that usually takes the trend out of a baseline. To use it, you just subtract one value from the next value in the baseline — that's why it's called *differencing.* The results of the subtractions are called *differences.* Occasionally, you may need to difference the differences — that's called *second differencing.* You may find you have to do that if your original series grew exponentially — that is, it looks not like a straight-line trend, growing at a roughly fixed amount from period to period. Instead, it's a curve that gets steeper the farther you get into the baseline.

Figure 17-2 shows an example of a baseline with a linear, straight-line trend and the baseline's first differences. The first differences form what's often called a *stationary* series of values.

Notice in Figure 17-2 that the original baseline trends up very strongly. But the first differences form a horizontal, stationary series.

I know what you're thinking. "If I'm supposed to make a forecast from the transformed, stationary baseline, that forecast is going to be under $100,000, but the next actual value will be close to $1,000,000. What's the deal?"

Good question. Toward the end of this chapter, there's a section called "And All the King's Men: Putting a Baseline Together Again." That section shows you how to undo the first differencing — often called *reintegrating* the differenced values.

You don't see it all the time, but you do occasionally, so have a look at Figure 17-3 for an example of a baseline that requires second differencing.

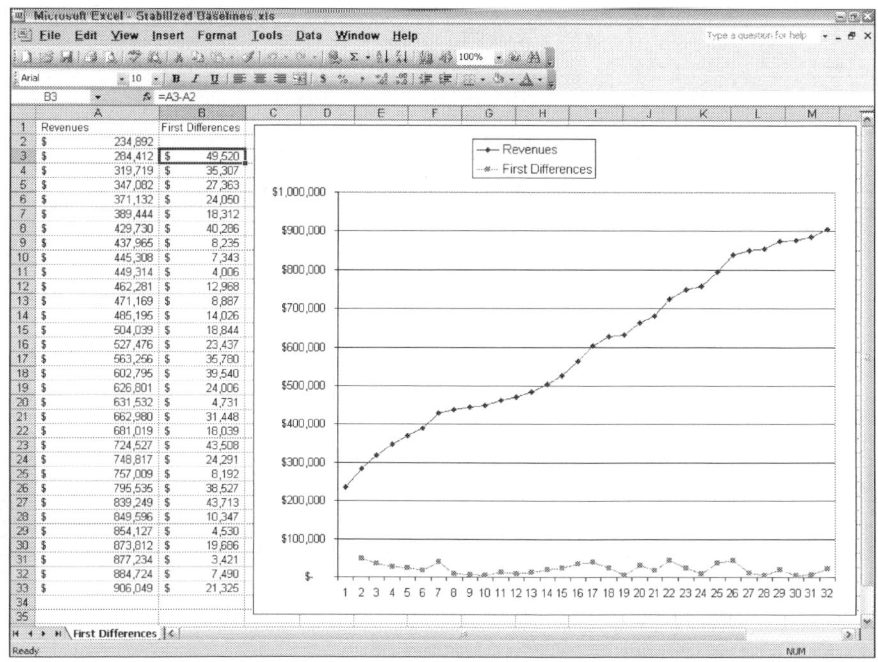

Figure 17-2: Just by subtracting one value from the next, you can take the trend out of the baseline.

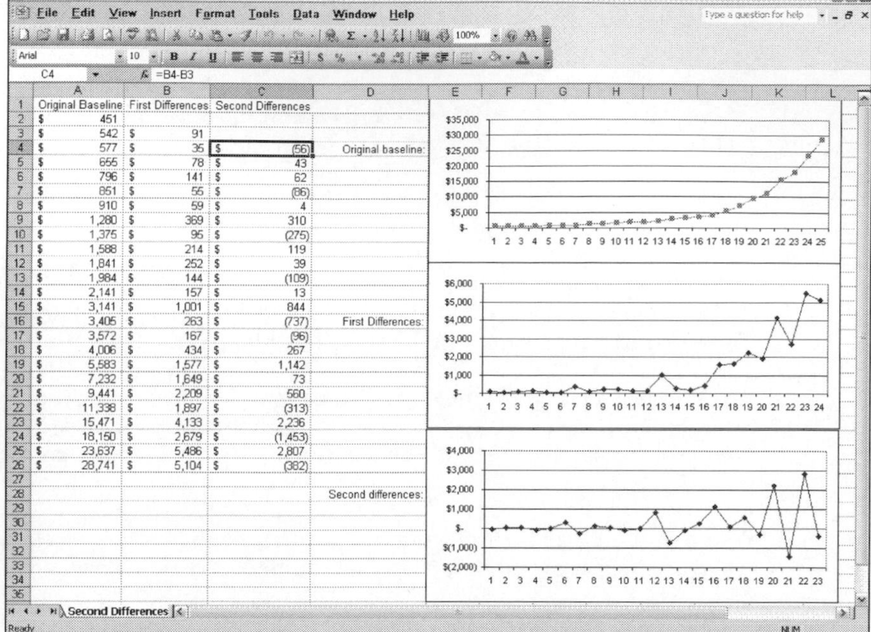

	A	B	C
1	Original Baseline	First Differences	Second Differences
2	$ 451		
3	$ 542	$ 91	
4	$ 577	$ 35	$ (56)
5	$ 655	$ 78	$ 43
6	$ 796	$ 141	$ 62
7	$ 851	$ 55	$ (86)
8	$ 910	$ 59	$ 4
9	$ 1,280	$ 369	$ 310
10	$ 1,375	$ 95	$ (275)
11	$ 1,588	$ 214	$ 119
12	$ 1,841	$ 252	$ 39
13	$ 1,984	$ 144	$ (109)
14	$ 2,141	$ 157	$ 13
15	$ 3,141	$ 1,001	$ 844
16	$ 3,405	$ 263	$ (737)
17	$ 3,572	$ 167	$ (96)
18	$ 4,006	$ 434	$ 267
19	$ 5,583	$ 1,577	$ 1,142
20	$ 7,232	$ 1,649	$ 73
21	$ 9,441	$ 2,209	$ 560
22	$ 11,338	$ 1,897	$ (313)
23	$ 15,471	$ 4,133	$ 2,236
24	$ 18,150	$ 2,679	$ (1,453)
25	$ 23,637	$ 5,486	$ 2,807
26	$ 28,741	$ 5,104	$ (382)

Figure 17-3: When the original baseline isn't linear, you may need to take second differences.

In Figure 17-3, the curve in the baseline is so pronounced that the first differences also have a curve to them. (A gentler original curve would usually produce first differences that looked more like a straight-line trend.) But the second differences are finally horizontal. These are the values you'd use to make your forecast. Then you'd reintegrate that forecast twice so you could compare it to the original baseline's scale. (See the section later in this chapter, "And All the King's Men: Putting a Baseline Together Again.")

Dividing one value by another

Another approach to stabilizing a baseline that has trend is to divide, rather than subtract, one value by the previous value. The result forms a series of what are called *link relatives.* Figure 17-4 shows the link relatives for the baseline used in Figures 17-1 and 17-2.

To get Excel to calculate link relatives, follow these steps:

1. **Using the layout in Figure 17-4, select cell B3.**
2. **Type** =A3/A2 **and press Enter.**
3. **Select cell B3 and choose Edit ⇨ Copy.**
4. **Select the range B4:B26 and choose Edit ⇨ Paste.**

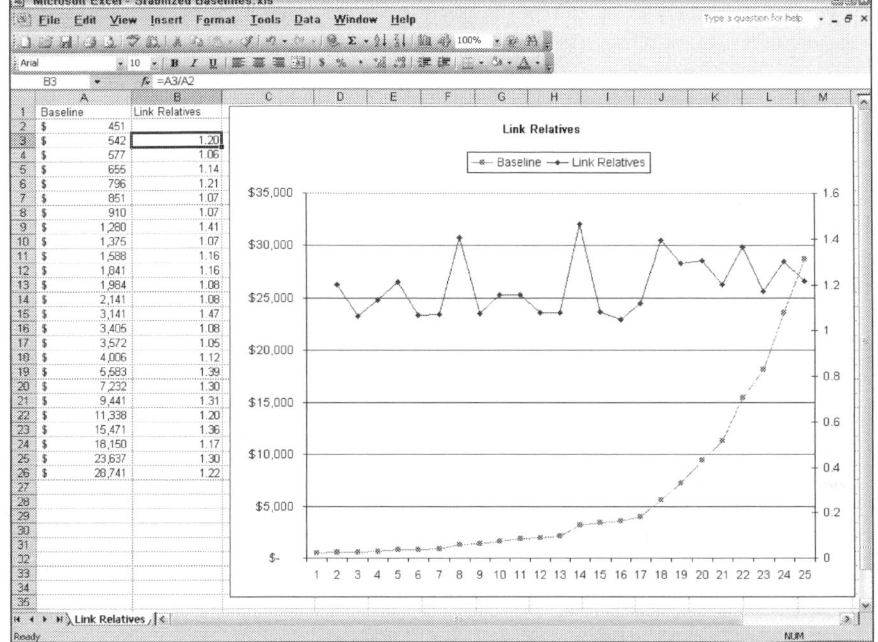

Figure 17-4: This chart uses two different vertical axes.

Now you have the link relatives. You should have already charted the original baseline to determine whether it's already stationary (if it is, you don't need to be doing this — the only point to calculating either first differences or link relatives is if the original baseline had an up or a down trend). To get the link relatives into that chart, do the following:

1. **Select the entire range of link relatives, including its column header.**

   In Figure 17-4, that's the range B1:B26.

2. **Click on Link Relatives, hold the mouse button down, drag through to the final value, and release the mouse button.**

   Yes, that means that you'll include a blank cell, B2, in the selected range. By selecting the blank cell, you arrange to line up the two data series properly on the chart. By including the Link Relatives column header, you give the series that name, which will appear in the chart legend.

3. **Click anywhere on the heavy border around the range and hold the mouse button down.**

4. **Drag your mouse pointer into the chart, and release the mouse button.**

   You'll see the Paste Special dialog box, as shown in Figure 17-5.

5. **Given the layout in columns A and B, you should accept the defaults in the dialog box: Add Cells as New Series, Values (Y) in Columns, and Series Names in First Row.**

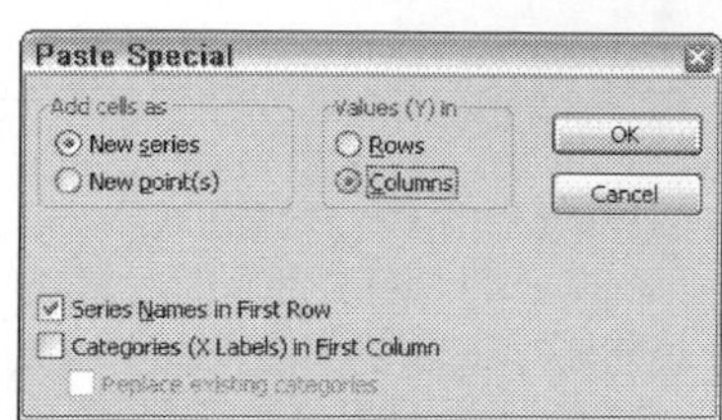

Figure 17-5: If you choose New Points, Excel will append the data you're dragging into the chart to an existing data series.

6. **Click OK.**

Because they're ratios of one baseline value to the preceding baseline value, link relatives usually range from 0 to 2. So if you want to chart them along with the original baseline values, as in Figure 17-4, you may need to use two different vertical axes. If you use one axis only, the values of the link relatives often get mashed down into the horizontal axis (see Figure 17-6).

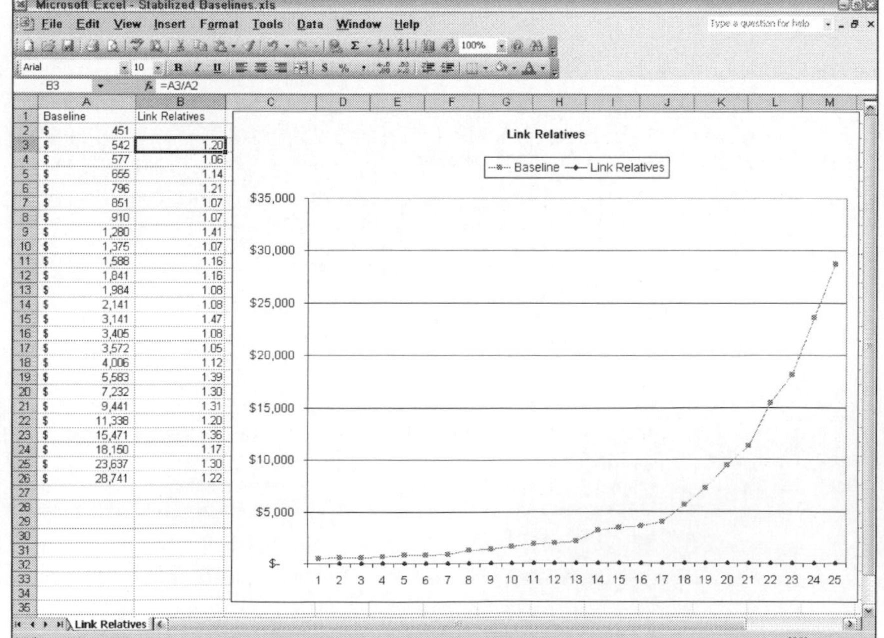

Figure 17-6: The solution to this problem is to use two axes, as is done in Figure 17-4.

Notice that the scale for the original baseline is so large that values between 1 and 2 get swallowed up, and you can't see what's going on with them in the chart.

To get a second axis, as Figure 17-4 shows, do the following:

1. **Click the chart to activate it.**

   You'll see square handles on the corners and on the sides of the chart.

   To resize a chart, put your mouse pointer over one of those handles, press and hold down the mouse button, and drag in a direction that will expand or shrink the chart.

2. **To select the chart, click on the series that's been buried by the scale of the vertical axis.**
3. **Choose Format ⇨ Selected Data Series.**
4. **Select the Axis tab.**
5. **Click the Secondary Axis radio button, and then click OK.**

   There will now be a primary axis for one series on the left of the chart's plot area, and a secondary axis for another series on the right, just as in Figure 17-4, and you can now see what's going on in both series.

It's a good idea to have Excel calculate and chart both first differences and link relatives, and verify that neither shows visual evidence of a trend.

Getting rates

Another way to make a trended baseline stationary is to change it to a rate of some sort. For example, outside the area of sales forecasting, you may want to forecast the number of traffic accidents that will occur during the next quarter. If you were to divide the number of accidents in your baseline by the number of licensed drivers during that quarter, it's quite likely that the ratio would form a stationary baseline.

This is a sort of per-capita ratio, and people tend to understand per-capita ratios more easily than first differences or link ratios.

But if you adopt this approach to detrending a baseline, you'll need to forecast both the accident rate and the number of licensed drivers, and then apply the forecast rate to forecast of drivers. Forecast errors in each baseline will then tend to compound one another.

The downside of differencing

Take another look at Figures 17-1 and 17-3. You'll notice that you lose one value from the beginning of the baseline of first differences, as well as that of link relatives. The reason is that, in each case, you're converting two values into one.

This is yet another reason to put some effort into getting as lengthy a baseline as you can. When your baseline contains only ten values, first differencing (or link relatives) causes you to lose 10 percent of your data. If you've managed to collect 50 values without spending half a career doing so, first differencing loses only 2 percent — not usually a major loss.

It's not just the raw number of values that are lost, it's also the power of the statistical tests that you may apply to determine whether you've really removed the trend (see Chapter 4). The smaller the number of data points involved in the test, the less sensitive the test.

But there's more. Whenever you difference a baseline, the amount of forecast error increases. Have a look at Figure 17-7.

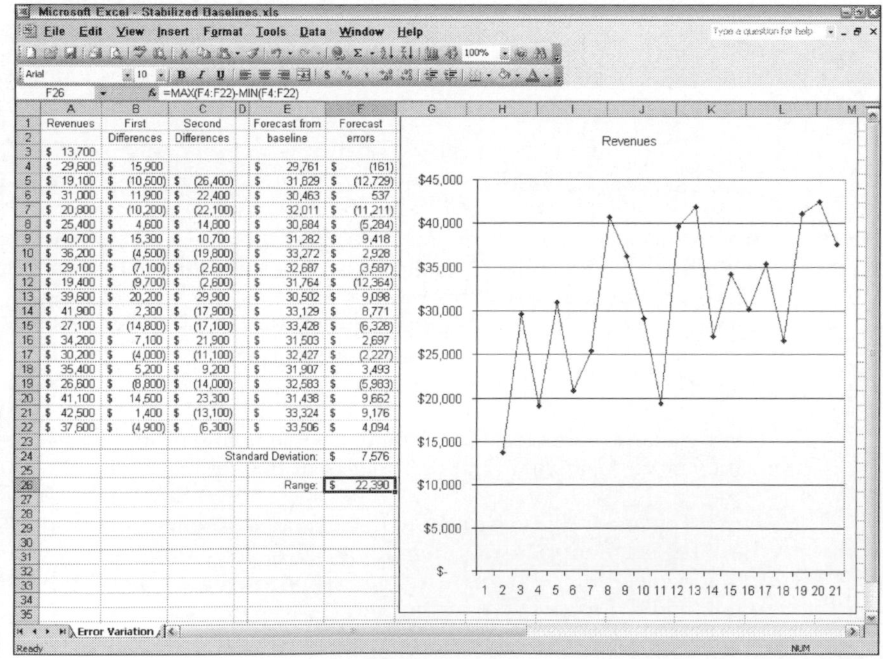

Revenues	First Differences	Second Differences	Forecast from baseline	Forecast errors
$ 13,700				
$ 29,600	$ 15,900		$ 29,761	$ (161)
$ 19,100	$ (10,500)	$ (26,400)	$ 31,829	$ (12,729)
$ 31,000	$ 11,900	$ 22,400	$ 30,463	$ 537
$ 20,800	$ (10,200)	$ (22,100)	$ 32,011	$ (11,211)
$ 25,400	$ 4,600	$ 14,800	$ 30,684	$ (5,284)
$ 40,700	$ 15,300	$ 10,700	$ 31,282	$ 9,418
$ 36,200	$ (4,500)	$ (19,800)	$ 33,272	$ 2,928
$ 29,100	$ (7,100)	$ (2,600)	$ 32,687	$ (3,587)
$ 19,400	$ (9,700)	$ (2,600)	$ 31,764	$ (12,364)
$ 39,600	$ 20,200	$ 29,900	$ 30,502	$ 9,098
$ 41,900	$ 2,300	$ (17,900)	$ 33,129	$ 8,771
$ 27,100	$ (14,800)	$ (17,100)	$ 33,428	$ (6,328)
$ 34,200	$ 7,100	$ 21,900	$ 31,503	$ 2,697
$ 30,200	$ (4,000)	$ (11,100)	$ 32,427	$ (2,227)
$ 35,400	$ 5,200	$ 9,200	$ 31,907	$ 3,493
$ 26,600	$ (8,800)	$ (14,000)	$ 32,583	$ (5,983)
$ 41,100	$ 14,500	$ 23,300	$ 31,438	$ 9,662
$ 42,500	$ 1,400	$ (13,100)	$ 33,324	$ 9,176
$ 37,600	$ (4,900)	$ (6,300)	$ 33,506	$ 4,094
			Standard Deviation:	$ 7,576
			Range:	$ 22,390

Figure 17-7: Note that the baseline of revenues has a clear upward trend.

In Figure 17-7:

- Column A contains the original baseline. The chart shows that the baseline is trended, so you would consider detrending it.
- Column B contains the first differences of the original baseline. For example, cell B4 contains the difference between A4 and A3, B5 contains the difference between A5 and A4, and so on.
- Column C contains the second differences of the original baseline. For example, cell C5 contains the difference between B5 and B4, C6 contains the difference between B6 and B5, and so on.

With that data in columns A, B, and C, you can do some forecasting. Excel's TREND worksheet function comes in handy here. TREND does the following:

- It takes some actual values that you already know, such as a baseline of sales revenues.
- It takes some associated predictor values that you also already know.
- It calculates a regression equation between the predictor values and the actual values.
- It applies that equation to the predictors and returns the forecasts calculated by the regression equation.

In Figure 17-7, column E contains the TREND function. Its actual values are the revenues in cells A4:A22. Its predictor values are the revenues in cells A3:A21. In words, the TREND function forecasts the 2nd through 20th values in the baseline, using the 1st through 19th values as predictors.

This is classic autoregression, where you forecast based on the variable itself — you use a prior value to forecast a later value. Formally, you should detrend the series first. (This first example is not detrended, to make a point about increasing the errors when you do so.)

You enter the TREND function as an array formula. In Figure 17-7, you select E4:E22 and type the following equation:

```
=TREND(A4:A22,A3:A21)
```

You array-enter a formula not by pressing Enter, but by pressing Ctrl+Shift+Enter.

Several functions in Excel are concerned with regression and require that you array-enter them:

- **LINEST:** This function returns the regression coefficients as well as several statistics that help you evaluate how accurate the regression equation is likely to prove.
- **TREND:** See the discussion earlier in this section.
- **MINVERSE:** This function returns the inverse of a matrix. It's the multiple-value version of a regular inverse — for example, 2/7 is the inverse of 7/2.
- **MMULT:** This function returns the product of two matrixes.

You also use array formulas outside the context of regression. Array formulas, properly designed, can return results that are both elegant and impossible to achieve any other way.

For example, in cell E4 of Figure 17-7, you see $29,761. This is the result of plugging the first actual value, $13,700, into the regression equation. E5, $31,829, is the result of plugging the second actual, $29,600, into the equation.

Column F in Figure 17-7 is the difference between the forecasts in column E and the actuals in column A. These are the forecast errors. The less the variability — the spread — in the forecast errors, the more precise your forecast.

Cell F24 contains the standard deviation of the forecast errors in the range F4:F22. The standard deviation is one measure of the amount of spread in a set of numbers. If you're not familiar with standard deviations, you can instead look at the range in cell F26: the difference between the maximum and minimum values in a set of numbers.

Now do the same thing with the first differences of the baseline, shown in column B of Figure 17-7. The result appears in Figure 17-8.

Figure 17-8 adds two columns to Figure 17-7. Column H uses the TREND function just as column E does, except that it forecasts using the first differences. It develops an equation that uses a prior first difference to forecast a subsequent first difference.

Don't get lost in the fun house here. Right now, the main point is not the meaning of a forecast first difference; the point is the amount of extra error you induce when you difference a baseline.

Column I shows the difference between the forecasts and the first differences. Look at cells I24 (the standard deviation of the forecast errors) and I26 (the range of the forecast errors). Both are larger than for the forecast errors based on the original baseline, shown in F24 and F26. The act of differencing the baseline has increased the variability in the forecast errors.

	A	B	C	E	F	H	I
1	Revenues	First	Second	Forecast from	Forecast	Forecast from	Forecast
2		Differences	Differences	baseline	errors	First Differences	errors
3	$ 13,700						
4	$ 29,600	$ 15,900		$ 29,761	$ (161)		
5	$ 19,100	$ (10,500)	$ (26,400)	$ 31,829	$ (12,729)	$ (5,770)	$ (4,730)
6	$ 31,000	$ 11,900	$ 22,400	$ 30,463	$ 537	$ 5,703	$ 6,197
7	$ 20,800	$ (10,200)	$ (22,100)	$ 32,011	$ (11,211)	$ (4,032)	$ (6,168)
8	$ 25,400	$ 4,600	$ 14,800	$ 30,684	$ (5,284)	$ 5,573	$ (973)
9	$ 40,700	$ 15,300	$ 10,700	$ 31,282	$ 9,418	$ (859)	$ 16,159
10	$ 36,200	$ (4,500)	$ (19,800)	$ 33,272	$ 2,928	$ (5,510)	$ 1,010
11	$ 29,100	$ (7,100)	$ (2,600)	$ 32,687	$ (3,587)	$ 3,095	$ (10,195)
12	$ 19,400	$ (9,700)	$ (2,600)	$ 31,764	$ (12,364)	$ 4,225	$ (13,925)
13	$ 39,600	$ 20,200	$ 29,900	$ 30,502	$ 9,098	$ 5,355	$ 14,845
14	$ 41,900	$ 2,300	$ (17,900)	$ 33,129	$ 8,771	$ (7,639)	$ 9,939
15	$ 27,100	$ (14,800)	$ (17,100)	$ 33,428	$ (6,328)	$ 140	$ (14,940)
16	$ 34,200	$ 7,100	$ 21,900	$ 31,503	$ 2,697	$ 7,572	$ (472)
17	$ 30,200	$ (4,000)	$ (11,100)	$ 32,427	$ (2,227)	$ (1,946)	$ (2,054)
18	$ 35,400	$ 5,200	$ 9,200	$ 31,907	$ 3,493	$ 2,878	$ 2,322
19	$ 26,600	$ (8,800)	$ (14,000)	$ 32,583	$ (5,983)	$ (1,120)	$ (7,680)
20	$ 41,100	$ 14,500	$ 23,300	$ 31,438	$ 9,662	$ 4,964	$ 9,536
21	$ 42,500	$ 1,400	$ (13,100)	$ 33,324	$ 9,176	$ (5,162)	$ 6,562
22	$ 37,600	$ (4,900)	$ (6,300)	$ 33,506	$ 4,094	$ 531	$ (5,431)
23							
24				Standard Deviation:	$ 7,576		$ 9,186
25							
26				Range:	$ 22,390		$ 31,100

Figure 17-8: The variability or spread in the error values of the forecast first differences increases.

Finally, Figure 17-9 shows that the same effect continues with second differencing. The forecasts, using the TREND function on the values in column C, are in column K, and the forecast errors — the differences between the second differences and the forecast second differences — are in column L. Notice that in cells L24 and L26, both the standard deviation and the range are larger than those for the first differences.

Why is this important? Because the greater the error variation, the less precise your forecast. And that's the trade-off involved in detrending a series:

- You can use one of the simpler approaches to forecasting — moving averages or exponential smoothing — by detrending the series. But then you're inducing more variability into the forecast errors, making your forecast less precise.
- You can leave the trend in place and use a regression approach, typically using time period as the predictor variable. But then you're making more-restrictive assumptions about your data, which ideally you should test, and those tests can be time consuming and not necessarily easy to interpret.

My own tendency is to do it both ways and see which one seems to provide the more accurate forecasts. (Also, the diagnostic tests involved in checking the regression assumptions go pretty quickly, because I've been doing this for so many years.)

Microsoft Excel - Stabilized Baselines.xls

L6 =C6-K6

	A	B	C	E	F	H	I	K	L
1	Revenues	First	Second	Forecast from	Forecast	Forecast from	Forecast	Forecast from	Forecast
2		Differences	Differences	baseline	errors	First Differences	Errors	Second Differences	Errors
3	$ 13,700								
4	$ 29,600	$ 15,900		$ 29,761	$ (161)				
5	$ 19,100	$ (10,500)	$ (26,400)	$ 31,829	$ (12,729)	$ (5,770)	$ (4,730)		
6	$ 31,000	$ 11,900	$ 22,400	$ 30,463	$ 537	$ 5,703	$ 6,197	$ 14,718	$ 7,682
7	$ 20,800	$ (10,200)	$ (22,100)	$ 32,011	$ (11,211)	$ (4,032)	$ (6,168)	$ (12,767)	$ (9,333)
8	$ 25,400	$ 4,600	$ 14,800	$ 30,684	$ (5,284)	$ 5,573	$ (973)	$ 12,296	$ 2,504
9	$ 40,700	$ 15,300	$ 10,700	$ 31,282	$ 9,418	$ (859)	$ 16,159	$ (8,487)	$ 19,187
10	$ 36,200	$ (4,500)	$ (19,800)	$ 33,272	$ 2,928	$ (5,510)	$ 1,010	$ (6,177)	$ (13,623)
11	$ 29,100	$ (7,100)	$ (2,600)	$ 32,687	$ (3,587)	$ 3,095	$ (10,195)	$ 11,001	$ (13,601)
12	$ 19,400	$ (9,700)	$ (2,600)	$ 31,764	$ (12,364)	$ 4,225	$ (13,925)	$ 1,313	$ (3,913)
13	$ 39,600	$ 20,200	$ 29,900	$ 30,502	$ 9,098	$ 5,355	$ 14,845	$ 1,313	$ 28,587
14	$ 41,900	$ 2,300	$ (17,900)	$ 33,129	$ 8,771	$ (7,639)	$ 9,939	$ (16,991)	$ (909)
15	$ 27,100	$ (14,800)	$ (17,100)	$ 33,428	$ (6,328)	$ 140	$ (14,940)	$ 9,931	$ (27,031)
16	$ 34,200	$ 7,100	$ 21,900	$ 31,503	$ 2,697	$ 7,572	$ (472)	$ 9,480	$ 12,420
17	$ 30,200	$ (4,000)	$ (11,100)	$ 32,427	$ (2,227)	$ (1,946)	$ (2,054)	$ (12,486)	$ 1,386
18	$ 35,400	$ 5,200	$ 9,200	$ 31,907	$ 3,493	$ 2,878	$ 2,322	$ 6,101	$ 3,099
19	$ 26,600	$ (8,800)	$ (14,000)	$ 32,583	$ (5,983)	$ (1,120)	$ (7,680)	$ (5,333)	$ (8,667)
20	$ 41,100	$ 14,500	$ 23,300	$ 31,438	$ 9,662	$ 4,964	$ 9,536	$ 7,734	$ 15,566
21	$ 42,500	$ 1,400	$ (13,100)	$ 33,324	$ 9,176	$ (5,162)	$ 6,562	$ (13,274)	$ 174
22	$ 37,600	$ (4,900)	$ (6,300)	$ 33,506	$ 4,094	$ 531	$ (5,431)	$ 7,227	$ (13,527)
24				Standard Deviation:	$ 7,576		$ 9,186		$ 13,967
26				Range:	$ 22,390		$ 31,100		$ 55,617

Error Variation

Figure 17-9: The farther you get from the original baseline, the greater the error variation.

And All the King's Men: Putting a Baseline Together Again

If you decide to difference a baseline, to make it stationary before you use it to make a forecast, you have a little more work to do before you're ready to announce that forecast.

As you've seen, when you difference a baseline you usually wind up with much smaller values in the first differences than are in the original baseline. In Figure 17-9, for example, the first differences in column B are much smaller than the original baseline values in column A.

And, as this chapter explains, the idea behind differencing is to remove the trend from a baseline prior to forecasting with one of the single-variable methods like moving averages and exponential smoothing. They're more effective when you deploy them on a stationary baseline.

So, when you make your forecast, it's in first-difference units, not the original baseline's units (see Figure 17-10).

Microsoft Excel - Stabilized Baselines.xls

D6 =0.3*C5+0.7*D5

Time Period	Revenues	First Differences	Forecast Differences
1	$ 674		
2	$ 625	$ (49)	#N/A
3	$ 586	$ (39)	-$49
4	$ 514	$ (72)	-$46
5	$ 473	$ (41)	-$54
6	$ 428	$ (45)	-$50
7	$ 343	$ (85)	-$48
8	$ 236	$ (107)	-$59
9	$ 278	$ 42	-$74
10	$ 231	$ (47)	-$39
11	$ 215	$ (16)	-$41
12	$ 209	$ (6)	-$34
13	$ 269	$ 60	-$25
14	$ 299	$ 30	$0
15	$ 382	$ 83	$9
16	$ 461	$ 79	$31
17	$ 442	$ (19)	$46
18	$ 375	$ (67)	$26
19	$ 370	$ (5)	-$2
20	$ 396	$ 26	-$3
21	$ 439	$ 43	$6
22	$ 419	$ (20)	$17
23 forecast			$6
Smoothing constant:		0.30	
Damping factor:		0.70	

Figure 17-10: Exponential smoothing forecasts a value of $6 in cell D25. You still need to reintegrate the forecasts with the original baseline.

You can't report a forecast for period 23 of $6. People won't understand when you say you're forecasting a first difference. They'll go back to the guy with the pointy hat with the stars and moons on it.

You need to reintegrate your forecast first difference with the baseline first. This is shown, along with a chart of the baseline and the reintegrated forecast, in Figure 17-11.

You got the first differences by subtracting a baseline value from the value that follows it. Now that you've made your forecast of the first differences (including the forecast of $6 for the 23rd period), you need to add them back to the baseline. This is how you get back to the original scale. In this example, the original scale in the baseline runs from $209 to $674, and the scale of the forecast differences runs from a negative $107 to a positive $83.

Combining the baseline and the forecast differences is easy. Using the example in Figure 17-11, enter the following formula in cell E5:

```
=B4+D5
```

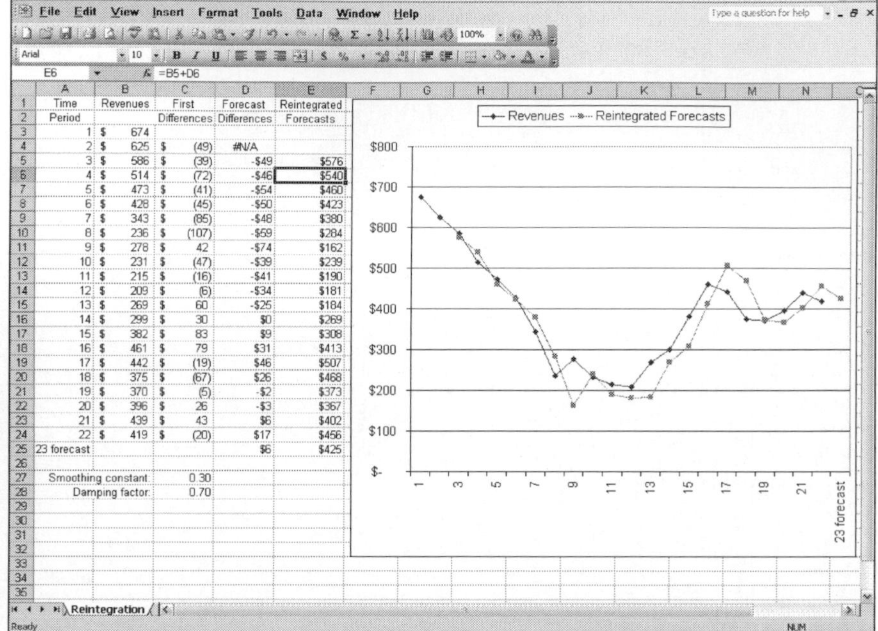

Time Period	Revenues	First Differences	Forecast Differences	Reintegrated Forecasts
1	$ 674			
2	$ 625	$ (49)	#N/A	
3	$ 586	$ (39)	-$49	$576
4	$ 514	$ (72)	-$46	$540
5	$ 473	$ (41)	-$54	$460
6	$ 428	$ (45)	-$50	$423
7	$ 343	$ (85)	-$48	$380
8	$ 236	$ (107)	-$59	$284
9	$ 278	$ 42	-$74	$162
10	$ 231	$ (47)	-$39	$239
11	$ 215	$ (16)	-$41	$190
12	$ 209	$ (6)	-$34	$181
13	$ 269	$ 60	-$25	$184
14	$ 299	$ 30	$0	$269
15	$ 382	$ 83	$9	$308
16	$ 461	$ 79	$31	$413
17	$ 442	$ (19)	$46	$507
18	$ 375	$ (67)	$26	$468
19	$ 370	$ (5)	-$2	$373
20	$ 396	$ 26	-$3	$367
21	$ 439	$ 43	$6	$402
22	$ 419	$ (20)	$17	$456
23 forecast			$6	$425
Smoothing constant:		0.30		
Damping factor:		0.70		

Figure 17-11: The damping factor of 0.7 is fairly large, and the forecasts track the baseline quickly.

Here you're taking the value in the baseline, which is the basis for the differencing, and adding back into it the difference that you've forecast for the current period. The result is that you return to the original scale of the baseline.

This chapter has already mentioned the two principal downsides to differencing: loss of at least one value (first differencing a 20 value baseline, for example, results in 19 first differences), and greater variability in the forecast errors. When you then use exponential smoothing to make your forecast, you lose yet another value. As Chapter 15 shows, you can't make a forecast from the value in the baseline that precedes the first one, because it doesn't exist. So your first forecast value is always not available — or in Excel worksheet terms, `#N/A`.

The upshot is that you're going to wind up with two fewer forecast values than values in your baseline: one lost to first differencing, one lost to exponential smoothing. The loss can be even greater with moving averages, depending on how many baseline values go into each moving average.

Chapter 18

Same Time Last Year: Forecasting Seasonal Sales

In This Chapter

- Recognizing seasonal patterns in your exponential smoothing
- Calculating your first forecast
- Modifying the formulas to finish your forecast

Years have their seasons, and seasons make their mark on sales — particularly in the retail sector. If you're going to forecast sales in a business segment that has seasonal peaks and valleys, you're going to need a topo map. And you can get that map by accounting for seasons in your smoothing. It's just a step more complicated than regular old exponential smoothing. Your seasonal forecast is based not only on the most recent observation, but also on the last time this season came through on the calendar.

So, as you start to get a ways into the baseline, there are two components to a seasonal forecast, and one is the *level* component. This component is analogous to the previous actual baseline value used in exponential smoothing, described in Chapter 15. The current baseline level needs some adjustment before you apply the smoothing constant, in order to remove the seasonal factor from the previous actual.

The second component is *seasonal.* The idea is that, every year, the seasons have similar effects on sales. In preparing to make a forecast, we need to quantify those effects. You assign a number to each season — that is, you might've found that, over time, you experience a $2,000,000 falloff during spring and a $4,000,000 boost during winter. You can use that information to improve the accuracy of your forecasts. And not incidentally, you can use it to extend the number of future time periods you can forecast into.

Finally, in this chapter, I show you the difference between forecasts that are within the baseline periods and forecasts that extend past the end of the baseline — the ones you're really interested in. And I show you how to use a utility that I wrote to unburden you: It relieves you of having to put the equations into a worksheet.

Doing Simple Seasonal Exponential Smoothing

Simple seasonal exponential smoothing builds on concepts you use in exponential smoothing. The difference between the two is that you often recognize a seasonal pattern, like colder weather during winter, or increases in retail sales during the winter holidays.

Then you need to consider bringing a more complicated approach to bear on the forecasting problem. By "consider," I mean that you need to try both approaches and see which one works best for you.

I do suggest, though, that if you haven't looked through this book's chapters on simple exponential smoothing, you do so before you get into this chapter. It will be a lot easier to follow if you've already thought about things like smoothing constants and diminishing influences.

Relating a season to its ancestors

Think back to how exponential smoothing works. It uses a formula like this one to base the next forecast in part on the prior actual and in part on the prior forecast:

New Forecast = (0.3 × Prior Actual) + (0.7 × Prior Forecast)

This amounts to a weighted average of two prior figures — the actual and the forecast. This particular formula gives a good bit more of the weight to the forecast than to the actual. You have to experiment around some with a particular baseline to get the right smoothing constant (that's the 0.3 in the formula) and the right damping factor (that's the 0.7 in the formula).

The idea here is that one time period in the baseline is going to be closely related to the following time period. If today's high temperature were 70°F, you'd have to show me an approaching cold front to convince me that tomorrow's high will be 50°F. Without additional, contradictory information, I'd prefer to bet on 70°F. Yesterday tends to forecast today, and today tends to forecast tomorrow.

But let's shift to months. The general weather patterns follow changes in months much more closely than they do changes in days. If May's average daily high were 70°F, I'd still lean toward 70°F for June, but before I put any money down on it I'd want to know what *last* June's average daily high was.

So here's what I'm going to do: Instead of using just one smoothing constant, I'll use two. Instead of using only one constant in conjunction with the immediately prior baseline value, I'll use one for the prior value, and one for the season that's one year back from this one.

Figure 18-1 shows a seasonal sales baseline, and the associated forecasts, in practice.

Notice in Figure 18-1 how the sales invariably head up during the third quarter of each year, and spike during the fourth quarter. Then the bottom falls out during the first and second quarters. The figure also shows the forecasts, which have captured the seasonal pattern in a smoothing equation, making the forecasts that much more accurate.

What if I used regular exponential smoothing, the sort covered in Chapter 15? Figure 18-2 gives some of the bad news.

Here, the smoothing constant is 0.3, and the forecasts are relatively insensitive to fluctuations in the actuals from the baseline. The forecasts do nod in passing to the peaks and valleys in the baseline, but it's a dismissive sort of nod.

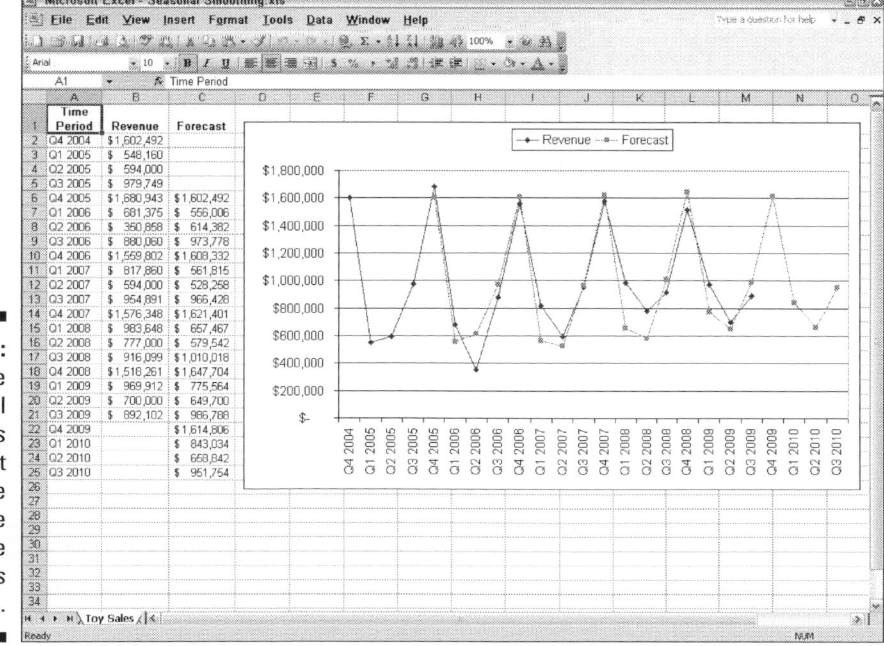

Time Period	Revenue	Forecast
Q4 2004	$1,602,492	
Q1 2005	$ 548,160	
Q2 2005	$ 594,000	
Q3 2005	$ 979,749	
Q4 2005	$1,680,943	$1,602,492
Q1 2006	$ 681,375	$ 556,006
Q2 2006	$ 350,858	$ 614,382
Q3 2006	$ 880,060	$ 973,778
Q4 2006	$1,559,802	$1,608,332
Q1 2007	$ 817,860	$ 561,815
Q2 2007	$ 594,000	$ 528,258
Q3 2007	$ 954,891	$ 966,428
Q4 2007	$1,576,348	$1,621,401
Q1 2008	$ 983,648	$ 657,467
Q2 2008	$ 777,000	$ 579,542
Q3 2008	$ 916,099	$1,010,018
Q4 2008	$1,518,261	$1,647,704
Q1 2009	$ 969,912	$ 775,564
Q2 2009	$ 700,000	$ 649,700
Q3 2009	$ 892,102	$ 986,788
Q4 2009		$1,614,806
Q1 2010		$ 843,034
Q2 2010		$ 658,842
Q3 2010		$ 951,754

Figure 18-1: The seasonal forecasts cannot start until one sequence of baseline seasons has passed.

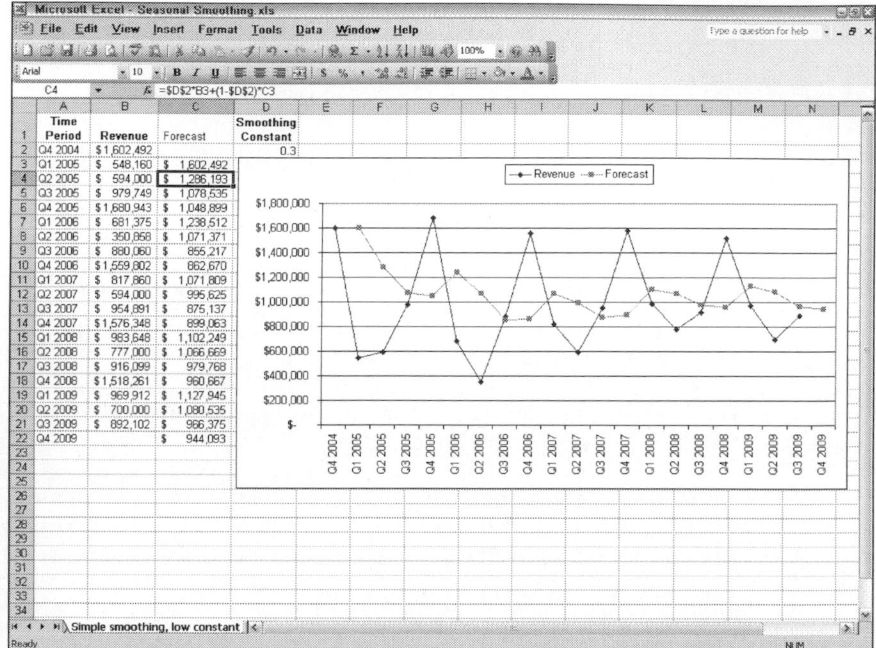

	A	B	C	D
1	Time Period	Revenue	Forecast	Smoothing Constant
2	Q4 2004	$1,602,492		0.3
3	Q1 2005	$ 548,160	$ 1,602,492	
4	Q2 2005	$ 594,000	$ 1,286,193	
5	Q3 2005	$ 979,749	$ 1,078,535	
6	Q4 2005	$1,680,943	$ 1,048,899	
7	Q1 2006	$ 681,375	$ 1,238,512	
8	Q2 2006	$ 350,858	$ 1,071,371	
9	Q3 2006	$ 880,060	$ 855,217	
10	Q4 2006	$1,559,802	$ 862,670	
11	Q1 2007	$ 817,860	$ 1,071,809	
12	Q2 2007	$ 594,000	$ 995,625	
13	Q3 2007	$ 954,891	$ 875,137	
14	Q4 2007	$1,576,348	$ 899,063	
15	Q1 2008	$ 983,648	$ 1,102,249	
16	Q2 2008	$ 777,000	$ 1,066,669	
17	Q3 2008	$ 916,099	$ 979,768	
18	Q4 2008	$1,518,261	$ 960,667	
19	Q1 2009	$ 969,912	$ 1,127,945	
20	Q2 2009	$ 700,000	$ 1,080,535	
21	Q3 2009	$ 892,102	$ 966,375	
22	Q4 2009		$ 944,093	

Figure 18-2: The forecasts emphasize the signal in the baseline.

What if I boosted the smoothing constant so that the forecasts track the actuals more than they smooth them? That situation is shown in Figure 18-3, where the smoothing constant is 0.7.

In Figure 18-3, the peaks and valleys are represented more clearly — but they lag one period behind. Compare Figure 18-3 and its tardy forecasts with Figure 18-1 and its on-time forecasts. The forecasts in Figure 18-1 can show up on time because they pay attention to what happened last year. And you know that showing up is 85 percent of life. (Don't bother to Google it: The Web pages disagree wildly over the statistic that Woody Allen cited.)

Figure 18-4 shows how I combine the components to get a forecast value. Don't worry, the source of the components and what they mean become clear as I walk through developing the seasonal forecast.

From examining the formula in cell C7 of Figure 18-4, you can see that the forecast for Quarter 1 of 2006 is the sum of two quantities:

- The prior estimate of the level of the baseline (see cell E6)
- The prior estimate of the effect of Quarter 1 in 2005 (see cell F3)

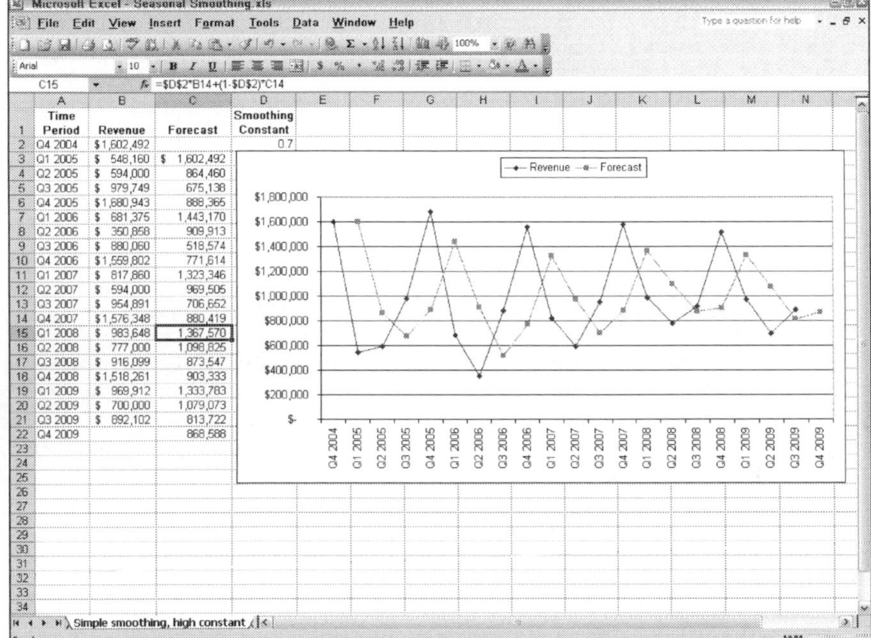

	Time Period	Revenue	Forecast	Smoothing Constant
2	Q4 2004	$1,602,492		0.7
3	Q1 2005	$ 548,160	$ 1,602,492	
4	Q2 2005	$ 594,000	864,460	
5	Q3 2005	$ 979,749	675,138	
6	Q4 2005	$1,680,943	888,365	
7	Q1 2006	$ 681,375	1,443,170	
8	Q2 2006	$ 350,858	909,913	
9	Q3 2006	$ 880,060	518,574	
10	Q4 2006	$1,559,802	771,614	
11	Q1 2007	$ 817,860	1,323,346	
12	Q2 2007	$ 594,000	969,505	
13	Q3 2007	$ 954,891	706,652	
14	Q4 2007	$1,576,348	880,419	
15	Q1 2008	$ 983,648	1,367,570	
16	Q2 2008	$ 777,000	1,098,825	
17	Q3 2008	$ 916,099	873,547	
18	Q4 2008	$1,518,261	903,333	
19	Q1 2009	$ 969,912	1,333,783	
20	Q2 2009	$ 700,000	1,079,073	
21	Q3 2009	$ 892,102	813,722	
22	Q4 2009		868,588	

Figure 18-3: The forecasts emphasize the changes in the baseline.

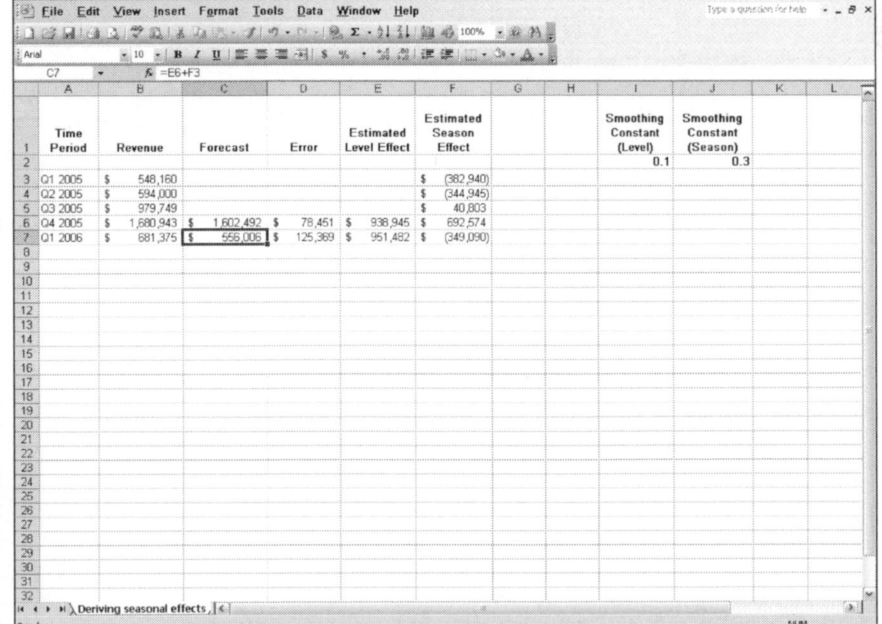

	Time Period	Revenue	Forecast	Error	Estimated Level Effect	Estimated Season Effect	Smoothing Constant (Level)	Smoothing Constant (Season)
2							0.1	0.3
3	Q1 2005	$ 548,160				$ (382,940)		
4	Q2 2005	$ 594,000				$ (344,945)		
5	Q3 2005	$ 979,749				$ 40,803		
6	Q4 2005	$ 1,680,943	$ 1,602,492	$ 78,451	$ 938,945	$ 692,574		
7	Q1 2006	$ 681,375	$ 556,006	$ 125,369	$ 951,482	$ (349,090)		

Figure 18-4: The seasonal effects are above (positive values) and below (negative values) the current overall level of the baseline.

The same is true of every forecast in Figure 18-1: It's the sum of the estimated level of the baseline and the estimated effect of the season. Comparing the seasonal smoothing forecasts in Figure 18-1 with the ordinary smoothing forecasts in Figures 18-2 and 18-3 wouldn't hurt. Clearly, you're better off if you can estimate the seasonal effect *before* it takes place. This is what is happening in Figure 18-4, which combines the level that's attributable to a season with the general level of the baseline to get the current season's forecast *before* the season takes place.

Using the smoothing constants

This section walks you through a demonstration of how you get forecasts that are seasonally smoothed. There's some math in it, but nothing more complicated than arithmetic. It's a little tedious — or it would be if you had to smooth each forecast in the way I show you here. But there's a workbook named Seasonal Smoothing.xls, with code in it, that you can download from `www.dummies.com/go/excelsffd`. When you run that code, you'll be prompted for some information, like where your baseline data is and the values you want to use for the smoothing constants. When you click OK, you'll get the seasonally smoothed forecasts.

If you decide you'd like to do the forecasting on the worksheet, using the formulas I set out in this section, there's just the upfront work to do. When you're a couple of periods into the forecast region, the process turns into a simple copy and paste.

So getting a seasonally smoothed forecast is not as onerous as it's going to seem by the time you've reached the end of this section. When you've gotten there, you'll have a better understanding of what's going on, and you can steam ahead.

Seasonal smoothing uses not one but two smoothing constants: one for the current level of the baseline and one for the current seasonal effect.

Actually, there are three smoothing constants: for the current level, for the current season, and for the slope in the baseline. To keep things straightforward, I assume that either there's no slope in the baseline, or I'm working with a baseline that I've already differenced and, thus, made stationary. If you read other books on forecasting, you may see the level constant referred to as *alpha* and the seasonal constant referred to as *delta*.

Figure 18-5 shows an example of the smoothing equation for the forecast's *level* component.

Bear in mind that, to forecast revenue in Q2 2006, you want to do your data gathering and apply your formulas during Q1 2006. So, you're working with information that's available to you by the end of Q1 2006.

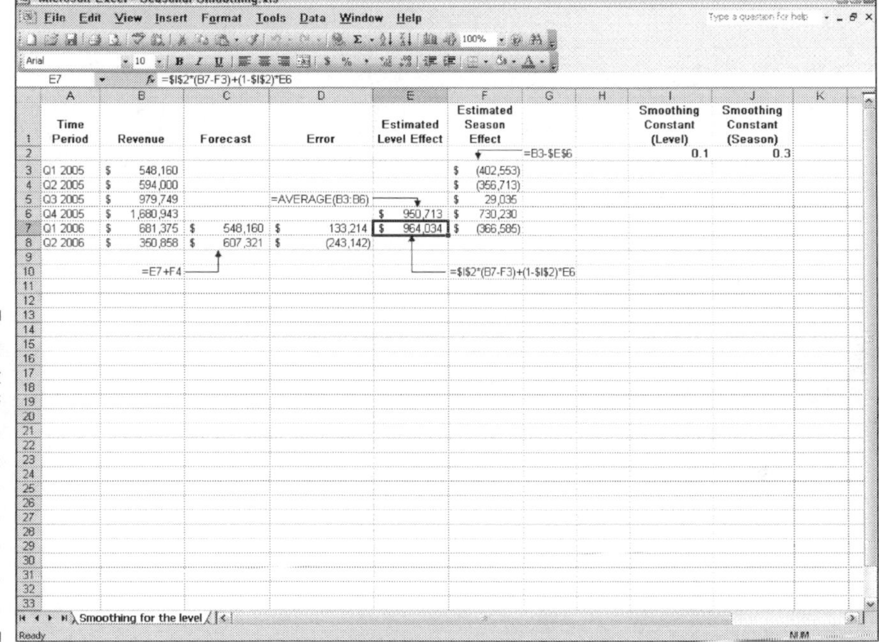

Figure 18-5: The first estimate of the baseline's level is the average of the revenues in the first year, in cell E6.

Estimating the season's effect

Work forward from cell F3. That cell contains the initial estimate of the effect of being in the first quarter. It's nothing more than the actual revenue in Q1 2005 less the average for all quarters in 2005. In terms of formulas, that's the following:

```
=B3-$E$6
```

where B3 contains the actual revenue for Q1 2005, and E6 contains the average quarterly revenue for 2005.

Similar formulas are used to get Q2 through Q4 of 2005. So, the formula for Q4 2005 is:

```
=B6-$E$6
```

Estimating the effect of the baseline's level

So far, you've quantified the effect of Q1 on the total revenue (and, thus, the quarterly average revenue) for 2005. You still need an estimate of the level of the baseline as of Q1 2006, and cell E7 shows that figure. Its formula is:

```
=$I$2*(B7-F3)+(1-$I$2)*E6
```

Does that look at all familiar? It may if you've looked at Chapter 15 recently. It's a smoothing equation, and it has two parts:

- In the first part, you multiply the smoothing constant (in cell I2) times the difference between B7 and F3: the actual revenue in Q1 2006 less the actual effect of being in Q1 2005. Just as with the (nonseasonal) exponential smoothing discussed in Chapter 15, you're multiplying the smoothing constant times an actual.
- In the second part, you're multiplying the damping factor times an estimate. In this case, the estimate is the level for 2005, the average of the four quarters in 2006 in E6.

The damping factor is 1 minus the smoothing constant.

Finally, you get your forecast for Q2 2006 by adding the estimate of the seasonal effect to the estimate of the level of the baseline:

```
=E7+F4
```

or $607,321.

Reviewing the process

Here's a review of what you've done: You have an estimate of the effect on revenue of being in Q1. Your best estimate of that, in Q1 2006, is what happened in Q1 2005. Then, $ (402,553) was the effect of being in Q1.

There are several ways to display a negative amount in currency. The default U.S. English method is to enclose the amount in parentheses, and because I'm a default kinda guy, I'm using that method. So $ (402,553) means a negative number of dollars.

Put another way, the company made $402,553 *less* than the average quarter in 2005. Relative to each quarter's average, Q1 was a bad quarter to be in, to the tune of $402,553. In terms of cell addresses:

```
$ (402,553) = B3 - E6
```

and in terms of the dollar values in those cells:

```
$ (402,553) = $548,160 - $950,713
```

so that's your seasonal effect, at least as of Q1 2006.

Also, you've smoothed an actual and an estimate to get a measure of the current level of the baseline:

- You used the smoothing constant of 0.1 on the difference between revenue for Q1 2006 and the seasonal effect. You take revenue to be the combined effect of the current level of the baseline and the seasonal effect.

  ```
  Revenue = Level + Season
  ```

  So the difference between the revenue and the seasonal effect is a measure of the level of the baseline:

  ```
  Revenue - Season = Level
  ```

- You used the damping factor of (1.0 – 0.1), or 0.9, on the estimate of the baseline level. As in Chapter 15, the damping factor is used on the prior period's estimate. In this case, that's the average of all four quarters in 2005: your best estimate of the level of the baseline at this point. You smooth those two — the actual and the estimate — together. In terms of cell addresses (and bear in mind that the smoothing constant is in cell I2):

  ```
  $964,034 = I2*(B7-F3)+(1-I2)*E6
  ```

  and in terms of the dollar values in those cells:

  ```
  $964,034 = 0.1 * ($681,375 - $ (402,553)) + 0.9 *
          $950,713
  ```

Finally, you total the smoothed estimate of the baseline level and the estimate of the seasonal effect, to get the forecast for Q2 2006. In terms of cell addresses:

```
$607,321 = E7 + F4
```

and in terms of the dollar values in those cells:

```
$607,321 = $964,034 + $(356,713)
```

Getting Farther into the Baseline

Chapter 15 is where this book first really digs into exponential smoothing. There you can find that the first forecast made by exponential smoothing is just the first value in the baseline. Nothing is available earlier than the first value on which to base a forecast, so exponential smoothing uses the first value instead.

Calculating the first forecast

If you prefer to look at the effect of there being no prior value here, instead of going to Chapter 15 for it, Figure 18-6 shows an example of what I'm talking about.

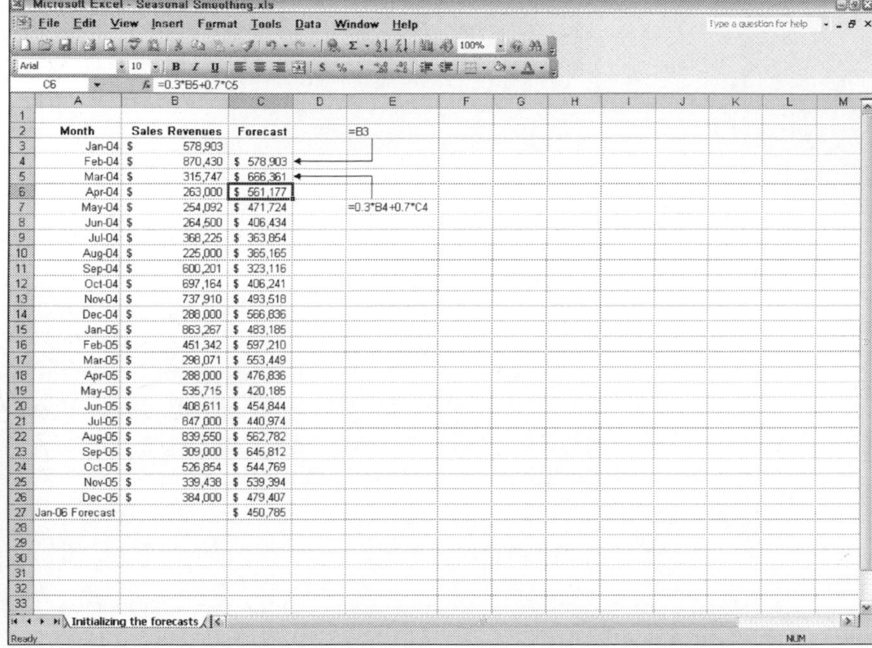

Month	Sales Revenues	Forecast
Jan-04	$ 578,903	
Feb-04	$ 870,430	$ 578,903
Mar-04	$ 315,747	$ 666,361
Apr-04	$ 263,000	$ 561,177
May-04	$ 254,092	$ 471,724
Jun-04	$ 264,500	$ 406,434
Jul-04	$ 368,225	$ 363,854
Aug-04	$ 225,000	$ 365,165
Sep-04	$ 600,201	$ 323,116
Oct-04	$ 697,164	$ 406,241
Nov-04	$ 737,910	$ 493,518
Dec-04	$ 288,000	$ 566,836
Jan-05	$ 863,267	$ 483,185
Feb-05	$ 451,342	$ 597,210
Mar-05	$ 298,071	$ 553,449
Apr-05	$ 288,000	$ 476,836
May-05	$ 535,715	$ 420,185
Jun-05	$ 408,611	$ 454,844
Jul-05	$ 847,000	$ 440,974
Aug-05	$ 839,550	$ 562,782
Sep-05	$ 309,000	$ 645,812
Oct-05	$ 526,854	$ 544,769
Nov-05	$ 339,438	$ 539,394
Dec-05	$ 384,000	$ 479,407
Jan-06 Forecast		$ 450,785

Figure 18-6: The first forecast in smoothing is usually the first value in the baseline.

Notice first cell C5 in Figure 18-6. It contains the classic formula for exponential smoothing:

```
=0.3*B4+0.7*C4
```

That is:

- The smoothing constant, 0.3 in this case, times the prior actual value in cell B4
- The damping factor (1.0 minus the smoothing constant) times the prior forecast in cell C4
- The sum of the two multiples

Suppose you copied and pasted that formula one cell higher in the worksheet — which would amount to starting to use the formula one month earlier, in February 2004 rather than March 2004. It would be:

```
=0.3*B3+0.7*C3
```

From the point of view of the worksheet structure, the problem is that there's no value in cell C3 to multiply by the damping factor. That is, this portion of the formula:

```
0.7*C3
```

is 0 because C3 is empty.

From the point of view of the logic of forecasting by way of exponential smoothing, the problem is that you've gone back too far in the baseline. Exponential smoothing needs a weighted average of a prior actual and a prior forecast. But as of the first time period in the baseline, no forecast is available: There is no value prior to the first time period on which to base a forecast.

So, the first forecast, found in cell C4 in Figure 18-6, is not a smoothed forecast. It takes the first value in the baseline to be the best estimate of the first forecast, and in this case its formula is:

```
=B3
```

This is called *initializing* the forecast.

A method called *backcasting* forecasts backward into the baseline's first time period, and — if the forecaster wants — even farther back. I don't get into it here, but at some later point you may want to know that the technique exists, or at least recognize the term.

What does all this have to do with *seasonal* smoothing? The problem at the start of the series is extended, because you have not just one but several forecasts to initialize. Those are the initial estimates of the seasons.

The preceding section mentions briefly how this is done, but I want to put it in the context of the worksheet and the formulas to give you a better feel for what's going on.

To initialize the forecasts for the level of the baseline and the seasons, you start by getting the average of the quarterly revenues for the earliest full year, in cell E6 of Figure 18-7. You use this value in two places:

- Later, when you start smoothing to get new estimates of the level of the baseline
- Now, when you initialize the seasonal effects based on the first year

Time Period	Revenue	Forecast	Error	Estimated Level Effect	Estimated Season Effect			Smoothing Constant (Level)	Smoothing Constant (Season)
Q4 2004	$ 1,602,492							0.1	0.3
Q1 2005	$ 548,160				$ (402,553)		=B3-$E$6		
Q2 2005	$ 594,000		=AVERAGE(B3:B6)		$ (356,713)		=B4-$E$6		
Q3 2005	$ 979,748				$ 29,035		=B5-$E$6		
Q4 2005	$ 1,680,943			$ 950,713	$ 730,230		=B6-$E$6		
					$0		=SUM(F3:F6)		

Figure 18-7: The seasonal effects show how the individual revenue figures vary around the *average* revenue figure.

To get your initial estimates of the seasonal effects, you calculate in cells F3:F6 the results of subtracting the average quarterly revenue for 2005 from the actual revenue during each quarter. No offense to the numbers, but these are called *deviations.*

Notice in cell F8 that the sum of these deviations is zero, and this is always true (and is easily proven). So each deviation isolates from the current level of the baseline the effect of its season above or below that level:

- The effect of Q1 on revenue is $ (402,553). The level of the baseline, $950,713 plus the seasonal effect of $ (402,553), is $548,160, the revenue for Q1 2005.
- The effect of Q2 on revenue is $ (356,713). The level of the baseline, $950,713 plus the seasonal effect of $ (356,713), is $594,000, the revenue for Q2 2005.
- The effect of Q3 on revenue is $29,035. The level of the baseline, $950,713 plus the seasonal effect of $29,035 is $979,748, the revenue for Q3 2005.
- The effect of Q4 on revenue is $730,230. The level of the baseline, $950,713 plus $730,230 is $1,680,943, the revenue for Q4 2005.

Because these four deviations sum to zero, adding them to the level of the baseline has no effect on that level for the full year — just for the revenue during each quarter.

I've started the calculations using Q1 through Q4 of 2005, even though Q4 2004 was available. I did this to keep the notions of seasons in a year straightforward: It's easier to think of a year as starting in Q1 than to think of it as starting in Q4. But the quarterly designations are just labels and have no effect on the forecasting process. Besides, your company might well have a fiscal year that begins on October 1. So there's no special technical reason to start the forecasting in Q1, and there can be good reasons to start it in some other quarter (or monthly period, or bimonthly period).

Smoothing through the baseline level

After the initial estimates are made, you're ready to start getting three actual forecasts:

- The smoothed forecast of the revenue itself
- The smoothed forecast of the level of the baseline
- The smoothed forecast of the level of the season

Figure 18-8 shows how the smoothed forecast of the baseline level is calculated.

By the way, to keep things from looking more cluttered than they already do in Figures 18-8 through 18-10, I haven't used dollar signs in the formulas. But I urge you to do so when you're referencing the smoothing constants, turning them into absolute references. That way you can copy and paste your formulas down the worksheet and find that, no matter how far down you go, they're still making reference to the correct cell addresses. You don't want to freeze the other addresses, because they *need* to adjust as you paste the formulas down the sheet.

In Figure 18-8, column G shows the contents of the formulas that are used in column E. Column G shows that the formulas follow the pattern you've established for smoothing. In cell E7 and as shown in G7, the formula uses:

- A smoothing constant, often called *alpha* and found in cell I2, times an actual value — the actual revenue for Q1 2006 less the actual seasonal effect of Q1 2005
- A damping factor times the prior estimate of the same variable — that is, 1.0 minus the smoothing factor, times the estimate of the baseline level as of Q4 2005

Microsoft Excel - Seasonal Smoothing.xls

E7 =I2*(B7-H3)+(1-I2)*E6

	Time Period	Revenue	Forecast	Error	Estimated Level Effect			Estimated Season Effect	Smoothing Constant (Level)	Smoothing Constant (Season)
2	Q4 2004	$ 1,602,492							0.1	0.3
3	Q1 2005	$ 548,160						$ (402,553)		
4	Q2 2005	$ 594,000						$ (356,713)		
5	Q3 2005	$ 979,749						$ 29,035		
6	Q4 2005	$ 1,680,943			$ 950,713	←	=AVERAGE(B3:B6)	$ 730,230		
7	Q1 2006	$ 681,375	$ 548,160	$ 133,214	$ 964,034	←	=I2*(B7-H3)+(1-I2)*E6	$ (366,585)		
8	Q2 2006	$ 350,858	$ 607,321	$ (256,464)	$ 938,388	←	=I2*(B8-H4)+(1-I2)*E7	$ (425,958)		
9	Q3 2006	$ 880,060	$ 967,424	$ (87,364)	$ 929,652	←	=I2*(B9-H5)+(1-I2)*E8	$ 5,447		
10	Q4 2006	$ 1,559,802	$ 1,659,882	$ (100,080)	$ 919,644	←	=I2*(B10-H6)+(1-I2)*E9	$ 703,209		
11	Q1 2007	$ 817,860	$ 553,059	$ 264,801	$ 946,124	←	=I2*(B11-H7)+(1-I2)*E10	$ (295,089)		
12	Q2 2007	$ 594,000	$ 520,165	$ 73,835	$ 953,507	←	=I2*(B12-H8)+(1-I2)*E11	$ (406,023)		
13	Q3 2007	$ 954,891	$ 958,954	$ (4,064)	$ 953,101	←	=I2*(B13-H9)+(1-I2)*E12	$ 4,350		
14	Q4 2007	$ 1,576,348	$ 1,656,310	$ (79,961)	$ 945,105	←	=I2*(B14-H10)+(1-I2)*E13	$ 681,619		
15	Q1 2008	$ 983,648	$ 650,016	$ 333,632	$ 978,468	←	=I2*(B15-H11)+(1-I2)*E14	$ (205,008)		
16	Q2 2008	$ 777,000	$ 572,445	$ 204,555	$ 998,923	←	=I2*(B16-H12)+(1-I2)*E15	$ (350,793)		
17	Q3 2008	$ 916,099	$ 1,003,273	$ (87,175)	$ 990,206	←	=I2*(B17-H13)+(1-I2)*E16	$ (19,187)		
18	Q4 2008	$ 1,518,261	$ 1,671,825	$ (153,564)	$ 974,850	←	=I2*(B18-H14)+(1-I2)*E17	$ 640,157		
19	Q1 2009	$ 969,912	$ 769,842	$ 200,070	$ 994,857	←	=I2*(B19-H15)+(1-I2)*E18	$ (150,989)		
20	Q2 2009	$ 700,000	$ 644,063	$ 55,937	$ 1,000,450	←	=I2*(B20-H16)+(1-I2)*E19	$ (335,690)		
21	Q3 2009	$ 892,102	$ 981,263	$ (89,161)	$ 991,534	←	=I2*(B21-H17)+(1-I2)*E20	$ (43,261)		

Leveling the baseline

Figure 18-8: Wait for a year's worth of actuals in the baseline before starting seasonal smoothing.

These two values are summed to get the smoothed forecast of the baseline level as of Q1 2006.

'Tis the seasonal component

Figure 18-9 shows how the smoothed forecast of the seasonal effect is calculated.

The same approach is used: the smoothing constant times an actual, plus the damping factor times the prior estimate. Starting in cell F7 and continuing down through F21, the same pattern is in place, differing only in the location of the prior actuals and the prior estimates. In cell F7, the formula uses:

- A smoothing constant, often called *delta* and found in cell J2, times an actual value — the actual revenue for Q1 2006 less the actual baseline level as of Q1 2005. Note that this leaves the seasonal effect based on actuals.
- A damping factor times the prior estimate of the same variable — that is, 1.0 minus the smoothing factor, times the estimate of the seasonal effect as of Q1 2005.

Again, these two values are summed to get the smoothed forecast of the seasonal effect of the first quarter, as of Q1 2006.

Microsoft Excel - Seasonal Smoothing.xls

F7 =J2*(B7-E7)+(1-J2)*F3

	A	B	C	D	E	F	G	H	I	J
1	Time Period	Revenue	Forecast	Error	Estimated Level Effect	Estimated Season Effect			Smoothing Constant (Level)	Smoothing Constant (Season)
2	Q4 2004	$ 1,602,492							0.1	0.3
3	Q1 2005	$ 548,160				$ (402,553)				
4	Q2 2005	$ 594,000		=AVERAGE(B3:B6)		$ (356,713)				
5	Q3 2005	$ 979,749				$ 29,035				
6	Q4 2005	$ 1,680,943			$ 950,713	$ 730,230				
7	Q1 2006	$ 681,375	$ 548,160	$ 133,214	$ 964,034	$ (366,585)		=J2*(B7-E7)+(1-J2)*F3		
8	Q2 2006	$ 350,858	$ 607,321	$ (256,464)	$ 938,388	$ (425,958)		=J2*(B8-E8)+(1-J2)*F4		
9	Q3 2006	$ 880,060	$ 967,424	$ (87,364)	$ 929,652	$ 5,447		=J2*(B9-E9)+(1-J2)*F5		
10	Q4 2006	$ 1,559,802	$ 1,659,882	$ (100,080)	$ 919,644	$ 703,209		=J2*(B10-E10)+(1-J2)*F6		
11	Q1 2007	$ 817,860	$ 553,059	$ 264,801	$ 946,124	$ (295,089)		=J2*(B11-E11)+(1-J2)*F7		
12	Q2 2007	$ 594,000	$ 520,165	$ 73,835	$ 953,507	$ (406,023)		=J2*(B12-E12)+(1-J2)*F8		
13	Q3 2007	$ 954,891	$ 958,954	$ (4,064)	$ 953,101	$ 4,350		=J2*(B13-E13)+(1-J2)*F9		
14	Q4 2007	$ 1,576,348	$ 1,656,310	$ (79,961)	$ 945,105	$ 681,619		=J2*(B14-E14)+(1-J2)*F10		
15	Q1 2008	$ 983,648	$ 650,016	$ 333,632	$ 978,468	$ (205,008)		=J2*(B15-E15)+(1-J2)*F11		
16	Q2 2008	$ 777,000	$ 572,445	$ 204,555	$ 998,923	$ (350,793)		=J2*(B16-E16)+(1-J2)*F12		
17	Q3 2008	$ 916,099	$ 1,003,273	$ (87,175)	$ 990,206	$ (19,187)		=J2*(B17-E17)+(1-J2)*F13		
18	Q4 2008	$ 1,518,261	$ 1,671,825	$ (153,564)	$ 974,850	$ 640,157		=J2*(B18-E18)+(1-J2)*F14		
19	Q1 2009	$ 969,912	$ 769,842	$ 200,070	$ 994,857	$ (150,989)		=J2*(B19-E19)+(1-J2)*F15		
20	Q2 2009	$ 700,000	$ 644,063	$ 55,937	$ 1,000,450	$ (335,690)		=J2*(B20-E20)+(1-J2)*F16		
21	Q3 2009	$ 892,102	$ 981,263	$ (89,161)	$ 991,534	$ (43,261)		=J2*(B21-E21)+(1-J2)*F17		

Smoothing the seasons

Figure 18-9: After the end of the first full year, you switch from deviations to smoothing for seasonal estimates.

You now have the two components that determine the seasonally smoothed forecasts: a smoothed baseline level and a smoothed seasonal effect. You can add them together to come up with the forecast for the subsequent time period. For example, the formula for the forecast for Q2 2006 is:

```
=E7+F4
```

Referring to Figure 18-9, you have two columns with static values: the label that identifies the time period in column A and the actual revenue for each time period in column B. These columns would have to be filled in manually (usually by copy-and-paste methods). They may also get their values from an external data range that points to another data source such as a database, or via a pivot table that summarizes to quarter, month, or some other time period.

The remaining columns in Figure 18-9, columns C through F, contain formulas. These formulas are special for rows 3 through 6, where you're calculating the seasonal effects directly in F3:F6 and the baseline level directly in E6.

The remaining rows, row 7 through row 21, contain formulas that you can copy and paste. (The one column that you haven't considered in detail is column D, which is simply the difference between the actual revenue and the forecast revenue. It's useful for calculating the overall error associated with the values you've chosen for the smoothing constants, alpha and delta.)

If you want to copy and paste the formulas, though, you'll want to replace the relative references to alpha and delta with absolute references.

A relative reference adjusts itself when you copy and paste it to another row or column. If =C2 is in cell D2 and you copy and paste that formula into E2, it becomes =D2. If you copy and paste it into D1, it becomes =C1. You make a relative reference absolute by putting dollar signs in it. The formula =$C$2 remains =$C$2 no matter what cell you copy it into.

So, still referring to Figure 18-9, to prepare to copy cell F7 you would want to change the formula from this:

```
=J2*(B7-E7)+(1-J2)*F3
```

to this:

```
=$J$2*(B7-E7)+(1-$J$2)*F3
```

In this way, you make sure that, when you paste the formula into F8:F21, all the new instances of the formula still refer to $J$2. For example, in cell F21 the formula would be:

```
=$J$2*(B21-E21)+(1-$J$2)*F17
```

Suppose that you're on a cross-country flight and the plane hits some chop just as you're trying to position the mouse pointer between the J and the 2 in the cell address J2. It's not easy, is it? It *is* easier to drag across J2 in the Formula Bar, and press the F4 key. This changes the relative reference J2 to the absolute reference $J$2. Continuing to press F4 cycles you through J$2, $J2, and then back to J2. This frees up one hand so you can press the call button for the flight attendant to ask for a drink — not that anyone will come.

Finishing the Forecast

When you get to the end of the baseline, a minor modification is needed to complete the forecasts. It's these forecasts, the ones that extend beyond the end of the baseline, that are the real focus of your work. After all, by now you have the actual revenue values for the periods that have already come and gone.

Modifying the formulas

Figure 18-10 illustrates what's going on at this point.

Microsoft Excel - Seasonal Smoothing.xls

C25 =$E$21+F21

	A	B	C	D	E	F	I	J
1	Time Period	Revenue	Forecast	Error	Estimated Level Effect	Estimated Season Effect	Smoothing Constant (Level)	Smoothing Constant (Season)
2	Q4 2004	$ 1,602,492					0.1	0.3
3	Q1 2005	$ 548,160				$ (402,553)		
4	Q2 2005	$ 594,000		=AVERAGE(B3:B6)		$ (356,713)		
5	Q3 2005	$ 979,749				$ 29,035		
6	Q4 2005	$ 1,680,943			$ 950,713	$ 730,230		
7	Q1 2006	$ 681,375	$ 548,160	$ 133,214	$ 964,034	$ (366,585)		
8	Q2 2006	$ 350,858	$ 607,321	$ (256,464)	$ 938,388	$ (425,958)		
9	Q3 2006	$ 880,060	$ 967,424	$ (87,364)	$ 929,652	$ 5,447		
10	Q4 2006	$ 1,559,802	$ 1,659,882	$ (100,080)	$ 919,644	$ 703,209		
11	Q1 2007	$ 817,860	$ 553,059	$ 264,801	$ 946,124	$ (295,089)		
12	Q2 2007	$ 594,000	$ 520,165	$ 73,835	$ 953,507	$ (406,023)		
13	Q3 2007	$ 954,891	$ 958,954	$ (4,064)	$ 953,101	$ 4,350		
14	Q4 2007	$ 1,576,348	$ 1,656,310	$ (79,961)	$ 945,105	$ 681,619		
15	Q1 2008	$ 983,648	$ 650,016	$ 333,632	$ 978,468	$ (205,008)		
16	Q2 2008	$ 777,000	$ 572,445	$ 204,555	$ 998,923	$ (350,793)		
17	Q3 2008	$ 916,099	$ 1,003,273	$ (87,175)	$ 990,206	$ (19,187)		
18	Q4 2008	$ 1,518,261	$ 1,671,825	$ (153,564)	$ 974,850	$ 640,157		
19	Q1 2009	$ 969,912	$ 769,842	$ 200,070	$ 994,857	$ (150,989)		
20	Q2 2009	$ 700,000	$ 644,063	$ 55,937	$ 1,000,450	$ (335,690)		
21	Q3 2009	$ 892,102	$ 981,263	$ (89,161)	$ 991,534	$ (43,261)		
22	Q4 2009		$ 1,631,691		=E21+F18			
23	Q1 2010		$ 840,545		=E21+F19			
24	Q2 2010		$ 655,844		=E21+F20			
25	Q3 2010		$ 948,273		=E21+F21			

Back to the future

Figure 18-10: Past the baseline, the estimates of baseline levels become a constant.

The forecasts that extend beyond the end of the baseline are in the range C22:C25. They're different from earlier forecasts in that they don't incorporate an estimate of the baseline's level from the prior period. The most recent level estimate is in cell E21, for Q3 2009.

And this continues to be your best estimate for any forecasts that extend past Q3 2009, when you got your most recent actual. So subsequent forecasts use it as the level estimate. You can see that in the forecasts for Q4 2009 through Q3 2010. Each of them uses the value in cell E21 for the level component of the forecast.

In contrast, you have estimates of the seasonal effects from Q4 2008 through Q3 2009. These are available to you for use in the forecasts from Q4 2009 through Q3 2010. And that's what the formulas in C22:C25 do: They make use of the most recent estimate of the level of the baseline, and add to it the current values of the seasonal effects.

Of course, as the next quarter's actuals become available, you can reestimate the current level of the baseline and update the forecast for Q4 2009, using the new information. You can also get a new season effect estimate for Q4 and extend the future forecasts into Q4 2010, which will occupy cell C26.

Using the worksheet

If you want to view the intermediate calculations that come into play — in particular, the calculation of the seasonal effects and the baseline level — you can plug a new baseline into the worksheets illustrated by Figures 18-8 through 18-10. You just need to remember to make a few adjustments:

- **If you're using a different time period in your baseline than quarters, you'll want to change the time period labels in column A.** That's not necessary for the actual forecasting, but it'll help keep you straight with which data goes where.
- **Your forecasts, the values in column C, will start no sooner than the first row after the first year's worth of actuals have completed.** In Figures 18-8 through 18-10, the forecasts actually start one quarter later than that, but — as I mention earlier — that's just to keep the discussion straightforward and avoid having forecast years straddle two calendar years. There's no other reason that you couldn't have started with Q4 2004. The forecasts would have been somewhat different, of course, because the initial values for the level and the seasons would have started earlier in the baseline.
- **You'll want to adjust the way you calculate the first estimate of the baseline level, shown in Figures 18-8 through 18-10 in cell E6.** There, the formula is the average of cells B3:B6. But if you were using monthly actuals in your baseline, it might be the average of cells B3:B14. And in that case, your forecasts and your errors would begin in cells C15 and D15 — all due to the fact that there are eight more months in a year than there are quarters.
- Be sure that your estimates of the level effect in column E, and the seasonal effects in column F, point back to the correct time period. For example, in Figure 18-10, the formulas in cells E7 and F7 make use of the value in cell F3. That's the most recent estimate of the effect of being in Q1, so it's the appropriate estimate to use for a forecast of the next Q1 revenue. If you're using months as your time period, your level and seasonal estimates for, say, January will need to point back to the preceding January's seasonal effect.

If you prefer, you can name the cells that contain the smoothing constants — it's convenient to name one of the cells Alpha and the other cell Delta. Names are by default absolute references, so you don't need to worry about putting dollar signs in your formulas, and they can look a little more self-documenting — for example:

```
=Delta*(B7-E7)+(1-Delta)*F3
```

Using the workbook

You can download an Excel workbook from www.dummies.com/go/excelsffd. It's named Seasonal Smoothing.xls and was mentioned in "Using the smoothing constants" earlier in this chapter. The workbook contains code that will do all the seasonal exponential smoothing calculations for you. It's much faster than the workbook approach, but it's also less informative if you really want to dig into what's happening. Its output includes this information:

- The baseline values
- The forecast values
- The values of alpha and delta that you used

All you need is a baseline. Then, with the add-in opened, choose Data➪Smooth to display the Seasonal Exponential Smoothing dialog box. Figure 18-11 shows how it might look.

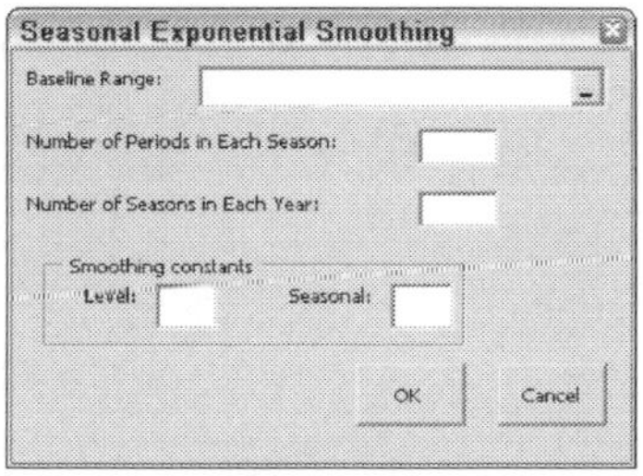

Seasonal Exponential Smoothing

Baseline Range:

Number of Periods in Each Season:

Number of Seasons in Each Year:

Smoothing constants

Level:

Seasonal:

OK

Cancel

Figure 18-11: If you use text as a list header, don't include it in the baseline range.

With the dialog box and your baseline showing, follow these steps:

1. **In the dialog box, click the reference edit box labeled Baseline Range, and drag through the cells containing your baseline.**

   In Figure 18-11, that would be B2:B21.

2. **In the Number of Periods in Each Season box, enter the appropriate number.**

   For example, if you're treating a quarter as a season and your baseline has one period for each quarter, you would enter the number 1. If you're treating a quarter as a season and your baseline has monthly data, you would enter the number 3.

3. **In the Number of Seasons in Each Year box, enter the appropriate number.**

   If you want to treat each quarter as a season, enter 4 in the box — regardless of whether your baseline range shows the data on a monthly basis or a quarterly basis.

4. **Put the values you want to use for alpha and delta in the appropriate boxes, and click OK.**

   The results are put in a new worksheet, inserted before the active worksheet (the one where you have the baseline). Figure 18-12 shows the results for the baseline in Figure 18-11, and assumes that the seasons are quarters and that each time period in the baseline represents one quarter.

Notice that the smoothing constants are shown in row 1. You can run the analysis repeatedly, for different values of alpha and delta. Then calculate the errors in the forecasts and put them through the same analysis discussed in Chapter 15. This will help you determine which combination of alpha and delta gives you the smallest amount of error in your forecasts.

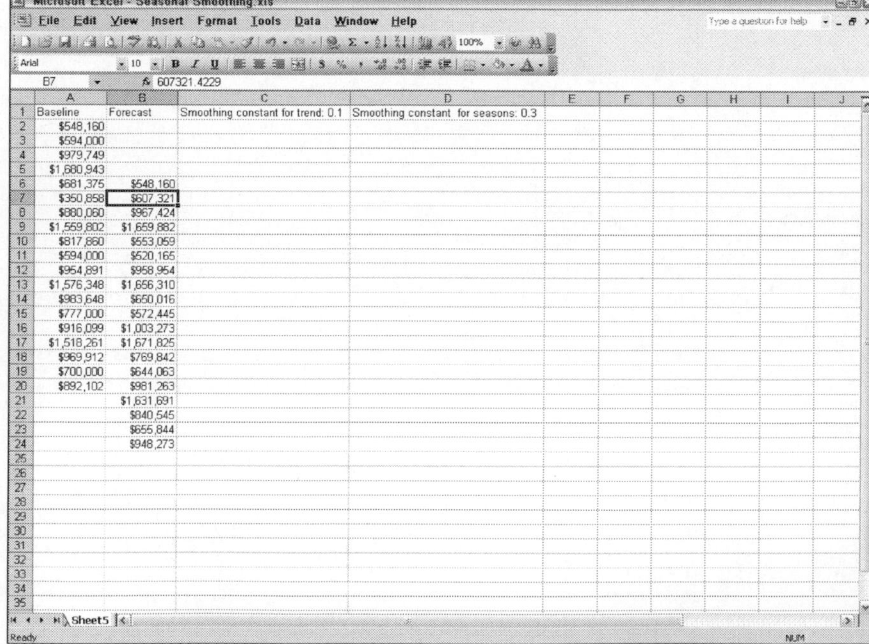

	A	B	C	D
1	Baseline	Forecast	Smoothing constant for trend: 0.1	Smoothing constant for seasons: 0.3
2	$548,160			
3	$594,000			
4	$979,749			
5	$1,680,943			
6	$681,375	$548,160		
7	$350,858	$607,321		
8	$880,060	$967,424		
9	$1,559,802	$1,659,882		
10	$817,860	$553,059		
11	$594,000	$520,165		
12	$954,891	$958,954		
13	$1,576,348	$1,656,310		
14	$983,648	$650,016		
15	$777,000	$572,445		
16	$916,099	$1,003,273		
17	$1,518,261	$1,671,825		
18	$969,912	$769,842		
19	$700,000	$644,063		
20	$892,102	$981,263		
21		$1,631,691		
22		$840,545		
23		$655,844		
24		$948,273		

Figure 18-12: Compare the forecasts from the add-in with the forecasts from the worksheet in Figure 18-10.

Part V
The Part of Tens

In this part . . .

This Part of Tens doesn't focus specifically on sales forecasting. It does hit on some problems, traps, tips, and tricks that you'll find helpful in setting up your forecasts. I take this chance to tell you about some very helpful tools that you may not have explored before. I also gripe about some problems in Excel that I think you're going to want to dodge when you use pivot tables to set up your forecasts.

Chapter 19

Ten Pivot Table Troubles — and How to Overcome Them

In This Chapter

- Selecting parts of a pivot table
- Working with fields
- Performing special calculations
- Managing the data cache

This book has a fair amount to say about Excel's pivot tables — with good reason. Pivot tables are a great way to pull baseline data into an Excel workbook and summarize the baseline by whatever time period you want.

But they're not perfect. Most of their warts have to do with how you define the pivot table in the first place, how you select parts of the table, working with fields, performing special calculations, and managing what's called the *cache*. You don't need to memorize how to deal with these problems. Just keep in mind that there are ways to do so and that I cover them here — and keep this book close to your computer.

Importing External Data

Your sales data may very likely be stored in a database, and you may want to pull that sales data into Excel to prepare your forecasts and other analyses. If you're going to do that efficiently, you really need to use Microsoft Query.

Microsoft Query is an application that comes with Microsoft Office. Query helps you find the data source, such as a database, and choose the data that you want to get into your pivot table. Better yet, after you've set up your pivot table, you don't need to do it again — Excel remembers where the data source is and which data it should get. So all you need to do is refresh the pivot table (and that's just a matter of clicking one button).

But you need to make sure you have Microsoft Query installed. Since Office 2000, it's been located in the Office Tools category on your installation disk.

Saving the Password

I like to store my data in a database and let Excel analyze it. This approach makes the best of both applications — a database to store and retrieve, and Excel to do the number crunching.

Microsoft Access isn't the best database management system, but it is convenient because it comes along with Excel in the Office suite.

If you're going to store sales data in Access, protecting the database with a password often makes sense. And it also makes sense to save the password in the Excel workbook that relies on the Access database for its data.

After you create a pivot table that uses an external data source, right-click in any of the pivot table's cells, choose Options, and select the Save Password check box. The password is saved in a hidden name in the workbook and can't be viewed as it would be in a DSN file.

DSN stands for Data Source Name. A DSN file contains information about the data source — its filename (such as the name of a database), its location, and other information, including a password if one is needed. But it's a text file, which means that anyone can open it with a utility as simple as Notepad. So a DSN file isn't secure enough to store a password to a file with confidential information. You're much better off storing the password with the pivot table because it's *much* harder to get to. I may as well admit that I've tried and failed.

Protecting an Access database with a password isn't the best protection you can give it. I do a lot of work with databases that contain information like social security numbers and physicians' Drug Enforcement Administration numbers — sensitive stuff. If you work with sensitive information, and if you're storing data in Microsoft Access, have a look at User-Level Security. *User-Level Security* is a series of steps you take to make an Access database very difficult to break into. If you set it up right, Access security is much stronger than is generally thought. For more information see "Frequently Asked Questions about Microsoft Access Security for Microsoft Access," by Mary Chipman and Andy Baron et al, in Microsoft's Knowledge Base at `http://support.microsoft.com`.

Refreshing the Data when the File Opens

Refreshing the data in a workbook is a constant headache. If you've built a workbook for someone else, calling for its pivot table — or, more likely, tables — to automatically update when that someone else opens it is considerate: You're likely to know a lot more about pivot tables than the other person is (especially after reading this book!), so you want to call for an automatic update.

You set a pivot table to update automatically by right-clicking any cell in the pivot table, choosing Table Options, and selecting the Refresh On Open check box. Be sure to save the workbook. Now, when someone opens the workbook, the pivot table will check its data source and update the results if the data has changed. This normally happens when the pivot table is based directly on an external data source, like a database, but it can happen in other circumstances as well.

The problem comes in when you have a huge database, or a really slow network connection (often due to a router that's been set up badly), or a whole bunch of pivot tables in the workbook. It can take what feels like forever for the data to refresh.

Because refreshing can be time consuming, I like to give my users a choice. In those circumstances, I don't set the pivot tables to Refresh On Open. I use the VBA code in this section. It asks the user if he wants to update the data. If — and only if — he clicks the Yes button, the pivot tables get refreshed. The point is that the user chooses whether he has time to wait for the refreshes to finish. Here's how to give your users that choice:

1. **Choose Tools ➪ Macro ➪ Visual Basic Editor.**
2. **In the Project Explorer, right-click This Workbook and choose View Code.**
3. **In the left drop-down list, choose Workbook.**
4. **In the right drop-down list, choose Open.**

   This causes the code to run when the workbook opens, unless the user bypasses it.

5. **Enter the following code in the blank module:**

```
Option Base 1
Option Explicit

Private Sub Workbook_Open()
Dim Wks As Worksheet, pt As PivotTable, i As Integer
Dim CheckWithUser As Variant, Msg As String

Msg = "Do you want to refresh the pivot tables?"

CheckWithUser = MsgBox(Msg, vbYesNoCancel)
```

```
If CheckWithUser = vbYes Then
    Application.DisplayAlerts = False
    For Each Wks In ThisWorkbook.Worksheets
         Wks.Activate
         For i = 1 To Wks.PivotTables.Count
               Wks.PivotTables(i).RefreshTable
         Next i
    Next Wks
    Application.DisplayAlerts = True
End If

End Sub
```

In plain English, this code first asks the user if she wants to refresh the pivot tables, by means of a message box. If the user clicks the Yes button, then the code goes through every worksheet in the workbook, and every pivot table on every sheet, and refreshes it. You use `Application.DisplayAlerts` to keep the user from having to respond to every alert that a pivot table has changed due to a refresh.

Bear in mind that this code is designed to stand in for a setting that causes pivot tables to refresh themselves automatically.

The code may have nothing to do with refreshing the pivot tables, but instead with the *results* of refreshing the tables. Keep in mind that code that runs when the workbook opens takes effect *before* any automatic refreshes either of pivot tables or external data ranges. I once cost myself $1,000 because I didn't know that and had to spend hours fixing things for free. The code assumed that the refreshes had already taken place, but I discovered, to my chagrin, that they hadn't.

Drilling to Details

A major reason to use pivot tables is to summarize data — to get sums, averages, and so on. But if you base your pivot table on an external data source and you want to see the underlying data, doing so can be a little clumsy.

The way to see the underlying data when you're relying on an external data source is to double-click the pivot table cell that you're interested in. Excel adds a new worksheet to the workbook and shows the individual records that are summarized in the cell you clicked.

To make sure this works, you need to have the Enable Drill to Details check box selected, in the Table Options dialog box, but that's the default. To make sure it's selected, right-click any cell in the pivot table and select Table Options from the shortcut menu.

Formatting Fields

Even when you base a pivot table on a formatted Excel list, the pivot table doesn't automatically show those formats. So if your list shows revenue numbers and they're formatted as Currency, when you build a pivot table by using that list, the numbers just get a General format. But you can fix this formatting issue easily:

1. **Right-click any one of those unformatted numbers.**
2. **Choose Field Settings from the shortcut menu.**
3. **Click the Number button.**
4. **Select the format you want.**
5. **Click OK, and then click OK again to get back to the worksheet.**

Pivot Tables: Things That Go Bump in the Day

Stick two pivot tables onto one worksheet. Put one higher up than the other. Say, one starts in A1 and has five rows and the other starts in A6. Now you refresh their data and, as a result, the first pivot table gets another row — maybe another month has passed, so its results show up in the pivot table.

Excel is going to scold you. Pivot tables aren't allowed to overlap one another, and that added row in the first table is going to bump into the first row of the second table.

Someone at Microsoft should look into automatically inserting a new row between the two tables so as to keep them apart. If you can invent something as elegant as pivot tables, you can figure out how to maintain their separation when they get bigger. This is particularly aggravating when you want the tables to refresh themselves automatically, such as when you open the workbook. You shouldn't have to pay so much attention to managing their locations. Of course, the same problem can occur when you put the tables side by side, if they have column fields.

This may not seem like such a problem — you can probably find a way to separate the tables so that they're unlikely to bang into each other when they refresh. But what if you have to print them? That can lead to a very awkward report layout. My best advice is to write VBA code that will copy the pivot tables and paste them into a blank worksheet so that they'll have just enough separation, and print that worksheet.

If you do use VBA code to reposition the pivot tables, you'll find this VBA command useful:

```
ActiveSheet.Cells.SpecialCells(xlCellTypeLastCell).Select
```

You can use it each time you paste a pivot table, to find where the worksheet's last cell is now — that is, the cell that occupies its rightmost column and bottommost row. Knowing that helps your code decide where to paste the *next* pivot table.

Naming Fields

Excel names a field in a pivot table, by default, using the type of data summary you've chosen — for example, "Sum Of Revenues" or "Average of Units Sold." Some users don't want to see labels like "Sum" or "Average" because they know what they've asked for, or because it's obvious from the numbers themselves.

If you right-click in the pivot table's data area, you'll get a menu with an item called Field Settings. Click that item and the PivotTable Field dialog box, shown in Figure 19-1, appears.

Suppose that your pivot table's data source — whether it's part of the workbook or coming in from a database — has a field named Revenues, and that you're pulling it into the pivot table. If you now try to use the PivotTable Field dialog box to rename the field as Revenues, Excel stumps you. It already has a field named Revenues, which it got from the data source, and it won't let you rename Sum Of Revenues to Revenues because it already has a Revenues field.

I like to rename Sum Of Revenues to Revenues with a blank space after the last letter (after the *s*). This makes it a different and unique name, Excel doesn't worry about it, and my pivot table looks better.

Figure 19-1: Use the PivotTable Field dialog box to control how the field appears on your worksheet.

Calculating Fields

Pivot tables give you a way of calculating fields that aren't part of the data source. Maybe your data source has monthly revenues and the number of salespeople on staff each month. If you're looking to forecast the average revenues per salesperson, you can get the pivot table to calculate that for you. The result is called a *calculated field*, and here's how to set it up:

1. **Create a pivot table.**

   In this example, you might create one that shows the sum of revenues and sum of salespeople.

2. **Select one of the pivot table's cells.**
3. **Choose View⇨Toolbars and click Pivot Table.**
4. **On the Pivot Table toolbar, choose Pivot Table⇨Formulas⇨Calculated Field.**
5. **Give the field a name — or don't — in the Name box.**

   In this example, that might be Revenues per Salesperson.

6. **Leave the equal sign alone in the Formula box.**
7. **Click the name of a field in the Fields box, click Add, and complete the formula — something like this:**

   ```
   =Revenues / Salespeople
   ```

8. **Click OK.**

Now you have a brand-new field in the data area.

Be careful how you arrange your calculation. It can depend on the order in which you do the calculations. For example, if you're after average revenue, you need to distinguish between this approach:

Average = Sum of Revenues ÷ Sum of Salespeople

which is the approach taken by a pivot table's calculated field, and this approach:

Average = Average (Revenues ÷ Salespeople)

which is one way that you might do it on the worksheet. The two approaches give the same result only if the same number of salespeople was involved in each sale.

Calculating Items

In a pivot table, a *field* is a variable such as the sum of revenues, or the names of your salespeople, or the dates when sales were made. An *item* is a particular value of a field, and it usually refers to values of row, column, or page fields. An item may be the name of a salesperson, or a particular month, or a particular product.

Again, getting those items directly from your data source, whether it's in a workbook list or a database, is usually cleaner. But you can also do it in the pivot table if that's more convenient for you.

There's a problem here, though, that you're likely to incur if you're doing sales forecasting. If you're using a pivot table to create a forecast baseline, you're probably grouping on a date field, to get all January sales together, all February sales together, and so on. And when you have a grouped field, you can't create a calculated item. Calculated field, yes, but not a calculated item.

So, if you've grouped on a pivot table field such as revenue date, start by ungrouping the field. If you haven't, you have no worries.

There are plenty of situations in which you want to forecast the next time period on the basis of the prior periods. This book's chapters on exponential smoothing and moving averages talk about that. Suppose you have sales data on January through March and you want to forecast April by averaging the first three months. (That's too short a baseline for a decent forecast, of course, but this is just to illustrate the approach.) With your pivot table in place, take these steps:

1. **Select a cell in a row or column field in the pivot table.**
2. **Click the Pivot Table drop-down list on the pivot table toolbar, and choose Formulas ➪ Calculated Item.**
3. **If you want, change the name of the calculated item to something such as April Forecast.**
4. **In the Formula box, enter this:**

```
=(January + February + March) / 3
```

5. **Click OK.**

Now you have a new, and calculated, item in your date field: a forecast for April, based on the first three months of the year. Again, bad idea to base a forecast on just three months, but I think you get the basic idea.

Subtotaling Inner Fields

An *inner field* is similar to any row or column field in a pivot table. The main difference between an inner field and an outer field is that the inner field's items get repeated for each value of the outer field. The inner field is *nested within* the outer field. For example, in Figure 19-2, Year is an outer row field and Product is an inner row field.

When you have inner fields, you don't automatically get subtotals for them. Notice in Figure 19-2 that you get a subtotal by Year, but not by Product, in the pivot table that starts in column A. But in the pivot table that starts in column G, you can see subtotals for the two product lines at the bottom of the table. These subtotals are called *block totals.*

To get block totals, do this:

1. **Right-click a cell in the Product column (more generally, the inner field).**
2. **Choose Field Settings from the shortcut menu.**
3. **Under Subtotals, click Custom.**

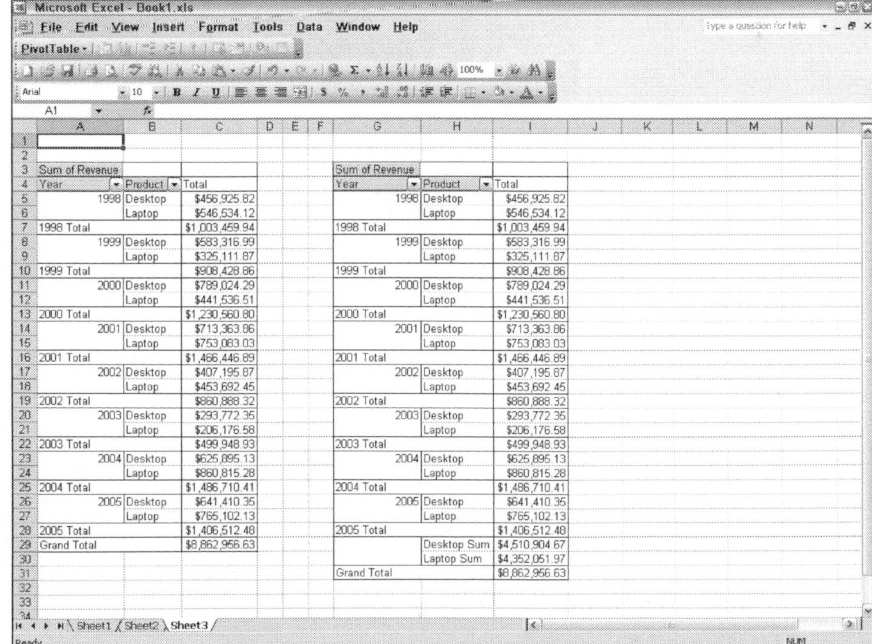

Sum of Revenue		
Year	Product	Total
1998	Desktop	$456,925.82
	Laptop	$546,534.12
1998 Total		$1,003,459.94
1999	Desktop	$583,316.99
	Laptop	$325,111.87
1999 Total		$908,428.86
2000	Desktop	$789,024.29
	Laptop	$441,536.51
2000 Total		$1,230,560.80
2001	Desktop	$713,363.86
	Laptop	$753,083.03
2001 Total		$1,466,446.89
2002	Desktop	$407,195.87
	Laptop	$453,692.45
2002 Total		$860,888.32
2003	Desktop	$293,772.35
	Laptop	$206,176.58
2003 Total		$499,948.93
2004	Desktop	$625,895.13
	Laptop	$860,815.28
2004 Total		$1,486,710.41
2005	Desktop	$641,410.35
	Laptop	$765,102.13
2005 Total		$1,406,512.48
Grand Total		$8,862,956.63

Sum of Revenue		
Year	Product	Total
1998	Desktop	$456,925.82
	Laptop	$546,534.12
1998 Total		$1,003,459.94
1999	Desktop	$583,316.99
	Laptop	$325,111.87
1999 Total		$908,428.86
2000	Desktop	$789,024.29
	Laptop	$441,536.51
2000 Total		$1,230,560.80
2001	Desktop	$713,363.86
	Laptop	$753,083.03
2001 Total		$1,466,446.89
2002	Desktop	$407,195.87
	Laptop	$453,692.45
2002 Total		$860,888.32
2003	Desktop	$293,772.35
	Laptop	$206,176.58
2003 Total		$499,948.93
2004	Desktop	$625,895.13
	Laptop	$860,815.28
2004 Total		$1,486,710.41
2005	Desktop	$641,410.35
	Laptop	$765,102.13
2005 Total		$1,406,512.48
	Desktop Sum	$4,510,904.67
	Laptop Sum	$4,352,051.97
Grand Total		$8,862,956.63

Figure 19-2: Outer fields get subtotals automatically. On the PivotTable toolbar, use PivotTable➪Field Settings to manage the subtotals.

4. **Choose the type of subtotal you want (Sum, Count, Average, and so on) and click OK.**

   Now you'll have block subtotals at the bottom of the table for your inner field.

Managing the Data Cache

One reason that pivot tables are so effective has to do with the *cache.* The cache saves the underlying data, whether it's in an Excel list or in an external data source, in a way that lets the pivot table recalculate in a flash.

When you right-click a cell in a pivot table, one of your choices is Table Options. In the Table Options dialog box, you'll see the Save Data with Table Layout check box.

Back when data storage on drives was at a premium, clearing this check box sometimes made sense — it saved space. When you needed to, you could refresh the pivot table from its original data source, without having to resave the data in a cache.

Today, with drives that are bigger than Montana, clearing the Save Data with Table Layout check box doesn't make sense. Save the data in the pivot table's cache. It'll save you time. It won't save you space, but then you're not fenced in anymore.

Chapter 20

The Ten Best Excel Tools

In This Chapter

- Getting the most out of Excel
- Customizing Excel to make it work for you

If you're like most people, you probably don't get the most out of Excel, because you don't know what it has to offer. I've used Excel for years, but I didn't know about some of the tools in this chapter until I read about them in online forums. Cell Comments, AutoComplete, toolbar customization — these will all save you time and maybe even grief.

Cell Comments

When you use Cell Comments, you can make notes about the contents of a worksheet cell. You can document where the information came from, how confident you are of its accuracy, whether it might need revision and when. All this information can be important in building a baseline for a forecast.

If several people are entering data and formulas in a workbook, Cell Comments are really helpful. You don't have to see them unless you want to, but when you want to see them, they can provide great backup.

To enter a Cell Comment, follow these steps:

1. **Select the cell where you want to make a comment.**
2. **Either right-click the cell and choose Insert Comment, or choose Insert ⇨ Comment.**

3. **Type anything that will help explain what's in that cell and click another cell in your worksheet to close the comment.**

   Now the cell will have a small triangle in its upper-right corner, signifying that a comment is there.

To read a comment, you can just put your pointer over the cell with the comment in it, and the comment pops up for you to read. Or you can right-click on the cell and select Show/Hide Comments.

You can deal with comments in a variety of ways. Start by choosing Tools➪Options and clicking the View tab. In the Comments section, you have three options:

- **None:** Click the None radio button if for some reason you don't want to see that any cell has a comment.
- **Comment Indicator Only:** Click the Comment Indicator Only radio button if all you want to know is whether a cell has a comment in it — but you don't want to actually see the comment itself (if you choose this option, you'll see the little triangle in the upper-right corner).
- **Comment & Indicator:** Click the Comment & Indicator radio button if you want the comments themselves to always be visible (Figure 20-1 shows an example of this option in action).

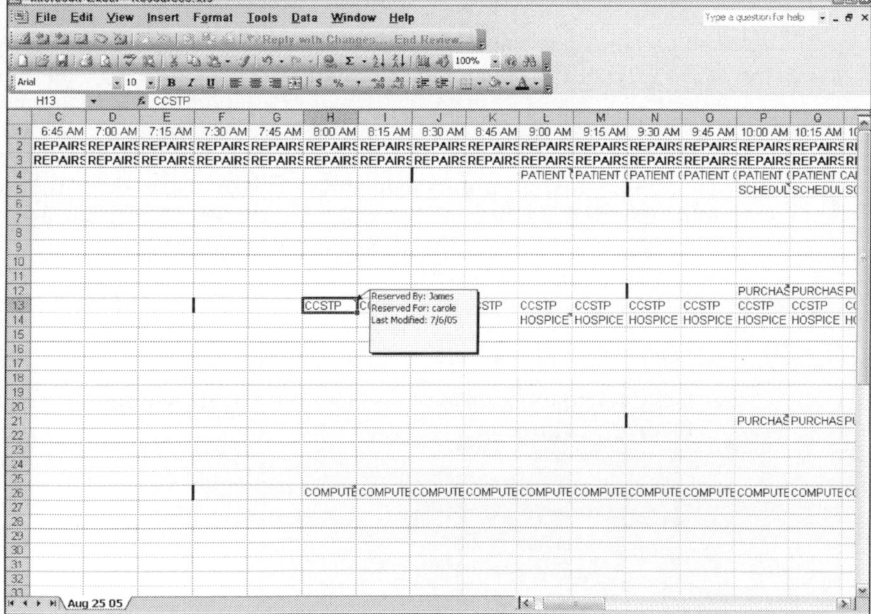

Figure 20-1: Using Cell Comments can help you document where and when the data came from.

AutoComplete

I keep my company's income statement in an Excel workbook. The deposits and the payments are associated with just a few clients and vendors — for example, my main sources of revenue, my bank, my broker, my office building, my accountant.

Being able to type just **My** in the cell where I show the payee, and having Excel complete the rest of the name is really handy. AutoComplete saves time and helps keep me from mistyping. Suppose the person you lease an office from is named Latimer, and your broker's name is Larry.

In column C, let's say you already have a cell that contains Latimer (but no cell that contains another value beginning with *L*). Now, if you type **L** in column C (the case doesn't matter), Excel offers to finish it off with "atimer". All you have to do now is press Enter. If you don't want to type Latimer (for example, and you do want to type Larry), you just keep typing what you want.

If column C already has a Latimer *and* a Larry, and you type **La** in a cell in column C, Excel waits — it doesn't know yet whether you mean Latimer or Larry. As soon as you type another letter — in this case, *t* or *r* — that distinguishes the two existing entries, Excel finishes the entry for you.

AutoComplete works only with entries in the same column, not the same row.

Macro Security

Microsoft had a shock a few years ago when it turned out that someone with too much time on his hands could write VBA code that would make Excel (or any Office application, for that matter) go nuts. This little monster is called a *macro virus.* The first one that showed up displayed a message box that said "I think this makes my point."

I confess that I've written one or two macro viruses, but I swear I've never distributed them. They can be nasty, and you want to protect yourself.

Excel now has four levels of virus protection, and you can choose the one you want to use.

If you never share Excel workbooks with anyone else (that means co-workers, clients, your Uncle Joe), you can save some time this way:

1. **Choose Tools ⇨ Options.**
2. **Select the Security tab, and then click the Macro Security button.**

3. **Choose the Low option and click OK.**

   Note: Microsoft doesn't recommend this option because, if you ever do get a workbook from somewhere else, you could be in trouble: If the workbook has a macro virus, you won't be warned.

If you *do* share workbooks with other people, or open workbooks that other people have created, you can arrange to be warned that a workbook has potentially hazardous macros by choosing the Medium option on the Security tab. When you've chosen the Medium security setting, Excel warns you that the workbook you're opening has macros in it, and you can decide to open the workbook (which enables the macros), not to open it, or to open it but to disable the macros.

Opening the workbook but disabling the macros is a good option if you think you know where your workbooks come from, but you're not certain of the good intentions of the source.

If you want even more security, you can choose the High option on the Security tab. If the file doesn't contain a digital signature, Excel will open it but will not run any macros that it contains. If the file does contain a digital signature, things get complicated and what happens depends on the source of the file.

If you're really concerned, choose Very High on the Security tab. That way, Excel won't run a workbook's macros unless the developer is on your trusted list — whether or not it's signed.

The Customizable Toolbar

Lots of experienced Excel users think, understandably, that the toolbars are inflexible. But they're not. You can take any button off a toolbar, and you can put any button on a toolbar.

For years, I wasted time by not customizing my toolbars. For example, I frequently searched for a particular value in a worksheet. I used to choose Edit ➪ Find and type in the value I was looking for. If you do that, you want to put the Binoculars button on your main toolbar, as I've done on mine. Here's how:

1. **Choose View ➪ Toolbars ➪ Customize.**
2. **Select the Commands tab.**
3. **In the Categories box, select Edit.**
4. **Scroll down in the Commands box until you see the Find command.**

5. **Click the Find command and, while holding down the mouse, drag it onto the toolbar where you want it to appear, and then release the mouse button.**

   You've now installed the Find button on the toolbar.

If there's another task that you do frequently, put its button on the toolbar following the same steps.

Evaluate Formula

I admit I've never been a big fan of Excel's formula auditing. In some instances, being able to choose Tools ➪ Formula Auditing ➪ Trace Precedents to see which cells a formula refers to is helpful. For example, if cell C8 has the following formula

```
=A1 + Q37
```

the Trace Precedents command can help a bit if you need to find the values that are involved.

But I haven't found much use for it. The more recent Evaluate Formula command, though, is a different story. I love it.

Start by selecting a cell with a formula. Then choose Tools ➪ Formula Auditing ➪ Evaluate Formula, and you can see step by step how Excel evaluates that formula. This is a wonderful way to help figure out how you've gone wrong in entering a formula. And believe me: It's happened to me a lot.

Worksheet Protection

These days, almost everyone has workbooks that other people use. Whether the workbooks are shared by others (I don't recommend this) or they're just available to others through shared folders, your colleagues probably have access to your work. And that means you need to look after your work.

Excel makes protecting your work pretty easy. With your workbook open, choose Tools ➪ Protection ➪ Protect Sheet. The Protect Sheet dialog box appears, giving you various options for what to protect.

Make sure to select the Protect Worksheet and Contents of Locked Cells check box. Provide a password in the Password to Unprotect Sheet box. If you do this, you're better protected against other users changing your values and formulas.

Worksheet protection isn't completely secure. You can buy a *password cracker* — software that figures out your password — and if *you* can buy it, that means other people can buy it, too. Free VBA code is floating around the Web that will do the same thing. But unless you need to protect your work from someone who's both knowledgeable and really determined, Excel's protection is probably sufficient.

Unique Records Only

Excel has a way to show you individual unique values that are in a list. This feature can be helpful when you have repeated values in that list, and you want to view the specific unique values. For example, if you have a list of dates when sales were recorded, those dates are probably repeated.

To get a list of unique individual dates, follow these steps:

1. **Select the cells in your list, or, if no data is adjacent to the list, just select any cell in your list.**
2. **Choose Data ➪ Filter ➪ Advanced Filter.**

   The Advanced Filter dialog box appears.
3. **Select the Unique Records Only check box.**
4. **Click OK.**

I like to use the Copy to Another Location option so my original list is left as is — but be careful if you do so. Suppose you choose to copy to another location, and you specify, say, cell F1. If there's data in column F, it can be overwritten by the new filtered list — and you can't undo it.

List Management

Excel 2003 has more tools for list management than earlier versions. After you've created a list, click any cell in the list and choose Data➪List to get to a new menu with various items that help you manage your list. When you use the Create List menu item, for example, Excel automatically puts a border around your list and adds a cell at the bottom of the list, with an asterisk, where you can add new values to the list.

Among other things, the list management options make it easy to:

- Resize your list when you add or remove cells
- Add a row at the bottom that shows any of several summaries, like a count, an average, or a sum of the values in the list

- Filter your list — you automatically get an AutoFilter in the top cell of the list

Quick Data Summaries

If you don't like typing formulas — and who does? — you can quickly get data summaries on the Status Bar. These summaries just show you the result — they don't save anything. Suppose you want to know the smallest number (or the largest number, or the average, or the sum, and so on) in a list. Just follow these steps:

1. **Choose the View menu and make sure that the Status Bar is enabled.**
2. **Right-click the Status Bar — you'll find it at the bottom of the Excel window — to get a shortcut menu.**
3. **Choose None (to display no summary value) or Average, Count, Count Nums, Max, Min, or Sum.**

   Now, when you select a range of cells on the worksheet, the Status Bar will display the summary value that you chose.

Help with Functions

Ever had trouble remembering what information you need to provide to an Excel function? For some functions, like SUM and AVERAGE, no problem: You just enter the name of the function, and then an open parenthesis, drag through the cells involved, and enter a close parenthesis.

But for more-complicated functions such as PMT (which shows you the amount of a recurring payment for a given loan amount, interest rate, and number of payments) or HYPERLINK (which you use to put a hyperlink into a worksheet), remembering what the inputs are and what order to enter them can be difficult. The order in which you enter the inputs is important because, for example, Excel will interpret this:

```
=PMT(360,.005,100000)
```

as meaning that the interest rate is 360 percent and that you're going to make only 0.005 payments. Instead, you need to enter something like this:

```
=PMT(.005,360,100000)
```

which means that the interest rate is one half of 1 percent per payment period, and you're going to make 360 payments.

The Insert Function tool can be helpful for these more-complex functions. To the left of the Formula Bar, you'll see the Insert Function button (labeled f_x). Click the Insert Function button to get to the Insert Function Wizard, which lets you first select the function you want to use, and then guides you through entering the inputs you want to use — in the correct order.

Index

• Symbols and Numerics •

• A •

• B •

• C •

• D •

• E •

• J •

• L •

• M •

• Q •

• R •

• S •

• T •

• U •

• V •

• W •

• X •

• Y •

• Z •

BUSINESS, CAREERS & PERSONAL FINANCE

Grant Writing
FOR
DUMMIES
A Reference for the Rest of Us!

0-7645-5307-0 0-7645-5331-3 *†

Also available:

- Accounting For Dummies † 0-7645-5314-3
- Business Plans Kit For Dummies † 0-7645-5365-8
- Cover Letters For Dummies 0-7645-5224-4
- Frugal Living For Dummies 0-7645-5403-4
- Leadership For Dummies 0-7645-5176-0
- Managing For Dummies 0-7645-1771-6
- Marketing For Dummies 0-7645-5600-2
- Personal Finance For Dummies * 0-7645-2590-5
- Project Management For Dummies 0-7645-5283-X
- Resumes For Dummies † 0-7645-5471-9
- Selling For Dummies 0-7645-5363-1
- Small Business Kit For Dummies *† 0-7645-5093-4

HOME & BUSINESS COMPUTER BASICS

Windows XP
FOR
DUMMIES
A Reference for the Rest of Us!

0-7645-4074-2

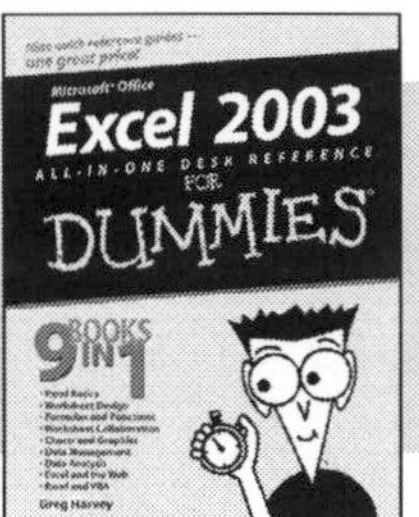

Excel 2003
ALL-IN-ONE DESK REFERENCE
FOR
DUMMIES
9 BOOKS IN 1

0-7645-3758-X

Also available:

- ACT! 6 For Dummies 0-7645-2645-6
- iLife '04 All-in-One Desk Reference For Dummies 0-7645-7347-0
- iPAQ For Dummies 0-7645-6769-1
- Mac OS X Panther Timesaving Techniques For Dummies 0-7645-5812-9
- Macs For Dummies 0-7645-5656-8
- Microsoft Money 2004 For Dummies 0-7645-4195-1
- Office 2003 All-in-One Desk Reference For Dummies 0-7645-3883-7
- Outlook 2003 For Dummies 0-7645-3759-8
- PCs For Dummies 0-7645-4074-2
- TiVo For Dummies 0-7645-6923-6
- Upgrading and Fixing PCs For Dummies 0-7645-1665-5
- Windows XP Timesaving Techniques For Dummies 0-7645-3748-2

FOOD, HOME, GARDEN, HOBBIES, MUSIC & PETS

Feng Shui
FOR
DUMMIES
A Reference for the Rest of Us!

0-7645-5295-3

0-7645-5232-5

Also available:

- Bass Guitar For Dummies 0-7645-2487-9
- Diabetes Cookbook For Dummies 0-7645-5230-9
- Gardening For Dummies * 0-7645-5130-2
- Guitar For Dummies 0-7645-5106-X
- Holiday Decorating For Dummies 0-7645-2570-0
- Home Improvement All-in-One For Dummies 0-7645-5680-0
- Knitting For Dummies 0-7645-5395-X
- Piano For Dummies 0-7645-5105-1
- Puppies For Dummies 0-7645-5255-4
- Scrapbooking For Dummies 0-7645-7208-3
- Senior Dogs For Dummies 0-7645-5818-8
- Singing For Dummies 0-7645-2475-5
- 30-Minute Meals For Dummies 0-7645-2589-1

INTERNET & DIGITAL MEDIA

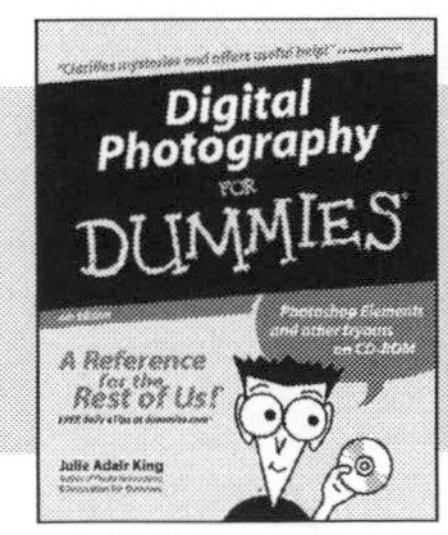

0-7645-1664-7

0-7645-6924-4

Also available:

- 2005 Online Shopping Directory For Dummies 0-7645-7495-7
- CD & DVD Recording For Dummies 0-7645-5956-7
- eBay For Dummies 0-7645-5654-1
- Fighting Spam For Dummies 0-7645-5965-6
- Genealogy Online For Dummies 0-7645-5964-8
- Google For Dummies 0-7645-4420-9
- Home Recording For Musicians For Dummies 0-7645-1634-5
- The Internet For Dummies 0-7645-4173-0
- iPod & iTunes For Dummies 0-7645-7772-7
- Preventing Identity Theft For Dummies 0-7645-7336-5
- Pro Tools All-in-One Desk Reference For Dummies 0-7645-5714-9
- Roxio Easy Media Creator For Dummies 0-7645-7131-1

*** Separate Canadian edition also available**
† Separate U.K. edition also available

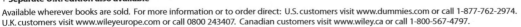

Available wherever books are sold. For more information or to order direct: U.S. customers visit www.dummies.com or call 1-877-762-2974. U.K. customers visit www.wileyeurope.com or call 0800 243407. Canadian customers visit www.wiley.ca or call 1-800-567-4797.

SPORTS, FITNESS, PARENTING, RELIGION & SPIRITUALITY

0-7645-5146-9

Parenting For Dummies

0-7645-5418-2

Also available:

- Adoption For Dummies 0-7645-5488-3
- Basketball For Dummies 0-7645-5248-1
- The Bible For Dummies 0-7645-5296-1
- Buddhism For Dummies 0-7645-5359-3
- Catholicism For Dummies 0-7645-5391-7
- Hockey For Dummies 0-7645-5228-7
- Judaism For Dummies 0-7645-5299-6
- Martial Arts For Dummies 0-7645-5358-5
- Pilates For Dummies 0-7645-5397-6
- Religion For Dummies 0-7645-5264-3
- Teaching Kids to Read For Dummies 0-7645-4043-2
- Weight Training For Dummies 0-7645-5168-X
- Yoga For Dummies 0-7645-5117-5

TRAVEL

0-7645-5438-7

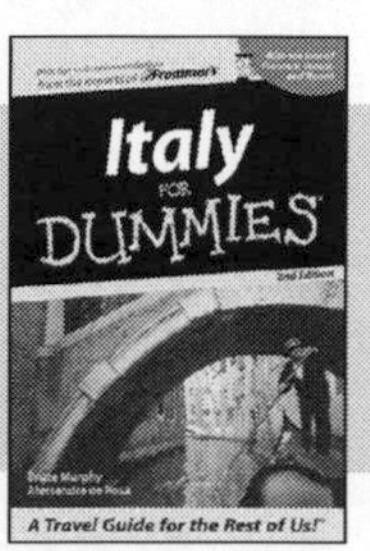

0-7645-5453-0

Also available:

- Alaska For Dummies 0-7645-1761-9
- Arizona For Dummies 0-7645-6938-4
- Cancún and the Yucatán For Dummies 0-7645-2437-2
- Cruise Vacations For Dummies 0-7645-6941-4
- Europe For Dummies 0-7645-5456-5
- Ireland For Dummies 0-7645-5455-7
- Las Vegas For Dummies 0-7645-5448-4
- London For Dummies 0-7645-4277-X
- New York City For Dummies 0-7645-6945-7
- Paris For Dummies 0-7645-5494-8
- RV Vacations For Dummies 0-7645-5443-3
- Walt Disney World & Orlando For Dummies 0-7645-6943-0

GRAPHICS, DESIGN & WEB DEVELOPMENT

0-7645-4345-8

0-7645-5589-8

Also available:

- Adobe Acrobat 6 PDF For Dummies 0-7645-3760-1
- Building a Web Site For Dummies 0-7645-7144-3
- Dreamweaver MX 2004 For Dummies 0-7645-4342-3
- FrontPage 2003 For Dummies 0-7645-3882-9
- HTML 4 For Dummies 0-7645-1995-6
- Illustrator CS For Dummies 0-7645-4084-X
- Macromedia Flash MX 2004 For Dummies 0-7645-4358-X
- Photoshop 7 All-in-One Desk Reference For Dummies 0-7645-1667-1
- Photoshop CS Timesaving Techniques For Dummies 0-7645-6782-9
- PHP 5 For Dummies 0-7645-4166-8
- PowerPoint 2003 For Dummies 0-7645-3908-6
- QuarkXPress 6 For Dummies 0-7645-2593-X

NETWORKING, SECURITY, PROGRAMMING & DATABASES

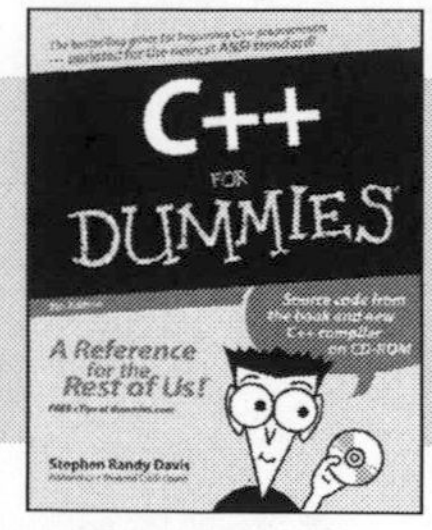

0-7645-6852-3

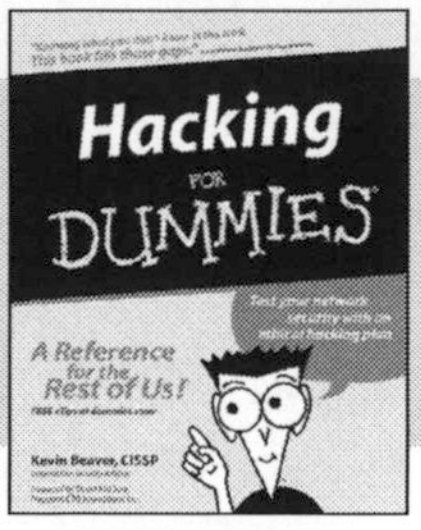

0-7645-5784-X

Also available:

- A+ Certification For Dummies 0-7645-4187-0
- Access 2003 All-in-One Desk Reference For Dummies 0-7645-3988-4
- Beginning Programming For Dummies 0-7645-4997-9
- C For Dummies 0-7645-7068-4
- Firewalls For Dummies 0-7645-4048-3
- Home Networking For Dummies 0-7645-42796
- Network Security For Dummies 0-7645-1679-5
- Networking For Dummies 0-7645-1677-9
- TCP/IP For Dummies 0-7645-1760-0
- VBA For Dummies 0-7645-3989-2
- Wireless All In-One Desk Reference For Dummies 0-7645-7496-5
- Wireless Home Networking For Dummies 0-7645-3910-8

HEALTH & SELF-HELP

0-7645-6820-5 *†

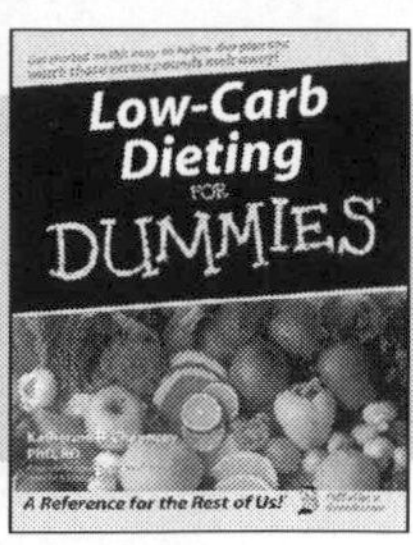

0-7645-2566-2

Also available:

- Alzheimer's For Dummies 0-7645-3899-3
- Asthma For Dummies 0-7645-4233-8
- Controlling Cholesterol For Dummies 0-7645-5440-9
- Depression For Dummies 0-7645-3900-0
- Dieting For Dummies 0-7645-4149-8
- Fertility For Dummies 0-7645-2549-2
- Fibromyalgia For Dummies 0-7645-5441-7
- Improving Your Memory For Dummies 0-7645-5435-2
- Pregnancy For Dummies † 0-7645-4483-7
- Quitting Smoking For Dummies 0-7645-2629-4
- Relationships For Dummies 0-7645-5384-4
- Thyroid For Dummies 0-7645-5385-2

EDUCATION, HISTORY, REFERENCE & TEST PREPARATION

0-7645-5194-9

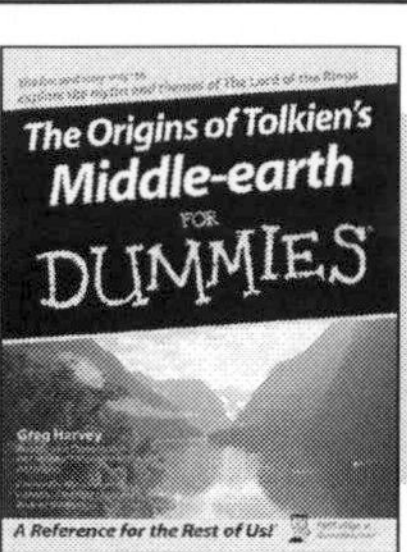

0-7645-4186-2

Also available:

- Algebra For Dummies 0-7645-5325-9
- British History For Dummies 0-7645-7021-8
- Calculus For Dummies 0-7645-2498-4
- English Grammar For Dummies 0-7645-5322-4
- Forensics For Dummies 0-7645-5580-4
- The GMAT For Dummies 0-7645-5251-1
- Inglés Para Dummies 0-7645-5427-1
- Italian For Dummies 0-7645-5196-5
- Latin For Dummies 0-7645-5431-X
- Lewis & Clark For Dummies 0-7645-2545-X
- Research Papers For Dummies 0-7645-5426-3
- The SAT I For Dummies 0-7645-7193-1
- Science Fair Projects For Dummies 0-7645-5460-3
- U.S. History For Dummies 0-7645-5249-X

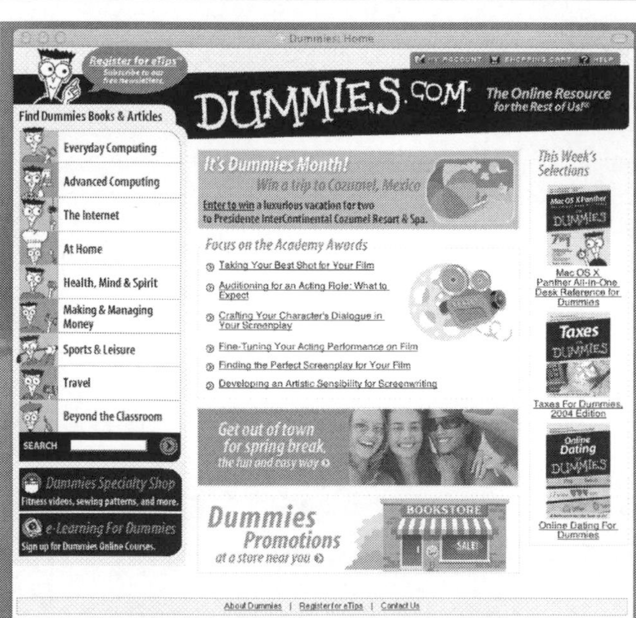

Get smart @ dummies.com®

- **Find a full list of Dummies titles**
- **Look into loads of FREE on-site articles**
- **Sign up for FREE eTips e-mailed to you weekly**
- **See what other products carry the Dummies name**
- **Shop directly from the Dummies bookstore**
- **Enter to win new prizes every month!**

*** Separate Canadian edition also available**
† Separate U.K. edition also available

Available wherever books are sold. For more information or to order direct: U.S. customers visit www.dummies.com or call 1-877-762-2974. U.K. customers visit www.wileyeurope.com or call 0800 243407. Canadian customers visit www.wiley.ca or call 1-800-567-4797.

Printed in Great Britain
by Amazon.co.uk, Ltd.,
Marston Gate.